Caught In-Between

Edinburgh Studies in Film and Intermediality
Series editors: Martine Beugnet and Kriss Ravetto
Founding editor: John Orr

A series of scholarly research intended to challenge and expand on the various approaches to film studies, bringing together film theory and film aesthetics with the emerging intermedial aspects of the field. The volumes combine critical theoretical interventions with a consideration of specific contexts, aesthetic qualities, and a strong sense of the medium's ability to appropriate current technological developments in its practice and form as well as in its distribution.

Advisory board
Duncan Petrie (University of Auckland)
John Caughie (University of Glasgow)
Dina Iordanova (University of St Andrews)
Elizabeth Ezra (University of Stirling)
Gina Marchetti (University of Hong Kong)
Jolyon Mitchell (University of Edinburgh)
Judith Mayne (The Ohio State University)
Dominique Bluher (Harvard University)

Titles in the series include:

Romantics and Modernists in British Cinema
John Orr

Framing Pictures: Film and the Visual Arts
Steven Jacobs

The Sense of Film Narration
Ian Garwood

The Feel-Bad Film
Nikolaj Lübecker

American Independent Cinema: Rites of Passage and the Crisis Image
Anna Backman Rogers

The Incurable-Image: Curating Post-Mexican Film and Media Arts
Tarek Elhaik

Screen Presence: Cinema Culture and the Art of Warhol, Rauschenberg, Hatoum and Gordon
Stephen Monteiro

Indefinite Visions: Cinema and the Attractions of Uncertainty
Martine Beugnet, Allan Cameron and Arild Fetveit (eds)

Screening Statues: Sculpture and Cinema
Steven Jacobs, Susan Felleman, Vito Adriaensens and Lisa Colpaert (eds)

Drawn From Life: Issues and Themes in Animated Documentary Cinema
Jonathan Murray and Nea Ehrlich (eds)

Intermedial Dialogues: The French New Wave and the Other Arts
Marion Schmid

The Museum as a Cinematic Space: The Display of Moving Images in Exhibitions
Elisa Mandelli

Theatre Through the Camera Eye: The Poetics of an Intermedial Encounter
Laura Sava

Caught In-Between: Intermediality in Contemporary Eastern European and Russian Cinema
Ágnes Pethő (ed.)

www.edinburghuniversitypress.com/series/ESIF

Caught In-Between
Intermediality in Contemporary Eastern European and Russian Cinema

Edited by Ágnes Pethő

EDINBURGH
University Press

Edinburgh University Press is one of the leading university presses in the UK. We publish academic books and journals in our selected subject areas across the humanities and social sciences, combining cutting-edge scholarship with high editorial and production values to produce academic works of lasting importance. For more information visit our website: edinburghuniversitypress.com

© editorial matter and organisation Ágnes Pethő, 2020, 2021
© the chapters their several authors, 2020, 2021

Edinburgh University Press Ltd
The Tun – Holyrood Road
12(2f) Jackson's Entry
Edinburgh EH8 8PJ

First published in hardback by Edinburgh University Press 2020

Typeset in 11/13 Adobe Garamond Pro
IDSUK (DataConnection) Ltd

A CIP record for this book is available from the British Library

ISBN 978 1 4744 3549 9 (hardback)
ISBN 978 1 4744 3552 9 (paperback)
ISBN 978 1 4744 3550 5 (webready PDF)
ISBN 978 1 4744 3551 2 (epub)

The right of Ágnes Pethő to be identified as the editor of this work has been asserted in accordance with the Copyright, Designs and Patents Act 1988, and the Copyright and Related Rights Regulations 2003 (SI No. 2498).

Contents

List of Figures	vii
The Contributors	x
Introduction: The Art of In-Betweenness in Contemporary Eastern European Cinema *Ágnes Pethő*	1

Part 1 Entangled Sensations, Cinema in-between the Arts

1. Intermedially Emotional: Musical Mood Cues, Disembodied Feelings in Contemporary Hungarian Melodramas — 27
   Hajnal Király

2. Black-and-White Sensations of History and Female Identity in Contemporary Polish and Czech Cinema — 45
   Judit Pieldner

3. Sculpture and Affect in Cinema's Expanded Field. From Aleksey Gherman's *Hard to Be a God* to Aleksey Gherman Jr's *Under Electric Clouds* — 65
   Ágnes Pethő

4. Intermedial Densities in the Work of Jan Švankmajer: A Media-Anthropological Case Study — 91
   Mareike Sera

Part 2 Immersions into Memory, Culture and Intermediality

5. Trickster Narratives and Carnivalesque Intermediality in Contemporary Romanian Cinema — 109
   Christina Stojanova

6. Photographic Passages to the Past in Eastern European Non-Fiction Films — 127
   Melinda Blos-Jáni

7. Trauma, Memorialisation and Intermediality in Jasmila Žbanić's *For Those Who Can Tell No Tales* — 147
   Katalin Sándor

8 An Immersive Theatrical Journey through Media and
Time in Alexander Sokurov's *Russian Ark* 163
Fátima Chinita

Part 3 Reflections upon Reality, Representation and Power

9 The Real and the Intermedial in Alexander Sokurov's
Family Trilogy 185
Malgorzata Bugaj

10 This is Not Magritte: Corneliu Porumboiu's Theory of
Representation 203
Zsolt Gyenge

11 Intermedial *Détrompe l'Oeil* and Contemporary Polish
Narrative Cinema 219
Gabriel Laverdière

12 Superhero Genre and Graphic Storytelling in Contemporary
Hungarian and Russian Cinema 237
Bence Kránicz

Index 255

Figures

0.1	Attila Damokos and Marcell Nagy: *Homunculus* (2012). Film, photography, installation art and opaque symbolism alloyed in a single image paraphrasing the *Pietà*	7
0.2	A paraphrase of Andrea Mantegna's painting, *The Lamentation over the Dead Christ* in Radu Jude's *Scarred Hearts* (2016)	8
0.3	An allusion to Rembrandt's *The Anatomy Lesson of Dr. Tulp* in *Scarred Hearts* (2016): an extreme emphasis on corporeality and aestheticism in the images of 'bodies dying into art'	9
1.1	The elevator as 'a musical time capsule' in *Adrienn Pál* (2010)	35
1.2	Liza dancing and singing in her own 'musical bubble' in *Liza, the Fox Fairy* (2015)	35
1.3	The mother listening to her 'own music' in *Fresh Air* (2006)	37
2.1	*I, Olga Hepnarová* (2016). Massive figures displayed in a frontal tableau shot: grey on grey	49
2.2	*The Reverse* (2009). The female protagonist set in the context of a variety of generic patterns amalgamated in the film and against various patterns of grey fabric	52
2.3–2.4	*Papusza* (2013). Frames that look like high definition, black-and-white renditions of Romantic genre paintings	53
2.5	*Cold War* (2018). The performance of the folk ensemble Mazurek: the grotesquely heavy black-and-white portrait of Stalin hovering above the stage	56
2.6–2.7	*Ida* (2013). Wanda's close-up in 'black on black' and Ida enveloped in grey in-between light and darkness	60
3.1	Aleksey Gherman, *Hard to Be a God* (2013): sculptural bodies covered with mud	69
3.2	Aleksey Gherman, *Hard to Be a God* (2013): a world in-between flesh, mud, clay and stone with life-sized sculptures blending in with the live figures	70

3.3	Aleksey Gherman, *Hard to Be a God* (2013): sculptural objects thrust into close-up, frames cluttered with the entanglement of bodies and objects	76
3.4	Aleksey Gherman Jr, *Under Electric Clouds* (2015): the skeleton-like frame of an unfinished skyscraper that looms in the distance over an urban wasteland	79
3.5	A gloomy, unfinished statue in *Under Electric Clouds* (2015)	81
3.6	Aleksey Gherman Jr, *Under Electric Clouds* (2015): the discarded statue of Lenin	82
4.1–4.2	*The Flat* (1968): everyday objects that fail to function. The initials on the wall of Švankmajer and his wife, as well as their son, Václav Švankmajer	95
4.3–4.4	The design of *The Ossuary* (1970): the bizarre tableau of bones. The signature of the designer	97
4.5–4.6	*Dimensions of Dialogue* (1983): encounters between vegetables, kitchen objects, scientific tools and Arcimboldian heads	101
6.1	*Crulic. The Path to Beyond* (2011): Crulic's longing for his home is represented with a drawing of a house that imitates a photograph	133
6.2	*Felvidék. Caught in Between* (2014): photographs and moving images are projected on real-world surfaces in order to construct their meaning in the present	135
6.3	*I Made You, I Kill You* (2016): one of the few childhood photographs of the director is collaged into a hypermediated landscape	136
6.4	*Paperbox* (2011): close-up of still visible details on a photograph in decomposition. This image focusing on the hands of the soldiers returns several times during the film, until its recognisable parts vanish totally	139
6.5	*Dead Nation* (2017): an example of the gelatin coat in decay. The photograph of the men standing in front of their carriage becomes a metaphor for stillness due to the voice-over	142
7.1	*For Those Who Can Tell No Tales* (2013): framing the gaze	155
7.2	*For Those Who Can Tell No Tales* (2013): performing a site of trauma	157
8.1	Tableau-like shot showing an affinity to theatrical practices	167
8.2	*Tableau dramatique*: allegorical theatrical stasis	167
8.3	*La vie en rose*: Nicholas II and his family	169

8.4	Historical tableau: watching the spectacle from the outside	177
9.1	Painterly influences in *Mother and Son* (1997) are highlighted through the film's reliance upon long takes and long shots employed to place the subjects within a wider context	188
9.2	*Father and Son* (2003) pursues its preoccupation with the human corporeality by focusing on the sculpted bodies of two soldiers. The film can be viewed as a certain glorification of the male physique, but remains ambiguous as to whether these are displayed for the erotic gaze	191
9.3	This image of a flayed human form in *Father and Son* (2003) points to early anatomical drawings and their distinctive aesthetic take on medicine intertwining the scientific with the artistic. It is also yet another way of emphasising the body of the character	194
9.4	*Alexandra* (2007): juxtaposing the elderly woman with young soldiers. A series of opposing pairs explored in the film calls attention to the physical properties of the main character's body	196
10.1	*Police, Adjective* (2009): the chalkboard and the definition of 'conscience' in the handwriting of the detective	212
11.1	*Suicide Room* (2011): the grainy digital images of webcam communications convey the troubled teenage protagonist's fears	229
11.2	*Suicide Room* (2011): the final images of the film show the footage of the boy's suicide posted online, with the comments of the viewers below	231
12.1	György Pálfi's *Sha-Man Vs. Ikarus* (2003), a self-reflexive superhero movie made in a style inspired by comic books	241
12.2	Flying Volga above the Red Square in *Black Lightning* (2009)	247

The Contributors

Melinda Blos-Jáni is Assistant Professor of Film Studies at the Film, Photography and Media Department of Sapientia Hungarian University of Transylvania, Cluj-Napoca, Romania. Her research interests are home videos and amateur films, autobiographical and found footage documentaries, silent film history, contemporary silent films, media genealogy. She earned her PhD in Anthropology with a thesis on the domestication of moving image technologies and media practices in familial contexts which was published in book form in Hungarian in 2015.

Malgorzata Bugaj has recently completed her PhD thesis *Visceral Material: Cinematic Bodies on Screen* (University of Edinburgh, 2014). She currently teaches at the University of Stirling and the University of Edinburgh. Her academic interests revolve around Eastern European film, cinematic presentations of the body and the senses, as well as avant-garde cinema.

Fátima Chinita is Associate Professor at the Theatre and Film School of the Lisbon Polytechnic Institute, Theatre and Film School, in Portugal. She recently finished her postdoctoral research, which was partly conducted at the University of Linnaeus, in Växjö, Sweden, in the Research Centre for Intermediality and Intermodality. She is the author of the book *The (In)visible Spectator: Reflexivity From the Film Viewer's Perspective in David Lynch's Inland Empire* (published in Portuguese).

Zsolt Gyenge is Associate Professor at the Institute for Theoretical Studies of the Moholy-Nagy University of Art and Design, Budapest, Hungary, where he teaches courses in film theory, film history and visual communication theory. His fields of research include interpretation theories (phenomenology, hermeneutics), experimental films and video art. He is the editor of the scholarly journal on design and visual culture, *Disegno*. He is the author of a book published in Hungarian dealing with the theory of phenomenological film analysis.

Hajnal Király is a senior researcher at the Institute for Hungarian Literary and Cultural Studies, Eötvös Lóránd University of Budapest. Besides contemporary Hungarian and Romanian cinema, her research interests are medium theory, literary re-mediations and intermediality. Her most important publications include a book on adaptation theory in Hungarian and several essays in volumes on intermediality, literary adaptations and cultural approaches to Eastern European Cinema, most recently in *The Cinematic Bodies of Eastern Europe and Russia. Between Pain and Pleasure* (ed. Ewa Mazierska, Matilda Mroz and Elżbieta Ostrowska, 2018) and in *Popular Music and the Moving Image in Eastern Europe* (ed. Ewa Mazierska and Zsolt Győri, 2018).

Bence Kránicz completed his Film Studies MA at Eötvös Loránd University, Budapest, where he is a PhD student at the Film, Media and Contemporary Culture Program. His articles on film and comics have been published in various journals and magazines since 2009.

Gabriel Laverdière graduated from Laval University, Quebec (Canada) where he completed his thesis on homosexuality in contemporary Polish cinema. His other research interests include digital cinema, nationalities in film, and the philosophy of film. He published articles in the Mexican journal *Unidiversidad* on a film by Robert Lepage, in *Klesis – Revue philosophique* on the ontology of digital images, and in *Nouvelles Vues* on queer figures of Quebec narrative cinema. He also translated into French a book by Camille Paglia, published under the title *Introduction à Personas sexuelles* by Presses de l'Université Laval, 2017.

Ágnes Pethő is Professor of Film Studies at the Sapientia Hungarian University of Transylvania in Cluj-Napoca (Romania) where she is currently head of the Department of Film, Photography and Media. She is also the executive editor of the English language international peer-reviewed journal, *Acta Universitatis Sapientiae: Film and Media Studies*. Her most important publications include the book, *Cinema and Intermediality. The Passion for the In-Between* (2011) and the edited volumes: *Words and Images on the Screen: Language, Literature, Moving Pictures* (2008), *Film in the Post-Media Age* (2012), *The Cinema of Sensations* (2015) published by Cambridge Scholars Publishing.

Judit Pieldner is Associate Professor at Sapientia Hungarian University of Transylvania, Department of Humanities, Miercurea Ciuc, Romania. Her research interests are related to intermediality, experimental cinema and screen adaptation. She has published several articles on film and literature and has contributed to the volumes *Words and Images on the Screen: Language, Literature, Moving Pictures* (2008), *Film in the Post-Media Age* (2012) and

The Cinema of Sensations (2015), edited by Ágnes Pethő and published by Cambridge Scholars Publishing. She is co-editor of the volume *Discourses of Space* (Cambridge Scholars Publishing, 2013) and assistant editor of the journal *Acta Universitatis Sapientiae: Philologica*.

Katalin Sándor is Assistant Professor at Babeș-Bolyai University, Cluj-Napoca, Romania. Her research interests include theories of intermediality, intermediality in literature and film. She has published articles on film, literature and visual poetry and has contributed to the volumes *Discourses of Space* (Cambridge Scholars Publishing, 2013) and *The Cinema of Sensations* (Cambridge Scholars Publishing, 2015). Her monograph, *Nyugtalanító írás/képek. A vizuális költészet intermedialitásáról* [Unsettling Image/Texts: The Intermediality of Visual Poetry] was published in 2011.

Mareike Sera graduated with a BA in Visual Theories and an MA in Film History and Criticism from the University of East London, with Professor Michael O'Pray as one of her main supervisors. She has obtained a doctoral degree from the Humboldt University of Berlin, Department of Slavonic Studies, where she was supervised by Professor Peter Zajac. Her research focuses on symbolic 'mixed' textures and how the hermeneutical approach of Paul Ricœur can be seen to broaden and enrich film-phenomenological thinking.

Christina Stojanova is Associate Professor at the Department of Film, University of Regina, Canada. She is a media historian specialising in philosophical, ideological, and analytical-psychological aspects of narrative modes and fictional representation in the cinemas of Quebec, interwar Germany, and Eastern and Central Europe. Since 2005 she has contributed twenty chapters to internationally acclaimed publications. She is the co-editor of *Wittgenstein at the Movies* (2011), *The Legacies of Jean-Luc Godard* (2014), and the editor of *The New Romanian Cinema* (Edinburgh University Press, 2019). She is currently working on a monograph about the Canadian animator Caroline Leaf.

Introduction: The Art of In-Betweenness in Contemporary Eastern European Cinema
Ágnes Pethő

CONVERGING APPROACHES

At a time when all sorts of transitions are taking place in the post-communist societies of Europe, when former borders have collapsed but differences remain, when the relationship between the cultures of the East and the West have become more complicated, paradoxical or tense than ever before, when the idea of national cinemas has been eroded by transnational productions, yet films still address issues grounded in local realities, in short: when in-betweenness has become the key term in almost all aspects of life, quite a lot of Eastern European films seem to resort, time and again, to a diversified poetics of intermediality, i.e. to an aesthetic highlighting cinema's relationship with the other arts and the media complexity of moving images. Even in less ostentatious and more covert forms, intermediality – as a veritable art of in-betweenness – appears as a way to register all kinds of ambivalences that pervade the culture of the region and is capable of becoming an efficient catalyst of self-reflection.

Despite the major historical events that swept away the past regimes and clearly marked the beginning of a new era, the slice of time referred to as 'contemporary', as we see in the title, is not easy to delimit, for historical events seldom coincide with paradigm shifts in the arts and aesthetic phenomena often persist across the ages. The term was therefore applied with certain flexibility in the selection of works analysed (or referred to) in this volume. Not only films that were made after the collapse of the Iron Curtain were considered, but also works of highly influential authors whose *oeuvre* connect the period before the fall of communism with that of the new generations of filmmakers, and which are important for understanding the major strategies of cinematic intermediality visible in the Eastern European cinemas of today.

The ways in which these cinemas harness the potential of intermedial and inter-art relations is not a widely researched subject in film (or media) studies. There are, however, important forerunners of the essays published in this book that need to be pointed out. In what follows, I will proceed with a concise survey of these previous researches in which such a subject has emerged so far[1] taking into consideration their main goals, the topics that have been discussed, and how they have enriched our knowledge of intermediality in Eastern European cinemas. Such an examination, inevitably, brings forth first of all the heterogeneity of the scholarly literature on intermediality. Defined as a subject area, as a research concept that we seek to understand and not as a particular theory, intermediality has always been addressed from diverse standpoints.[2] Furthermore, researches vary from explicitly focusing on the key notion of intermediality to only indirectly touching upon relevant issues connected to it, and also, from more abstract theorisations to in-depth analyses of specific instances examined in their historical context. Viewing this wide spectrum of approaches as they converge around questions of intermediality in contemporary Eastern European cinemas, and starting with concept-based studies, we see that although far from featuring prominently as a source of inspiration, films from this region have provided some examples even for the scholarship that aims to forge a more general theory of intermediality. Such scholarship pursues the study of intermediality through the identification of a set of categories describing media relations and interactions, a methodology which stems from semiotics and is informed by a broader perspective of media studies. Lars Elleström's researches have systematically contributed to laying the foundations of intermediality studies understood in this way through the clarification of its basic concepts. His analysis (2014: 62–86) of three films by Jan Švankmajer may reveal both the strengths and the limitations of this kind of approach. He uses the films of the Czech author of animated short films as examples to hold up a theoretical construction, and offers a close reading of these films with the purpose of explaining the 'general media transformation principles' (2014: 63) that he outlines. Accordingly, Elleström deliberately refrains from interpreting the films.[3] A similar methodology is employed by Asunción López-Varela Azcárate (2015), who explores Švankmajer's *Jabberwocky* (1971) as an inventive, contemporary form of *ekphrasis* comparing it to Lewis Carroll's poem with the same title included in the novel *Through the Looking-Glass* and Simon Biggs's 2010 digital video installation *reRead*, inspired by the same literary text. These studies identify specific types of media connections and the fact that these occur in moving images is of secondary importance to them seeking no connections with theories of film. The films themselves are observed *in vitro* (extracting them from their 'live/natural environment'), and therefore the fact that they come from Eastern Europe also becomes irrelevant. They are not interested in what intermediality can convey in the context of a specific aesthetic, culture or reality, instead, such approaches seek to unravel it through a conceptual framework applicable across media and pursue refined analyses of media relationships on a more abstract level.

We also find examples for the reverse, in which case analyses of films from the recent history of these cinemas touch upon questions regarding the connections of moving images with other arts and media without necessarily or exclusively applying the categories elaborated in the theoretical writings on intermediality. Articles that we can include under this umbrella deal with: strategies of literary adaptations in the region (e.g. Gelencsér 2008)[4]; the creative transformations and hybridisations of moving images in the realm of experimental cinema (e.g. Müllner 2008, Gilić 2010, Dánél 2015, Gelencsér 2015, Lipiński 2015); types of word-and-image relations (e.g. Varga 2008), the inspiration of paintings for the creation of sets and the overall atmosphere of the images (e.g. Zvonkine 2015); the role of music (e.g. Mazierska and Győri 2018); the appearance of new media within films (Kosmala 2014); the exploration of new media forms in feature-length experimental films (i.e. incorporating the multi-screen moving picture installation format into a painterly essay film by Benedek Fliegauf, analysed by Faluhelyi 2011; and the mixing of fiction film, documentary and interactivity offered by a DVD in György Pálfi's *I'm not Your Friend*-project, discussed by Stőhr 2012).

At the same time, we may note, that along with a variety of topics of interest both for the history of film and for intermedial studies, there are also certain authors whose works seem to invite an approach from an intermedial viewpoint and whose films have drawn attention to the relevance of intermedial phenomena in the region, prompting many scholars to investigate their intermedial style more explicitly. Béla Tarr, one of the leading figures in contemporary Eastern European film, has emerged at the same time as one of the key authors whose films have informed our understanding of intermediality (see Király 2008, 2010, 2015b, 2016a, and Pethő 2014b, 2015b, 2016). Lech Majewski, the versatile Polish author, active as a visual artist, poet, composer and film director, has been the subject of several articles (e.g. Tes 2013; Pethő 2014a: 483–8, 2015a: 157–72; Chakravorty 2015; Twardoch 2015). Other authors of interest in this respect include Alexander Sokurov, whose films appear like a palimpsest of the visual arts (see the essays of Hänsgen 2011 and Rascaroli 2017: 26–47), or Andrzej Żuławski (who interweaves the reflexive use of photography with a sophisticated array of literary allusions, according to Bene 2015). Directors of New Romanian cinema, who received much acclaim after 2000 with a series of successful films at international film festivals, brought about a re-evaluation of Romanian cinema as a whole, including the appreciation of their intermedial features (see Király 2016b and Sándor 2016, 2019 on Lucian Pintilie's films; Pethő 2011b on Mircea Daneliuc, Pfeifer 2017 and Pethő 2019 on Corneliu Porumboiu; Pieldner

2016b and Mironescu 2017 on Radu Jude; Blos-Jáni 2019, on the films of Nae Caranfil; Lutas 2019 on the works of Cristi Puiu).

Unravelling the Cinematic Poetics of Intermediality

Many of the contributors to this book have laid the groundwork for pursuing the poetics of cinematic intermediality more directly through their previous publications written within the framework of two consecutive research projects hosted by the Sapientia Hungarian University in Cluj-Napoca and funded by the Romanian Ministry of National Education between 2013 and 2019.[5] The first concentrated on figurations of intermediality in Central and Eastern European films, the second, assuming a wider perspective, aimed to contextualise these within changing forms of in-betweenness in contemporary cinema.[6] The comparative analyses which have been published and which draw parallels among authors in Eastern Europe or within an even broader circle in world cinema, describe general trends in which stylistic variations with specific meanings could be discerned, and shift the focus from the director/author or the artwork in a traditional film historical context to the interpretation of particular figurations of cinematic intermediality explored along the avenues opened up under the horizon of post-structuralism and more recent philosophies of film.[7] These studies, which can be seen as immediate predecessors of this book, are concerned less with an abstract set of relationships (i.e. a kind of grammar viewed in semiotic terms), and more with the unique configurations of intermediality and their sensuously perceivable excess, uncovering at the same time the way the poetics of intermediality can connect not only arts or media, but also art and life. They take into consideration the ways that media relations enable us to grasp the complexity of reality and culture, to observe various tensional (emotional, existential, etc.) states of in-betweenness, along with anxieties, relations of power and conflict characteristic of Eastern Europe. Implicitly, they assess the significance of intermediality regarding the cinemas of Eastern Europe by looking at it as something that actively 'performs' something, and not merely 'is'.[8] Without summing up in detail all the articles published previously that could be mentioned here, I will briefly attempt to outline the main clusters of ideas which we can distinguish around figurations of intermediality as 'a poetics of in-betweenness', and which have significantly shaped the aesthetic of contemporary Eastern European films.[9]

A significant import of these kind of researches has been to reveal intermedial practices which yield meditations upon history and time, cultural and personal identity through remediating (thus revitalising) or imitating archive imagery, earlier forms of moving images and photography, and through an emphasis on multisensual aspects of the moving image. The in-depth analyses written by Judit Pieldner (2014a, 2015) of films made by the Hungarian auteurs Gábor Bódy and András Jeles in the decades that preceded and immediately followed the fall of communism, demonstrate how the archaeology of cinema performed in such films, i.e. the confrontation with cinema's materiality, historicity and temporality can create productive tensions between the documentary value of the image and its rhetorical dimension. By resisting the canonical representational modes of history, they reveal a more intimate relationship with both historical past and the history of the cinematic medium itself. 'Sensing the texture, the fabric of the film, surrendering to lack of perfection, incompletion, distortion and disappearance' (Pieldner 2014a: 74) in Bódy's *American Torso* (*Amerikai anzix*, 1975) can activate a kind of 'non-figurative consciousness' through which the film becomes 'capable of telling our own story, our own disappearance' (Pieldner 2014a: 74). Melinda Blos-Jáni (2018) investigates similar techniques in a selection of contemporary Eastern European found footage films dealing with the socialist past and the regime changing events. She argues that by deliberate reframing and intensifying the medium-specific (i.e. both auditory and visual) 'noises' of the archival sources, or by an artificially created visual precariousness a new type of spectatorial awareness is created that goes hand in hand with a type of historical consciousness that is not yet solidified. Such films 'seem to challenge the concept of the frame as a container of images, or the frame as the boundary of a meaningful whole, instead they feature the image as a surface' (Blos-Jáni 2018: 154). Imperfections and noises veiling, rupturing or erasing the images become strategies of excess intended to reject 'the comforts of visibility in order to lure the viewers into their own quest for hidden meanings and memories' (Blos-Jáni 2018: 155).

Archival footage is combined with a series of literary, painterly and musical allusions in András Jeles's *Parallel Lives* (*Senkiföldje*, 1993), a film rendering the ineffable experience of the Holocaust from the perspective of a child. Pieldner finds the dense cultural references and the media hybridity of the film indicative of 'the impotence of art and aesthetics in the face of inhumanity' and of 'the incommensurability of the cohabitation – of the "parallel lives" – of the two faces of human culture, the scale of inhumanity and the aesthetic regime of culture' (Pieldner 2015: 137–8). Katalin Sándor (2016) looks at Lucian Pintilie's *The Oak* (*Balanţa*, 1992) and reveals in a close reading how the film confronts the communist past and the present marked by the after-effects of dictatorship. By incorporating a diegetic Polaroid camera and a home movie, *The Oak* displays a reflexive preoccupation with the mediality, the non-transparency and the sociocultural constructedness of the image. The analysis shows that the film can be regarded as a critical historical response to the social and representational crises linked to the communist era, but at the same time, it may be symptomatic of the social, cultural, political anxieties of post-1989 transition. The essay also elaborates on the way in which photographs may generate a media-reflexive discourse in a film as part of a reflection upon the intersections of personal and collective history.

The blending of photography and film into 'photofilmic' images, on the other hand, can be seen not only as a typical phenomenon of the so-called post-media age in which photography and film can be edited to morph into each other on their shared digital devices that produce and display them, but also as one of the most versatile figurations of intermediality in cinema with a special significance in the Eastern European context. Prolonged tableau shots framed to resemble a photograph or painting (sometimes also as direct references), the gesture of 'freezing into an image', the fascination with the arrested, tableau vivant-like pose perceptible on the border of stasis and movement (consequently, in-between photography, painting and moving image) have become hallmarks of a pictorial stylisation that conveys a whole spectrum of sensations and connotations linked to the tension between the inevitable transitions, displacements in the world or the transitoriness of life itself and a subjective state of paralysis and immobility. As a climax of an ever more polished visual form, Béla Tarr's last film, *The Turin Horse* (*A torinói ló*, 2011) performs exactly such a process of the moving images giving way to a series of photofilmic tableaux. 'Balancing between film and photography, and through a minimalist, repetitive narrative, Tarr stages no less than the end of the world itself as an ultimate "standstill"' (Pethő 2015b: 242), unfolding the still photographic frame from slow camera movements and long shots,[10] and fading away in the end into total darkness and imageless-ness. Hajnal Király (2016a) sees this preference for slowness and stillness primarily as a poetic technique within an allegorical mode of expression that prevails also in other contemporary Hungarian films, and interprets it, based on Julia Kristeva, as a figuration of melancholia and the manifestation of the Freudian 'death drive' described by Laura Mulvey, which underlies narratives advancing towards a halt or melodramatic ending involving death.

This recurring theme of imminent death aestheticised in an image is underscored by uncannily frequent imitations of Mantegna's and Holbein's famous paintings of the Dead Christ in the form of 'cadaverous tableaux vivants' in which a live body is displayed as a corpse. We have several studies that expound the rich signification of such performative images which excavate the visual repertoire of masterpieces in fine art and exert their mystifying magnetism even when appearing merely as fleeting sensations of déjà vu in the works of Péter Forgács (Sándor 2014a), Kornél Mundruczó, Benedek Fliegauf, Ágnes Kocsis (Király 2016a), Andrey Zvyagintsev (Pethő 2016: 246–9), or Cristi Puiu (Pethő 2018: 177–8).

A two-minute short film created by two young Hungarian filmmakers (Attila Damokos and Marcell Nagy) in 2012 with the title *Homunculus*[11] sums up the way such tableaux of 'live corpses' function in Eastern European films. The film consists of a poetic montage opening with images suggestive of the biological conception of life followed in quick succession by the close-up of an older man, a collage of picture frames, alchemical symbols and glimpses of a fashion photography session with a young black woman. It concludes with a composition in which film, photography and installation art are alloyed in a single image: we see the woman holding the man in the well-known pose of Michelangelo's *Pietà* (Figure 0.1), tracing in this way a trajectory of image associations from life to death, from biological to artistic creation, from bodies to images. The viewer may observe that the man facing the image of the inception of life and ending up as Christ in the *Pietà* is János Derzsi, whose statuesque, carved features have been engraved in our memory through the cinema of Béla Tarr. Thus, epitomising the 'insider' intertextual references woven into the films of Eastern Europe, the short film pays homage to the *Turin Horse* made just a year before, in which János Derzsi embodied a man facing not the beginning but the end of the world, and was shown in poses reminiscent of paintings. However, this connection to Tarr is not exclusive, more universal and non-localisable associations subvert the religious/painterly iconography and cinephile reference as we see that an enigmatic African woman is cradling a white man, a young fashion model is photographed with an old man in a decaying yet photogenic house. This reminds us how such a tableau can not only appear as a projection of a world slowly overcome by inertia or melancholia (as previously mentioned studies have demonstrated), but it can effectively pull the fictional world away from the reference frame

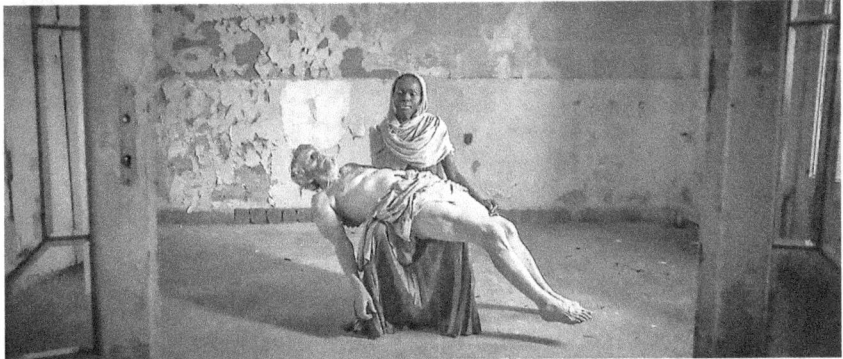

Figure 0.1 Attila Damokos and Marcell Nagy: *Homunculus* (2012). Film, photography, installation art and opaque symbolism alloyed in a single image paraphrasing the *Pietà*

of reality through the opaque amalgamation of symbolism, and can always aggregate different levels of abstract significations through the emblem-like density of the image.

There are also many instances in which the role of art references in images goes beyond confronting the mortality of the body with the immortality of art and opening up the image towards multiple philosophical interpretations. A striking example of this can be seen in Radu Jude's film, *Scarred Hearts* (*Inimi cicatrizate*, 2016), a story of a terminally ill young poet, whose tragic last months in a sanatorium are presented against the backdrop of the rise of fascism, and whose death is prefigured by a shot in which we see him in the hospital in the familiar foreshortened pose of Mantegna's Christ, with his father at his bedside (Figure 0.2). The film is loosely based on the autobiographical writings of Max Blecher, a multi-talented Romanian Jewish artist who died of bone tuberculosis in 1938, and whose drawings and thoughts are extensively quoted in the film in intertitles fragmenting the string of tableaux shot with a static camera and neatly composed into the confines of the Academy ratio, with rounded corners added as a further gesture of cinematic calligraphy imitating the cropped edges of old photographs.

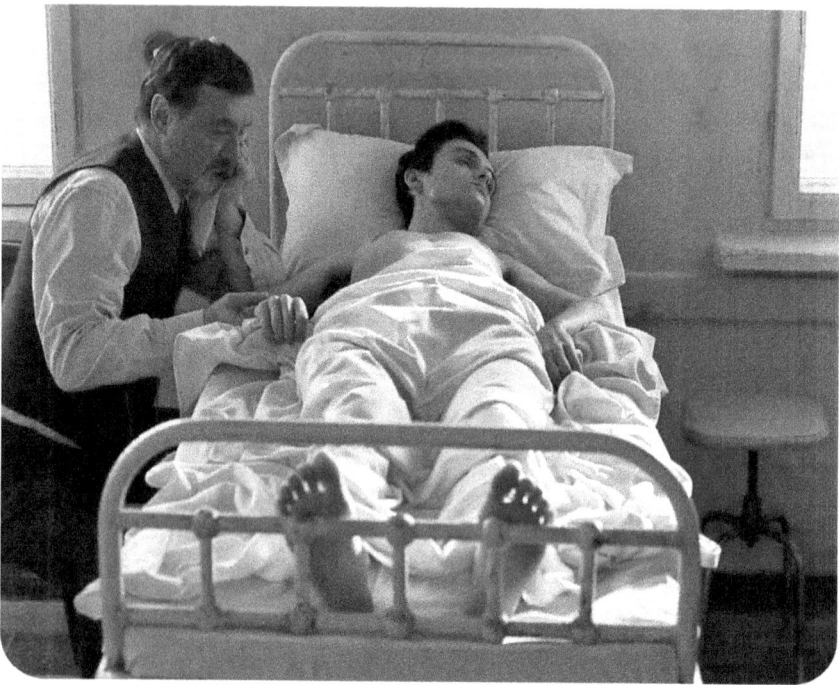

Figure 0.2 A paraphrase of Andrea Mantegna's painting, *The Lamentation over the Dead Christ* in Radu Jude's *Scarred Hearts* (2016)

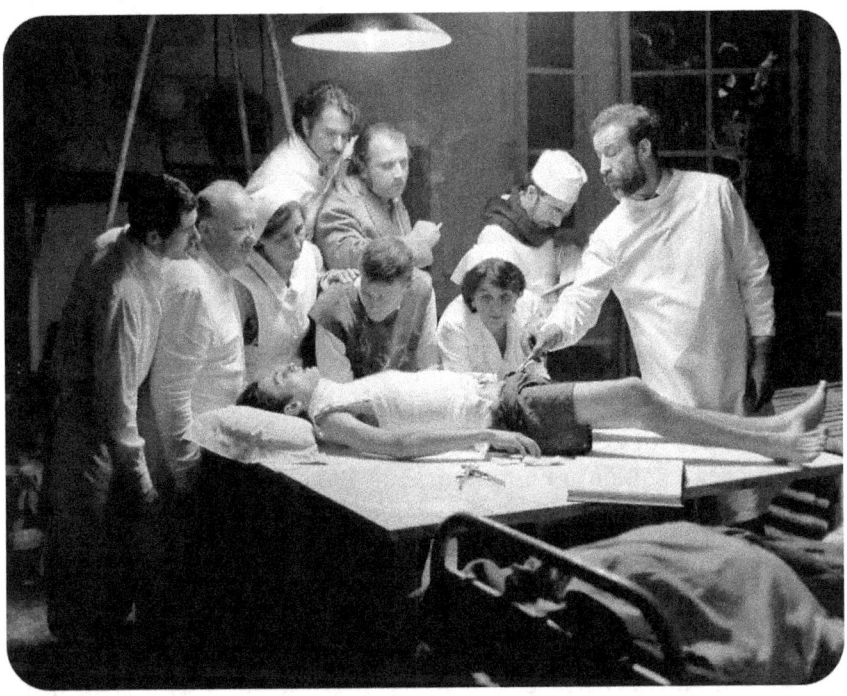

Figure 0.3 An allusion to Rembrandt's *The Anatomy Lesson of Dr. Tulp* in *Scarred Hearts* (2016): an extreme emphasis on corporeality and aestheticism in the images of 'bodies dying into art'

The beauty of the images in Jude's film is in stark contrast to the harrowing depictions of the torturous medical procedures the protagonist has to endure, as, for example, his torso is pressed into a body cast or an abscess is drained of pus with a giant needle. One of these terrible scenes appears as a paraphrase of Rembrandt's famous canvas, *The Anatomy Lesson of Dr. Tulp* (Figure 0.3). This picturesque frame may be symptomatic for another important role of such tableaux vivants, namely that despite the fact that they can always elevate these narratives into 'lessons', multi-layered allegories of a troubled existence in Eastern Europe,[12] the images of these bodies 'dying into art' often paradoxically intertwine almost irreconcilable extremes: from the emphasis on the sensation of corporeality, the visceral affect of the 'dissection' of the body to the distanciating effect of a conspicuous artificiality and aestheticisation. Thus they also combine the excessive attraction of the image through its well-crafted painterly beauty with the impulse to look away from something that is too painful to watch. György Pálfi's *Taxidermia* (2006), a gut-churning allegory of Hungary's history, is perhaps the most representative in this respect, in which three consecutive generations are presented and each of them is defined by exceedingly naturalistic scenes showing activities involving the body (and bodily fluids), i.e. animalesque sex, competitive eating and lastly, taxidermy. In its shocking finale we see a reversal of the process involved in the tableau vivant (i.e. the objectification of a live body as the replica of a painting) by a corpse 'coming alive' through art, as a sculpture literally made of flesh.

Such an extreme emphasis on corporeality and the mortality of the body intertwined with aestheticism and an intermediality combining painting, poetry, photography and cinema in order to tackle issues of Eastern European history and culture could be seen earlier as well. In some of the films made in the 1980s, in the final decade of communist rule, some of the filmmakers experimented with a Gesamtkunstwerk-like film form in order to channel the deep physical revulsion against a humdrum, humiliating life and an ideologically tainted art, along with a nostalgia for beauty, a Romantic-surrealistic desire for a freedom of artistic form that shunned conventions and explored the connections between the arts uninhibitedly. The most prominent examples of this are two films made in the 1980s in Hungary and Romania, Gábor Bódy's *Narcissus and Psyche* (*Nárcisz és Psyché*, 1980; analysed by Pieldner 2014b) and Mircea Daneliuc's *Glissando* (1984, interpreted as a paradigmatic work for the late communist period's 'politics of intermediality' alongside Daneliuc's subsequent films by Pethő 2011b). Sándor (2014a, 2014b) reveals how this tendency to link the experience of corporeality to the experience of intermediality takes shape in a couple of more recent Hungarian films. It appears as a philosophical meditation on liminalities of human existence and consciousness in Péter Forgács's 2008 adaptation of Péter Nádas's eponymous book, *Own Death*, which reflects on his near-death (bodily and spiritual) experiences, and it is connected to timely topics of post-colonialism, gender-based power, cultural and ethnic identity in Szabolcs Hajdu's *Bibliothèque Pascal* made in 2010. This latter is a surrealistic fable about storytelling as an escape from a harsh and pathetic reality, full of painterly constructed scenes that recount the misadventures and eventual magical deliverance of a half-Romanian, half-Hungarian woman ending up as a sex slave in a bizarre Liverpool brothel in which women pose in tableaux vivants referencing famous literary texts.

All these examples reveal the in-betweenness of body and image, implicitly, of life and art as a site where acute political, social or psychological issues can materialise in a sensuously layered and intellectually complex (also, covert and sublimated) form.[13] Moreover, this is also a site where another very important in-betweenness emerges underpinned by a general quest for identity connected to European culture. Although this has already been present in Eastern European and Russian literature and art throughout the nineteenth and the first half of the twentieth centuries,[14] after the fall of the Berlin Wall and the collapse of the communist ideology (which was based on the rejection of Western capitalism and on an all-pervasive propaganda promoting self-sufficiency and the new values of socialism), questions regarding self-definition vis-à-vis Western Europe resurfaced with renewed urgency in all areas of society, politics and culture, creating a context which cannot be disregarded when one seeks to understand the distinctive features of intermediality in contemporary Eastern European films. The penchant for inter-art allusions, more precisely, the frequent references to well-known European paintings, connect the cultures of the East with the West and highlight a kind of Europeanness in Eastern European cinemas which is both reaffirmed as an abstract set of ideals evoked by the shared cultural heritage of 'grand images' (usually reinforced by biblical or archetypal symbolism, therefore appearing as something stable, relatable and uncontested) while at the same time, they appear to be continuously questioned or undermined by narratives comprising situations of crises, and by images of disturbing, violated, dismembered, diseased bodies. These allusions to masterpieces of European art speak of an Eastern Europe struggling to redefine and reassert itself in-between East and West. On the one hand, they evoke the legacy of a bygone historical Europe before modern times united by a common Christian culture. On the other hand, they prolong and rely on a way of thinking inherited from the more recent, communist past, when art, paradoxically, constituted the only 'real' connection to Western Europe. While in most countries there were severe restrictions imposed on travelling and on concrete physical contact with the world beyond the Iron Curtain, quite surprisingly, there was no ban on the availability of high culture (world literature was translated, some foreign language books and periodicals were imported, people could buy music records and art history books, watch art-house films, there were quality theatre productions, cultural programmes on TV, etc.). In fact, the typical communist household of an Eastern European intellectual (and not only) was filled with bookcases, paintings and other artworks made by local artists, as culture was indeed affordable to the masses. Each such household became in this way a private cultural haven (sometimes a fortress of resistance) in which people, while living in isolation, could develop a deep-rooted and personal relationship with fragments of Western art and culture, a relationship that defined them as equals to those who had the good fortune to live in the free world.

These legacies coexist with the new global influences brought along with the collapse of state socialism and inform an art that reflects on specific issues arising from social changes, political instabilities and also economic mobilities involving large numbers of the populations moving back and forth in-between Western and Eastern Europe. Király argues that art references liberate contemporary Romanian films from provincialism, and initiate 'a discourse lamenting over the loss of Western, Christian and local values' (2016b: 67) endangered in the post-communist era. Direct references to sculptures by Romanian-born Constantin Brâncuși, for example, foreground the conflicting facets of the Europeanness of Eastern European art, the transient nature of values and a process of self-colonisation or 'self-othering'.[15] In the case of Romanian cinema, among others, Király (2016b) and Pieldner (2016a) have also revealed the relevance of allusions to Byzantine iconography mixed with Western pictorial references in highlighting the perplexing entanglement of cultural ties. The uncanny rituals of 'becoming an image' exemplified by the predilection for the use of tableaux vivants, may signal in this way a 'nostalgia for belonging', 'a yearning for a reintegration into something universal and lasting' (Pethő 2016: 252) amid acute crises of identity, precarious conditions for existence and artistic creation, together with a disillusioning clash of myth and reality implied also by the disturbing aspects of the depictions of corporeality mentioned earlier.

Beside 'regular' feature films, similar polarisations of bodies and images as well as cultural dialogues between Eastern and Western art can also be found in a unique corpus of 'post-cinematic' films directed by Lech Majewski, Sharunas Bartas and Ihor Podolchak. These authors from Poland, Lithuania and Ukraine have created films that consist of loosely connected tableau vivant-like scenes presented in mere succession which not only make them resemble art gallery movies but can also be displayed as installation art, and which emphasise a palpable interpenetration of art and life. Majewski's *The Garden of Earthly Delights* (2004), which unfolds a poignant love story retrospectively through the video recordings made by the protagonists, may be interpreted as a reflection upon the decomposition of cinema in the post-media age[16] and a celebration of the sensual wonders of both life and art through the repeated rituals of creating 'living pictures' based on Hieronymus Bosch's *Garden*. *The Mill and the Cross* (2011) mixes painted backgrounds, photographic techniques within a digital collage that presents in a self-reflexive and metaleptic loop (incorporating both the painter, Pieter Brueghel the Elder, and his models within the painting) the creation of *The Procession to Calvary* (1564) within a palimpsest of narratives (weaved from the story condensed into the painting coming to life in the film, the story of the painting as an artwork together with it art historical interpretations) and a juxtaposition of narrative modes (characteristic of painting, cinema, theatre, literature). Life is framed by the act of painting and, the other way round, the painting is framed by the anonymous, everyday life lived by the people depicted in the shadow of the 'grand narrative' of the Passion of Christ. *Glass Lips* (2007), assembled by Majewski from independent video shorts originally shown as a gallery installation with the title *Blood of a Poet* (as a deliberate homage to Jean Cocteau), offers variations on the interconnectedness of humans and the inanimate world, and repeatedly unfolds paintings into bodies and gestures, or representations into sensations of flesh. The common denominator in Majewski's *The Roe's Room* (*Pokój saren*, 1997), Sharunas Bartas's *The House* (*A Casa*, 1997), and Ihor Podolchak's *Las Meninas* (2008) is that in each of them there is a house as a setting of a kind of lyrical autobiography or dreamlike vision, as a space where sensual impressions, recollections are reshaped by an artistic imagination. The autonomous scenes of everyday activities in these works, the lingering on details of the *mise en scène* and gestures create a world in which 'art, perception and memory, present and past become parts of the same organic rhizomatic network' (Pethő 2015a: 175). There is an oscillation between 'the logic of sensation' in a Deleuzian sense disfigurating the image into mere 'flesh and nerve' (Deleuze 2003: 45), or by 'thinking' directly through gestures of the body (Deleuze 1989: 189) and the constant re-composition of the frames to resemble paintings. By building tableau compositions around details of bodies these films perform at the same time a continuous recovery of the 'lost gestures' that Agamben (2000: 49–63) claimed to be the essential 'element' of cinema.

We see an increased emphasis on gestures in slightly more traditionally conceived narratives as well, in two films set in typically cramped Eastern European apartments. *It's Not the Time of My Life* (*Ernelláék Farkaséknál*, directed by Hajdu Szabolcs in 2016), a film about a couple returning after a failed immigration to stay with their relatives, and *Sieranevada* (directed by Cristi Puiu in the same year), depicting a lengthy family gathering commemorating the death of the father, exemplify, however, another type of 'contaminated' form. This time we do not have a mixture between film and gallery art, but one that makes the viewer part of an experience resembling something in-between reality TV and site-specific theatre (in which plays are staged within the confined space of people's homes), and in which art 'bleeds' into the perception of reality and vice versa. Hajdu's film is in fact a rewriting of an actual immersive, site specific theatre production that he wrote, directed and acted in, performed both before and after making the film, so the two works (film and theatre play) became companion pieces, expansions of each other. Puiu's *Sieranevada* was also accompanied by another work, this time a seemingly autonomous series of mostly landscape photos shot at the outskirts of Bucharest, the product of an artistic photography project prompted by the search for a poster image for the film and exhibited with the same title as the film, first in two major cities in Romania then in Paris.

This complex relationship of interrelated artworks conceived in different media attests to the commitment of contemporary Eastern European directors to experiment with intermediality in refreshing new forms, an experimentation that has a special affinity with current trends in the visual arts. A further eminent example of this is Corneliu Porumboiu's *The Second Game* (*Al doilea joc*, 2014), which recycled an old TV broadcast of a soccer match in its entirety with the only addition being the audio track commentary of the dialogue between the director and his father who was the referee of the televised game. The result is an exercise of slow cinema bordering on installation art, and a peculiar imprint of both past and present, visible and invisible, historical and private[17] (see Blos-Jáni 2018: 152–4; Pethő 2019).

Finally, in trying to assess the productivity of employing the viewpoint of intermediality within the study of any kind of films, in this case within the study of Eastern European cinema, we have to keep in mind two interconnected questions: what does the analysis of intermediality reveal about the films (i.e. about their power to present and represent), and, reversely, what does the analysis of these particular films reveal about intermediality? As all of these previous studies have shown – by relying on the expressivity, the cultural associations and the interplay of the arts – intermediality can deliver inexhaustibly rich resources for introspection. Techniques of intermediality are seldom deployed solely as art for art's sake aestheticism or formal experimentation in contemporary Eastern European films. Although the works of Lech Majewski (an author, who can arguably be situated in-between East and West, having made films both abroad and at home) are often criticised by his fellow countrymen as empty exercises in style,[18] such a reception of his *oeuvre* ultimately only underscores the potential of intermediality to elicit controversies through a clash of expectations, and to provoke discussions about the relationship between art and life. Whenever it is most effective, intermediality always operates on tensions palpable in sensuous forms that raise questions to which there are no easy answers, in several instances through a perspective lodged in-between personal experience and aesthetic distance.

Contributions in this Volume

This collection of essays proposes the examination of intermedial strategies in the cinemas emerging after the collapse of the former Eastern Bloc.[19] Its aim is to offer neither a comprehensive survey of these cinemas, nor an exhaustive compendium of stylistic devices deployed in various genres or authorial *oeuvres*, but to open up new perspectives in their interpretation through a series of essays combining in-depth case studies, comparative analyses and theoretical investigations. Intermediality is explored in this book, in this way, at the cross-section of film history and theory. The chapters seek not only to enrich our knowledge of the cinemas of Eastern Europe and Russia, but in equal measure – in the spirit of the two, interlocked questions posed before – to contribute to the understanding of intermedial phenomena (their role, their diversity and their possibilities of interpretation) in contemporary cinema as a whole. Through different theoretical approaches and thematic focuses, the book attempts to map meaningful areas of in-betweenness including the intermedial and inter-art relations connecting cinema, music, theatre, photography, painting, sculpture, literature, language and the technologies of the moving image. All of these appear in the context of other tensional interrelationships on the level of the narratives, and become manifold passageways both to palpable, even visceral experiences (or imaginary extensions) of the real, and to more abstract reflections upon life.

The first part of the book is dedicated to the foregrounding of sensations and affects through perceivable modulations of the cinematic medium absorbing the expressivity of other arts. This part, entitled, 'Entangled Sensations, Cinema in-between the Arts', comprises four chapters. The first, 'Intermedially Emotional. Musical Mood-Cues, Disembodied Feelings in Contemporary Hungarian Melodramas', written by Hajnal Király, presents a distinct group of films that can be considered as melodramas presenting female protagonists struggling with a patriarchal society. However, instead of abiding by the conventions of the genre involving the representations of emotions, these films often operate with mood cues, visual and auditory (most prominently musical) figurations of a melancholic sense of loss and helplessness which compensates for the lack of bodily excess and ensures spectatorial embodiment through the congruency, contrast or competition between image and sound. In a similar vein, Judit Pieldner's chapter, 'Black-and-White Sensations of Intermediality and Female Identity in Contemporary Polish and Czech Cinema', addresses the monochrome image as a place suspended between the real and the mediated, action and emotion, past and present. It demonstrates how female characters are shaped through the aesthetic of black-and-white against the backdrop of distinct periods of twentieth-century history, and vice versa, analyses ways in which the encounter of the female topic and the monochrome template has produced modes of representation that enhance the amalgamation of media, creating cine-photographic universes of particular atmosphere.

In the next chapter, 'Sculpture and Affect in Cinema's Expanded Field', Ágnes Pethő unravels the intermedial and inter-art admixture of sculpture and cinema in the posthumously released magnum opus of Aleksey Gherman, and the subsequent work of his son, Aleksey Gherman Jr. The films of the two Ghermans share the ambition to expand the cinematic experience towards the plastic arts but in two different, yet equally paradigmatic ways, revealing two distinct ways in which an 'intermedial sensibility' may emerge in contemporary cinema. *Hard to Be a God* (*Trudno byt bogom*, 2013) provides unique insights into the performative value and the phenomenology of what we can conceive as the cine-sculptural. *Under Electric Clouds* (*Pod elektricheskimi oblakami*, 2015), on the other hand, foregrounds sculptures in film more literally within the context of contemporary culture and the productive overlaps between the domains of cinema and installation art. The essay also examines how these connect to specific Russian traditions and how the sculptural images and images of sculptures activate different relations to language. Mareike Sera continues to describe the expressivity of sculptural masses within film in Chapter 4, in the films of the world-renowned Czech animator, Jan Švankmajer. Through case studies that span several decades of his activity, she offers a media anthropological and philosophical incursion into his works which are intersections of theatrical, photographic, musical, graphic, poetic, sculptural and architectural worlds. She discusses gestures through which stop-motion animation engages with objects, and film as an excessive and hybrid medium is able to assimilate multiple medial 'densities' resulting in a fragile ontological status of multiple worlds.

Part 2 of the book, 'Immersions into Memory, Culture and Intermediality', groups together essays about films which seem to combine some kind of symbolic journey into the realm of personal or collective history with laying out variations of specific intermedial relations. Christina Stojanova's chapter, 'Trickster Narratives and Carnivalesque Intermediality in Contemporary Romanian Cinema' pulls together the Jungian and post-Jungian understanding of an archetype and the principles of Bakhtinian dialogism and identifies a carnivalesque form of intermediality in contemporary Romanian cinema. She discusses the fascination with re-enactments and the variety of (amateur, improvised, non-professional) audio-visual inserts, displayed both by the masters of the Old and New Romanian cinema, which emphasise through their 'unrefined' and even 'vulgar' status, and their association with Trickster narratives, the unlimited abilities of cinema to imitate and to become truly polyphonic while playfully venturing into unexpected cultural and psychological depths.

The next chapter, written by Melinda Blos-Jáni with the title 'Photographic Passages to the Past in Eastern European Non-fiction Films', investigates Eastern European 'memory films' that experiment with photo-collages weaved into moving images in order to visualise the exterior and the inner realities of their subjects. Three different types of photo-filmic hybridities are identified in Hungarian, Romanian, Polish and Slovak non-fiction films which draw on both the photograph's failure to represent its object in totality (its lacanuary relationship to the truth, theorised along the ideas of Georges Didi-Huberman) and its 'graphic' expressivity, thus redefining the correlation between photographic representation and traumatic experiences of the past. Katalin Sándor's essay examines a similar incursion into the past through the case study of Jasmila Žbanić's *For Those Who Can Tell No Tales* (2013), a filmic memorialisation of crimes, atrocities and mass rapes committed during the 1992–5 Bosnian war that have not been officially recognised. Frames that disclose the cinematic image in its sensible fusions with photography, the non-cinematic practice of private video diary and fragments of performance art are discussed as constituents of an intermedial cinematic discourse conveying a personal engagement with collective trauma in a particular socio-historical context as well as a mode of addressing the aporia of its representation.

Fátima Chinita has chosen to analyse a film that epitomises digital cinema as an ultimate immersive hyper-medium, a container for the arts and media. In Chapter 8, she describes Alexander Sokurov's *Russian Ark* (*Russkiy kovcheg*, 2002) not just as a technical tour de force on account of being shot in one uninterrupted segment of ninety minutes, but as a voyage through time and media. Her analysis unravels the fictional journey of a French marquis of the nineteenth century and an unseen contemporary character through the rooms of the State Hermitage Museum in St Petersburg as a sensorial experience leading the viewer through a series of variations of tableaux, in which the metaleptic intermingling of human beings from different time periods and 'realities' combine immersion with immediacy in a way that is similar to contemporary immersive theatrical performances.

The third and final part of the book, 'Reflections upon Reality, Representation and Power', comprises four chapters that deal more explicitly and critically with the relation between the experiences of the real, the corporeal and various media representations. First, Malgorzata Bugaj examines how the distinctive style of Alexander Sokurov's family trilogy is marked by a certain oscillation between the immediate and the (re)mediated. The painterly effect of the images of *Mother and Son* (*Mat i syn*, 1997) is combined with the extreme close-ups exploring the skin. In *Father and Son* (*Otets i syn*, 2003) cinema stages a dialogue between the biological dimension of corporeality and the medical representation of the body. While *Alexandra* (2007), set within a clear sociopolitical context, explores the senses of touch and smell, and thus emphasises the trace of the physical presence on screen.

Zsolt Gyenge proposes a discussion about the conceptual aspects of a film made by one of the leading directors of New Romanian Cinema with the essay, 'This is Not Magritte. Corneliu Porumboiu's Theory of Representation'. He breaks down the theoretical implications of Porumboiu's 'visual philosophy' through the close analysis of several scenes. In doing so he aims to move beyond the usual discourse on realism and minimalism that has almost completely dominated the critical reception of New Romanian Cinema for some time. Instead, he focuses on the (inter)mediality of communication and representation in order to bring into relief the implicit philosophy of power in Porumboiu's meta-cinema, and to provide a more nuanced media theoretical interpretation of his films.

Gabriel Laverdière's essay, 'Intermedial *Détrompe l'Oeil* and Contemporary Polish Narrative Cinema', examines three contemporary Polish films, *The Wedding Banquet* (*Wesele*, 2004), *The Egoists* (*Egoiści*, 2000) and *Suicide Room* (*Sala samobójców*, 2011), in which the grainy DV images prompt the viewer to briefly detach from the film's referential construction (i.e. the inherent *trompe l'oeil* effect of the cinematic medium), creating a kind of *détrompe l'oeil*, the unveilment of a more raw, direct experience of the real. Through a combination of glossy, high-definition digital images and low-resolution video, the films are able to articulate a critical commentary on contemporary society enmeshed by practices involving digital technologies.

The final chapter of the book, Bence Kránicz's 'Superhero Genre and Graphic Storytelling in Contemporary Hungarian and Russian Cinema', confronts the questions of the real and the intermedial on another level. It examines how certain contemporary Eastern European films use superhero figures rooted in American comic books, and adapt the aesthetic of graphic storytelling. The essay also deals with questions concerning post-socialist interpretations of superheroes, while also touching on the connections between national mass culture, folklore and contemporary genre films.

This collection does not aim to test the validity of a limited number of theoretical categories that could be applied to a selected group of works in a standard methodology of analysis. It aims specifically to present intermediality as a phenomenon of in-betweenness that resists containment and allows glimpses into an instable and densely layered world experienced with often contradictory perceptions. By proposing a series of different vantage points for analysis and interpretation, the essays in this book investigate the variety of intermedial strategies employed by contemporary Eastern European and Russian films as effective means to communicate how the cultures of the region are caught in-between East and West, past and present, emotional turmoil and more detached self-awareness. They demonstrate how a focus on intermediality can not only reveal a cross section of representations and media within cinema, but also a variety of sensuous or intellectual modes for addressing important issues of art and society, identity and history.

Acknowledgment: *Research for this book was funded by grants of the Romanian Ministry of National Education, CNCS – UEFISCDI, awarded for projects number PN-II-ID-PCE-2012-4-0573 and PN-III-P4-ID-PCE-2016-0418.*

NOTES

1. The survey is limited to studies written in English. I am aware that this may not represent all the scholarship of the region, nevertheless, due to the fact that recently more and more Eastern European scholars publish in English (while relying in their researches on sources that include relevant scholarship in their mother tongue as well), the overall picture may not be too distorted.
2. For a possible typology of intermedial researches laying out the pivotal notions which define them and the main avenues pursued by such studies, see Pethő (2018).
3. In an article that further exemplifies this method, Lutas (2017) provides examples of intermediality gleaned from several contemporary Eastern European and Russian films and classifies them according to Elleström's terms of 'transmediation' and 'media representation'.
4. Articles about literary adaptations could in fact be the subject of a different review, as adaptation studies – although having many connections with the study of intermediality – can already be considered a highly prolific and autonomous area of scholarly researches.
5. Some of the chapters in this book (as indicated in the acknowledgements at the end of the texts) are also outputs of these research projects.
6. The series of international film and media studies conferences organised at the Sapientia Hungarian University of Transylvania in Cluj-Napoca as parts of these research projects also contributed to the debate around issues of intermediality. Detailed information about these conferences are available at <http://film.sapientia.ro/en/conferences>, linked to a selection of the presentations made accessible on YouTube, on the Sapientia Film Conferences Channel at <https://www.youtube.com/channel/UCOAHvaV2kCOSqQ9XrumoIRQ> (last accessed 12 June 2019).
7. See more about this in Pethő (2018: 168–74).
8. See Pethő (2011a: 41–2) where, based on the works of Henk Oosterling (1998) and Joachim Paech (2002), performativity is presented from several points of view as one of the key aspects of intermediality. The trailblazing research activity of Lúcia Nagib (e.g. 2013) has further elaborated on this idea by foregrounding the political aspects of cinematic intermediality as something inseparable from its aesthetic dimension.
9. Here I would like to apologise to the reader for the numerous self-references in this overview that I could not avoid. This summary was written with the purpose of offering an introduction into the key ideas and methodologies emerging from previous literature in the field, as well as providing a list of publications that could be used by other researchers interested in the intermediality of Eastern European

cinemas as stepping stones in their future work if they decide to explore similar issues or debate these ideas.
10. The essay compares Tarr to Pedro Costa who employs a similar yet slightly different aesthetic strategy in his Fontainhas trilogy, portraying people 'whose entire lives are defined by deep and unsettling changes, yet their days are consumed by immobility and inertia' (Pethő 2015b: 251).
11. The film is available on Vimeo at < https://vimeo.com/52296851> (last accessed 12 January 2019).
12. See the allegorical features of intermediality in Hungarian and Romanian cinema explored in further analyses by Király (2016b) and Sándor (2016).
13. In several Hungarian films made after 2000, as Király explains (2015a), the emphasis on the senses (e.g. the avoidance of touch versus the representation of smell and the control of the gaze) acts as a similarly indirect way of depicting social or political problems.
14. See, for example, the opposition of Slavophiles to Westernisers in nineteenth-century Russia (and the famous literary quarrel between Fyodor M. Dostoevsky and Ivan S. Turgenev in this context), or the Francophilia of nineteenth-century Romania aspiring to become 'the Belgium of the East' with Bucharest defined as 'little Paris', the ambivalent feelings of the Hungarians towards the Austro-Hungarian empire, and so on.
15. See articles dealing with the topic of the legacies of the past, Europeanisation and practices of self-colonisation in East-Central European Fiction Film (between 1980 and 2000), but not including techniques of intermediality, in Volume 9 issue 1 (2018) of the journal, *Studies in Eastern European Cinema*.
16. The analysis of Majewski's film (Pethő 2014a) proposing this interpretation is part of a larger essay in which three films, inspired by Hieronymus Bosch's famous painting, *The Garden of Earthly Delights*, are used to exemplify three film historical models of intermedial 'in-betweenness'.
17. This blending of the historical with the private appears also (in different ways) in the films of Hajdu and Puiu mentioned before, which combine a fictional yet highly typical story that could be anyone's in Eastern Europe with some deeply personal elements. Hajdu shot the film *It's Not the Time of My Life* in his own home with the participation of his own family, Puiu was inspired by his own father's death in creating *Sieranevada*, and included photos of his daughter and home in his exhibition of photography. For a comparison of Puiu's film and series of photographs see Pethő (2018).
18. The stunning visual style of Paweł Pawlikowski, another author working abroad and held in high esteem internationally, is often met with a similar dismissal (as I have learned from several informal conversations with people from Polish academia).
19. Although the phenomenon of intermediality cannot be seen as something specific to this region, examining it in this context follows the lead of Ewa Mazierska, Matilda Mroz and Elżbieta Ostrowska's edited volume, *The Cinematic Bodies of Eastern Europe and Russia*, who contend that looking at the countries of the

former Eastern Bloc makes sense on account of their shared history and culture, 'which remains distinct even after the fall of the Berlin Wall', having 'been shaped by similar ideologies and systems of government' (2016: 2).

WORKS CITED

Agamben, Giorgio (2000), *Means without End. Notes on Politics*, Minneapolis and London: University of Minnesota Press.
Bene, Adrián (2015), 'Intermediality and Reflexivity in Andrzej Żuławski's Fidelity', *Acta Universitatis Sapientiae: Film and Media Studies*, Vol. 11, pp. 181–93.
Blos-Jáni, Melinda (2018), 'Sensing History. On the Uses of Medium-Specific Noise in Eastern European Found Footage Films', *Acta Universitatis Sapientiae: Film and Media Studies*, Vol. 15, pp. 137–62.
Blos-Jáni, Melinda (2019), 'Ephemeral History and Enduring Celluloid – Fictions about Romanian Film History', in Christina Stojanova (ed.), *The New Romanian Cinema. A Reader*, Edinburgh: Edinburgh University Press, pp. 93–107.
Chakravorty, Swagato (2015), 'Real Bodies in (Un)real Spaces: Space, Movement, and the Installation Sensibility in Lech Majewski's *The Mill and the Cross*', *Acta Universitatis Sapientiae: Film and Media Studies*, Vol. 11, pp. 7–27.
Dánél, Mónika (2015), 'Inf(l)ection of the Medium: Sándor Kardos's Films in Between Eye and Hand'. *Alphaville: Journal of Film and Screen Media*, Issue 9 (Summer), <http://www.alphavillejournal.com/Issue9/HTML/ArticleDanel.html> (last accessed 12 January 2019).
Deleuze, Gilles (1989), *Cinema 2. The Time-Image*. London: The Athlone Press.
Deleuze, Gilles (2003), *Francis Bacon: The Logic of Sensation*, London and New York: Continuum.
Elleström, Lars (2014), *Media Transformation: The Transfer of Media Characteristics Among Media*, London and New York: Palgrave Macmillan.
Faluhelyi, Krisztián (2011), 'Cinema, DVD, and Video Installation. The Medial Forms of Benedek Fliegauf's Milky Way', *Acta Universitatis Sapientiae: Film and Media Studies*, Vol. 4, pp. 63–74.
Gelencsér, Gábor (2008), The Relationship of Film and Literature in Post-War Hungarian Cinematic Art, in Ágnes Pethő (ed.), *Words and Images on the Screen. Language, Literature, Moving Images*, Newcastle upon Tyne: Cambridge Scholars Publishing, pp. 28–41.
Gelencsér, Gábor (2015), 'Continuing the Deviating Tradition of Hungarian Experimental Film Art: András Jeles's – Scenes from a Peasant Bible', *Alphaville Journal of Film and Screen Media*, Issue 9 (Summer), <http://www.alphavillejournal.com/Issue9/HTML/ArticleGelencser.html> (last accessed 12 January 2019).
Gilić, Nikica (2010), 'Revolution, Cinema, Painting: Creative Recycling of Images in the Films of Tom Gotovac (Antonio Lauer)', *Studies in Eastern European Cinema*, Vol. 1, No. 1, pp. 71–84.
Hänsgen, Sabine (2011) 'Sokurov's Cinematic Minimalism', in Birgit Beumers and Nancy Condee (eds), *The Cinema of Alexander Sokurov*, London and New York: I. B. Tauris, pp. 43–59.
Király, Hajnal (2008), 'Making Meaning in Béla Tarr's Adaptation Satan Tango', in Ágnes Pethő (ed.), *Words and Images on the Screen. Language, Literature, Moving Images*, Newcastle upon Tyne: Cambridge Scholars Publishing, pp. 58–76.
Király, Hajnal (2010), 'The Dance of Intermediality: Attempt at the Semiotic Approach of Medium Specificity and Intermediality in Film', in Lars Elleström (ed.), *Media Borders, Multimodality and Intermediality*, New York: Palgrave Macmillan, pp. 199–210.

Király, Hajnal (2015a), 'The Alienated Body: Smell, Touch and Oculocentrism in Contemporary Hungarian Cinema', in: Ágnes Pethő (ed.), *The Cinema of Sensations*, Newcastle upon Tyne: Cambridge Scholars Publishing, pp. 185–209.

Király, Hajnal (2015b), 'The Beautiful Face of Melancholia in the Cinema of Béla Tarr', in Eve-Marie Kallen (ed.), *Tarr 60 – In the Honour of a Distinguished Cinéaste*, Budapest: Underground, pp. 179–96.

Király, Hajnal (2016a), 'Playing Dead: Pictorial Figurations of Melancholia in Contemporary Hungarian Cinema', in Ewa Mazierska, Matilda Mroz, Elżbieta Ostrowska (eds.), *The Cinematic Bodies of Eastern Europe and Russia: Between Pain and Pleasure*, Edinburgh: Edinburgh University Press, pp. 67–89.

Király, Hajnal (2016b), 'Looking West: Understanding Socio-Political Allegories and Art References in Contemporary Romanian Cinema', *Acta Universitatis Sapientiae: Film and Media Studies*, Vol. 12, pp. 67–87.

Kosmala, Katarzyna (ed.) (2014), *Sexing the Border: Gender, Art and New Media in Central and Eastern Europe*, Newcastle upon Tyne: Cambridge Scholars Publishing.

Lipiński, Kamil (2015), 'On the Re-Emergence of Motion and Innovations in the Gábor Bódy's Intermedia Experiments', *Journal of Aesthetics & Culture*, Vol. 7, <https://doi.org/10.3402/jac.v7.28394> (last accessed 12 January 2019).

López-Varela Azcárate, Asunción (2015), 'Transmedial Ekphrasis. From Analogic to Digital Formats', *International Journal of Transmedia Literacy*, Vol. 1, No 1, pp. 45–66.

Lutas, Liviu (2017), 'Transmediation or Media Representation? Media Transformation in Recent Eastern European Films', *Ekphrasis*, No. 2, pp. 47–61.

Lutas, Liviu (2019), Remediation and Minimalism in New Romanian Cinema: The Example of Cristi Puiu, in Christina Stojanova (ed.), *The New Romanian Cinema. A Reader*, Edinburgh: Edinburgh University Press, pp. 107–23.

Mazierska, Ewa and Zsolt Győri (eds) (2018) *Popular Music and the Moving Image in Eastern Europe*, London: Bloomsbury Publishing.

Mazierska, Ewa, Matilda Mroz and Elżbieta Ostrowska (eds) (2016), *The Cinematic Bodies of Eastern Europe and Russia: Between Pain and Pleasure*, Edinburgh: Edinburgh University Press.

Mironescu, Andreea (2017), 'In-Between Histories: Intermedial Configurations in Radu Jude's Collage Film "The Dead Nation"', *Jazyk a kultúra*, No. 31–2, pp. 103–11.

Müllner, András (2008), 'Films not Shot but Bloodied: "Material" Projections in Hungarian Experimental Films and Neoavantgarde Works', in Ágnes Pethő (ed.), *Words and Images on the Screen. Language, Literature, Moving Images,* Newcastle upon Tyne: Cambridge Scholars Publishing, pp. 228–42.

Nagib, Lúcia (2013), 'The Politics of Impurity', in Lúcia Nagib, Anne Jerslev (eds), *Impure Cinema: Intermedial and Intercultural Approaches to Film*, London: I. B. Tauris, pp. 21–40.

Oosterling, Henk (1998), 'Intermediality. Art between Images, Words, and Actions', in Bartolomeu Marí, Jean-Marie Schaeffer (eds), *Think Art. Theory and Practice in the Arts of Today*, Rotterdam: Witte de With, Center for Contemporary Art, pp. 89–100.

Paech, Joachim (2002), 'Intermediale Figuration – am Beispiel von Jean-Luc Godard's *Histoire(s) du Cinéma*, in Jutta Eming, Annette Jael Lehmann, Irmgard Maassen (eds), *Mediale Performanzen*, Freiburg: Rombach, pp. 275–97.

Pethő, Ágnes (2011a), *Cinema and Intermediality. The Passion for the In-Between*, Newcastle upon Tyne: Cambridge Scholars Publishing.

Pethő, Ágnes (2011b), 'Message in the (Intermedial) Bottle. The Politics and Poetics of Intermediality in Eastern Europe: the Case of Mircea Daneliuc', in *Cinema and Intermediality. The Passion for the In-Between*, Newcastle upon Tyne: Cambridge Scholars Publishing, pp. 395–417.

Pethő, Ágnes (2014a), 'The Garden of Intermedial Delights: Cinematic 'Adaptation' of Bosch, from Modernism to the Postmedia Age', *Screen*, (Winter) Vol. 55, No. 4, pp. 471–89.

Pethő, Ágnes (2014b), 'The Tableau Vivant as a 'Figure of Return', in Contemporary East European Cinema', *Acta Universitatis Sapientiae: Film and Media Studies*, Vol. 9, pp. 51–76.

Pethő, Ágnes (2015a), '"Housing" a Deleuzian "Sensation": Notes on the Post-Cinematic Tableaux Vivants of Lech Majewski, Sharunas Bartas and Ihor Podolchak', in Ágnes Pethő (ed.), *The Cinema of Sensations*, Newcastle upon Tyne: Cambridge Scholars Publishing, pp. 155–85.

Pethő, Ágnes (2015b), 'Figurations of the Photofilmic: Stillness versus Motion – Stillness in Motion', in Brianne Cohen, Alexander Streitberger (eds), *The Photofilmic. Entangled Images in Contemporary Art and Visual Culture*, Leuven: Leuven University Press, pp. 221–43.

Pethő, Ágnes (2016), 'The 'Chemistry' of Art(ifice) and Life: Embodied Paintings in East European Cinema', in Ewa Mazierska, Matilda Mroz, Elżbieta Ostrowska (eds), *The Cinematic Bodies of Eastern Europe and Russia: Between Pain and Pleasure*, Edinburgh: Edinburgh University Press, pp. 239–57.

Pethő, Ágnes (2018), 'Approaches to Studying Intermediality in Contemporary Cinema', *Acta Universitatis Sapientiae: Film and Media Studies*, Vol. 15, pp. 165–87.

Pethő, Ágnes (2019), '"Exhibited Space" and Intermediality in the Films of Corneliu Porumboiu', in Christina Stojanova (ed.) *New Romanian Cinema*, Edinburgh: Edinburgh University Press, pp. 65–80.

Pfeifer, Patricia (2017), 'The Spectator in the Interval: Corneliu Porumboiu's *The Second Game* (2014) and Marta Popivoda's *Mass Ornament #1* (2013)', *Studies in Eastern European Cinema*, Vol. 8, No. 3, pp. 232–51.

Pieldner, Judit (2014a), 'Remediating Past Images. The Temporality of "Found Footage" in Gábor Bódy's *American Torso*', *Acta Universitatis Sapientiae: Film and Media Studies*, Vol. 8, pp. 59–78. Article republished in *Revista Laika*, Vol. 3, No. 6; and also in Ágnes Pethő (ed.) (2015), *The Cinema of Sensations*, Newcastle upon Tyne: Cambridge Scholars Publishing, pp. 323–43.

Pieldner Judit (2014b), 'Remediated Bodies, Corporeal Images in Gábor Bódy's *Narcissus and Psyche*', *Ekphrasis*, Vol. 12, No. 2, pp. 45–60.

Pieldner, Judit (2015), 'Performing the Unspeakable. Intermedial Events in András Jeles's *Parallel Lives*', *Acta Universitatis Sapientiae: Film and Media Studies*, Vol. 11, pp. 127–42.

Pieldner, Judit (2016a), 'Magic Realism, Minimalist Realism and the Figuration of the Tableau in Contemporary Hungarian and Romanian Cinema', *Acta Universitatis Sapientiae: Film and Media Studies*, Vol. 12, pp. 87–115.

Pieldner, Judit (2016b), 'History, Cultural Memory and Intermediality in Radu Jude's *Aferim!*', *Acta Universitatis Sapientiae: Film and Media Studies*, Vol. 13, pp. 89–105.

Rascaroli, Laura (2017), 'Medium: Liquid Image, Fluid Camera', in *How the Essay Film Thinks*, Oxford: Oxford University Press, pp. 22–47.

Sándor, Katalin (2014a), '"Own Deaths" – Figures of the Sensable in Péter Nádas's Book and Péter Fogács's Film', *Acta Universitatis Sapientiae: Film and Media Studies*, Vol. 8, pp. 21–40. Republished in Ágnes Pethő (ed.) (2015), *The Cinema of Sensations*, Newcastle upon Tyne: Cambridge Scholars Publishing, pp. 303–23.

Sándor, Katalin (2014b), 'Corporeality and Otherness in the Cinematic Heterotopias of Szabolcs Hajdu's Film, *Bibliothèque Pascal* (2010)', *Ekphrasis*, Vol. 12, No. 2, pp. 79–93. Republished in Andrea Virginás (ed.) (2016), *Spaces, Bodies, Memories. Cultural Studies Approaches in the Study of Eastern European Cinema*, Newcastle upon Tyne: Cambridge Scholars Publishing, pp. 71–9.

Sándor, Katalin (2016), 'The Polaroid and the Cross. Media-Reflexivity and Allegorical Figurations in Lucian Pintilie's *The Oak* (1992)', *Acta Universitatis Sapientiae: Film and Media Studies*, Vol. 12, pp. 45–67.

Sándor, Katalin (2019), 'Filming the Camera – Media-Reflexivity and Reenactment in Lucian Pintilie's *Reconstruction* (1969) and *Niki and Flo* (2003)', in Christina Stojanova (ed.), *The New Romanian Cinema. A Reader*, Edinburgh: Edinburgh University Press, pp. 80–93.

Stőhr, Lóránt (2012), 'New Forms of Narrativity and Documentary on DVD, György Pálfi's *I'm not Your Friend*-Project', in Ágnes Pethő (ed.), *Film in the Post-Media Age,* Newcastle upon Tyne: Cambridge Scholars Publishing, pp. 357–81.

Tes, Ursula (2013), 'Cultural Context of the Film *Angelus* by Lech Majewski', in Renata Szczepaniak (ed.), *Media Convergence – Approaches and Experiences,* Frankfurt am Main: Peter Lang, pp. 151–9.

Twardoch, Ewelina (2015), 'The various faces of intermediality in Lech Majewski's works', *International Journal of Humanities and Cultural Studies*, Vol. 1, No. 4, pp. 524–39.

Varga, Zoltán (2008), 'Wordless Words? Some Notes on the Verbality in Animated Films through the Use of Verbality in Péter Szoboszlay's Animated Films', in Ágnes Pethő (ed.), *Words and Images on the Screen. Language, Literature, Moving Images,* Newcastle upon Tyne: Cambridge Scholars Publishing, pp. 242–57.

Zvonkine, Eugénie (2015), 'The Artistic Process of Aleksei German', *Studies in Russian and Soviet Cinema*, Vol. 9, No. 3, pp. 154–83.

Part 1

Entangled Sensations, Cinema in-between the Arts

CHAPTER 1

Intermedially Emotional: Musical Mood Cues, Disembodied Feelings in Contemporary Hungarian Melodramas

Hajnal Király

A NEW AGE OF WOMEN'S PICTURES

Contemporary Hungarian cinema presents a growing number of films that can be called melodramas in terms of their plot and formal excess compensating for the few dialogues and passivity of the protagonists. Many of these films belong to feminine sub-genres, more specifically maternal melodramas or the melodramas of single women. However, these films are not domestic melodramas in the sense that family and a home are invariably missing from them. Home ceases to be a place where these characters can make themselves understood without much difficulty, which triggers the typical melodramatic paradox scenario that they cannot be at home and be themselves at the same time (see more about this in Király 2015: 178). In contrast with the classic melodrama where the milieu appeared as an imprint of the character's psychological condition, the decor of the places they move in or away from does not or only partially reflects their state of mind, which calls for other expressive, often aural solutions. Additionally, in the Eastern European context, work-related mobility and post-communist disorientation leads to changing constructions of 'womanhood', of the 'maternal' and the 'feminine'. With the opening borders after the change of regime and EU membership, many Eastern European women – single or married – chose to leave the country and their homes for varying lengths of time, attracted by a better labour market in Western European countries. This new, work-related mobility creating a similarly mobile notion of home challenges the traditional roles of woman- and motherhood that were still valid under communism.[1]

There are seven films that I will be referring to in my analysis, three of which are maternal melodramas: Ágnes Kocsis's *Fresh Air* (*Friss levegő*, 2006), Peter Strickland's *Katalin Varga* (*Varga Katalin balladája*, 2009), Szabolcs Hajdu's *Bibliothèque Pascal* (2010), and four are single woman-melodramas: Kornél Mundruczó's *Johanna* (2005), Ágnes Kocsis's *Adrienn Pál* (2010), Károly Ujj-Mészáros's *Liza, the Fox Fairy* (*Liza, a rókatündér*, 2015) and

Ildikó Enyedi's *Of Body and Soul* (*Testről és lélekről*, 2017). What is intriguing about these films is their general lack of emotion: not only that violent emotional outbursts are completely missing, but (despite the huge pressure of their social circumstances) the female protagonists remain expressionless, moving around with blank faces and minimal gestures, almost speechless. Even in *Bibliothèque Pascal*, the story of a single mother applying for the custody of her daughter, told from her very subjective point of view at the Children's Welfare Office, the tears of the protagonist can appear suspicious after the visually alienating fantasy-sequences which make up an important part of the narrative. These films seem to resist Linda William's definition of melodrama as 'body genre', offering 'the spectacle of a body caught in the grip of intense sensation or emotion', and the portrayal of weeping women (Williams 1991: 4). As Williams argues, this genre presents a body beside itself with overpowering sadness, sobs of anguish, asking for an emotional mimicry of the person watching the film. It seems, however, that in these Hungarian films, excessive emotion is channelled towards audio-visual excess, mostly musical signifiers, resulting in the melodrama's 'visceral, non-conceptual aesthetic energy' (Gledhill 1990: 3). Often strong, repressed emotions that characters cannot reach are replaced by sensual stimuli. In Ágnes Kocsis's *Fresh Air*, a film depicting severe alienation between a single mother working in a public lavatory and her teenage daughter, smell becomes the apparent cause of distanciation between the two women and a metaphor of a problematic primary bonding. Similarly, in *Adrienn Pál*, directed by the same Ágnes Kocsis, we see a nurse working in the intensive care ward in a hospital, and the smell of dying bodies becomes figurative of the protagonist's troubled relationship with her own body and repressed emotions, symptomatically reflected by her eating disorder. Touch is appreciated by Laura Marks (2000) as a sense much in focus in non-Western non-fiction films on women made by women. In these films, the depiction of touching different materials and textures (of fabrics and clothes) ensures spectatorial embodiment and represents a missing link to repressed or forgotten emotions and memories of characters. The representation of sensual (other than visual) experiences as an intermediary stage towards emotions is epitomised by Ildikó Enyedi's film, *Of Body and Soul*, in which the autistic single female protagonist asks for professional help following her aborted efforts to connect with a colleague at the slaughterhouse, where she works. She is then encouraged by her psychiatrist to learn to feel different materials before engaging physically in a romantic relationship. Ironically, the deeper, miraculous bonding between the man and the woman is achieved visually in their converging, sensual dreams (both the woman and the man see themselves as deer who meet each other by a spring, in a snowy forest).

These shared visual fantasies stop as soon as the spiritual attraction is sexually fulfilled.

Instead of excessive, spectacular representations of emotions, these films operate with what Robert Sinnerbrink calls mood cues (Sinnerbrink 2012: 20); visual, auditory (musical), tactile and even olfactory figurations of a melancholic sense of loss and helplessness. This is in line with David N. Rodowick's argumentation regarding the melodrama's displacements, discontinuities and dissonances resulting in gaps and tears in the text: what the text cannot solve through action, dialogue or emotional confession, it has to displace onto another (stylistic) level (Rodowick 1990: 269). In what follows, after a short overview of the role of stylistical, visual and aural excess as signifier of displaced emotions of the melodrama genre, I will primarily focus on the role of diegetic and non-diegetic music as mood cue in these feminine melodramas. I will also argue that in the films under analysis excessive audiovisual stylisation is not only depicting character's moods, but it compensates for the lack of bodily excess and ensures spectatorial embodiment through an intermedial figuration based on congruency, contrast or competition between image and diegetic music.

Visual and Musical Displacement

As Thomas Elsaesser (1990) and David Rodowick (1990) point out, the melodramatic genre greatly relies on the lack of language. In melodramas the incapacity to speak and to articulate problems verbally gives way to alternative solutions. Rodowick speaks about 'displacements, dissonances, discontinuities, abjurations, eloquent silences that the text cannot solve thus has to displace and work out on another level', pointing out that the 'greater the repression of desire in the narrative the greater the energy of its displacement as violence against the textual system' (Rodowick 1990: 272). Christine Gledhill picks up on Peter Brooks's metaphor describing melodrama as a 'text of muteness' (Brooks 1976) in which visual and musical excess reaches meanings that cannot be generated with language (Gledhill 1990: 36). The verbal inefficiency, the impossibility to communicate emotions through dialogue or gestures and the failure to deal with emotional tension result in a kind of functional muteness that in these films is reflected upon (often subversively, with too long silences or dialogue lines that simply don't match) and is overcome with visual, compositional or other aural solutions. Elsaesser argues that the role of musical scenes and recorded music as mood cues evoking (with displacement) missing emotions becomes crucial, allowing conflicts to surface 'by displaced emphasis' and 'metaphoric connections' (Elsaesser 1990: 59).

In the theatrical representations of early seventeenth-century popular melodramas the spectacle ensured by music, colours and visual excess was meant to compensate for the lack of dialogue, the so-called dumb show. Besides spectacle and performance, music constituted a third non-verbal dimension (Gledhill 1990: 17). In addition to the inclusion of popular songs and ballads, music, 'often written and performed with great care was meant to clarify the action and enhance the dramatic effect' (Elsaesser 1990, 18–20). An apparent formal regression to this early stage of the melodrama as theatrical genre is detectable in the verbal minimalism in many of these Hungarian films, which is compensated by vivid colours, exuberant visual style or diegetic songs. In *Bibliothèque Pascal*, for example, the story of the main character Mona, a prostitute who returns from abroad to Romania to claim the custody of her daughter, appears in a series of flashbacks. Among other episodes, the unspeakable (because traumatic or shameful) circumstances under which Mona's daughter was conceived appear as a silent dream loaded with excessive, eclectic ethnic visual motifs. In this motionless image depicting symbolically the union between Mona and Viorel, who keeps her hostage, the two appear facing each other at a table with empty plates and glasses, as well as a jug of red wine. Both of them are dressed in exquisite ethnic costumes: Mona's robe and head accessory is reminescent of Hungarian folk costumes, mostly due to their vivid colours – red, white and green – while Viorel wears the costume of a Spanish toreador, with golden ornaments. The lack of dialogue is emphasised by the irritating buzz of a fly, a possible allusion to the uncanny nature of this encounter, balancing on the verge of real and surreal, familiar and unfamiliar. Ethnicity here, just like in *Katalin Varga*, becomes, together with femininity, a correlate of identity and power dynamics. As a signifier of otherness, ethnic identity is a core melodramatic ingredient in both films not only because it adds to the vulnerability of the two main female protagonists, but also because it makes them more interesting for the person watching the film. As Christine Gledhill argues, the interest in 'socially and morally different others' is fuelled by 'our curiosity and desire to feel what it is like to be a particular kind of person in a particular situation – essential in the generation of empathy and intersubjectivity' (Gledhill and Williams 2018: xxii). Both films are set in Transylvania (*Katalin Varga* entirely, *Bibliothèque Pascal* partly), a Romanian region with historical tensions between Romanians and a large Hungarian minority. They present maternal melodramas fuelled by the taboos and rules of more archaic, village communities (in *Katalin Varga*), as well as the clash between two worlds, Eastern and Western Europe (in *Bibliothèque Pascal*, Mona as an exotic 'other' becomes the object of desire for the Western clientèle of the exquisite brothel).

On the other hand, intriguingly, bilingualism, as a consequence of the ethnic minority status, also becomes a tool of empowerment for both Mona and Katalin. When questioned by the Romanian Viorel, Mona claims her bilingual background ('fifty-fifty' Hungarian-Romanian, as she says defensively) in an effort to hide her vulnerability both as a woman and as an ethnic minority. Later on, when claiming the custody of her daughter, she is able to speak a formal Romanian when describing the circumstances in which the child was conceived and born. Similarly, *Katalin Varga* is also set in Romania, and is about an ethnic Hungarian woman chased away by her husband when he finds out that years ago she was raped and that he is not the father of their child. She sets off together with her son on a journey through Romanian villages to take revenge on the two men who raped her, skilfully using her knowledge of both Hungarian and Romanian languages to acquire information and get closer to them. In this film, diegetic Hungarian popular songs, sung either by Katalin or her teenage son, have the role to enhance the dramatic effect and balladesque tension. The coded language of songs about losing a soulmate and about a shepherd and wolves speaks of repressed emotions, secrets, taboos and traumas of both the individual and the ethnic community. The Hungarian title of the film is actually *The Ballad of Katalin Varga* (*Varga Katalin balladája*), pointing at a hybrid genre, an epic poem with lyrical effects (or affects) strongly resonating with the melodrama genre, an amalgam between *melos* (meaning music in Greek) and drama.

Visual excess and musical moments channelling emotional tensions are also epitomised by Károly Ujj-Mészáros's *Liza, the Fox Fairy* and Kornél Mundruczó's *Johanna*. The former is the story of a single woman who, under the curse of Japanese fox fairies becomes a femme fatale against her will: all men she dates fall dead in banal accidents when visiting her at home (by choking, being crushed by a huge chandelier or from electric shock). The surreal parts are conveyed with an up-to-date, twenty-first-century image technology (e.g. an animation sequence shows the landing on the moon, special visual effects are used to create the interiors mixing retro and futuristic elements especially in the scenes taking place in the Mekkburger, a post-communist Hungarian version of KFC or Burger King, and also to render their destruction). All of which is in striking contrast with the musical oldies that Liza plays repeatedly in the film using old-fashioned tape recorders. The film mixes colours, pictures from Japanese illustrated books, a vintage visual style and decor, as well as technical, cartoonish effects, conferring a touch of magic to the claustrophobic interiors and images of a quasi-utopian, post-communist capitalist Hungary. However, there is no direct reference to a certain period: the furniture and decoration of the interiors is vaguely old-fashioned, only the outside world, the Mekkburger and Western products like the Cosmopolitan magazine point to capitalist influence after the change of régime.

Johanna is an opera film evoking the legend of Saint Joan with the story of a nurse who counters a patriarchal system represented by doctors in a hospital. After being rescued from an overdose, the amnesiac Johanna (a young drug addict, who is an extra in a film shooting at the hospital) is retained there as a nurse. She refuses the love of her controlling mentor, a young doctor, and starts healing patients with her own body by having sex with them. In the end, she is killed by the hospital personnel, doctors and nurses who rely in their work on a different kind of perception of the flesh, on scientific medical results and sophisticated technological instruments objectifying the human body. Their alienating approach based on technical images is in striking contrast to the sensuality of Johanna's healing methods, based on intimate contact. Besides a distorted colouring due to the greenish visual effect characteristic of the whole film, the contemporary, atonal, recitativo opera style is figurative of a decaying patriarchal milieu ready to repress emotions and stop compassionate healing. Johanna's arias, sung during sexual intercourse, are the sole signifiers of her emotions, contrasting with her blank face and lack of gestures. In *Adrienn Pál* the striking visual effect is conveyed by a complete lack of colour, *extracted* from the image together with the emotions through profilmic stylisation, the choice of settings and environments filled with monochrome, colourless objects. In this film, the repression of emotions is represented in scenes of excessive eating in sterile, all-white environments: emotions are swallowed down with huge quantities of equally colourless food, only to resurface as (self) destructive moods. As Thomas Elsaesser points out, 'wherever characters are seen swallowing and gulping their drinks as if they were swallowing their humiliations along with their pride, vitality and the life-force have become palpably destructive, and a phoney libido has turned into real anxiety' (Elsaesser 1990: 65).

Excessive visual minimalism metaphorically represents the blockage of expression conceived as a missed communication between body and soul in Ildikó Enyedi's film, *On Body and Soul*. This is an unconventional love story between two people who have difficulty in reaching their own feelings and sensing their own bodies: the young woman is just learning to do so (by rehearsing situations with miniature figures and by touching different materials), while the man is trying to retrieve what he has lost: hope and the vitality of his body (he has a numb arm). The visually sterile interiors (homes and offices) are counterbalanced with sensual dreams and images abounding with blood and raw meat at the slaughterhause where both the male and female protagonists are working. 'The text of muteness' of the melodrama establishes a clear parallel between the silence of protagonists who cannot reach their feelings and desires, and the eviscerated bodies of animals. This is also in line with Elsaesser's observation on melodrama's visual symbolism that suggests an environment trapping the protagonists incapable of externalising themselves into action (Elsaesser 1990: 54).

In Enyedi's film the tension created by the gap between body and soul leads to the violent, suicidal action of the female protagonist, who is turned against her own body: she slashes her veins in the bathtub, 'opening up' her body in a gesture echoing the slaughterhouse images. Attempted suicide or severely self-destructive behaviour as an outcome of a repeated failure to communicate in an assertive way with men and authority, or a failure to express strong emotions is present, in addition to Enyedi's film, also in *Johanna, Adrienn Pál* and *Liza, the Fox Fairy*). In all films under analysis, excessively loud music (e.g. the brass band in *Bibliothèque Pascal*), foolishness (in the case of *Liza*), melancholic or nostalgic emotional value (in *Adrienn Pál, On Body and Soul*) or strange tonality (in *Johanna*) appear as a valve that can release both emotions and the protagonists from a visually and symbolically overdetermined environment that keeps them entrapped. In *Bibliothèque Pascal* Mona's narration, which is rich in fantastic elements, tells about her being kidnapped and taken as a sex slave to an exquisite brothel enacting literary scenes in Liverpool, from where she is rescued by a loud brass band 'dreamed' by her daughter. The (sexual) victimisation of the female body, just like in *Johanna* or *Katalin Varga*, is not central to the narrative, it is avoided as a repressed memory and emotions are channelled through excessive visual style and/or music.

The old apartment inherited by Liza from her employer is an environment bearing the imprint of previous generations, suggestive of their nostalgia for their youth represented in old-fashioned objects and souvenirs, many of them from Japan. She tries to escape from this heritage by listening to Japanese pop music, and later is rescued (by a man addicted to Finnish country music) from the evil spirit of the Japanese pop singer Tomy Tany. This singer, only visible to Liza, takes control over her life in the same way as the curse of the legendary fox fairies operates: anyone in love with them is bound to die. Johanna's arias sung while she is healing patients with sex speak about a detachment from her very monotonous and limited tasks as a medical nurse prescribed by a routine and controlled by doctors. Nostalgic recorded music in *Adrienn Pál* also serves as an escape when she leaves her workplace, the hospital, and meets old schoolmates. In these films music has a thematic, rather than functional, structural significance; it belongs to the expressive content because it is used to formulate certain moods: sorrow, dread, suspense or happiness, respectively.

Sonorous, Enveloping Moods

Besides articulating the emotions of the characters, music triggers moods in the people watching the film. Unlike emotions, however, moods are diffuse tendencies towards emotional states and are longer lasting than emotions. The emphasis is on the bodily experience that appears in the encounter/interaction between bodies: the affecting and the affected body (in the case of film experience, between the film itself and the person watching it). Music and image framing as poetical tools can act as mood cues through which moods are experienced ('embodied') by the person watching the film. As Robert Sinnerbrink argues, music can trigger 'autonomous or enveloping moods' that transfigure narrative meaning. (Sinnerbrink 2012: 161). Music as 'enveloping' mood cue in these Hungarian films can appear as a 'paranarrative expressive dimension' (Sinnerbrink 2012: 155), that isolates the character from the narrative (often from her own life) and affects the person watching the film.

In the case of *Katalin Varga* an ambient musical score, characteristic of many contemporary films, ensures an embodiment that mediates signification responsible for bodily states in the person watching the film. A trauma that remains unrevealed until the very end haunts the film, imprinted on the soundtrack that, as Andrea Virginás describes, 'is composed of distorted noise, monotonous musical base, looped and lengthened human moaning, highlighting such aspects of temporality as before-after, or repetition (through monotony)' (Virginás 2014: 159). This disembodied voice signifying pain and fear of not only an individual, but of a community as well (that is, of all those involved in the shameful events, the rape and the exclusion) envelops Katalin and her son whenever we see them on the road with the carriage. By repetition and by its attachment to specific scenes, this soundtrack becomes an autonomous mood cue, triggering anxiety, fear in the person watching the film and exemplifies what Juan Chattah calls 'the path-expectation schema' (2015: 91): while we see Katalin and her son on the road, the soundtrack plays on the spectatorial expectation to find out the truth at the end. A scene very representative of this enveloping, musical mood cue is the one depicting Katalin and her son approaching the threatening forest that, as a menacing face, looks back at a visibly terrified, voiceless Katalin in a sequence of shot-countershot, while the soundtrack, as a disembodied voice, contains her unspeakable emotions (shame and pain over being expelled from the community) displaced into music.

While in *Katalin Varga* disembodied, extradiegetic, ambient sounds enclose the protagonist in her fear caused by traumatic memories, in the other films the retreat into an emotional, either melancholic or nostalgic 'bubble' is often facilitated by diegetic recorded music. The image of a tape recorder, a radio, a CD player or some other musical device is also a common cinematic prop used in the depiction of the female subjectivity, labelled by Pamela Robertson

Wojcik as 'the trope of the girl with the phonograph' (2001: 434). In the scenes corresponding to this trope, the female protagonist is generally alone or in the company of another woman or other women. Piroska in *Adrienn Pál* steps into the elevator, a kind of time capsule where together with a silent colleague they are listening to nostalgic music playing from the tape recorder (Figure 1.1). Liza, on the other hand, is not only a passive listener, she is dancing along and singing, or lip-synching the songs she plays on the record player (Figure 1.2). Unlike the married women and mothers mentioned in most studies about gender and phonographs, the women in these scenes are often single. Therefore, domesticity in this new type of melodrama is not at issue here. Instead of domestic use, the phonograph in such scenes signals a range of uses related to the woman's unexpressed desire (cf. Robertson Wojcik 2001).

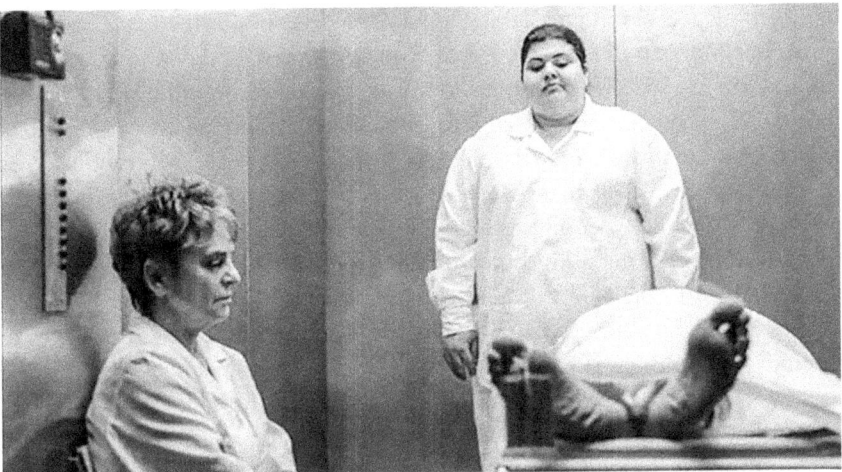

Figure 1.1 The elevator as 'a musical time capsule' in *Adrienn Pál* (2010)

Figure 1.2 Liza dancing and singing in her own 'musical bubble' in *Liza, the Fox Fairy* (2015)

As Robertson Wojcik argues, the phonograph functions not only as the perfect synecdoche of the audiovisual, but also as an overloaded gender signifier: 'it is a shorthand for female transgression and lack' (2001: 441), employed to mark sexual desire. Accordingly, it has a compensatory value: the music and the act of playing it is a consolation for depression, with lyrics telling about unspeakable feelings and acting as mood cues for the person watching the film. The songs signify the fantasy world of female characters, who are either 'bad' or 'sad' girls (2001: 445). In *Liza* suspense is sustained by an ongoing oscillation between the two types: while people watching the film get to know her as naive, the police see her as dangerous, a vamp and a serial killer. All female characters of these films are seen by society either as morally bad or at least unfitting at some point of the narrative. Similarly, Katalin Varga, Johanna and Mona are considered fallen women, Piroska is accused of performing acts of euthanasia, the female character of *On Body and Soul* is, in turn, misunderstood and considered a freak by her colleagues.

In *Liza* the scenes of listening to music with or without a headphone but not dancing, suggest emotional repression. The headphone is emblematic of enclosure of the music into the silent body, while the body is immobilised by the musical device (Liza can't move away from the cassette player or dance/move freely while listening because her movement is restricted by the headphone cable, creating a kind of intimate dependency). Such scenes alternate with moments when Liza decides to step out from her musical bubble and, after a radical change in her image (she puts on a sexy lace dress, a replica of a model she finds in the *Cosmopolitan* magazine), she becomes desiring and desirable. Similarly, apparently it is through music, through Laura Marling's songs that the autistic female protagonist from *Of Body and Soul* finally experiences emotions. In the CD shop she is recommended one of Marling's albums and it is while listening to the song *What he Wrote* that, in an act of despair, she attempts suicide in the bathtub. The lyrics are expressive of her difficulty to connect verbally and physically with the man, who is as 'broken' as she is, but whose bodily proximity (touch and smell) she craves; 'He cut out my tongue / There is nothing to say // Love me? Oh lord, he threw me away. / He laughed at my sins, in his arms I must stay // He wrote, I'm broke / Please send for me / But I'm broken too, / And spoken for . . .'

Listening to recorded music in *Liza*, represented as a 'safe bubble' for the lonely and unspoken protagonist, also attracts the concept of sonorous envelope. David Schwarz defines this as a fantasy connected with oceanic pleasure (the dissolution of boundaries separating the body from the external world) that can 'remind' us of something we can only imagine and can function as a space 'where thresholds are crossed and enunciated' (Schwarz 1997: 8). Resonating with the psychoanalytical concept of sonorous womb, represented by the maternal voice as pleasurable milieu, a fantasy, sonorous envelope refers to moments when we construct ourselves as listening subjects. In *Liza, the Fox Fairy*, the retreat of the two protagonists into their own musical bubble reveals, at the same time, the paradoxical nature of the sonorous envelope, characterised by both expansive oneness and containment. The sonorous envelope can also produce threshold crossing – a crucial component of listening as space: crossing the threshold between 'a clearly marked-off adult body and a fantasy of a familiar but archaic body less distinctly marked off from the external world than its adult counterpart' (Schwarz 1997: 8). We have seen how in *Katalin Varga* music stands for the state of mind of the character that is not expressed verbally and becomes, at the same time, an enveloping mood cue ensuring spectatorial embodiment. In *Of Body and Soul* music as sonorous envelope and mood cue is complemented by the image of a suicidal protagonist in the bathtub, a visual equivalent of a sonorous womb, listening to Marlings's melancholy song, in a scene that deliberately depicts death as birth or resurrection to a new life. Diegetic recorded music as mood cue, presented together with visual cues, such as colours and composition, isolating framing and de-framing also appears in Kocsis's *Fresh Air*, where both protagonists have their own musical bubble: the mother is shown at her workplace, a public toilet, listening and dancing with a small radio held to her ear, while the music gradually becomes louder and by visibly taking over her mind and body, turns into her 'own music,' i.e. the sound of her feelings (Figure 1.3). The daughter is seen in the dark of her room listening to a melancholy pop song that sounds like a prayer for 'not being misunderstood'. The loud music, in striking contrast with the silence of the daughter, can be also heard in the room where the mother is and appears as an unconscious wish of (and a desperate cry for) reconciliation.

Figure 1.3 The mother listening to her 'own music' in *Fresh Air* (2006)

Audio-Visual Meaning Making

These semantic correspondences between the visual and the aural, characteristic of these films and figurative of disembodied emotions correspond to what Juan Chattah calls metaphoric mappings and a congruency understood as the 'association of visual and musical movements' (2015: 65). Besides semantic congruency, reflected in conceptual metaphors like 'psychological tension is loudness' (the case of *Katalin Varga*), 'soft music is relaxed state of mind' (in *Fresh Air*, for example) or 'psychological tension is consonance-dissonance' (exemplified by *Johanna*) (Chattah 2015: 88), these films also exemplify a semantic contrast between the visual and the musical, or even a competition between the two domains, as it is the case of *Liza, the Fox Fairy*. As we have seen, congruency is applicable to *Fresh Air*, where colours and composition depict metaphorically the same isolation and impossibility to communicate as the tunes played by the protagonists. Similarly, in *Johanna* the alienating, de-humanising effect of greenish lights and the display of medical instruments is in semantic congruency with the dissonant opera music. The same pattern appears in *Katalin Varga*, where the loud, atmospheric music stands for the tension of the main protagonist. But in the case of *Bibliothèque Pascal* and *Adrienn Pál* there can be a contrast between the semantic content of the visible and audible: in the first film the loud brass band music dreamed by the daughter appears as an aggressive intrusion into the visually sterile scene of a ritual execution. In a similar vein, the all-white and metal environment and the protagonist's blank and pale face in *Adrienn Pál* is in striking contrast with the emotional, nostalgic Italian pop music about a little girl, played on the tape recorder in the hospital elevator. In both cases loud music is meant to connect the protagonists with their memories and feelings: in *Bibliothèque*, the mother returns home and applies for custody of her daughter; in the last scene of *Adrienn Pál* we see the nurse dancing and smiling, her body becoming (by re-embodiment) this time an expression of her emotions.

In *Liza*, the final 'battle' at the end of the film, between the song on the tape recorder (the Finnish western) and the sophisticated visual decor, ending with the triumph of the former, can be read as emblematic of the social reintegration process of the female protagonist. This closing scene depicts the heroic rescue mission undertaken by Sergeant Zoltán, a police officer who moves in with Liza in order to secretely supervise her and provide evidence that she is a serial killer. He falls in love with her and, in this scene, he is struggling through a number of obstacles in slow motion, accompanied by the western musical soundtrack, managing to save a suicidal Liza, trapped in the visual maze of melancholic isolation. The scene with the loud pop western and the predominantly visual scene depicting Liza's hallucinatory dream about her meeting with Tomy Tani in the Mekkburger (an ironic name for a post-communist Hungarian version of the global fast-food chain, McDonald's) are shown in a parallel montage. As the sergeant advances towards Liza in the flat, and Liza in her dream realises that her secret helper (who previously mended broken objects in the flat) was the sergeant, the illusionary world behind the windows of the Mekkburger, animated by the ghostly pop singer gradually disappears. At the end of the montage Zoltán's musical theme can already be heard in the scene of the meeting with Tomy Tani, marking the sergeant's presence. The decor falls as a wall that separates reality from illusion, truth from lie and we see the two men facing each other for a moment in Liza's room, like in a western: Zoltán advancing with his music and Tomy trying to maintain Liza in this hallucinatory state. The moment of transition between artificial visuality and a more realistic depiction of the room also marks Liza's return to (social) life.[2]

The audio-visual competition goes hand in hand with a duel of the two musical scores (male and female, associated with the two protagonists) and two old tape recorders that signify/symbolise the audiophilia of Liza and Sergeant Zoltán. The Finnish western, as a marginal pop-rock genre, just like the expressionless face of Sergeant Zoltán also evokes the male melodramas of Finnish director Aki Kaurismäki, in which emotional oldies have the same role to express, by displacement, the unspeakable emotions of 'stone faced' male characters.

The phenomenon of competition between the visual and the auditory can be also described with the concept of 'fold', connected by Deleuze to what Alfred Jarry calls 'audiovisual battle' (cf. Deleuze 1988: 112). The concept of the 'fold' is descriptive of an intermedial cinema represented by *Liza, the Fox Fairy*, that is, of the figurative interactions between the visual and auditory, stillness and movement, the artificial and the unmediated. As Ágnes Pethő points out, cinematic intermediality is

> the experience of some kind of juxtapositions, jumps, loops or foldings between the media representations and what we perceive as cinematic reality. This kind of intermedialization may take the form of diegetic reflexivity, or it may result in the world appearing as a media collage, it can be perceived as a marker for metaleptic leaps, intermediality may perform metaleptic contrasts between the 'natural', the seemingly 'unmediated' and the 'artificial' within the image, as well as 'folds' of the immediate and the mediated. (Pethő 2011: 6)

In *Liza, the Fox Fairy* the sonorous folding over the visual, the artificial over the unmediated, resulting in a constant interplay between the inside and outside, visible and invisible, also resonates with a Japanese cultural reference: the love for packaging of the Japanese, in which Roland Barthes used to admire the freedom from the Western obsession with meaning within objects, with signifieds within signifiers (Barthes 1982: 46).

Anti-melodramas?

The audio-visual figuration of emotions and an equivalence, contrast or competition between the visual and aureal delineate a highly aesthetic approach evocative of what Katherine Woodward labels as anti-melodramas, characteristic of the European cinematic modernism. As she argues, these anti-melodramas are distancing the viewer from the events portrayed in order to 'scrutinize their own melodramatic inclinations', 'thus eliciting contemplation rather than emotional identification' and transforming the 'alienating techniques into integral comments on the creation of melodramatic emotion' (Woodward 1991: 585). With the exception of *Katalin Varga* and *Johanna*, in which melodramatic conflict is constructed along the divide between good and evil, in the Hungarian films analysed above, characters are not presented in moral terms, but are, just like many characters of the modernist cinema, alienated and confused. These new Hungarian melodramas share many features of the films of Godard, Truffaut and Fassbinder listed by Woodward, that is, the intention to comment on melodramatic possibilities and many narrative features like the absence of home, rootlessness, the presence of strangers versus the all pervasive continuity of love. On the stylistical level we can also identify the dissociation of image and sound, the draining of narrative from emotional impact, a preference for strong heroines and a lack of real suspense and grand gestures. However, they do not share 'the total fusion between form and content and an analysis of the basic premise: the primacy of emotion' (Woodward 1991: 592–4). In these Hungarian films emotions are unseen and unspeakable, often dissociated from the bodies, displaced to a stylised aural/musical representation. But, as mentioned above, alienation is never complete: repressed emotions are surfacing and enveloping the viewers through visual and musical mood cues. While in the classic melodrama strong emotional outbursts counterbalanced the hero's impossibility to act, in these films, nostalgic and melancholic moods are not compensating for the lack of action, but often are figurative of a generalised helplessness. The double ending in some of these films – in *Bibliothèque Pascal, Adrienn Pál, Of Body and Soul* and *Liza, the Fox Fairy* – introduces a new narrative function of the musical scene: diegetic music has a breakthrough effect, it helps the protagonists to connect with their own repressed emotions, thus triggering a kind of emotional resurrection. As if, in order to be able to live their emotions, make soul and body meet, they need to almost die in an emblematic, musical scene. In order to let emotions surface, the inexpressive body needs to be destroyed, or at least hurt, cut open. The epilogues of these three films depict a state of emotional fulfilment, but only after emotions, all along replaced by mood cues, are embodied again. In *Adrienn Pál* for example, the final musical scene playing the very emotional popular song *Little Bird* (*Kismadár*), at a children's birthday party full of colours, shows the heroine's re-connection with her emotions, and is indicative of a kind of emotional resurrection, of a rebirth of her own. This is the first time we see her smiling. Providing a dramatic affirmation of the viewer's belief in the solution of the initial conflict is characteristic of the classic melodrama, while the anti-melodrama, according to Woodward, withholds that affirmation (that is, there is no solution to the initial conflict) (Woodward 1991: 587). Intriguingly, in these films, the re-embodiment of emotions is not presented as a spectacular breakthrough, a bodily act of excessive emotions. The representation of the emotional turn, (soft crying or smiling) is complemented visually and aurally with colours, composition or a highly emotional musical score, which places these films somewhere between classic and anti-melodramas, similar to those of Fassbinder and Kaurismäki.

Maternal or single female melodramas represent a very distinct group in the Hungarian cinema. The dramatic conflict they present is not a domestic one, induced by patriarchal order, but is related to the inner conflict of a female subjectivity in process of transformation, struggling to reach genuine emotions and a forgotten feminine identity. Music doesn't reinforce the bodily expression of emotions, nor does it complement visual stylisation: it rather appears independent and initiates a dialogue with the image in a contrasting, competing way. It is often responsible for enveloping moods that reflect on the image and affect the person watching the film. This unconventional image-sound relationship thematises the innovative figurative potential of cinematic intermediality.

Accepting Elsaesser's idea that melodrama is an 'expressive code' (1990: 51), we can argue that the thematisation of the characters' own and recorded music in these films can be seen as elements of interiorisation and personalisation of social and ideological conflicts. Melodrama is popular in periods of intense social, ideological crisis: in the case of Eastern Europe, we see a crisis of femininity as a symptomatic parallel of a crisis of masculinity triggered by the fall of a patriarchal communist order[3] and aggravated at times by problematic ethnic identity and issues of post-communist mobility (in *Bibliothèque Pascal*). This seems to exemplify what Matthew Buckley calls the myths of melodrama's revolutionary and moral foundational birth, through a relentless engagement with trauma, 'taking form from the crisis of a traditional order' (Buckley 2018: 20–4). However, this crisis should not be seen as a loss, but as an affirmation of the force of morality, and of a new type of masculinity and femininity. Both contemporary Hungarian and Romanian films often thematise the process of understanding and rejection of the obsolete social roles of previous generations.[4] In comparison with contemporary Romanian, mostly male melodramas, where the transgenerational male conflicts are conveyed by iconic abstractions of the three Orthodox Patriarchs and painterly references,[5] in Hungarian female melodramas music becomes the missing link between body and soul in the recovery process of sensuality and emotions. The different intermedial articulations of the same post-communist crisis of patriarchy – that could be the subject of another essay – testifies for the perception of melodrama not simply as a genre, but as a transcultural modality (as Gledhill suggests, 2018), fulfilling our relentless interest in otherness.

This work was supported by a grant of the Romanian Ministry of National Education, CNCS – UEFISCDI, project number PN-III-P4-ID-PCE-2016-0418.

Notes

1. Many women and families working abroad commute between Hungary and their new homes. In this respect, the variable form of the Hungarian word for 'home': 'itthon' (literally meaning something like 'here-home') and 'otthon' ('there-home') can be seen as highly suggestive. On the phenomenon of post-communist placelessness represented in Hungarian and Romanian films see Király (2015).
2. See a more detailed analysis of this scene in an other essay (Király 2018) comparing the film with another post-communist Hungarian musical, *Dollybirds* (*Csinibaba*, Péter Tímár, 1997), where musical scenes are analysed as figurations of nostalgia (and belonging to a community in Tímár's film) and melancholia (isolation from the community in *Liza*).
3. This crisis is often represented as a disorientation, an identity quest of sons, their strained and ambivalent relationship to a (distant or missing) father figure in many Hungarian films from the early 2000s to the present. In a Hungarian context, the male melodramas of Kornél Mundruczó are the most representative in this respect: *This I Wish and Nothing More* (*Nincsen nekem vágyam semmi*, 2000), *Szép napok* (*Pleasant Days*, 2002), *Delta* (2008), *Tender Son. The Frankenstein Project* (*Szelíd teremtés. A Frankenstein-terv*, 2010).
4. See for example the Hungarian films, *Father's Acre* (*Apaföld*, 2009), the already analysed *Johanna* as female melodrama, or the Romanian films *Child's Pose* (*Poziția copilului*, Călin Peter Netzer, 2013) and *Sieranevada* (Cristi Puiu, 2016)
5. The frequent reminiscences of Byzantine, triangular iconograpy in the New Romanian Cinema have been discussed as specific intermedial techniques by Király (2016) and Pieldner (2016).

Works Cited

Barthes, Roland (1982), *Empire of Signs*, New York: Hill and Wang.
Brooks, Peter (1976), *The Melodramatic Imagination: Balzac. Henry James, Melodrama and the Mode of Excess*, New Haven: Yale University Press.
Buckley, Matthew (2018), 'Unbinding Melodrama', in Christine Gledhill and Linda Williams (eds), *Melodrama Unbound: Across History, Media and National Cultures*, New York: Columbia University Press, pp. 15–30.
Chattah, Juan (2015), 'Film Music as Embodiment', in Maarten Coegnarts and Peter Kravanja (eds), *Embodied Cognition and Cinema*, Leuven: Leuven University Press, pp. 81–113.
Deleuze, Gilles (1988), *Foucault*, Minneapolis: University of Minneapolis Press.
Elsaesser, Thomas (1990), 'Tales of Sound and Fury. Observations on Family Melodramas', in Christine Gledhill (ed.), *Home is Where the Heart Is: Studies in Melodrama and the Woman's Film*, London: BFI Publishing, pp. 43–69.
Gledhill, Christine (1990), 'The Melodramatic Field: An Investigation', in Christine Gledhill (ed.), *Home is Where the Heart Is*, London: BFI Publishing, pp. 43–69.
Gledhill, Christine and Linda Williams (eds) (2018), *Melodrama Unbound: Across History, Media and National Cultures*, New York: Columbia University Press.
Király, Hajnal (2015), 'Leave to Live? Placeless People in Contemporary Hungarian and Romanian Films of Return', *Studies in Eastern European Cinema*, Vol. 6, No. 2, pp. 169–84.
Király, Hajnal (2016), 'Looking West: Understanding Socio-Political Allegories and Art References in Contemporary Romanian Cinema', *Acta Universitatis Sapientiae: Film and Media Studies*, Vol. 12, pp. 67–87.
Király, Hajnal (2018), 'Pop Music, Nostalgia and Melancholia in *Dollybirds* and *Liza, the Fox Fairy*', in Ewa Mazierska and Zsolt Győri (eds), *Popular Music and the Moving Image in Eastern Europe*, New York, London, Oxford, New Delhi: Bloomsbury Academic, pp. 83–98.
Marks, Laura (2000), *The Skin of the Film. Intercultural Cinema, Embodiment, and the Senses*, Durham, NC and London: Duke University Press.
Pethő, Ágnes (2011), *Cinema and Intermediality. The Passion for the In-Between*, Newcastle upon Tyne: Cambridge Scholars Publishing.
Pieldner, Judit (2016), 'Magic Realism, Minimalist Realism and the Figuration of the Tableau in Contemporary Hungarian and Romanian Cinema', *Acta Universitatis Sapientiae: Film and Media Studies*, Vol. 12, pp. 87–115.
Robertson Wojcik, Pamela (2001), 'The Girl and the Phonograph; or the Vamp and the Machine Revisited', in *Soundtrack Available: Essays on Film and Popular Music*, ed. Pamela Robertson Wojcik and Arthur Knight, Durham, NC: Duke University Press, pp. 433–53.
Rodowick, David N. (1990), 'Madness, Authority and Ideology. The Domestic Melodramas of the 1950's', in Christine Gledhill (ed.), *Home is Where the Heart Is: Studies in Melodrama and the Woman's Film*, London: BFI Publishing, pp. 268–82.
Schwarz, David (1997), *Listening Subjects: Music, Psychoanalysis, Culture*, Durham, NC and London: Duke University Press.
Sinnerbrink, Robert (2012), 'Stimmung: Exploring the Aesthetics of Mood', *Screen*, Vol. 53, No. 2 (Summer) pp. 155–63.
Virginás, Andrea (2014), 'Female Trauma in the Films of Szabolcs Hajdu, David Lynch, Cristian Mungiu and Peter Strickland', *Studies in Eastern European Cinema*, Vol. 5, No 2, pp. 155–68.

Williams, Linda (1991), 'Film Bodies: Gender, Genre, and Excess', *Film Quarterly*, Vol. 44, No. 4 (Summer), pp. 2–13.
Woodward, Katherine S. (1991), 'European Anti-melodrama: Godard, Truffaut, and Fassbinder', in Marcia Landy (ed.), *Imitations of Life. A Reader on Film and Television Melodrama*, Detroit: Wayne State University Press, pp. 586–95.

CHAPTER 2

Black-and-White Sensations of History and Female Identity in Contemporary Polish and Czech Cinema
Judit Pieldner

BLACK-AND-WHITE SPOTS ON THE MAP OF CONTEMPORARY CINEMA AND THE DIGITAL MONOCHROME

If asked to reflect on black-and-white films made today, some of us would most probably think of a type of tableau image such as the one encountered in Michael Haneke's *The White Ribbon* (*Das weiße Band*, 2011), rendering a solitary, empty landscape accompanied by the voice-over of the retrospective narrator. A still image inserted, as part of a series, into the texture of narration, lingers as a moment of stasis within the moving image. This momentary arresting of time reveals the subjective construct of the past that condenses in its enigmatic tranquillity and fixity the tense atmosphere that precedes World War I. An image of the irretrievable past, a moment of fragile beauty – this is what the photographic still within the film carries in itself, together with the potential of becoming memorable as an image, burnt in the beholder's mind. The Hanekean still may be highlighted as incorporating those qualities that are most commonly associated with the contemporary use of the black-and-white film, namely the evocation of both the past and high artistry. The logic of evocation of the past is actually carried out via the logic of transposition: the effect of calling forth a bygone world is achieved through the mimicry of a past mode of representation and through the quality of the photographic within film. The Hanekean example marks out the terrain that this essay addresses, namely the intermedial sensation, implying the conjunction of photography, painting and film, emerging in the aesthetic of the contemporary black-and-white cinema.

In the digital age, in the spirit of proliferation of a kind of vintage aesthetic, the use of black and white as a tendency to revert to earlier forms of representation has been refashioned with new impetus. The revival of the black-and-white filmmaking is a worldwide phenomenon. Beyond its exceptional diversity motivated by various intents, the aesthetic of the black-and-white image can be traced back to the perceptual otherness that has defined the monochrome art of all times, not only analogue cinema, but also classical photography and monochrome painting. The digitally created monochrome (with its nuances perceptible within the colour range between black and white)[1] establishes a fruitful connection with the heritage of monochrome artistic representation. The black-and-white image carries in itself the potential to make the viewer rethink the relationship between 'reality' and representation, to be engaged in a process of abstraction, being elevated from the 'real', and in parallel, to also reflect on the nature of spectatorial experience. Such images are perceived in the in-betweenness of the analogue and the digital, the natural and the artificial, the cinematic and the photographic. They are part of the vertiginous digital adventure that is coined by Philip Rosen as the regime of the 'digital mimicry', referring to 'the capacity of the digital to imitate [. . .] preexisting compositional *forms* of imagery' (Rosen 2001: 309, italics in the original). Rosen defines the digital image as being determined by two fundamental and apparently contradictory drives: 'the sundering from origins and unprecedented manipulability of pictorial and compositional elements are two of the founding thematics in arguments for the radical novelty of the digital on the plane of images' (Rosen 2001: 307). What is of interest for us here with regards to the black-and-white mode of representation is that when it appears in the digital age, the spectator's awareness of simulation is activated. Simulation is situated at the core of the digital image: 'to make its "simulations", the digital had to mime previously known instruments that functioned as reliable imprints of the world', that is 'to reproduce nondigital image configurations' (Rosen 2001: 310, 313). In the spirit of simulation, the appropriation of the old, in our case the black-and-white image as the erstwhile mode of recording, always appears conjointly with the viewer's awareness of simulation, resulting in Rosen's terms, in the 'hybridizations of old and new' (2001: 315). In this way, the digital mimicry is a mode that induces hybridity, impurity, as a consequence, 'one would have to seek the digital in the contradictory junctures of idealized purities and impure hybridities' (Rosen 2001: 315).

Lara Thompson (2010) discusses digital black-and-white cinema in terms of the 'inherent nostalgia for the optical and ontological qualities of the analogue, black and white photograph'. As she states, digital black-and-white cinema is driven by

> a longing not for the past, but for a past mode of representation. Contemporary critics seem to be mourning not the loss of actual photographic realism, but rather the emotional loss of a kind of imagined, fetishised photographic truth and aura, elevated by Susan Sontag and Roland Barthes, the most visible element of which is a monochrome palette. (Thompson 2010)

The awareness of simulating photographic representation in the contemporary cinematic image subtly overwrites the sense of photorealism even in the most realistic forms of representation, thus the rendition of the past – as in most cases the monochrome image is associated with the past – turns up in the form of constructed, artificial, stylised realities: 'the black and white image is a constructed version of reality. It envisions a past that has been stripped of colour, a past that has been re-imagined in form and line, in contrast and shadow' (Thompson 2010).

Female Identities in the Fore of a Monochrome Past

This essay proposes to look into a segment of contemporary black-and-white East-Central European cinema productions, formed by a set of Polish films with female protagonists, namely, in chronological order: *Hi, Tereska!* (*Cześć, Tereska*, Robert Gliński, 2001), *The Reverse* (*Rewers*, Borys Lankosz, 2009), *Ida* (Paweł Pawlikowski,[2] 2013), *Papusza* (Joanna Kos-Krauze and Krzysztof Krauze, 2013) and *Cold War* (*Zimna wojna*, Paweł Pawlikowski, 2018). In addition, a Czech film with Polish connections,[3] *I, Olga Hepnarová* (*Já, Olga Hepnarová*, Tomáš Weinreb and Petr Kazda, 2016), will also be examined. In them, the use of the black-and-white representational mode seems to conform to one of the major conventions of the digital monochrome, namely the evocation of the past via mimicking a past mode of representation, creating thus more iconic, more memorable figures than a colour version could perhaps render.

From a generic perspective, the black-and-white image proves to be applicable in a wide range of genres. Robert Gliński's *Hi, Tereska!* is a coming-of-age story (a dark Eastern European mumblecore perhaps), which is an emerging subgenre in postsocialist countries reflecting, through the representation of the 'transitory' age, adolescence, the abysses of the transitory period after the fall of the communist regimes in Eastern European countries. Borys Lankosz's *The Reverse* differs from the drama-type films in that it is a bizarre dark comedy, a parody of the film production of the 1950s and also of crime movies. It constructs a caricaturesque world, showing the respective period from its 'reverse', constructing a storyline that evolves from burlesque, through romance, to horror. Set in the 1960s, Paweł Pawlikowski's *Ida*, the story of a nun in quest of her true identity and hidden past, combines the features of memory film and road movie; Pawlikowski continues his cinematic investigation of the past in *Cold War*, a blend of historical period drama, melodrama and musical film, in which the love story between the singer and dancer Zula and the musician Wiktor Warski appears closely interwoven with the chilling East-West political relations in the 1950s. Joanna Kos-Krauze and Krzysztof Krauze's *Papusza* is a biopic about the Gypsy poetess, Bronisława Wajs, set against the backdrop of historical events before, under and after the World War II; and finally, Tomáš Weinreb and Petr Kazda's *I, Olga Hepnarová* is an existential drama that takes the viewer back to the 'grey' shades of Czechoslovakia under communist rule in the 1970s.

The five Polish films from the examined corpus attest to the profound preoccupation of Polish cinema with the historical past, forming part of the contemporary Polish 'cinema of national remembrance', the term coined by Magdalena Nowicka and Wiktor Mrozek, referenced and thoroughly substantiated by Elżbieta Durys, who argues that 'historical movies made since 2007 form one of the most (or even the only) noticeable and critically discussed trend in recent Polish cinema' (2017: 281–2). The burdened Polish history provides an inexhaustible storehouse for film directors who seek ways to access recent or most distant segments of the past, phenomena that mark the collective identity of Polish society. Taken together, the mosaics of these films, characterised by an exceptional diversity, provide an ampler insight into the stormy and traumatic history of the twentieth century, spanning from before the World War II to post-communism experienced in the eastern side of Europe.

The other predominant feature of the digital monochrome, namely the indication of artistry, also characterises these films. The association of artistry with the black-and-white image in contemporary cinema can be identified as a reconnection to European modernist art-house cinema. Even in the more commercial *The Reverse*, black-and-white photography is the marker of quality and sophistication. Furthermore, the black-and-white image that appeals to diverse photographic and painterly solutions can be seen in close association with the sensibilities presupposed by the representation of stories of women in the grip of history. In general, there is an underlying tension between the palpable and the sensuous commonly associated with the feminine on the one hand, and the distancing effect, flatness, abstraction and stylisation inherent in achromatic representation, on the other. In their own specific ways, each of these films goes against the visual pleasure that is conventionally linked to the image of the woman in the classical Hollywood-type film narrative. In them, what is withdrawn from the realm of the feminine as the object of the male gaze, is released at the level of seductive 'imageness' that Laura Mulvey conceptualises as 'the "feminization" of the spectator's gaze' (2006: 155). As she asserts, 'with the weakening of narrative and its effects, the aesthetic of the film begins to become "feminized" with the shift in spectatorial power relations dwelling on pose, stillness, lighting and the choreography of character and camera' (2006: 154).

Among the discussed films, there are illustrative instances of the 'anti-pretty' rhetoric. The least 'pretty' and the most visceral images are in *Hi, Tereska!*, in which a sombre story of an adolescent girl in a downward moral spiral unfolds against the backdrop of a post-communist urban ghetto in Warsaw, and *I, Olga Hepnarová*, an unsettling story of a young girl at odds with all family and social bonds, inspired by the real events around the last executed death sentence of a woman in Czechoslovakia in 1975. Both protagonists end up as murderers, committing their crimes as covert (in *Hi, Tereska!*) and overt (in *I, Olga Hepnarová*) indictments against the social milieu. In the two stories of radical alienation the austere imagery of the 1990s and the 1970s respectively, stress the hostile atmosphere in which the developing female identities are derailed, but also the deranged inner processes that are revealed by extreme antisocial behaviour in both cases.

In *Hi, Tereska!* the obnoxious handicapped friend, who will end up as the innocent victim of the protagonist's *action gratuite*-type unprecedented violent outburst, is in fact Tereska's alter ego, who provides a possibility for her to channel her inner tensions. In *I, Olga Hepnarová* the protagonist does not feel comfortable in her body and suffers a pathological case of deviation as regards both social and gender roles, originating from childhood traumas and schizophrenia; having been the victim of bullying, she drives her truck into a group of people in a Prague bus stop, killing eight of them, in a manner highly similar to today's terrorist acts, but with a different aim, planned not on religious or political grounds to inflict terror and fear, but as a personal revenge against the society that has shown, as she perceives it, an impassive and hostile attitude towards her throughout her short life. The massive, antagonistic forces of society are suggested, for example, in the jam-packed and boxed-in tableau shot of the trial, in which we see the people sitting in front of a dark grey curtain and with their backs to the viewer, not so much in black and white, but in nuances of 'grey on grey', conferring a heavy, sculptural quality to the image (Figure 2.1).

Figure 2.1 *I, Olga Hepnarová* (2016). Massive figures displayed in a frontal tableau shot: grey on grey

In elaborating their 'anti-pretty' imagery, both *Hi, Tereska!* and *I, Olga Hepnarová* resort to the desaturated version of the digital black-and-white image; however, while the former conforms to the conventions of quasi-documentary realism, the latter employs a perceivably more subversive style. In creating *Hi, Tereska!*, Robert Gliński worked with amateur actors who themselves came from the depicted social environment, including Aleksandra Gietner, who played the protagonist, Tereska;[4] the film recorded their improvised dialogues against the backdrop of typically post-communist, drab scenery. In this respect the film strives for authenticity by returning to the grounds of Italian neorealism, characterised by the employment of non-professional actors, for instance, simple workers as in the famous *Bicycle Thieves* (*Ladri di biciclette*, Vittorio de Sica, 1948) performing fictitious stories set in a documentary-like milieu. Robert Gliński carried his especially mobile DV camera in the manner of the Dogme 95 filmmaking style, with unconcealed educationalist purposes. He treated his subject matter objectively; the low-key black-and-white images were meant to render the greyness of life in the represented suburban ghetto, proving especially suitable for the realistic claim of representation and situating the story in between documentary realism and fiction (Mazierska 2007: 149).

The making of *I, Olga Hepnarová* is also motivated by an intent to realistically represent a controversial past event, creating the script based on confessions of witnesses and those personally involved in the story; the elaboration of the film is, however, more dramatic, more shattering, relying on carefully composed, heavy static shots (like the one in Figure 2.1). Olga Hepnarová's anomalous conduct, which pushes her towards a radical political act, is conveyed by an unsettling monochrome imagery, whereby sensing differently is the essence of Rancière's concept of political *dissensus*, 'an activity that cuts across forms of cultural and identity belonging and hierarchies between discourses and genres, working to introduce new subjects and heterogeneous objects into the field of perception' (Rancière 2010: 2). Lúcia Nagib proposes to rethink Rancière's concept of *dissensus* in relation to the intermediality, the 'impurity' of cinema stating that the employment of other media in film 'suspends the pedagogical character of representational narratives by introducing a dilemma, or "dissensus", in Rancière's terms, which, rather than giving univocal lessons, multiplies the meaning of the referent' (2014: 31). Nagib uses the term 'impure' with reference to André Bazin's 1951 essay *Pour un cinema impur: défense de l'adaptation*, in the sense of cinema's intermedial connections and potential for hybridisation. The digital black-and-white cinema, standing out as an 'impure' form due to its appeal to old forms while being in fact new does introduce ambivalence and *dissensus*, multiplying the modalities of its perception. *I, Olga Hepnarová* can be taken as an excellent example that illustrates the multi-layeredness of the contemporary black-and-white image, since the artistry of the film extensively draws on the simultaneous harshness and subtlety of the monochrome image, hard and soft, ruthless and sensitive as Olga Hepnarová herself is.

In the films that use a glossier type of monochrome imagery, the perception of this kind of digital mimicry activates a double register in another way: the black-and-white image arouses analogue nostalgia by evoking the medium of a particular era, but a glaze of digital polish overwrites this sensation, turning the illusion of the erstwhile medium into a contemporary awareness of the artificial. Such is Borys Lankosz's *The Reverse*, set in Warsaw in the 1950s; its black-and-white cinematography (by Marcin Koszałka) imitates, on the one hand, the cinema of the period evoked, e.g. Andrzej Munk's comedy *Bad Luck* (*Zezowate szczęście*, 1960), and has an evident contemporary lustre, on the other. This yields a perceptual in-betweenness of the illusion of analogue production and, at the same time, the awareness of digital simulation. In addition, the mixed use of black-and-white and colour images indicates the difference between the past and the present, resulting in the heterogeneity of the moving image, which inscribes, again, a certain degree of *dissensus* into its perception. The colour images show Sabina, the protagonist at an old age, as a survivor, after all that happened in her youth, shown in black and white: committing the murder of her suitor under bizarre circumstances and hiding the remains of the body in the foundations of Warsaw's highest and most representative building, the Palace of Culture and Science, under construction at that time. Thus, the film subtly interweaves the motif of ordinary lives of ordinary people (Durys 2017) with a caricature image of the power mechanisms of Stalinist times, when everybody had to bend the truth, to pretend, to circumvent the system, a heritage that profoundly marks today's post-communist Eastern European culture. At the same time, Sabina's queer caricature figure, the clumsy spinster who embodies a 'pretty anti-pretty' feminine image (that might be connected to the *Frances Ha*-type trend of the awkward female character, epitomised by Noah Baumbach's 2012 film) is incorporated into a hybrid generic pattern that amalgamates and subverts, with Thomas Schatz's (1981) categories, the feminine genres of integration (comedy, melodrama) and the masculine genres of order (crime movie, the secret-agent suitor's macho behaviour being reminiscent of gangster films). Nevertheless, in this ingenuous comedy the monochrome mostly remains at the level of playful stylisation (see the patterns of grey fabric framing the protagonist in Figure 2.2), marking the shifts of time between the past and the present.

In her elaboration of the 'pretty' as an aesthetic category, Rosalind Galt points at its troublesome character, arising from a 'quality of discomfort

Figure 2.2 *The Reverse* (2009). The female protagonist set in the context of a variety of generic patterns amalgamated in the film and against various patterns of grey fabric

with a style of heightened aesthetics that is too decorative, too sensorially pleasurable to be high art, and yet too composed and "arty" to be efficient entertainment' (Galt 2011: 12). The glossy, ornamental, exoticising images and Gypsy-ethno orientalism of Joanna Kos-Krauze and Krzysztof Krauze's *Papusza*, the only film in the corpus that is also made by a female film director, qualifies through the in-betweenness with which Galt characterises the 'pretty' image. The choice of shooting in monochrome underpins the film's express non-racist attitude in depicting the nomadic Polish Romani community on the brink of dissolution, as in a world of light and shadow the differences of skin colour are blurred. The film relates the rise and fall of the Polish Romani poetess Bronisława Wajs or Papusza, discovered by the Polish poet, writer and translator Jerzy Ficowski, prominent personality of Polish literature. It sensitively transposes the light from the central, canonical literary figure of Jerzy Ficowski to the marginal figure of Papusza, a literate Gypsy woman endowed with poetic talent, and through her, to the social fresco of the Polish Romani people, in times of crisis that threaten the existence of the community. Papusza's identity drama arises from her ethnicity, in close interconnection with her immediate community which considers the poetess as a traitor who has betrayed the Romani identity. As the reviewer Bartosz Staszczyszyn (2013) notes, the film 'has the structure of a white poem', 'it's a filmic crystal that lacks shortcomings, it's a poem recorded on celluloid tape'. This poetic quality is achieved through a non-chronological ordering of events, through flashbacks, but perhaps more importantly, through long takes and a balanced, rhythmic pulsation of decorative, crystal-clear, high contrast, decidedly black-and-white (and never grey tone) images, creating a correspondence between the filmic, the painterly and the photographic. Several scenes look like high definition, high contrast, black-and-white renditions

Figures 2.3–2.4 *Papusza* (2013). Frames that look like high definition, black-and-white renditions of Romantic genre paintings

of genre paintings with Gypsies shown in dynamic scenes against picturesque landscapes (Figure 2.3) or ruins, gathered around the camp fire (Figure 2.4), thus showing reverence for an ethnic group and its traditions in a romanticised fashion.

Albeit profoundly distinct in terms of genre and approach, *Papusza* and Paweł Pawlikowski's much-discussed *Ida* – both dealing with history through the prism of female fates, Gypsy and Jewish respectively – are similar in their use of glossy monochrome tableaux and in their poetic character achieved through the inflections of the photographic and the painterly. Set in the

1960s, *Ida* has as its protagonist a young novice, Anna, her story being intertwined with that of her aunt, Wanda; the traces of her unknown past lead to the Holocaust. The orphan novice is told, before taking a vow to become a nun, to visit her only living relative, 'red Wanda', a former communist state prosecutor now living a mundane and promiscuous life. Wanda informs her about her real name, Ida Lebenstein, her Jewish heritage and the fate of her deceased parents. It is at this point that they embark on a journey, in the spirit of a road movie, to find out where Ida's parents are buried. Their quest leads back to her parental home expropriated by the Polish family, who turn out to have killed them. In exchange for Ida's renouncing the claim for the parental house and estate, the Polish man shows them the burial place in the forest and exhumes the bones, among them also the remains of Wanda's son, which Anna and Wanda will rebury in a Jewish cemetery. Under the burden of the unprocessed trauma Wanda commits suicide, and Ida literally steps in her shoes, briefly identifying with her, before she returns to take the vow. Shooting the film in black and white, together with a minimalist setting and the Academy 4:3 ratio, successfully conjures up the dreary environment of post-Stalinist Poland, and, on the other hand, carries a self-reflexive potential, evoking the cinematic language of the period it is set in, the 1960s, reminiscent of films by Bresson, Wajda and Kieślowski. Ida's final return to the confines of the monastery conveys the film's rather conservative message: although she puzzles out her actual identity and is deeply affected by the experience of her identity quest, still, she does not choose a new path for herself but resumes her convent identity and the thread of her former life; she gets assimilated as there seems to be no other viable alternative for her as a Jewish woman in post-war Poland. This conservative strain is reinforced by the film's adjustment to the highly esteemed artistic model of modernist art cinema's monochrome style. Its highly calibrated, saturated images are most memorable, as their compositions revive the artistry of Carl Theodor Dreyer's Christian masterpiece, *The Passion of Joan of Arc* (*La passion de Jeanne d' Arc*, 1928), in which the shots, executed with careful precision, radiate with preternatural clarity, arousing the contemporary filmgoer's cinephilia.

Loosely inspired by his parents' personalities and relationship, Pawlikowski's masterful *Cold War* continues the aesthetic constitution of *Ida* by applying the Academy 4:3 ratio and the black-and-white format, but with a significant difference, namely that it enthralls the viewer by the exceptionally wide spectrum of black-and-white image types, from the high definition, saturated monochrome to desaturated, grainy images. In our classification this film represents a synthesis in that it aims at exploring to the full the possibilities of the black-and-white image in contemporary art-house cinema; it does not choose between the glossy or the dirty version but it embraces both and also the scale in between, like distinct variations on a theme in a musical piece. There is a strong interconnection between the music-related topic of the film and the perceivably musical orchestration of polished black-and-white compositions. Pawlikowski offers yet another story in which the contours of a historical period are shaped in parallel with the unfolding of a private story, marked by the presence of a strong female character, Zula. Her musical talent is discovered by Wiktor and Irena, who are recording authentic folk music and searching for singers and dancers in rural Poland with the aim of establishing a folk ensemble in the late 1940s. Zula and Wiktor are passionately attracted to each other and their relationship evolves in parallel with the rising success of the folk ensemble Mazurek, which soon finds itself under political pressure and is forced to include pieces eulogising Stalin. The images of the performing ensemble with Stalin's portrait floating above their heads become emblematic of the case of art compromised by political propaganda in the 1950s. Albeit performed with Wiktor and Irena's profound disagreement, the performance of Mazurek placed in the service of politics is illustrative of how the communist regime involved folk art in politics and appropriated it to make it an agent of transmitting ideology, revealing the 'distribution of the sensible' (Rancière 2004) based on which the social order operated at that time. The duality of the performance is underscored by the disproportionately large portrait of Stalin hovering above the stage, the filmic image acquiring thus an ambivalent, grotesque quality, simultaneously floating and heavy, radiating and obnoxious, glaring and grey. The effect of the black-and-white template, in this case, is to degrade and homogenise the individuals as the political system itself attempted, and to reinforce the artificial effect of the composition (Figure 2.5). The success of Mazurek opens up the borders within the Eastern Bloc, and the opportunity of performing in Berlin gives Wiktor the chance of defection. However, Zula does not join him, thus the Iron Curtain is set between them, not just geopolitically, but also emotionally. The latter becomes a jazz music performer in a Paris club; further episodes of the story show the protagonists rhythmically together and apart. Conjointly with the musical modulations of the initial folk song, adapted to the spirit of jazz and then the French language, we see Zula undergoing a miraculous transformation from folk art performer to jazz singer. The black-and-white image sensitively accompanies the tensions of forced and deliberate border transgressions between Eastern and Western locations of the Cold War, the modulations of music and Zula's versatility. It acquires a twofold quality resulting from 'the presence of two worlds in one' as Rancière defines *dissensus* (2010: 37), the film incorporating crystal-clear images marked by depth of field and saturation mostly associated with the theme of folk music and collective singing in a choir, and also more indistinct

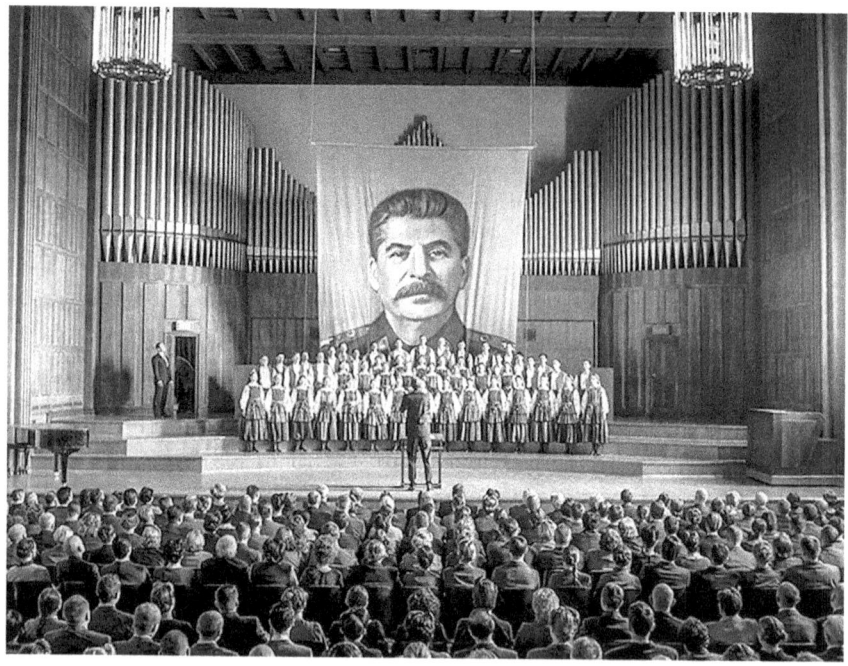

Figure 2.5 *Cold War* (2018). The performance of the folk ensemble Mazurek: the grotesquely heavy black-and-white portrait of Stalin hovering above the stage

ones displaying blunt background and dim nuances of grey aligned to the scenes of Zula's individual performances of jazz.

Jazz establishes a direct contact not only with the depicted period, but also with the mood and musical interferences of the French New Wave cinema. Pawlikowski shows his reverence for classical modernist cinema and *Nouvelle Vague* through an entire network of intertextual allusions, both covert and overt, thematic and stylistic, which turn the volatile relationship between Zula and Wiktor into a subtle variation of great modern love stories such as between Katherine (Ingrid Bergman) and Alex (George Sanders) in Roberto Rossellini's *Journey to Italy* (*Viaggio in Italia*, 1954), between Vittoria (Monica Vitti) and Piero (Alain Delon) in Antonioni's *The Eclipse* (*L'Eclisse*, 1962), between Camille (Brigitte Bardot) and Paul (Michel Piccoli) in Godard's *Contempt* (*Le Mépris*, 1963). More than that, some of the ways in which the allusions are woven into the texture of the black-and-white image, in the form of textual inscriptions, intertextual reference or film insert, can be perceived as a remediation of Godard's densely self- and media-reflexive style, itself full of cinematic and inter-art allusions.[5] Such *cinéphile* references can be detected in the name of the Paris jazz club, L'Eclipse, in the French title of a poem randomly popping up, '*Voyage en Italique*' [sic], playfully concealing the reference to the Italian film in the

French cultural context, or in the wig that Zula wears – reminiscent of Camille's wig in *Contempt* – in the scene that shows her as a cheap singer and wife of the much-hated servant of the system, Kaczmarek. Zula (Joanna Kulig) embodies the *noir*-ish femme fatale while remaining, at the same time, genuinely Polish, a re-embodiment of emblematic modernist female characters, while radiating with the contemporary glow of the black-and-white image.

Towards the Intermedialisation of the Digital Monochrome

Black-and-white cinema is obviously not merely black and white, it also implies the entire scale of grey in between. The extended perception of the nuances of grey is like 'hypervision', a concept set forth by contemporary Danish-Icelandic artist Olafur Eliasson, whose experiments with immersive spaces lit by monofrequency lamps, as in his *Room for One Colour* (1997), demonstrate that once relieved from the task of processing many colours, our eyes become capable of more powerfully perceiving the details and nuances:

> As our brain has to handle or digest less visual information due to the lack of other colors, we feel that we see details more easily than usual. This means that our eyes can detect more shades of gray in a black-and-white photograph than shades of color in a color image. We have, in other words, in this monochrome space, a sort of hypervision that gives us the feeling of having a particularly sharp detection of the space and people around us. (Eliasson 2006: 75)

The perception of a wider range of details in the black-and-white image, whether in the shades of grey or in compositional forms, morphs the monochrome cinematic surface into an immersive space, into a compositional and textural unit that activates both our intellectual and sensory awareness. This may elucidate the way in which even a most minimalist series of shots can easily turn into the sensation of visual overflow in black-and-white cinema, grasped as the materiality of the image that goes beyond the narrative logic and 'becomes a perceptual field of structures which the viewer is free to study at length, going beyond the strictly functional aspects' (Thompson 1986: 141).

Additionally, the black-and-white image is often associated with a kind of 'photographic' quality of film. 'The photographic' as an effect within the medium of cinema, conceptualised in its status of in-betweenness by Raymond Bellour (2008),[6] serves as the basis of the concept of the photofilmic, which implies that the photographic, the cinematic and the photofilmic are to be conceived along a spectrum. Photofilmic images 'layer, if not amalgamate, structures of existing media (photography and film) in order to provide new images of and on the world' (Streitberger and Van Gelder 2010: 50–1).

Among the various theoretical avenues to the photofilmic (e.g. Sutton 2009, Cohen and Streitberger 2016), Ágnes Pethő proposes an approach to the photofilmic from the perspective of its forms of occurrence, namely 'specific forms (or trans-forms) and rhetorical figurations emerging *within* either film or photography, through which on a perceptual level one medium seems to cross over into the territory of the other' (Pethő 2016: 234, italics in the original). She then takes stock of the figurations of the photofilmic, which she broadly identifies in cases when a still picture becomes a film frame as an insert within film, or when the moving image becomes frozen into a still picture, associated with slow movement and long takes, creating a sensation of the photographic within film. Bearing in mind the considerations above, a few photofilmic and photo-pictorial instances will be taken from the corpus of the analysed films in order to illustrate the implied artistic claim of the digital black-and-white image and its special inclination towards slow cinema. The films discussed here are frequently interspersed with insertions of, or references to, photographs, photographic compositions, freeze frames, static shots, long takes and tableau moments, which are eminent manifestations of the photofilmic. The photofilmic instances allow the perception of the black-and-white image as an intermedial fold, a subtle multimodal, reflexive layer.

Ida fully explores the figurative potential of the photofilmic. The stylised images, whether landscape tableaux, photographic interiors or facial close-ups, are instilled with slowness and immobility, making the boundary between the cinematic and the photographic transgressable. In her analysis concentrating on the visualisation of absence, loss and grief, Matilda Mroz argues that the photographic becomes the major structuring principle of the film, manifesting at different layers, from the entire film resembling an old photograph, through the presence of photographs as objects, to images also associated with framing light, such as windows. The presence of the photographic acquires multiple significations. Firstly, it serves as the indexical trace of former presence, as in the insertion of the photo of the absent mother and deceased family members, the lead glass rosette in the window of the barn belonging to the erstwhile parental home, painted by Ida's mother, Rosa – the most artistic rendering possible of the transcended presence of absence – or the empty window frame after Wanda commits suicide. Further on, the stillness of the photographic becomes the signifier of trauma and grief, while the photographic compositions that recurrently show the characters bisected by framing, 'point to the difficulty of rendering visible *Ida*'s particular narrative, as well as gesturing towards the broader loss of the Polish-Jewish community as a whole' (Mroz 2016). The tableau moments in *Ida* – picturesque landscapes of the forest foliage arching over the road in form of a Gothic vault, spectacles of fields under the immense Polish sky with the tiny figures pressed to the bottom of the image – simultaneously evoke the existentialist feel of Caspar David Friedrich's paintings and the atmosphere of the phantom-like Polish landscape in the spirit of Claude Lanzmann's *Shoah* (1985) or Władysław Pasikowski's *Aftermath* (*Pokłosie*, 2012).

The mutilation of bodies by *décadrage*, also evocative of modernist art, becomes a visual signifier of the unspeakable. The grieving protagonists, symbolically 'beheaded' by deframing in the scene of exhumation pour onto the screen the pain and sense of loss, the protagonists becoming lifeless torsos in a profound cinematic gesture of identification and empathy. The facial close-up of the grieving aunt preceding her suicide, arrested in a very dark freeze-frame, turns the living body into a still image showing the face as if in (a photographic) decomposition into various shades of black (Figure 2.6), turning motion into inertia, presence into anticipated absence. In an intensely aesthetic moment of the film, Ida, grieving through identification, performing a series of gestures belonging to the aunt, is symbolically transfigured into a 'moving' image by folding herself into the translucent curtain suspended between light and shadow, white and dark grey, as if entangled in the whirl of the past. The image of Ida's swirling body (Figure 2.7) may be perceived as condensing the essence of the 'photographic' and the 'cinematic', folding upon each other in the subtle texture of the black-and-white image.

In *Cold War* Lukasz Zal's camera further experiments with the potential of photographic black-and-white composition. The film unfolds before the viewer's eyes as a series of perfectly composed photographic images which visually convey what the narrative, devised in an episodic-economical manner, deliberately omits. The rhythm of the narrative is regulated by the counterpoint of quick cuts and slow takes, dynamic sequences of dance and static shots of photofilmic landscape tableaux. The film excels among contemporary productions in its utmost care for the beauty of the image. Purely descriptive inserts such as the boat trip on the Seine after the couple's reunion, with a night-time view of Notre Dame passing by, accompanied by silence, relieves the photographic still from its subordination to diegesis and reinforces its autonomy, 'image-ness'. Shown in a series of photographic stills, the scene with church ruins where Kaczmarek accidentally enters at the beginning of the story and where Zula and Wiktor themselves administer the marriage oath before they opt to cross the greatest, this time existential border together at the end of the film, provides the architectonic symmetry of the narrative. The final landscape tableau, showing Zula and Wiktor sitting together on a bench on the side of the road awaiting their final moments before eternity and then the empty bench after they move to the other side for the sake of 'a better view', reconnects to *Ida* in that it becomes, just like the lead glass rosette, the signifier of absence.

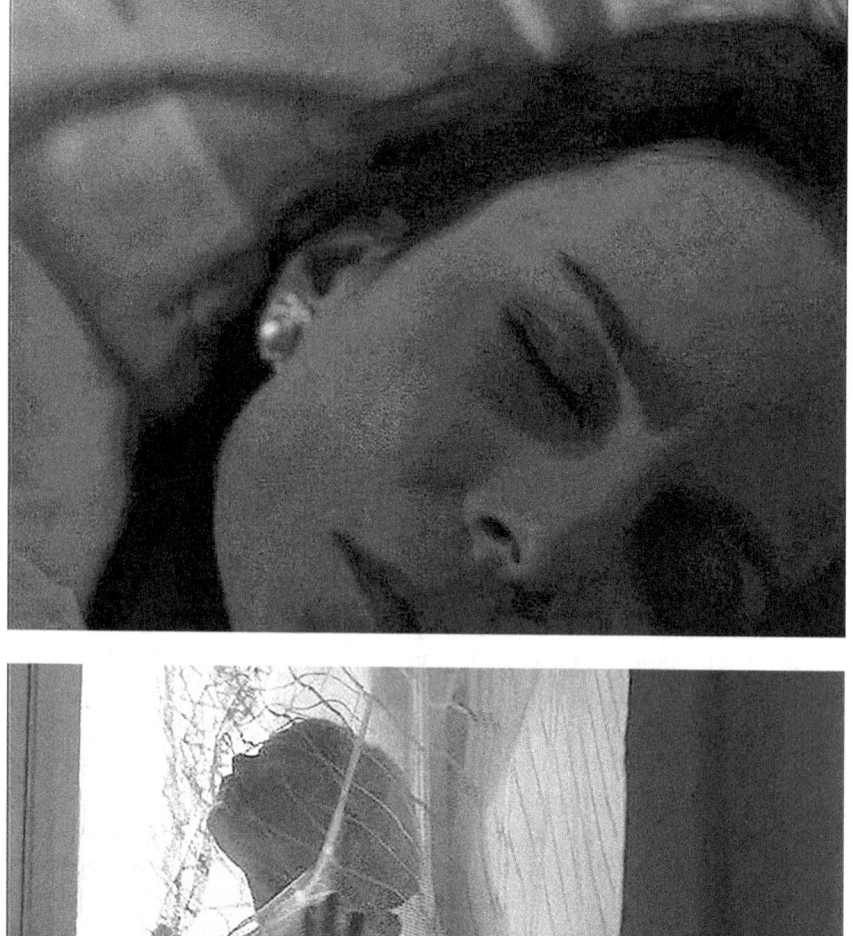

Figures 2.6–2.7 *Ida* (2013). Wanda's close-up in 'black on black' and Ida enveloped in grey in-between light and darkness

The experience of viewing *Papusza* is similar to leafing through a photo album containing black-and-white photos created with analogue technique. Impressive landscape tableaux alternate with genre images and close-ups, all recorded with fixed frontal camera position. Tableaux with Gypsy caravans on the road display an archaic way of life unfolding under the heavens, constant longing for moving further, and contrast the eternal patterns of nature with the ephemeral existence of the nomadic community. The landscape tableaux, providing various horizontal and vertical patterns drawn by clouds, water surfaces and forest trees, are meant to render the oneness of the Gypsy community with nature. The chiaroscuro effect intensely applied in these highly stylised photofilmic compositions (Figure 2.4) endow the film images with a painterly quality.

The slow pace of *I, Olga Hepnarová* is regulated by the rhythm of mostly static shots, recorded with fixed frontal camera position, in long and extreme long takes (e.g. Figure 2.1). The initiation of the viewer into the film's heavy atmosphere and its immersive use of the spectrum of greyness is provided by an extreme long take at the beginning of the film: through long moments of arrested time we can see the image of a corridor in the flat of Olga's family, Olga disappearing behind one door's room and long moments later her father appearing through the same door. Later in the film Olga confesses that she was harassed and beaten by her father. The extreme long take recorded with an unmoving camera – with intertextual resonances with a similar image of a hallway in Haneke's *The White Ribbon*, behind which the priest's children are punished, recorded in real time – becomes the site of childhood trauma, the signifier of the unspeakable that pushes Olga into the depth of alienation and solitude, and turns her against all those who bullied her throughout her life. The real time of (non-)narration transposes the cinematic image to another plane, that of the viewer's, the cinematic space turns thus into an ethically burdened, uncanny dimension. Paralysed images, suspended moments in-between stillness and motion become signposts of the ethical path the viewer is supposed to walk along.

Conclusion

The films discussed above connect the monochrome template with the issue of female identity at a crossroads, against the backdrop of historical-political events, social alienation and confrontation, and against turning points on a grand, historical scale that powerfully mark individual destinies. These films seem to be in search of reinvented and reflexive approaches to the past; through the fates and vicissitudes of the female protagonists, they allow for a more personal involvement in processes of history. The analysis has tried to shed light on the 'multicolouredness' of the digital monochrome as reflected by the analysed films. We encounter a great variety of stylistic options, but they converge in their attempt to delineate female figures at odds with themselves and negotiating their identity against the whims of history and society.

The black-and-white image, with its distinct degrees of saturation and in its specific compositional and textural forms, proves to be adaptable to a wide range of approaches, from documentary realism as in *Hi, Tereska!*, through stylisation in narrative construction as in *The Reverse*, to more refined mediareflexive forms that overtly play upon prior analogue cinematic discourses as, most of all, in *Ida* and *Cold War*. The aestheticising tendencies relying on the photographic quality of the black-and-white image also demonstrate an impressive diversity, from the employment of a more conservative, exoticising form of language that can be found in *Papusza*, through the ways in which *Ida* and *Cold War* play upon and evoke modernist cinematography, to an utterly stern and subversive monochrome combining photographic precision with the effect of slow cinema in *I, Olga Hepnarová*. In the highly saturated forms of the monochrome image, the various figurations of the photofilmic (mainly in *Ida*, *Papusza* and *Cold War*) train our eyes to see differently, to adapt to 'another kind of, more *tableau* orientated, rhythm' (Mulvey 2006: 155) that regulates these affective images. The photographic quality of the black-and-white picture results in a sensible, 'sensual' mode of intermediality, affording 'a type of cinematic image that displays its palimpsest like layers and that impresses the viewer with its fusion between the haptical and the optical' (Pethő 2011: 6).

The use of black-and-white photography proves especially suitable for rendering characteristic modes of Eastern European feeling. It enhances the documentary realism that connects the economic and moral void of post-communist social peripheries to the theme of adolescent crisis in *Hi, Tereska!*; further on, it conveys the tensions of the communist past marked by individual strategies of survival in *The Reverse*, the fate of an ethnic periphery in *Papusza*, the burden of the Holocaust and identity quest in *Ida*, the anxieties of a stormy relationship drifting along post-war political whirls and driven by contradictory impulses in *Cold War* and finally, the crisis leading to anti-social commitment in *I, Olga Hepnarová*. Through a great stylistic diversity, the discussed films all build on the perceptual heterogeneity of the digital monochrome, marked by an awareness of the old while sensing the new. Thus, they manage to create various sensations of in-betweenness to be conceived of not in terms of fixed dichotomies but rather as productive *dissensus*.

This work was supported by a grant of the Ministry of National Education, CNCS – UEFISCDI Romania, project number PN-III-P4-ID-PCE-2016-0418.

Notes

1. Although the term 'monochrome' may imply the exclusive use of nuances of any other single colour, the term 'digital monochrome' will be consistently used in this essay to refer to black-and-white film created with the procedures of digital technology.
2. The director Paweł Pawlikowski, of Polish origin, works in the UK, however, *Ida* and *Cold War* were directed in Poland as international co-productions – a prevailing filmmaking practice in Eastern Europe nowadays – and were nominated for an Oscar as films representing Poland. In 2015 *Ida* won the Oscar for Best Foreign Language Film.
3. The protagonist is played by a Polish actress (Michalina Olszańska) and some of its locations were filmed in Poland.
4. Aleksandra Gietner came from a juvenile delinquency institution. After the film was finished she disappeared for weeks, returning to the life she had led before.
5. For the ways in which the conflicting relationship between man and woman becomes an allegory of media confrontations, effecting a multi-layered (self-)reflexive and intermedial discourse in Godard's films created in the period of the *Nouvelle Vague*, see Pethő (2011).
6. '"The photographic," as I imagine it, is not reducible to photography even while borrowing part of its soul and the fate of which we believed photography to be the guardian. The photographic exists somewhere in-between: it is a state of "in-between-ness": in movement, it is that which interrupts, that paralyzes; in immobility, it perhaps bespeaks its relative impossibility' (Bellour 2008: 253).

Works Cited

Bellour, Raymond (2008), 'Concerning "the Photographic"', in Karen Beckman and Jean Ma (eds), *Still Moving: Between Cinema and Photography*, Durham, NC and London: Duke University Press, pp. 253–76.
Cohen, Brianne and Alexander Streitberger (eds) (2016), *The Photofilmic. Entangled Images in Contemporary Art and Visual Culture*, Leuven: Leuven University Press, Lieven Gevaert Series.
Durys, Elżbieta (2017), '*Film and Values: Polish Cinema of National Remembrance*', in Sabrina P. Ramet, Kristen Ringdal and Katarzyna Dośpiał-Borysiak (eds), *Civic and Uncivic Values in Poland. Value Transformation, Education, and Culture*, Budapest and New York: Central European University Press, pp. 281–301.
Eliasson, Olafur (2006), 'Some Ideas about Color', in Ismail Soyugenc and Richard Torcia (eds), *Olafur Eliasson: Your Colour Memory*, Exhibition Catalogue, Glenside, PA: Arcadia University Art Gallery, pp. 75–83.
Galt, Rosalind (2011), *Pretty. Film and the Decorative Image*, New York: Columbia University Press.
Mazierska, Ewa (2007), *Polish Postcommunist Cinema: From Pavement Level*, Oxford, Bern, Berlin, Bruxelles, Frankfurt am Main, New York, Wien: Peter Lang.

Mroz, Matilda (2016), 'Framing Loss and Figuring Grief in Pawel Pawlikowski's *Ida*', *Screening the Past*, Issue 41, <http://www.screeningthepast.com/2016/10/framing-loss-and-figuring-grief-in-pawel-pawlikowskis-ida/> (last accessed 27 January 2018).

Mulvey, Laura (2006), 'The Possessive Spectator', in David Green and Joanna Lowry (eds), *Stillness and Time: Photography and the Moving Image*, Brighton: Photoforum/Photoworks, pp. 151–63.

Nagib, Lúcia (2014), 'The Politics of Impurity', in Lúcia Nagib and Anne Jerslev (eds), *Impure Cinema. Intermedial and Intercultural Approaches to Film*, London and New York: I. B. Tauris, pp. 21–39.

Pethő, Ágnes (2011), *Cinema and Intermediality. The Passion for the In-Between*, Newcastle upon Tyne: Cambridge Scholars Publishing.

Pethő, Ágnes (2016), 'Figurations of the Photofilmic: Stillness versus Motion – Stillness in Motion', in Brianne Cohen and Alexander Streitberger (eds), *The Photofilmic. Entangled Images in Contemporary Art and Visual Culture*, Leuven: Leuven University Press, pp. 233–55.

Rancière, Jacques (2004), *The Politics and Aesthetics: The Distribution of the Sensible*, London and New York: Continuum.

Rancière, Jacques (2010), *Dissensus. On Politics and Aesthetics*, London and New York: Continuum.

Rosen, Philip (2001), 'Old and New: Image, Indexicality, and Historicity in the Digital Utopia', in *Change Mummified: Cinema, Historicity, Theory*, Minneapolis and London: University of Minnesota Press, pp. 301–449.

Schatz, Thomas (1981), *Hollywood Genres: Formulas, Filmmaking, and the Studio System*, New York: Random House.

Staszczyszyn, Bartosz (2013), 'Papusza – Krzysztof Krauze, Joanna Kos-Krauze', <http://culture.pl/en/work/papusza-krzysztof-krauze-joanna-kos-krauze> (last accessed 27 January 2018).

Streitberger, Alexander and Hilde Van Gelder (2010), 'Photo-Filmic Images in Contemporary Visual Culture', *Philosophy of Photography*, Vol. 1, No. 1, pp. 48–53.

Sutton, Damian (2009), *Photography, Cinema, Memory. The Crystal Image of Time*, Minneapolis and London: University of Minnesota Press.

Thompson, Kristin (1986), 'The Concept of Cinematic Excess', in Philip Rosen (ed.), *Narrative, Apparatus, Ideology: A Film Reader*, New York: Columbia University Press, pp. 130–42.

Thompson, Lara (2010), 'Monochrome Now: Digital Black and White Cinema and the Photographic Past', *Screening the Past*, Issue 29, <http://tlweb.latrobe.edu.au/humanities/screeningthepast/29/monochrome-now.html> (last accessed 27 January 2018).

CHAPTER 3

Sculpture and Affect in Cinema's Expanded Field: From Aleksey Gherman's Hard to Be a God *to Aleksey Gherman Jr's* Under Electric Clouds

Ágnes Pethő

SCULPTURE, CINEMA, INTERMEDIALITY

Sculpture, the quintessential plastic art, with its immobility and palpable materiality seems to be the opposite of cinema which unfolds an intangible world of images in perpetual motion, conjured up by a mere play of shadows and light. Nevertheless, there are several intriguing possibilities in which these two arts and media have come into contact, both literally: in the form of sculpture appearing in film (or its reverse, film or film projection used in the construction of a sculptural art object),[1] and figuratively: film viewed in terms of sculpture. Both of these literal and figurative contact zones constitute extremely wide and rewarding fields of study.

This essay narrows down this wider perspective to the analysis of two films made by Aleksey Gherman and his son, Aleksey Gherman Jr, *Hard to Be a God* (*Trudno byt bogom*, 2013) and *Under Electric Clouds* (*Pod elektricheskimi oblakami*, 2015) not because the authors are related, but because sculpture and cinema rarely mix in such a complex intermedial and interart entanglement as we see in the works of these Russian auteurs. The films of the two Ghermans could not be more different, yet both of them share the ambition to break the conventional 'moulds' of narrative films and to expand the cinematic experience to enfold sensations of the plastic arts through the intervention of sculptural elements. The aim of joining the two analyses is to define and compare how this intervention can happen by exploiting the sensuous impressions of malleable physical matter, the statuary appearance of both living beings and inanimate things, or the expressivity of sculptural artefacts amassed within the cinematic frame. The ways in which these films 'expand' cinema conveys in each case a highly critical, universal vision of humanity, art and society. At the same time, they also rely on specific cultural traditions and, as the analyses will show, they refashion a typically ideology-laden area of interart relationships in Russian cinema by experimenting with an aesthetic based on the phenomenology of the cine-sculptural (Gherman Sr) and by using sculpture as a link between cinema and contemporary art (Gherman Jr). The films reveal two distinct ways in which an 'intermedial sensibility' may become prominent in contemporary cinema and in a wider context in which, in their own way, sculpture and cinema both have already undergone various processes of 'expansion'.

Sculpture, as Rosalind Krauss's seminal essay (1979) has revealed, has become 'placeless' and 'nomadic' in the postmodern age. It has become 'largely self-referential [. . .] through the representation of its own materials or the process of its construction' (Krauss 1979: 34). The set of oppositions (such as, sculpture versus landscape, sculpture versus architecture) between which the modernist category of sculpture used to be suspended, according to Krauss, have become problematic in an 'expanded field', where sculpture can also be combined with arts that are 'not sculpture' (i.e. architecture or landscape). In a culture that is able 'to think the complex', she wrote: 'sculpture is no longer the privileged middle term between two things that it isn't. Sculpture is rather only one term on the periphery of a field in which there are other, differently structured possibilities' (1979: 38). At the same time, cinema has gone through a similar process of expansion through new technologies, dislocation from its previous institutions and diffusion through new forms of moving images.[2] It has established new associations with the arts, gravitating at times towards painting, performance, or installation art. The two Gherman films connect to these processes of expansion through the transgression of the cinematic into the sculptural and drawing on the performative value of 'nomadic' sculptures.

Although Krauss conceived the 'expanded field' as a result of an increasingly more intricate matrix of structural parameters, we may also shift the emphasis from the spatial metaphor to the process itself, from sculpture understood in terms of autonomous figural form to the emergence of the sculptural, i.e. sculpture 'operating more prolifically, as a quality that informs spatial practices as a whole' (Droth 2009: 4). Thus, instead of mapping the area of interconnections between the arts, we can consider the aesthetic strategies involved in the 'expansions', the 'processes of becoming'[3] taking place and the way we perceive them. The perspective proposed here for the double analysis of the two films that concentrates on the overlapping realms of sculpture and cinema makes it possible to explore the phenomenon of intermediality in this way as a kind of 'opening out', as a sensation of expansion: a sensuous enhancement, a multiplication of the perceptual and conceptual layering of the cinematic experience. From this point of view, we can consider cinema as 'becoming intermedial' when we are made aware that a moving image is not just an image, but something more: a photograph that moves, a canvas painted with vivid colours, a space of exhibition, a stage for (inter)action, a container for statuesque figures, a choreography of bodies in motion, an architectural construction, and so on. Cinema does not seamlessly absorb features of the other arts and media (on the level of set design or the elements of the diegetic world), but it becomes augmented by their affordances and connotations, even to a degree of excess or saturation.

BECOMING SCULPTURAL: A WORLD IN-BETWEEN FLESH AND CLAY

Aleksey Gherman, regarded by some film historians to be 'the last Soviet auteur'[4] (Anemone 2016), considered the making of *Hard to Be a God* at almost every stage of his creative life. The film, which took thirteen years to complete[5] and became his final work, turned out to be the culmination of his art, his *chef-d'œuvre*, a monumental endeavour in every respect: as radical, uncompromising and grandiose as a last opus can ever be.

A loose adaptation of the eponymous science-fiction novel written by Arkady and Boris Strugatsky, *Hard to Be a God* presents an apocalyptic vision of a dystopian world. The film opens with a picturesque black-and-white shot of a winter landscape outside the walls of a construction that looks like a medieval castle; it is snowing and we see makeshift huts, scaffoldings and wheels, a fire, and tiny human figures moving around. The perspective is wide, like in a painting of Pieter Brueghel the Elder, but the narrator quickly informs us, that contrary to all appearances 'this is not the Earth. It's another planet, about 800 years behind'. What we see is a kind of alternate reality that unfolds on a small planet named Arkanar, where humanity is stuck in a grim, never-ending Dark Age. 'The Renaissance did not happen here' and there is 'a brutal hunt for thinkers, wisemen, bookworms and talented artisans', we find out from the voice-over. The university has already been destroyed, writers and scientists have been tortured and murdered. We can soon behold the aftermath of the carnage: the shocking display of their festering corpses hanging in public places. The protagonist of the film is Don Rumata (Leonid Yarmolnik), supposedly sent from Earth to this world on a peaceful (God-like) mission to help save the intellectuals and facilitate progress, but who instead becomes irreversibly involved in the all-pervasive violence which escalates into a gruesome, chaotic massacre.[6]

However, the film is not about telling his story or his adventures, it is not even about him. It is about presenting the world around him and about immersing the viewer into this world. According to the official press book of the film, Aleksey Gherman declared: 'I am not interested in anything but the possibility of building a world, an entire civilization from scratch.'[7] In his desire to do so, Gherman thus joins the great modernist artists whose ambition was to conjure up visions that comprehend nothing less than the totality of the human condition. Furthermore, he is not content with creating a cinematic universe of incredible authenticity in which each detail 'is developed with an all-or-nothing approach',[8] (re)constructing objects, clothes, weaponry, every minor detail belonging to medieval life just as they would have been some 700 years ago, he also created a uniquely naturalistic and idiosyncratic cinematic language, one that would subject the viewers to an experience of an unparalleled intensity. Jonathan Romney's (2015) insightful observation captures the essence of this latter feature in this way: 'his previous film *Khrustalyov, My Car!* – a Fellini-like nightmare about Stalin's purges – was a daunting monolith of often inscrutable extremity. If that film was the *Ulysses* of Russian cinema, *Hard to Be a God* is surely its *Finnegans Wake*.'

Paradoxically, while Gherman succeeded in his endeavour to create an entire world, this world (not unlike Joyce's *Finnegans Wake*) is a world 'in the making'. If we consider the original narrative devised by the Strugatsky brothers, what we are supposed to be presented with is the evolution of history, but what we behold instead is an endless process of suspended gestation (or labour): the turmoil of a world that is oversaturated, ripe for change yet not actually changing. We are shown fragments of the same horrid reality from beginning to the end in claustrophobic close-ups. Although Don Rumata and his entourage are forever on the move, making their way through narrow, overcrowded spaces, they seem to make no headway, while corpses pile up and more and more repulsive actions take place around them in macabre, gut-wrenching detail.

Gherman's overwhelming and overblown vision is generated by a poetic strategy that forges a language of in-betweenness, expanding the cinematic into the realm of the sculptural. As we know, in several major religions, God creates man by way of moulding him from clay and dust. Hence, the act of divine creation in these mythologies brings to mind the act of a sculptor, by modelling moist clay into the semblance of flesh, and subsequently infusing life into a sculptural object. Gherman reminds us of this process when he intertwines the gestures of a sculptor with that of a filmmaker in crafting a never-before-seen cinematic world not as a picture, a representation, but as a full-blown alternate reality that he challenges the viewer to confront in its quasi palpable, sensuous physicality. Sculptural elements and the quality of the sculptural occur in the film on many levels: both literally (with sculptures, sculpturally ornate objects and bas-reliefs shown within the frames) and figuratively, constituting a visual language of enhanced cinematic plasticity that blends the phenomenology of the sculptural and the cinematic. The aims of this sculptural intervention in the cinematic world are manifold: to develop a complex, tangible impression of corporeality, to highlight the intensity of the physical creativity of this universe bursting with energy and violence, and to bring into relief its radical focus on materiality (this is a world that refuses transcendence into spiritual dimensions).

Hard to Be a God presents a world of viscous consistency oscillating in-between states of fluidity and solidity. As if to illustrate Jean-Paul Sartre's famous poetic description of viscosity as 'the agony of water' and a 'phenomenon in the process of becoming',[9] everything is drenched by rain, snow and slush amid the freezing cold of an implacable winter. People walk around the place with runny noses, or defecate in half-open outhouses, leaking corpses covered with icicles dangle from the gallows or lie about in the puddles. Muck, dirt and bodily fluids mix and soil all things. Flesh, stone and clay become indistinguishable, and the carnal is in continuous fusion (and chiastic con-fusion) with the sculptural. Sculptures placed in the courtyards are all life-sized and blend in with the live figures in the frames, while human bodies are overlain with the same mud that covers everything, thus making them look a lot like sculptures (Figures 3.1 and 3.2). What is more, people are often shown smearing themselves with slimy substances (or pouring icy water with glittering pieces of metal over stiffly frozen corpses, making them bizarrely ornate), thus reminding us how coating or glazing is a technique that may confer a sculptural aspect to any object.[10] A statue seems to come alive as a sexual body when the viewer notices a detail such as an erect penis in one of the first scenes of the film. Animal and human body parts are isolated as autonomous sculptural forms. The first striking example of this is the head of Rumata appearing above the table when we first meet him, displayed as part of a still-life arrangement featuring several handcrafted objects.[11] Masterfully carved body armours, shields and weaponry that prosthetically expand the human bodies, along with devices of torture attached to them (e.g. wooden pillories), which transform people into composite entities of man

Figure 3.1   Aleksey Gherman, *Hard to Be a God* (2013): sculptural bodies covered with mud

Figure 3.2 Aleksey Gherman, *Hard to Be a God* (2013): a world in-between flesh, mud, clay and stone with life-sized sculptures blending in with the live figures

and sculpture. Whole body parts become substituted by artefacts, or artefacts are fashioned akin to body parts: we see metal studded gloves, giant wooden fists used as battering rams, heads covered by elaborate helmets and masks with horns or beaks (blending man, object and animal). The film is packed with decorative objects with intricate bas-reliefs. Even parts of the slaughtered animals consumed during the feasts seem like bizarre flesh-sculptures.

This is a precarious universe in which the borders between liquidity and rigidity, formlessness and artfully designed form, life and death, organic and mineral, repulsive and aesthetic are disconcertingly blurred. The most astonishing manifestations of this blurring are the human figures themselves. Gherman deliberately sought out odd-looking and corpulent people with malformations, protruding bumps and disfiguring scars to populate his monstrous universe. The result is an incessant pageant of expressive faces looking like 'living gargoyles'[12] that make them, together with their bizarre accessories, worthy descendants not only of the paintings of the Brueghel dynasty but of the hellish visions of Hieronymus Bosch, as well. Deformity appears as a manifestation of the queer twists in the creative force of nature combined with human aggression,[13] and as something we recognise not only as an agency that distorts (and in the process, potentially dehumanises) the regular body, but also one that turns the misshapen and amorphous into the sculptural.

Expanding to all the things, animate or inanimate, truncated and crammed into the close-up frames, the formless can be perceived as the agony of matter (if we were to paraphrase Sartre's metaphor), and is caught in-between the insidious, uncontainable viscosity of the world presented in the film and the combination of the multitude of shapes in the process of becoming sculptural.[14]

At the same time, this sculptural vision of life in barbaric times also descends from a distinguished tradition in Russian cinema that dates back to the great plasticity of close-ups and the expressive accumulation of sculptural objects in the historical films of Sergei Eisenstein. It also continues, more excessively, the mud-soaked war nightmare in Elem Klimov's *Come and See* (*Idi i smotri*, 1985). But most of all, it appears as a response to Andrei Tarkovsky's *Andrei Rublev* (1966), which unravels a similarly grandiose fresco of a violent medieval world shown in landscapes sodden with rain and snow. It resonates especially with its awe-inspiring final chapter depicting the casting of the giant church bell. In this chapter, we see Boriska, a young boy undertaking the daunting assignment of supervising the casting of the bell. Threatened by the Prince to be killed if he fails, Boriska risks his life by pretending to know what he is doing, despite the fact that his father had died without passing on to him the secret of the trade. Yet, somehow, miraculously, he succeeds in the near impossible endeavour of finishing the job. Although he is almost crushed by the enormity of the task and sinks into intense emotional agony, he descends into a mud-drenched hellhole, finds the right clay that can be moulded, organises the work, fires up the furnaces and forges a magnificent sculptural object capable of producing a perfectly clear, angelic sound. Boriska's daring and daunting labour climaxing in the cathartic scene of ringing the bell is an ode to artistic creation as an act of passion (and the performance of a kind of secularised, lay Passion). It is a demonstration of art born from suffering, faith and endurance, as well as a testament to the redeeming powers of such an art (inspiring Andrei Rublev to break his vow of silence and to resume painting). It also seems to be the opposite of what happens in *Hard to Be a God*.

While Tarkovsky's hero digs himself into a slimy pit only to elevate clay, dirt, sweat, blood and tears into art, with the sublime chimes of the bell hoisted high up in the church tower signifying the triumph of spirit over matter, Gherman denies his hero and his world any possibility of transcendence or redemption. Rumata's journey seems to be, ironically, the opposite of Boriska's destiny. In contrast to Boriska who has to rely on his instincts because he does not actually know how to make a bell, Rumata is granted a higher degree of knowledge than his peers and a connection to a superior civilisation, yet he still fails in his mission, as he cannot use his advantage and succumbs to the savage instincts driving the chaos around him. The words of Psalm 40: 2 from the Bible apply to the parable of the young bell caster in Tarkovsky's film: 'He lifted me out of the slimy pit, / out of the mud and mire; / he set my feet on a rock / and gave me a firm place to stand.'[15] In Gherman's world, however, having achieved no progress and having sparked not a flicker of enlightenment, Rumata remains forever bogged down in the dismal, slimy morass of Arkanar. As one of the observers of 'this shitty planet' muses: 'Where is the art?' 'And a Renaissance? Not here!' Gherman lays out almost the same context as the one we see in Tarkovsky's film: the raw reality of a turbulent history, violence, despair, carnage, humanity dragged into the muck. There are artfully carved objects everywhere, the whole viscous world appears to be in the process of being moulded from clay, everything is ornate, carved, reshaped, encrusted, decorated, but Gherman's character is right, there is no art of the kind we see in Tarkovsky's film.[16]

The quality of sculpturality may be omnipresent here, but this becoming sculptural remains in the in-betweenness of mere flesh and clay, of body and object. Form is forever conjoined with masses of viscous formlessness in the kind of 'base materialism' and the '*informe*' that Georges Bataille speaks about. For Bataille the formless (*informe*) 'is a lowering of form, a rendering into material, such that material comes to be as only material' (Hegarty 2003: 7). Furthermore, as Benjamin Noys explains, the formless is not the negation or absence of form, 'the formless (*informe*) is always in-form' (2000: 34). Thus, Bataille's *informe* can only be conceived as something in-between, forever suspended in the process of becoming.[17] If we consider Gherman's vision from Bataille's perspective, then it also becomes clear, that this is in fact not an antithesis of Tarkovsky's poetics and philosophy of art, but a radical alternative of it. Although the film shows us an 'excremental fantasy' (Bataille 1985: 78) in which we see 'a literalization of formlessness pictured as chaotic scatter, or detritus, or substances of disgust' (Krauss 1996: 95) that bring forth powerful affects of abjection[18] (repulsion, horror, nausea), this descent into what Bataille terms 'base matter' (and formlessness) may not necessarily signify the impossibility of transcendence, but the depiction of a world of a radically different order (after all, Gherman's premise does stipulate that, despite similarities, this is not the civilisation we know, but an alternative universe). Bataille's core concept of 'base materialism' dismantles the opposition between materialism and idealism, high and low. He writes: 'base matter is external and foreign to ideal human aspirations, and it refuses to allow itself to be reduced to the great ontological machines resulting from these aspirations' (1985: 51). In Tarkovsky's universe, in the words of Thorsten Botz-Bornstein, 'the matter or the mud [...] becomes spiritual itself' (2007: 24).[19] Gherman's world submerged in 'base matter', however, is not measured against and not driven by ideals but by the dynamic, fluctuating, never-settling force of the formless.

From the Plasticity of Forms to the Phenomenology of the Cine-sculptural

Unfolding a process of becoming sculptural, caught in the in-betweenness of watery substances, flesh and clay, *Hard to Be a God* defies the solidity and stability of sculptural objects not only through the ubiquity of slime, but most of all through the intense, uncontainable mobility of all the elements in the frame. The film keeps pushing the visible into the realm of tactile sensations, but also throws the viewer into a primal world of raw aggression and perpetual motion. There is always something going on in the frames, people walk around in their heavy armour, do their chores, eat, fight, commit horrible acts to kill, enslave, mutilate and debase each other, there are no melancholic landscape shots or meditative still-life compositions, there is no respite. The film may be a chronicle of Rumata's descent into a universe of tactility and sheer matter, but matter is far from dead in this film,[20] even the corpses appear eerily in motion, there is an immense, uncontainable energy that infuses everything to appear as a cinematic *danse macabre*, in keeping with the spirit of Bataille's 'virulent nihilism' (Land 1992). This paradoxical vitality subverts the traditional attachment of a death-in-life quality to the perception of the sculptural in Gherman's vision which is utterly (and non-judgmentally) 'torrential' in the sense described by Bataille. As he writes, there is 'a profound complicity with natural forces such as violent death, gushing blood, [. . .] the fall into stinking filth of what had been elevated, [. . .] a sadistic understanding of an incontestably thundering and torrential nature' (1985: 101).[21]

The most intriguing aspect of this astonishing vision of sculptural masses in perpetual, vigorous motion is the way Gherman's film can surpass the level of the plasticity of forms, and explore a more complex imbrication of sculpture and cinema that we may term as cine-sculptural. The cine-sculptural, in its most accomplished manifestation, can be seen in terms of a chiasmus (cinematic sculpturality and sculptural cinema): as the combination of the becoming sculptural of the cinematic world (through the introduction of sculptures, of a panoply of sculpturally ornate objects, the sensations of sculpturality in the frames) with the becoming cinematic of the sculptural plasticity emerging in the film (through various types of movements animating the sculptural masses). In Gherman's case, Bataille's *informe* is even more relevant from this perspective, because it is not a descriptive but a performative notion, and as such may be identified as a dynamic principle active in both of these processes of becoming. Renée Hoogland aptly emphasises that 'the *informe* is defined more by what it does than by what it is' (2014: 16). In the in-betweenness of flesh, mud, bodily fluids and sculptural objects in the film, 'the formless operates within different forms to destabilize the organizing principle of form' (Hoogland 2014: 16). This continuously destabilising, reshaping, slippery dynamism of the formless traverses the entire world, materialising in front of the viewer. Moreover, we can also identify it in the way Gherman frustrates the mobile, spatial perception of this world through the subversive intrusion of the phenomenology of sculpture into the kind of cinematic experience we are accustomed to.

How can we define this intrusion? The American abstract painter, Ad Reinhardt once defined sculpture as 'something you bump into when you back up to look at a painting' (quoted by Lichtenstein 2008: 198). The famous quip points to a very important aspect of the phenomenology of sculpture: to the fact that, in contrast to painting, which opens up a virtual space that the spectator can behold from a distance, sculpture appears as an obstruction, an intrusion in the art gallery that occupies space alongside the spectator. As such, perhaps the most defining feature of sculpture is not the stillness of form suspended from the flow of time (that we can contemplate as the ultimate Apollonian art according to Friedrich Nietzsche),[22] but its ability to stimulate the viewer's sense of bodily contact and touch (even when placed in a glass case), which also prompts the visitor to walk around the display and engage with the whole space around the sculpture. While painting usually posits the spectator in a fixed position in front of it, and invites the spectator's gaze 'inside', the spatial dynamics of sculpture is much more complex, based on the bodily in-betweenness of sculpture and viewer, as many theorists have noted (see Genosko 1998). According to Mark Paterson, it 'makes a space available to play', 'as an art of palpation, the haptic experience of sculpture is [. . .] bi-directional, its reciprocity stemming from the possibility of our touching an object and its touching us' (2007: 94). Rudolf Arnheim speaks of a space that is 'warmed by body heat' (1966: 250). Replacing Henri Focillon's (1934) notions of *'l'espace-limite'* (space as a limit) and *'l'espace-milieu'* (space as an environment), he describes the enfoldment of concave and convex forms in late Greek and baroque sculpture, as well as in Henry Moore's statues by coining a new term, *'l'espace-partner'*. He emphasises the performative aspect of sculptural body versus space interaction: 'from the centre of the figure bulging volumes push forward into empty space [. . .] making space an active partner of the figure' (Arnheim 1966: 252). In the same vein, David F. Martin believes that sculpture always inhabits an 'enlivened' space, where 'we invariably perceive the forces of a sculpture as if they were pressing on our bodies' (1981: 62), therefore the main feature of the phenomenology of sculpture is that it 'reveals our physical "withness" with things, our "being-with", much more vividly than painting' (1981: 28).

From a phenomenological point of view, cinema sets up a 'being-with' the world of moving images on two interconnected levels, as Vivian Sobchack writes, 'when we sit in a movie theater and perceive a film as sensible, as making sense, we (and the film before us) are immersed in a world and in an activity of visual being' (1992: 8). The viewer undergoes 'both a "real" (or literal) sensual experience and an "as-if-real" (or figural) sensual experience' (2004: 73). The incorporeal moving images are constantly fleshed out by our synesthetic capacity to combine what we see and hear with senses of touch, smell, taste, with feeling weight, dimension and movement in space. When Gherman clutters up his close-ups with sculptural bodies and forms while saturating each shot with filth or mud he not only creates a persistent atmosphere of claustrophobia, but effectively undermines the sensorial hierarchy involved in the cinematic experience. While, in Sobchack's words, as a rule, 'cinema uses our dominant senses of vision and hearing to speak comprehensibly to our other senses' (2004: 67), in Gherman's film these other senses become incredibly enhanced, it is the quasi tactile, olfactory experience of repulsively 'sculpted' bodies, people in shackles and elaborate pillories, cadavers on gallows doused by rain, animal carcasses, rotten food, overflowing cesspits and spilt guts that challenge the viewer (struggling with a recurring gag reflex) to construct a comprehensive picture of what is actually going on in this world. The fact that there is also a lack of clear, linear, cause-and-effect based narrative storytelling, and we are merely presented a chain of individual scenes of escalating abhorrence, only underscores the primacy of the 'sensible' over 'making sense'.

Figures displayed in a constant entanglement and movement produce a 'suffocating kinesis' (Jameson, 2016). They may also remind us of Vachel Lindsay's famous, poetic description of action cinema as 'sculpture in motion' (1916: 79–96) and his observation that in the process of viewing bodies in movement, 'the eye makes this journey, not from space to space, or fabric to fabric, but first of all from mass to mass' (1916: 91). Moving from one crowded frame to another, in Gherman's film, however, we do not only just move from body to body but we seem to experience through cinema what David F. Martin identified in the phenomenology of sculpture: a 'contact with the raw power of reality: the bumping, banging, pushing, pulling, soothing, palpitating tangibility of our witness with things' (1981: 78–9). What is more, this 'witness' can be felt not only through the dismantling effect of the tactile over the visual as the camera pores over the palpable details, but also through the characters' repeated glances into the camera which pull the viewer even more strongly into the cinematic world, as if they were leering directly in our face.[23]

Sculptural elements intervene aggressively in the shots, producing rudimentary 3D effects, with bulging faces, pieces of weaponry or bulky objects repeatedly thrust into the foreground of the close-up, occluding over and over again the camera's view and frustrating the viewers who can only behold

Figure 3.3 Aleksey Gherman, *Hard to Be a God* (2013): sculptural objects thrust into close-up, frames cluttered with the entanglement of bodies and objects

a fragment of the overstuffed background behind the things dangled in front of their eyes (Figure 3.3). This is, nevertheless, not a space appearing as an active partner of the figures in the cinematic frame, but the space of Bataille's *informe*. As the camera keeps moving forward, we keep bumping into bulky, formless masses pushing into the frame. This 'mobile disruption' connecting sculptural palpability with cinematic motion can be seen in terms of Bataille's subversive image. Defined by the *informe* such a subversive image, nevertheless, cannot absorb the formless which 'does not fit into the frame but spills over it', (Noys 2000: 35). As Noys remarks, 'matter for Bataille is always "active" [. . .], never settling within a frame or an image but always emerging from an image, a word or things' (2000: 35). Accordingly, in Gherman's film, with the disturbing, grinning faces turning towards the camera, or the weird shaped utensils popping up unexpectedly in the jam-packed frames, there is always a sensation of overspill, the tangle of body parts and sculptural objects becomes more and more confusing as the camera ambles around the chaos without being able either to contain or to unravel it.

The relentless horizontal movement and the mobile close-up frame, which very seldom opens up into a wider shot, or an above the eyeline perspective – a technique that operates on 'the same principles as the classical Chinese storytelling scrolls, or the bas-reliefs on ancient buildings and porticos' (Jameson 2016: 151) – is also consistent with the horizontality imposed by the perspective of base materiality and the actions of the formless. Commenting on Bataille, Rosalind Krauss notes:

> The vision of animals [is] focused on the horizontal ground on which they and their prey both travel, a vision that is therefore, in certain ways, merely an extension of the sense of touch [. . .] Qualified by its acknowledgement of the distance that separates the 'beholder' from his object, the gap built into the human perceptual relation is what provides a space for all those varieties of vision which separate man from animals: contemplation, wonder, scientific inquiry, disinterestedness, aesthetic pleasure. (Bois and Krauss 1997: 90)

So while Western culture promotes the supremacy of vision, the overview, as the highest intellectual comprehension of the world, the productivity of the formless can be seen, as Hegarty points out, 'in work that horizontalizes in order to remove the control of "what is to be seen" through mankind's "expanded" vision' (2003: 8). Such a horizontal, tactile, animalesque vision dominates Gherman's film, and creates the possibility both for the sculptural reconfiguration of the mobile cinematic universe, and for its reverse, the cinematic expansion of the sculptural in the film, combined in uniquely subversive and idiosyncratic strategies of the cine-sculptural.

Hard to Be a God unfolds an infernal world in a forever unfinished, turbulent process of becoming sculptural. The film ends the same way it begins, with a panoramic image of a foggy winter landscape. As we gradually leave behind the horrors of the massacre with the warriors packing and leaving, one man is lighting a camp fire and preparing his meal with a donkey tethered to the cart quietly watching him, the stiff carcass of a dog hanging by a noose at the campsite is the only thing left to remind us of all the grisly bodies we bumped into during the excruciatingly long movie. We slowly back up and observe from afar small human figures moving in the ghostly tableau enveloped in mist that encloses the film into a circular structure (as one more faint resemblance to *Finnegans Wake*, another masterpiece of 'virulent' formlessness). We could just as well start watching everything all over again as the cine-sculptural fades into the photo-pictorial in the final sequence. In the words of Michel Serres, 'chaos doesn't provide any markers, or we can't discern any there. Hence [. . .] the underworld has no door or window by which one can enter or leave' (2015: 191).

AROUND BODIES OF STATUES

Hard to Be a God presents an alternative universe modelled as a world trapped within an apocalyptic past, Aleksey Gherman Jr's film, *Under Electric Clouds*, with a somewhat similar ambition, devises a dystopian present with elements of a not-so-far, post-apocalyptic future. Working on it with interruptions over a period of more than four years while also helping to finish his father's last opus, Gherman Jr's film made as a Russian-Ukrainian-Polish co-production, is conceived as yet another complex allegorical vision of our times. Despite a few subtle correspondences,[24] however, the similarity ends here. From the point of view of the relationship between sculpture and cinema, *Under Electric Clouds* ventures into a totally different, yet equally exciting territory: it is less about the performative value or the phenomenology of the cine-sculptural, and more about statues themselves viewed in the context of contemporary culture, in an aesthetic of cinema expanding towards installation art. Gherman Jr places his characters around a slew of enigmatic statues perceivable not in terms of an in-betweenness of flesh, clay and stone, as we see in *Hard to Be a God*, but of an in-betweenness of sculpture, architecture and landscape.

The film continues and reflects on a long tradition in Russian cinema of assigning special emphasis to sculpture in films that dealt with social or historical themes (a tradition no doubt connected to the privileged status of sculpture as a tool for political propaganda in Soviet times and epitomised by the famous sculptural logo of Mosfilm).[25] At the same time, it also premiered not only following Gherman Sr's grandiose, sculptural movie, but within a year after Andrei Zvyagintsev's *Leviathan* (2014), which features as one of its most memorable images shot against the breathtaking scenery of the Barents Sea a huge skeleton of a whale stranded on the shore. Half buried in the mud, half exposed and polished clean by the wind, with its ambivalent connotations of power and loss of power, fusing nature and culture in an unsettling, monumental fossilised state of in-betweenness, the image is an enigmatic symbol that has been reproduced in all the publicity materials accompanying the film. The skeleton itself, a sculpture designed and built for the film, however, can be seen as meaningful not only within the film about the monstrosity of greed and corruption in today's Russia, but also within a larger perspective of contemporary Russian society and culture. After the shooting of the film, the giant prop, now a famous sculpture used to advertise the film (and advertised by the film), ended up as a piece of commodity: according to newspaper reports, it was bought by a businessman and placed on the lawn outside his house in Moscow.[26] This piece of entertainment news is significant especially in connection with Aleksey Gherman Jr's *Under Electric Clouds*, which was inspired by the new generations of well-to-do Russians for whom something like this would constitute an everyday gesture.

Gherman Jr deliberately sets his film in 2017, moving just a few years ahead in time, to coincide with the hundred-year anniversary of the Bolshevik Revolution. The vision is thus only slightly displaced, with a few futuristic

Figure 3.4 Aleksey Gherman Jr, *Under Electric Clouds* (2015): the skeleton-like frame of an unfinished skyscraper that looms in the distance over an urban wasteland

elements that sketch a mildly post-apocalyptic vision of Moscow. As if to resemble Zvyagintsev's whale, there is a skeleton-like frame of an unfinished skyscraper that looms in the distance over an urban wasteland (Figure 3.4). The eternally overcast sky displays electronic advertisements that float and disperse on the horizon. Underneath, colourful lights weave decorative patterns in a city appearing as a cluster of images. The tempo is slow, and unlike the congested shots of Gherman Sr's film, in which everything is entangled in constant motion, and the crisp black-and-white photography often emphasises slivers of white light in pitch darkness, etching the figures into space, *Under Electric Clouds* is photographed in tableau-style shots resembling impressionist paintings with pastel colours and soft veils of mist.[27] Each scene is constructed with painterly care and watching the film on a computer, one can barely resist the temptation to freeze the frames and admire the screenshots on their own as individual pictures.

The film consists of seven fragmentary chapters and parades a host of characters whose lives are loosely connected to the helix-shaped, unfinished skyscraper. We meet a Kyrgyz migrant worker who used to work at the construction site and now wonders around aimlessly. As he cannot speak Russian, he cannot communicate with passers-by. At the frozen river bank, he runs to the rescue of a woman who is getting stabbed by a stranger but arrives too late. There is a brother and a sister, the children of the deceased oligarch whose death halted the construction work on the skyscraper. They come to deal with the inheritance but have no plans to stay. The real estate lawyer, who was once involved in the purchase of the land for the building, is haunted by traumatic memories of the past. There is an art scholar now working as a tour guide at a museum nearby. The derelict building near the construction site hosts a group of drug addicts who take a young girl hostage. A young man who lost his family in the war in Ukraine helps the girl to escape. After an attempted suicide, the architect of the building invites people to celebrate his birthday but decides not to attend his own party. The recurring themes of the disconnected episodes are death, acts of suicide, violence, failure to communicate and connect, the experience of frustration, grief and senselessness.

'These are confusing times – the narrator informs us at the beginning – crucified between a great past and an equally large future, everyone seems to be waiting for a great war. Globalisation failed to unify the world.' Gherman Jr borrows the structure of meandering plot lines and several motifs from the great tradition of Russian nineteenth-century literature, most notably it revisits the theme of the 'superfluous man' in a sombre, slightly abstract setting and, occasionally, with absurd undertones. In the literary tradition established by authors like Aleksandr Pushkin, Mikhail Lermontov, Ivan Turgenev or Ivan Goncharov, the 'superfluous man' is a kind of Byronic hero, a talented and educated nobleman who cynically wastes his life in boredom. With explicit references weaved into the dialogues, Gherman Jr alludes to this tradition but also essentially reinterprets it: in his film, the 'superfluous man' is a person who has lost his foothold and who is adrift in a world falling apart culturally, socially and politically, he is the small individual lost in the big picture. Such men are, accordingly to the narrator: 'just people, no better or worse than the others. [. . .] Yet somehow nothing in this world happens without these people. Without them, there can be no picture of our world, our country, our time.' Hence, neither of the characters or their depressing stories are fleshed out, but we may find that the gloomy, entrancing pictoriality of the tableau shots are reminiscent of the atmosphere of languor and Romantic brooding of the literature evoked by the film.

In this respect, the film can also be seen in parallel with Alexander Sokurov's *Whispering Pages* (*Tikhiye stranitsy*, 1994), the third film in his trilogy of 'death and nothingness'[28] also based – as its subtitle indicates – on 'motifs from nineteenth century prose', and which shows his characters in a similarly slow perambulation within a fog-infused dreamscape, in images that look like stretched, damaged or colourised photographs. The film concludes with an astonishing slow sequence centred around a sculpture, displaying an uncanny intimacy between the protagonist and a huge, enigmatic statue of a lioness which appears to offer refuge and nurture within its cavernous, sculpted 'bodyspace'. Sokurov unfolds his haunting vision in a completely artificial, nightmarish world, as a cinematic *ekphrasis* of a few pages that one may vaguely remember from Russian literature, enhanced by his own poetic imagination.

In contrast, Gherman Jr's stylised vision, with its eerie digital sky, is ultimately anchored in the all-pervading aestheticisation of contemporary life that

Figure 3.5 A gloomy, unfinished statue in *Under Electric Clouds* (2015)

Frederic Jameson described as a 'near-total commodification of the world', 'an addiction, halfway between drugs and pornography and the mania of the pathological collector' (2016: 149). In the world of *Under Electric Clouds* art and, prominently, sculpture is everywhere. The setting includes a foggy riverbank littered with sculptures, some seem to be unfinished, some are already crumbling, or just outmoded. We have statues of all sizes and materials. There is a colossal, clunky, metal-plated, robot-like statue overlooking the city to open the film (with its eyes glowing in the dark reminiscent of the accessories of a second-rate sci-fi). We see antique torsos, classic busts in the collection of the dead oligarch, large-scale bas-reliefs in the park, half-finished statues, giant heads of concrete (Figure 3.5) and a horse made of metal framework on the outskirts of the town. Abstract sculptures and transparent, floating textures are combined with the hologram-like projection of a giant flying man as parts of a complex installation in an art gallery.

There is also the unavoidable, large statue of Lenin, discarded in what seems to be a veritable cemetery of statues. The imposing figure of Lenin carved in stone – along with a few smaller statues of what we assume to be other political dignitaries of the past (but cannot really make out in the foggy landscape) – appears as an ironic commentary on the traditional, ideologic use of sculptures in Russian history and historical movies. In this respect, we may remember, how Eisenstein's film, *October* (*Oktyabr*, 1928) opens with the statue of Nicholas II, the Czar of Russia, which the insurgent crowd pulls down from its pedestal as a symbolic act of rebellion against the royal dynasty. As Rosalind Krauss describes, in a film like this, people move in real space, ideologies 'are symbolized by means of statuary', 'sculptures are made into surrogate actors; and there is a consistent identification of particular icons with particular political views' (1981, 8). In the same vein, in recent cinema, the removal and destruction of the statues of Lenin was used time and again as a powerful image signifying the defeat of communism. In Theo Angelopoulos's film, *Ulysses's Gaze* (*To vlemma tou Odyssea*, 1995) there is a majestic tracking-shot sequence in which the pieces of a colossal statue of Lenin placed on a ship are floating down the Danube. The giant, petrified body appears as an embodiment of past political power and glory. Commodified and dismembered, displaced but still awe-inspiring, it offers a terrific spectacle to people watching on the shore as the ship passes by in a stately manner, as if it were a funeral procession. The German tragicomedy, *Good Bye, Lenin!* (2003) directed by Wolfgang Becker, reprises Federico Fellini's famous shot of *La dolce vita* (1960) featuring the statue of Jesus being transported by helicopter, with his arms stretched as if bestowing blessing over Rome. In one of the most touchingly ridiculous scenes in Becker's film, the upper half of an enormous statue of Lenin flies similarly above Berlin and seems to literally say goodbye with its arms stretched toward the bewildered mother who has no idea that communism has fallen and the two halves of Germany have been reunited.

In Gherman Jr's film, however, the statue of Lenin standing in the fog with his arms stretched, not only seems to point to nowhere (Figure 3.6), it simply does not seem to evoke the full weight of its historical status and past ideological charge. We can barely make out its silhouette among other figures in the falling snow. Without a particular emphasis, it stands there as not much more than a mass of stone in an adult playground, a surface for graffiti. The young heiress of the unfinished skyscraper climbs it and sits on the outstretched arm as if it were the branch of a tree, apparently just for the fun of it. Later, she also stands playfully on her head, balancing on top of the statue. The gesture is then reversed in the scene in which

Figure 3.6 Aleksey Gherman Jr, *Under Electric Clouds* (2015): the discarded statue of Lenin

another character places a small Buddha statue on his head while walking on the river bank. As a remainder of a historical figure fading into obscurity, losing its complex associations with nightmares of the past, thus, the statue of Lenin, just like the Buddha figurine, blends seamlessly into the hotchpotch of an exceedingly globalised Russian culture that we see burgeoning around it.

The disillusioned architect describes his work in the film as 'incredibly trendy but meaningless'. Similarly, all the statues we see strike us mostly as picturesque and decorative. They are symptomatic of our age in which we live in spaces where not only are nature and culture irreversibly enmeshed (exemplified by the unfinished construction as a crossover between skeleton, sculpture and architecture), but art can re-appropriate everything. The protagonists spend their time in art galleries and exhibitions, partying amid artworks scattered around the waterfront or near a heap of rubble, they are moving around in an environment in which a construction site, an artist's studio, a junkyard, an installation space or an artistically designed airport terminal become undistinguishable. Buildings are merely sculptures created on a larger scale. Industrial waste, everyday objects become intriguing as sculptural forms and assemblages. Historical statues and monuments are reclaimed and absorbed by nature as parts of a hybrid peri-urban landscape.

The 'nomadic' sculptures – to use Rosalind Krauss's famous expression for the 'expanded field of sculpture' (1979) – that populate the film, engulf life in the ever-expanding field of art. The film itself, with the multitude of artworks commissioned especially for its elaborate set design, becomes a host for a unique collection of artworks. This feature was underscored by the exhibition organised at the Moscow Museum of Modern Art with the title *Now 2017*, curated by the film's art director, Elena Okopnaia and video-art historian Antonio Geusa, in June 2015. Based on the film, the exhibition, showcased the painterly quality of the frames and documented the process of the combined creation of sculpture and cinema, also displaying some of the objects and sculptures used in the movie and explicitly engaging with the idea of expanded cinema. According to the curators' statement on the website of the MMOMA, expanded cinema can be seen in this case in the intertwining of the exhibition and the film as neither a new form of cinema 'nor a new form of contemporary art. It is the dialogue between the two. It may be even seen as a duet of art forms.'[29] Thus, we may add, the tandem of film and exhibition connects cinema and the plastic art in a process of dual expansion and mutual enfoldment. Cinema expands into a space for the arts, it becomes a virtual container of artworks displayed not only within the setting of the art gallery incorporated into the film, but also within the loosely connected open-air tableau sequences composed around them, blurring the line between episodic cinema and the moving tableaux of single channel video installations. The exhibition conceives the art gallery both as a repository that expands towards cinema, relocating several of the artworks created for the film and screening fragments of the movie, and as a portal in-between vision and reality: where the fictional world of the film 'explodes' into the real, sending its palpable 'debris' into the museum.

THE SILENCE OF SCULPTURES

According to the French philosopher Michel Serres, music and sculpture, two fundamental and most ancient forms of art that precede language, must be sought in 'the heart of chaos', where they 'maintain a secret relation of duality with one another' (2015: 191). But while, music (embodied in the mythological figure of Orpheus, who 'climbs back up from the underworld') is 'a procession toward the sublime', sculpture (embodied by the figure of Lot's wife turning around and becoming a statue) is 'a descent into the dense' (Serres 2015: 195). He writes:

> since statues remain indefinitely in silence, the monotheisms of speech and writing move away from them as they do from the underworld [. . .], you will not find, in history or the tradition, any general philosophical treatise on sculpture or statues. Language does not speak about silence. (Serres 2015: 198)

Both of the films analysed above explore chaotic, dystopian universes through harnessing the performative value of sculpturality and sculptures, as well as the 'density' of their silence. *Hard to Be a God* even doubles down on the negation of the culture of the words. On the one hand, it depicts a ferociously anti-intellectual society, where people are persecuted for as much as knowing how to read and write. At one point in the film, the protagonist, Rumata, the controversial and failed saviour coming from a more enlightened, learned world, quotes a few lines from Boris Pasternak's poem, *Hamlet*, which blends the figure of Christ on the eve of crucifixion with Shakespeare's pensive Danish prince. When asked who wrote those verses, he replies, mocking the illiteracy of the brutes around him, that it was him, and indeed there is no one to disprove him in this world that trumps Hamletian meditation with violence and pushes Rumata from his eloquent poetic reverie towards gory action. On the other hand, as we have seen, the plasticity of the depiction does not evoke 'the majesty of sculpture' that Vachel Lindsay (1916: 96) associated with the images of movies based on action. Rather, Gherman's method resembles how sculptors dig deep into dirt, mould the material, chisel away the stone in a constant tactile encounter with bare matter, and evokes Bataille's base materiality which is 'external and foreign' not only of 'ideal human aspirations' (1985: 61) as we have seen, but of the realm of language as well. If becoming sculptural in *Hard to Be a God* can be described through the notion of the *informe*, we have to keep in mind that formlessness is also basically inarticulate and escapes any clear-cut categorisation. In Bataille's words, the 'formless is not only an adjective having a given meaning, but a term that serves to bring things down in the world, generally requiring that each thing have its form' (1985: 31). *Hard to Be a God* takes us on a journey into this dense and formless 'underworld' experienced primarily through gut-churning, pre-reflective affects, it makes us descend into 'the world before words' (Serres 2015: 53).

Gherman Jr proposes a different perspective. How do you contemplate the Apocalypse? – he seems to ask in his film, and the answer is: by becoming a sculpture as when Lot's wife turns into a pillar of salt while looking back at Sodom and Gomorrah. The solitary statues, looking over a post-apocalyptic Moscow in *Under Electric Clouds*, refuse to tell any tales. Yet, they seem to be exhibit an uncanny mixture of the animate and the inanimate. Kenneth Gross remarks:

> Not unlike Roland Barthes's description of the photograph, the statue presents a body or a pose arrested in time, arresting time itself; it marks an absence or a loss through the presence of a thing that is yet irremediably, materially present – though a statue will tend to monumentalize and dehistoricize that arrest, conceal the absence, in a way a photograph does not. (Gross 1992: 15)

If Zvyagintsev's whale was a reminder of nature's inability to withstand the destructive forces of humanity, Gherman Jr's oversized statues appear as the petrification of the stasis, arrestedness, superfluousness and paralysis experienced in a society confronting a world in continuous and violent change, incommensurate with the powers of individuals. At the same time, these statues, with their half-carved, half-rugged or defaced surfaces, bear the traces of both human creative energy and destruction (not unlike the deformed faces of *Hard to Be a God*), making them objects animated through the conflicting affects they materialise in an anonymous and unqualified way.[30] 'These are some depressed statues' – one of the protagonists observes, reflecting on the general mood of melancholy. 'It's like Carthage' – another one says, reloading the stones with wider cultural signification. In this way, Gherman Jr's statuary does not emerge in opposition to language because it would be external or foreign to it, but because it absorbs and conceals it under its layers of signification. *Under Electric Clouds* presents a palimpsestic world, where even the sky is used as a surface to be inscribed with images and words, where statues are covered with graffiti and the whole urban landscape is imbued with opaque references to literature, history and the arts. Yet, all of these layers fail to make coherent sense, and introduce us (as a reversal of what we see in *Hard to Be a God*) to a world not 'before', but 'after the words', enhanced by all the stories of the episodes that remain fragmented, and leaving the picturesque quality of the tableaux and the silent expressivity of the statues to come to the fore.

In both films, the sculptural elements that infiltrate the cinematic image convey complex allegories of contemporary human existence, unravelling the very fabric of the world. In *Hard to Be a God* this is messy, physical and visceral, excluding the rational order of the logos; in *Under Electric Clouds*, it gives the impression of a cultural wasteland, oversaturated with signification.

This work was supported by a grant of the Romanian Ministry of National Education, CNCS – UEFISCDI, project number PN-III-P4-ID-PCE-2016-0418.

Notes

1. See the collection of essays written by Steven Jacobs, Susan Felleman, Vito Adriaensens and Lisa Colpaert (2017).
2. See, for example, Youngblood (1970), Bellour (2007) and Casetti (2015).
3. Somewhat similarly, Gene Youngblood declares: 'when we say expanded cinema we actually mean *expanded consciousness*. Expanded cinema does not mean computer films, video phosphors, atomic light, or spherical projections. Expanded cinema isn't a movie at all: like life *it's a process of becoming*' (1970: 41, my emphasis).
4. This is probably because Aleksey Gherman's life and work united the best and the worst with regards to the condition of the artist in the Soviet era: as the son of an acclaimed Soviet writer (Yuri Gherman), he grew up in Leningrad surrounded by all the privileges of the Stalinist cultural elite, yet working with a persistent refusal to compromise, he was in a constant struggle with censorship, being able to make only six films, many of which were harshly criticised, their production delayed for years, and even banned. Yet at the same time he also acquired a somewhat legendary status of a maverick author of masterpieces. According to Anthony Anemone: 'his struggles with a benighted cultural and political establishment provide a vivid commentary on the fate of cinema in Russia from the 1960s to the present' (2016: 543).
5. Gherman wanted to make an adaptation of the Strugatsky brothers' novel as his debut film, as early as 1964, but the project was postponed for different reasons until 2000. The shooting of the film took six years (during which time some of the older actors died), and the post-production work dragged on for an

additional seven years. Gherman himself became ill and passed away before the sound editing was completed, leaving his wife and son to apply the finishing touches to the film, which was released posthumously.

6. *The History of the Arkanar Massacre* was actually the working title of the film for some time before its completion.
7. Available at <http://14films.de/wp-content/uploads/2014/11/Presskit-Its-hard-to-be-a-god.pdf> (last accessed 12 January 2019).
8. Aleksey Gherman Jr's words, quoted from the pressbook of the film. Available at <http://14films.de/wp-content/uploads/2014/11/Presskit-Its-hard-to-be-a-god.pdf> (last accessed 12 January 2019).
9. See: 'Slime [*le visqueaux*] is the agony of water. It presents itself as a phenomenon in the process of becoming; it does not have the permanence within change that water has but on the contrary, represents an accomplished break in a change of state' (Sartre 1956: 604).
10. The sculptural effect of glazing was recently explored by James Franco's controversial video work commissioned to advertise Sotheby's 2016 exhibition entitled *Glazed: The Legacy of the Della Robbia*, in which glossy, transparent gel was poured over models in slow motion. Available at <http://www.sothebys.com/glazed> (last accessed 12 January 2019).
11. This image is grotesquely echoed in the sequence in which severed heads of corpses float around in the muddy puddles for children to poke and kick around.
12. The phrase is borrowed from Richard Brody's short review in *The New Yorker*. Available at <http://www.newyorker.com/goings-on-about-town/movies/hard-god-2> (last accessed 12 January 2019).
13. Cf. 'Nothing is seen that arouses the human spirit more, that ravishes the sense more, that horrifies more, that provokes more terror or admiration to a greater extent among creatures than the monsters, prodigies, and abominations through which we see the works of nature inverted, mutilated, and truncated' (Bataille quotes Pierre Boaistuau in his *Visions of Excess*, 1985: 53).
14. In this respect, Gherman's cinema remotely connects to tendencies in modern sculpture which conceive the sculptural as a trans-form based on the in-betweenness of autonomous body parts, tissues and inorganic matter, combining the raw sensation of the flesh with the craftsmanship of artisanal objects. For example, Louise Bourgeois's ambivalent sculptures (like *Le Regard*, 1966; *Janus fleuri, Fillette*, 1968; *Blind Man's Buff*, 1984), or the more recent 'flesh-objects' made by Jonathan Pyne, Russel Cameron, Felix Deac or Géza Szőllősi, as well as Mathew Barney's transgressive art that blends viscous, organic sculpture, cinema and performance.
15. New International Version, 2011. Available at <https://www.biblegateway.com/passage/?search=Psalm+40%3A2> (last accessed 12 January 2019).
16. *Andrei Rublev* can be considered perhaps the ultimate cinematic epic about the transcendence of art. In the episode of the casting of the bell, sculptural creation draws attention to the weight of physicality and materiality involved in the work of an artist, and bears out the essence of Tarkovsky's poetics: this is a sensuous cinema that is at the same time deeply spiritual, similar to icon

painting (see Dalle Vacche 1996), in which – in the absolute, transcendental sense of the word – the image (just like any other object of religious art) is a medium, an intermediary, making the invisible visible and palpable.

17. As Paul Hegarty explains: 'for something to stay outside the world of form requires that an object remain a process, disabling the imposition of form at all stages' (2003: 7).

18. Although we could also fit this into Julia Kristeva's (1982) concept of abjection, we have to keep in mind, as Benjamin Noys points out that 'Bataille's formless is "like a spider or spit" [. . .], mobile or fluid enough to evade classification and meaning, including as the abject' (2000: 34).

19. Botz-Bornstein also remarks: 'by reuniting the body of the hero with the mud, the "vision" of the hero ceases to be a vision in which a subject perceives an object. What has truly taken place, is a union of subject and object' in a neo-Platonic sense (2007: 25).

20. In his critique of 'classical materialism', Bataille points out that the notion of 'dead matter' has been conceived within a system of thought that he calls 'senile idealism' (1985, 15–16). Gherman's all-encompassing sculpturality also defies the concept of sculpture outlined by W. J. T. Mitchell, who considers that: 'sculpture, especially that modeled on the human body, is not only the first but also the most dangerous of the arts. It impiously elevates the human image to the status of a god, reifies mortal men into immortal idols, and degrades spirit into dead matter' (Mitchell 2005: 248).

21. Nick Land's poetic interpretation of Bataille, 'life is an exploration of death, [. . .] life smears itself across death' (1992: 128), may explain perhaps how the making of such a film filled with horrors could have meant a labour of love for Gherman.

22. For a comprehensive overview of Nietzsche's philosophy on sculpture, see Babich (2011).

23. These recurring camera-looks do not break the so-called fourth wall by directly addressing the camera as a kind of Brechtian alienation effect. Because of the intense sensorial experience, in fact, we have already been intensely absorbed into this world, we have already been 'pulled in' by the quasi-tactile and olfactory sensations, and these looks merely strengthen the viewer's engagement and embodied immersion.

24. For example, both films are unusually long and, in different ways, difficult to watch. They both create an entire fictional universe with a large cast of characters and refined visuals based on elaborate set designs and exquisite cinematography. Both start with an unidentified narrator only to abandon the narratorial voice after a few introductory statements, etc.

25. The *Worker and Kolkhoz Woman* holding a sickle and a hammer over their heads, which appeared in the logo, was a statue made by Vera Mukhina in 1937.

26. Available at <https://themoscowtimes.com/articles/russian-businessman-buys-leviathan-skeleton-for-moscow-lawn-43384> (last accessed 12 January 2019).

27. The connection with the art of painting is made explicit by the quotation from Paul Cézanne used as a motto that introduces the film.

28. The other two are: *The Second Circle* (*Krug tvoroy*, 1990) and *Stone* (*Kamen*, 1992).
29. Available at <http://www.mmoma.ru/en/exhibitions/gogolevsky/sejchas_2017/> (last accessed 12 January 2019).
30. In distinguishing between affect and emotion, Steven Shaviro quotes Brian Massumi for whom 'affect is primary, non-conscious, asubjective or presubjective, asignifying, unqualified, and intensive; while emotion is derivative, conscious, qualified, and meaningful, a "content" that can be attributed to an already-constituted subject. Emotion is affect captured by a subject, or tamed and reduced to the extent that it becomes commensurate with that subject. Subjects are overwhelmed and traversed by affect, but they have or possess their own emotions' (Shaviro 2010: 3).

Works Cited

Anemone, Anthony (2016), 'Aleksey Gherman: The Last Soviet Auteur', in Birgit Beumers (ed.), *A Companion to Russian Cinema*, Chichester and Malden: Wiley-Blackwell, pp. 543–65.

Arnheim, Rudolf (1966), 'The Holes of Henry Moore: On the Function of Space in Sculpture', in *Towards a Psychology of Art: Collected Essays*, Berkeley: The University of California Press, pp. 245–55.

Babich, Babette (2011), 'Zu Nietzsches Statuen: Skulptur und das Erhabene', in Beatrix Vogel and Nikolaus Gerdes (eds), *Grenzen der Rationalität: Teilband 2: Vorträge 2006–2009*, München: Allitera, pp. 391–421. English translation available online at <https://www.academia.edu/1099632/Nietzsche_and_the_Sculptural_Sublime_On_Becoming_the_One_You_Are> (last accessed 12 January 2019).

Bataille, Georges [1970] (1985), *Visions of Excess. Selected Writings 1927–1939*, Minneapolis: University of Minnesota Press.

Bellour, Raymond (2007), 'Of an Other Cinema', in Tanya Leighton (ed.), *Art and the Moving Image: A Critical Reader*, London: Tate Publishing & Afterall, pp. 406–23.

Bois, Yve-Alain and Rosalind Krauss (1997), *Formless: A User's Guide*, New York: Zone Books.

Botz-Bornstein, Thorsten (2007), *Films and Dreams: Tarkovsky, Bergman, Sokurov, Kubrick, and Wong Kar-Wai*, Plymouth: Lexington Books.

Casetti, Francesco (2015), *The Lumière Galaxy. Seven Key Words for the Cinema to Come*, New York: Columbia University Press.

Dalle Vacche, Angela (1996), 'Cinema as the Restoration of Icon Painting', in *Painting and Cinema: How Art is Used in Film*, Austin: University of Texas Press, pp. 135–61.

Droth, Martina (2009), *Finding Sculpture in the Decorative Arts*, Los Angeles: Getty Museum.

Focillon, Henri [1934] (1992), *The Life of Forms in Art*, New York: Zone Books.

Genosko, Garry (1998). 'The Sculptural Problem of the Between', in *Undisciplined Theory*, London: Sage, pp. 92–5.

Gross, Kenneth (1992) *The Dream of the Moving Statue*, Ithaca, NY and London: Cornell University Press.

Hegarty, Paul (2003), 'Formal Insistence', *The Semiotic Review of Books*, Vol. 13, No. 2: pp. 6–9.

Hoogland, Renée (2014), *A Violent Embrace: Art and Aesthetics after Representation*. Lebanon, NH: Dartmouth College Press.

Jacobs, Steven, Susan Felleman, Vito Adriaensens, Lisa Colpaert (2017), *Screening Statues: Sculpture and Cinema*, Edinburgh: Edinburgh University Press.

Jameson, Frederic (2016), 'Suffocating Kinesis. The Late Films of Aleksey German', in Seunghoon Jeong and Jeremi Szaniawski (eds), *The Global Auteur. The Politics of Authorship in 21st Century Cinema*, London, New York: Bloomsbury, pp. 149–59.

Krauss, Rosalind (1979), 'Sculpture in the Expanded Field', *October*, Vol. 8. (Spring): pp. 30–44.

Krauss, Rosalind [1977] (1981), *Passages in Modern Sculpture*, Cambridge, MA and London: The MIT Press.

Krauss, Rosalind (1996), '"Informe" without Conclusion', *October*, Vol. 78, (Autumn): pp. 89–105.

Kristeva, Julia [1980] (1982), *Powers of Horror. An Essay on Abjection*, New York: Columbia University Press.

Land, Nick (1992), *The Thirst for Annihilation: Georges Bataille and Virulent Nihilism*, London and New York: Routledge.

Lichtenstein, Jacqueline (2008), *The Blind Spot: An Essay on the Relations Between Painting and Sculpture in the Modern Age*, Los Angeles: Getty Research Institute.

Lindsay, Vachel (1916), *The Art of the Moving Picture*, New York: The Macmillan Company.

Martin, F. David (1981), *Sculpture and Enlivened Space: Aesthetics and History*, Lexington: University Press of Kentucky.

Mitchell, W. J. T. (2005), 'What Sculpture Wants. Placing Antony Gormley', in *What do Pictures Want. The Lives and Loves of Images*, Chicago and London: The University of Chicago Press, pp. 245–72.

Noys, Benjamin (2000), *Georges Bataille. A Critical Introduction*, London and Sterling, VA: Pluto Press.

Paterson, Mark (2007), *The Senses of Touch: Haptics, Affects and Technologies*, London and New York: Bloomsbury.

Romney, Jonathan (2015), *Hard to Be a God* Review – Art Cinema at its Most Heroically Extreme, *The Guardian*, 9 August, <https://www.theguardian.com/film/2015/aug/09/hard-to-be-a-god-film-review-heroically-extreme> (last accessed 12 January 2019).

Sartre, Jean-Paul [1943] (1956), *Being and Nothingness: An Essay on Phenomenological Ontology*, New York: Philosophical Library.

Serres, Michel [1987] (2015), *Statues. The Second Book of Foundations*, London and New York: Bloomsbury.

Shaviro, Steven (2010), *Post-Cinematic Affect*, Manchester and Washington DC: Zero Books.

Sobchack, Vivian (1992), *The Address of the Eye. A Phenomenology of Film Experience*, Princeton: Princeton University Press.

Sobchack, Vivian (2004), *Carnal Thoughts. Embodiment and Moving Image Culture*, Berkeley and London: University of California Press.

Youngbood, Gene (1970), *Expanded Cinema*, New York: P. Dutton & Co.

CHAPTER 4

Intermedial Densities in the Work of Jan Švankmajer: A Media-Anthropological Case Study
Mareike Sera

> *What characterizes gesture is that in it nothing is being produced or acted, but rather something is being endured and supported.* (Agamben 2000: 57)

INTERMEDIALITY AND THE CINEMA OF JAN ŠVANKMAJER

In film any object, gesture, emotion, rhythm or idea seems removed from its points of references in actual and imagined worlds. A smile on screen, for example, takes on a doubtful and fragile ontological status. It floats in space and time. The closer the camera gets, the stronger this effect occurs. The close-up enhances this ontological status of in-betweenness that characterises cinema. The image emerging is torn from its circumstances of production. Historic time and space is ruptured. Moreover, the fragility of the cinematic image extends to the subject and object worlds on-screen as well as off-screen. The dubious ontological state of the image (in)forms the subjects and objects represented. Ontological fragility opens communicative channels and creative potential.

The fragility of the ontological status of the cinematic image relates to the idea of intermedial density that the following discussion would like to put forward. A piece of wood on the palm of a hand, for example, purports densities in terms of material qualities: the wood weighs, smells and looks in a specific way as well as the hand radiates warmth, tenderness and humidity. Sensing these qualities and the contact between them, engaging with them and making sense of them is part of a dialogue emerging between the Self and the Object that requires a shared context between them. The piece of wood or the hand will not share anything about its qualities if there is no contact, no 'communicative' act. Inner and outer worlds open onto each other and merge into one another. The exchange of qualities between different medial worlds may function in a similar way. Object worlds, for example, bear painterly qualities as a result of a dialogue, of worlds opening up to one another and sharing a common ground. The intensity and intimacy of this dialogue blurs the distinction between subjectivity and objectivity. It is very difficult to discern the painterly qualities outside painting, in a physical environment in an objective manner, as the exchange subjectifies the communicative partners. A context of 'intercommunicability' is created, as the following discussion will point out in relation to the media-anthropological approach of Eduardo Viveiros De Castro (2004: 464).

In order to examine the idea of intermedial densities in relation to the work of Czech animator and artist Jan Švankmajer, as suggested in the title, it is worthwhile exploring the communicative and creative possibilities that the object animation process offers. Engagement plays a key role here, while a media-anthropological perspective helps to understand the degree of intimacy evolving in the process. The films by Švankmajer fascinate in the way they engage with object worlds. Objects are not approached as something already known. Rather, the films re-negotiate the conditions of communication. As Michael Richardson observes:

> As an animator Švankmajer has always been concerned to open up the inner life of object, both in relation to human activity (as repositories of memories and witness of events [. . .] and in terms of their own integrity that is independent of their human 'masters', in which they may be seen to have a life at variance with human objectives. Humans are not the centre of this world: life is fragile and objects are likely to have revenge on whoever abuses them. (2006: 127)

Švankmajer's films open up a breathing space that cuts ideas and media free of their naturalist obligation to represent and cohere.

Naturalist ontology sharply distinguishes between culture and nature and for this reason purports set terms for the what and the how of the relationship between the Self and the Other. In arguing for the existence of multiple realities, Viveiros De Castro draws on the Amerindian idea of perspectivism, which proceeds along the lines that the point of view creates the subject; whatever is activated or 'agented' by the point of view will be a subject (1998: 477). The interest of multiple interpretations of one world (multi-culturalism) shifts towards one interpretation of multiple worlds (multi-naturalism). The shift refocuses the interest in the direction of the means of exchange and translation and therefore in the direction of social concerns such as behaviour in relation to the Other. It personifies the object. As Viveiro De Castro (2004: 468) asserts 'to know' in the naturalist sense 'is to objectify [. . .] to desubjectify, to make explicit the subject's partial presence in the object so as to reduce it to an ideal minimum'. In Amerindian perspectivism, the approach to understanding is different.

'It is necessary to know how to personify nonhumans, and it is necessary to personify them in order to know' (Viveiro De Castro 2004: 469).

The shift towards a media-anthropological perspective recalibrates the level at which the spectator's and artist's engagement takes place. To open up, one takes oneself back, one commits to alterity and plurality, one submits to vulnerability and uncertainty. This allows one to move forward, to get in contact with the inner life of objects, their autonomous agency and ability to communicate. It means to enter a state of translation and comparison, a state of 'intercommunicability' (Viveiros De Castro 2004: 464). The term relates to a 'state of undifferentiation between humans and animal' (Viveiros De Castro 1998: 471). It creates a common context that allows a mix of human and animal attributes in order to be able to communicate and interact. Transferred to a media-anthropological context this means to create a shared context or common ground 'on eye level'. This pretence alters the terms of communication and interaction. The things said, felt, acted out, as well as the attributes associated with them, become accessible to any 'instance' (subject, object, animal, deity, artefact, medium, etc.) involved in the process/situation, as they lead to a shared sensibility. Moreover, they lead to a shared sociability. The subjectified 'Other' gains the status of a social 'quasi-being',[1] just like the de-subjectified human agent.

Intercommunicability allows us to understand more about the phenomenon of intermediality, which always implies dialogue and ambiguity. The films by Švankmajer serve as a rich example in this context. If one directs attention to how the artist engages with the material that he uses, Švankmajer's strong pretence to communicate 'on eye level' comes to the fore. Passion and devotion are important here. Švankmajer's love for the art of animation and the art of cinema is rarely discussed, which might come as a surprise if one considers how rich the discourse on his work is.[2] Švankmajer includes manifold references to other artists' works from different media contexts and he usually highlights the artists' passion and devotion. Theatrical, photographic, musical, graphic, poetic, sculptural, architectural worlds intersect in his films. The emphasis on artistic commitment, therefore, does not merely add representational layers to a pre-existing understanding of the materials, artefacts and works of art referred to. It rather immerses them in the natural, conceptual and artefactual layers of objecthood and acknowledges their ontological plurality. Švankmajer's engagement does not attempt to enclose 'being', but to open onto it, resulting in excess and fragmentation. The films engage with their objects in the mannerist sense of exploding senses of Selves. The sensual density emerges in relation to and in between the dramatisation of Object-Selves, dispersing and diverting abundance. Ontological differences and ambiguities are highlighted, which leaves multiple worlds to open and emerge. The media-anthropological approach, thus, attempts to retrace an intimate level of communication that challenges the naturalist and humanist divide between nature and culture. The ontological state of in-betweenness requires us to leave the naturalist percept behind as well as to open towards different modes of communication. Cinematic expression works with more than one medium, it adopts and appropriates media. The 'multi'-expressivity requires the artist to translate and compare between the plurality of media.

Švankmajer's *The Flat* (*Byt*), *The Ossuary* (*Kostnice*) and *Dimensions of Dialogue* (*Možnosti dialogu*) foreground the desire to reach beyond, to find a subtle way out, to expand one's visions. Capabilities to connect and diversify become central motifs. In *The Flat*, a man is thrown into a flat, which is fully furnished (Figure 4.1). Yet he fails to make use of the equipment and is unsuccessful in finding a subtle way out. There is a table with food, an oven to heat, a bed to sleep, etc. and arrows pointing the way. The illusion of being taken care of, however, is soon shattered. The everyday objects and the surroundings do not perform their familiar functions. When the man, for example, attempts to eat the soup, the spoon suddenly appears perforated, making it impossible to eat. The glass of beer rapidly changes size and shape so that when the glass reaches his mouth it is the size of a thimble with the according amount of beer. The other objects in the flat are similarly not working. The mirror does not show the face of the man, but – reminiscent of the famous painting by René Magritte – the back of the head. When he opens the oven, water pours out, and when he lies down to sleep, the bed and its covers begin to dissolve. Any need is frustrated, making the man more and more desperate to leave. A mysterious man with a bowler hat on his head appears and brings a rooster and an axe. The man freely enters the flat and leaves the axe with the prisoner. Equipped with this new tool, he chops the door down that the other man entered. Behind it, a solid wall appears with signatures on it. The man turns towards the camera, speaks in a nonsensical fashion, turns back to the wall and signs it, too. Among the signatures on the wall are Švankmajer's and his wife's (Figure 4.2; the initial V. Š. refers to their son, Václav Švankmajer). The flat's rebellious equipment and environment clearly suggest the idea of expanding one's vision and understanding. The dramatisation is intended to work against familiar ways of looking at the world. Yet this desire introduces passion, devotion and care. The fragile sense of Self driving creative/narrative curiosity allows one to place one's artistic signature despite failure or rather because of it. The artistic gesture depends on the failure of the signature, as passivity, naivety and vulnerability engage new possibilities (potentiality) of knowing the Other.

Intermedial Densities in the Work of Jan Švankmajer 95

Figures 4.1–4.2 *The Flat* (1968): everyday objects that fail to function. The initials on the wall of Švankmajer and his wife, as well as their son, Václav Švankmajer

INTERMEDIALITY: SENSES OF SELVES

Intermedial instances (bodily presence of the artefact/condition of production and perception/relation to space and time, etc.) share the blurriness of charged potentiality, withdrawing in ambiguity. The occurrence of a painting in a film, for example, leaves no doubt about the process of abstraction that takes place with the painting being transposed to film. As the painting's relation to time and space has been significantly altered and with this the mode of experience, the presence of the painting or the painterly still invites us to get in touch with the mode of expression itself, its qualities and limitation. The dialogue-partner (here the art of painting) is the quasi-object or quasi-density of the concrete instance of reference and the abstract notion of the mode of expression. The transposition reduces/explodes the medium's quality into the fragile ontological state of the 'quasi', developing ideas and potentiality.

Entering a state of 'intercommunicability' in artistic engagement with media/artefacts means to pass into a state of uncertainty, fragility and vulnerability. The 'I' or Self is only understood in its engagement with the Other, with bodies, with matter, with environments, with figures, with media, etc. It learns about itself by accommodating the Other, by engaging with it passionately and sociably. One gives oneself entirely, tenderly, with love and care. According to Agamben, 'potentiality [. . .] survives actuality and, in this way, *gives itself to itself*' (2000: 184, italics in the original). The utterance 'I speak' opens towards ontological variants – 'I speak with', 'I feel', 'I can' – thus giving way to understanding and expression.

Uncertainty, fragility and vulnerability in the context of creative and communicative potentiality are the central themes in *The Ossuary*. The film shows the famous Sedlec Ossuary near Kutná Hora, where the remains of thousands of victims of the Black Death are arranged in bizarre tableaux of bones. For ten years (1870–80) František Rint worked on this strange, yet beautiful design (Figure 4.3). Interestingly, Švankmajer's film, which relates to Rint's work, was released in two versions as the authorities banned the first one with a tour guide's voice as soundtrack. The second version features the poem *Pour faire le portrait d'un oiseau* (*To Paint the Portrait of a Bird*, 1949) by Jacques Prévert, presented in the most wonderful and breathtaking way by a singing female voice and set to music by the great Zdeněk Liška.[3] The poem reflects on how to achieve likeness in a painting. The painting of a bird is only successful if the bird begins to 'sing'. To attain this – according to the poem – the painter needs to draw a cage, imagine a fitting environment, and most importantly, has to be patient. Only patience will allow the bird to 'sing' and will entitle the artist to sign the painting. The poem ends on this note, as does the film, when it closes with Rint's signature on the wall (Figure 4.4). The poem reads:

Intermedial Densities in the Work of Jan Švankmajer 97

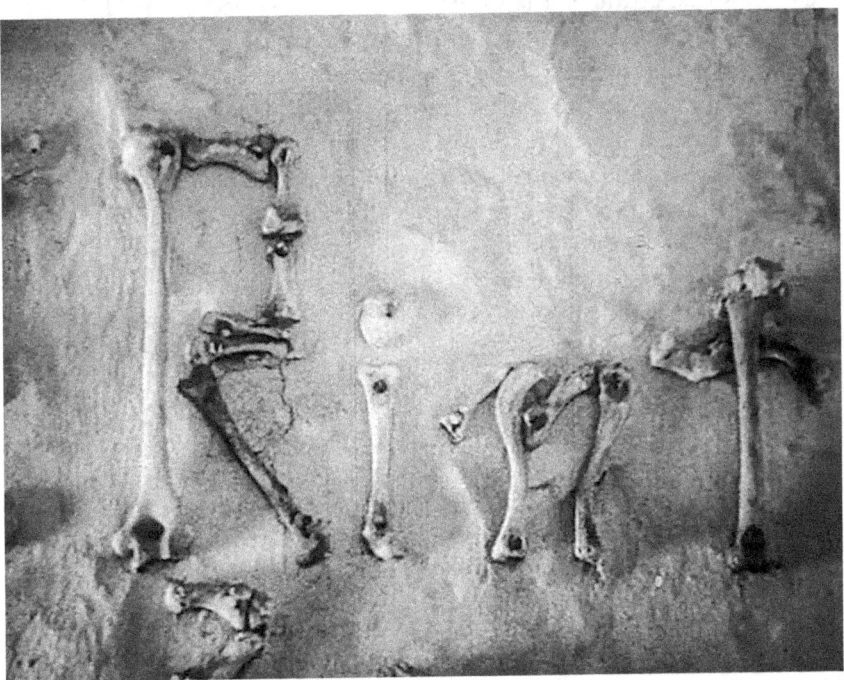

Figures 4.3–4.4 The design of *The Ossuary* (1970): the bizarre tableau of bones. The signature of the designer

puis et puis attendre que l'oiseau se décide à chanter. Si l'oiseau ne chante pas c'est mauvais signe mais s'il chante c'est bon signe signe que vous pouvez signer. Alors vous arrachez tout doucement une des plumes de l'oiseau et vous écrivez votre nom dans un coin du tableau.[4]

If one has the skill and patience, the bird will sing. The active/passive involvement draws the different instances together on the basis of desire, equipment and environment. Interiority and exteriority move onto and into one another.

GESTURES OF LOVE, COMMUNICATION AND QUASI-PALPABLE DENSITIES

The Ossuary underlines how representational sensuality (which is ontologically abstract and fragile) is permeated by the passion and devotion for the medium of expression that the artist chooses to work with; to which the artist chooses to give himself or herself entirely, with all the naivety, sensuality, sexuality and mysticism involved. The sensual density of *The Flat*, *The Ossuary* and *Dimensions of Dialogue* is intensely informed by the longing to transgress and expand the intermedial gesture, both in a personal and an impersonal sense. The ontological fragility and vulnerability gives way to a quasi-identity that requires patience and devotion to explore it, as well as a social attitude. The Other is to be approached 'on eye level'. The poem, the bizarre arrangement of the bones, the singing and the intense filmic presentation highlight how 'taking oneself back' and 'giving oneself entirely' submerge in the artistic gesture. The representational 'quasi-identity' is permeated by real pain, passion and care that 'gives life' and 'takes life' at the same time. Two perspectives merge here, one 'flying high', over-arching, without ever reaching completeness and the other 'deep under', from within, without ever being allowed to enter. The famous pool passage in *Mind and Eye* by Merleau-Ponty draws attention to this all-permeating character, that mediates between the personal and the impersonal, the above and the below:

> When through the water's thickness I see the tiled bottom of the pool, I do not see it despite the water and the reflection; I see it through them and because of them. If there were no distortions, no ripples of sunlight, if it were without that flesh that I saw the geometry of the tiles, then I would cease to see it as it is and where it is – which is to say, beyond any identical, specific place. [. . .] This inner animation, this radiation of the visible, is what the painter seeks beneath, the words *depth, space,* and *color.* (1993: 142, italics in the original)

Merleau-Ponty describes the impact of the inner desire of the creative gesture to expand and transgress towards dramatisation and vice versa. Exteriority and interiority move into one another without ever fully realising or becoming whole themselves. Seeing as a means of understanding, as a gesture of searching – just like feeling and touching – is not to be reduced to an instrument but opens towards a dynamic and pluralised ontological understanding of the world/worlds. The intermedia status of cinema addresses this. It engages – especially in relation to object animation and tactile exploration – a tension between bringing to life and bringing together. Ontologies different to naturalism, such as animism and analogism foreground this. Analogism as a mode of perception highlights the physical condition of discontinuity, and answers this in the gesture of searching, in bringing together different beings. While analogism implies wholeness, animism breaks on this pretence. Philippe Descola defines animism as an attribution by humans to non-humans that humanises plants and, above all, animals (2013: 70). The reason for this is that the soul endowing them 'allows them not only to behave in conformity with the social norms and ethical precepts of humans but also to establish communicative relations both with humans and among themselves' (2013: 70).

Bringing the analogue and the animate gesture together implies never achieving completeness. 'On the screen, the essential quality of a gesture is that it does not come to an end', according Jean Epstein (2012: 273). Gestures are fixed neither in terms of their ends nor in time, but in the process of engaging with the world. Animism and analogism embrace physical difference and plurality. As Viveiros De Castro points out, 'animism could be defined as an ontology which postulates the social character of relations between humans and non-humans: the space between nature and society is itself social' (1998: 473). Moreover, animism may emphasise love, care and tenderness. The gesture of animating implies turning towards communication partners, taking interest and engaging passionately and exhaustively with them. Švankmajer's films highlight this. In *The Ossuary*, giving and taking life is explored in multiple and diverse ways (worlds): the bones of the victims of the Black Death, the ornament, the poem, the painting of the bird, the song and the film retracing the communicative flows emerging between these worlds. The film's vivid editing and images set these flows in motion, expand and explore them with great attentiveness and humbleness, while the exhaustiveness of this excessive and multiple mobilisation is present at any moment as well. The artistic gesture giving way to exploration and mobilisation (submerging multiple worlds) appears as fragile and vulnerable as the bones of the victims and the representational quasi-identities emerging (poem, painting, song, film).

The reference to Merleau-Ponty and the gestures of 'flying high' and going 'deep under' intend to underline this tension between giving and taking life in relation to multiple worlds. One gives oneself entirely as well as exhaustively. The tension is also present in the third film under discussion, *Dimensions of Dialogue*. While the film refers more subtly to artistic struggle and passion, the sensual density appears just as strong as in the other two examples. This is especially true for the first episode of the film that famously cites one of the major influences on Švankmajer's work, the paintings by Giuseppe Arcimboldo.[5] The film is divided into three parts: factual dialogue, passionate dialogue and exhausting dialogue, according to the subtitles shown in the film. The first part consists of a series of encounters between Arcimboldian heads: one head composed of fruits and vegetables, one of art and scientific objects and one of kitchen equipment (Figures 4.5 and 4.6). These heads move towards each other, face to face, in tableau style. During each encounter one head throws itself on the other, consuming the materials, shredding and smashing them, while marking one head as superior and the other as inferior. The metal head with the kitchen tools, for example, crushes the vegetables, the scientific tools grind the kitchen equipment, and the vegetables decompose the scientific equipment. After each encounter the offensive head spits out the material of its adversary. The heads move along, but the materials of the inferior part have suffered considerably.

The idea of working through, of passionately engaging with materiality and mediality, is very explicit in this episode. In this respect, *Dimensions of Dialogue* is quite similar to *The Ossuary*. Physicality does and does not matter. One works with bones similarly as with space, words, sounds, visuals, rhythms, celluloid, etc. One works with these media encountering their specific physicality, one engages passionately with them, one tries to understand them, one is curious about them. The media body involves a physical dimension that the artist needs to engage with factually, intimately and exhaustively. *Dimensions of Dialogue* comprises these realms. It is quite interesting to read the film as an allegory on creativity, as the film is usually interpreted in terms of the human inability to communicate. As Julian Petley points out that '*Možnosti dialogu* translates rather better as *Possibilities of Dialogue* – possibilities which, according to the evidence on offer here, seem limited [due to] humankind's intolerance of otherness, the inhabitual, the non-conformist and the unexpected' (1986: 222).

The working with and through medial instances is what makes *Dimensions of Dialogue* quite memorable as film. The heads and bodies confronting each other factually, passionately and exhaustively (as the intertitles of the film state) stay for their strong physical presence with the viewer. In relation to the material presence, the viewer is made aware of the skill, equipment and environment needed to animate these materials: the painstaking effort, patience, and passion required of the artist. In relation to *The Ossuary* one realises that the physicality of different arts asks for specific techniques to

Intermedial Densities in the Work of Jan Švankmajer 101

Figures 4.5–4.6 *Dimensions of Dialogue* (1983): encounters between vegetables, kitchen objects, scientific tools and Arcimboldian heads

work with the material/medium (natural, artefactual and conceptual dimension of the object). Physicality evokes discontinuity, interstices, as it calls for different behavioural skills (intimately linked to environments). The art of painting requires a different skill set and bodily engagement than the art of music, or the art of cinema and animation.

On the other hand, the Archimboldian heads in the first episode of *Dimensions of Dialogue* act rather aggressively. They eat and spit each other out. This aggression does not contradict a caring attitude. It highlights the bodily difference that marks analogism and animism. Eating and spitting each other out describe processes of appropriation, of becoming Other. One absorbs in order to adopt. This is also true for media in film. *The Ossuary* adopts and appropriates a range of media 'bodies', violently dissecting and reassembling them: the female voice, the music, the poem, the painting, the design, the bones. This is most palpable in the rapid editing. The editing intersects in the sense of quasi-palpabilities cinema's hovering perspective from above (exteriority) and the bone's rooted view from below/within (interiority). The same is true for the instances of the music/voice and poem/painting, as levitating and earthing qualities supplement and object each other: the bodily dimension of voice and breath (rhythm) is countered by the abstract quality of painting, as the linearity of poetry is balanced by the texturality of painting. Bones in themselves already dispute interiority and exteriority, as they are within the living human being, outside the decomposed body and culturally/ritually supposed to be contained in the ground, in cloth, etc. The rearrangement of the bones to intricate ornamentation and the fast editing connote violent acts of dissecting and re-assembling. Passion goes along with appropriation. Passion also adds approximation, complements action with passivity. This means that one makes oneself aware of the passive naivety that the gesture of searching and intercommunicability (exchange of perspectives) requires. Different medial instances involve different sensibilities and densities that interweave them. Different bodies, milieus and skills evoke discontinuity and diversity. Interiority integrates on shared grounds, to the point where interiority/exteriority become interchangeable, collapse into one another. Accordingly, it seems possible to perceive the inter-media status of cinema as a state of 'bodily collapse', where the exchange in between media, the positioned quality of their specific perspectives is broken down to a state of utter exhaustion/enrichment and with this to the passivity of desire in creation/narration. The act of dispersal directs against common orders of representation that link to a naturalistically reduced world view. They expand the restrictions opposed on perception and understanding in view of the naturalist ontological orientation. The means of expansion is artistic engagement and its continuous desire to break 'through' the mere objective obligation to 'represent'. *The Flat,*

The Ossuary and *Dimensions of Dialogue* demonstrate this. Engaging with densities, sensibilities and perspectives means not only to approach them actively, but passively: to allow to be acted upon, to endure their appropriation and approximation. The naturalist perspective cuts these attempts of communication short. In this view, the behaviour of the defunct objects in *The Flat* are simply hostile and oppressive, the opponents in *Dimensions of Dialogue* simply arguing, the bones in *The Ossuary* simply communicating death (narrative layer). However, if one changes the perspective towards an (artistic) desire to expand means of communication and interaction in between instances, a different picture evolves. Defunct utility becomes tools that reach beyond. Acts of communication turn to gestures of searching and understanding. The natural, conceptual and artefactual object becomes a place to 'move in', to subjectify and dramatise. Moreover, intermediality highlights a social concern. The attitude of 'how' one challenges ways of perception becomes as important as 'what' the challenge directs at. To achieve a state of intercommunicability, of translation and comparison between different positions requires a specific attitude. 'Objects' (natural, conceptual, artefactual) do not invariably signify or stand for something else. This is what the recent ontological turn in anthropology intimates.[6] The commitment to plurality and difference presupposes a social attitude, an attitude that requires the ability to communicate.

Conclusion

How then to approach the intermediality of cinema in Švankmajer's films? This essay started with a quote by Agamben, claiming that the nature of the gesture is not to be understood in relation to products and acts, but to 'how' and 'what' a gesture endures and supports. The openness and fragility of the ontological status of the gesture and cinematic representation allows it to be brought in close association with the epistemological aim to radically open towards the object of knowledge and experience. In conjunction with intimacy, the desire to know the 'inner life', this act of 'radically opening' requires naive passivity and passion. The conjecture challenges the foundations of a naturalistic oriented epistemology. It allows more than simply cast multiple representational layers onto a – in principle – unified world, but to multiply the worlds in themselves. The gesture of searching (epistemology) commits to fragility and uncertainty (passivity, naivety and vulnerability) and merges in this commitment with the object of experience and knowledge (ontology). The condition of communication with the Other becomes negotiable and necessary to negotiate.

The media-anthropological perspective allows for a better understanding of the idea of a shared sensibility. The intermedial densities described in relation to the films form the intense and intimate experience of their sociability. Different worlds come together and create shared 'social' contexts to be explored. From this point of view, cinema emerges as a constellation of medial instances, continuously and concretely 'passing into the other', as a fragile Self that 'implies otherness to such an intimate degree that one cannot be thought of without the other' (Ricœur 1992: 3). Working through medial instances becomes understanding, while the desire to know moves towards the perception of bodily difference, wishing to engage with and accommodate bodily/objective multiplicity.

The artist's love, care and tenderness in relation to the 'Other', as intimated above, relates to this passive and passionate desire to understand on the basis of a shared sensibility and sociabilty. It relates to a shift from epistemological towards ontological concerns. It distances from 'representation' which focuses on the interpretation of fixed objects disconnected from culture. It rather attempts to radically open up towards the object of engagement and therewith to respect it in its ontological ambiguity, its being different, being in process, being in media. Embracing the possibility of ontological ambiguity does require one to give oneself entirely, to manoeuvre oneself in a schizophrenic and ecstatic state of being outside ('flying high') and inside ('working through'). Merleau-Ponty and Agamben have demonstrated this as quoted before. One does not simply immerse, but also abstract. One desires to know but is radically open to what one might learn. Furthermore, the object of experience/ knowledge is not only directed at actuality, but also open towards virtuality. Engagement with 'objects' relates not solely to opening up to the 'inner life' of historically located objects, pieces of art, literature, music, film, etc., but also their potential transformation in processes of translation and mutilation. The cinematic gesture and its intermedial character is predestined to enter such states of intercommunicability. Švankmajer's work shows this impressively.

Notes

1. Bruno Latour's notion of the quasi-object comes to mind here: 'In the first denunciation, objects count for nothing; they are just there to be used as the white screen onto which society projects its cinema. But in the second, they are so powerful that they shape the human society, while the social construction of the sciences that have produced them remains invisible. Objects, things, consumer goods, works of art are either too weak or too strong' (1993: 53).
2. The best resources in this respect are the books that evolved out of close collaboration with the director such as Švankmajer (1994), (2014) and Dryje and Schmitt (2012).
3. Liška and Švankmajer collaborated on many of Švankmajer's films until Liška's death in 1983.

4. Translation: 'and then wait for the bird to decide to sing. If the bird doesn't sing it's a bad sign, a sign that the painting is bad, but if he sings it's a good sign, a sign that you can sign. So then so very gently you pull out one of the feathers of the bird and you write your name in a corner of the picture.' The French original and English translation are cited from Prévert (1970: 64–5), translated and introduced by Lawrence Ferlinghetti.
5. Intermediality in Švankmajer's work often consists of an intimate link to a specific artist's work rather than an abstract notion of art and artistic medium. If his films refer to visual art, they envision artists like Arcimboldo and Leonardo Da Vinci (e.g. *A Game with Stones/Spiel mit Steinen*, 1965; *Leonardo's Diary/ Leonardův deník*, 1972); if his films engage with literature, they refer directly to texts by authors like Lewis Carroll (e.g. *Jabberwocky/Žvahlav aneb šatičky Slaměného Huberta*, 1971, *Alice/Něco z Alenky*, 1989), Edgar Alan Poe (e.g. *The Fall of the House of Usher/Zánik domu Usherů*, 1980; *The Pendulum, the Pit and Hope/Kyvadlo, jáma a naděje*, 1983; *Lunacy/Šílení*, 2005), etc. Another impressive example involving music, is *J. S. Bach Fantasy in G Minor/J. S. Bach – Fantasia g-moll*, 1965). This personal link intensifies the emphasis on artistic engagement, drawing various arts and media together.
6. See Henare, Holbraad and Wastell (2006) and Holbraad (2010).

Works Cited

Agamben, Giorgio (2000), *Potentialities: Collected Essays in Philosophy*, Stanford, CA: Stanford University Press.

Descola, Philippe [2005] (2013), *Beyond Nature and Culture*, Chicago: University of Chicago Press.

Dryje, František and Bertrand Schmitt (2012), *Jan Švankmajer: Dimensions of Dialogue/ Between Film and Fine Art*, Řevnice: Arbor Vitae.

Epstein, Jean [1921] (2012), *Jean Epstein: Critical Essays and New Translations*, Amsterdam: Amsterdam University Press.

Henare, Amiria, Martin Holbraad and Sari Wastell (eds) (2006), *Thinking Through Things: Theorising Artifacts Ethnographically*, London: Routledge.

Holbraad, Martin (2010), 'Ontology is Just Another Word for Culture: Against the Motion', *Critique of Anthropology*, Vol. 30, No. 2, pp. 152–200.

Latour, Bruno [1991] (1993), *We have Never Been Modern*, Cambridge, MA: Harvard University Press.

Merleau-Ponty, Maurice [1961] (1993), 'Eye and Mind', in J. A. Galen (ed.), *The Merleau-Ponty Aesthetics Reader: Philosophy and Painting*, Evanston, IL: Northwestern University, pp. 121–49.

Petley, Julian (1986), 'Dimensions of dialogue', *Monthly Film Bulletin*, Vol. 53, No. 630, pp. 222–3.

Prévert, Jacques [1965] (1970), *Selections from Paroles Jacques Prévert*, Harmondsworth: Penguin Books.

Richardson, Michael (2006), *Surrealism and Cinema*, Oxford: Berg.

Ricœur, Paul [1990] (1992), *Oneself as Another*, Chicago: University of Chicago Press.

Švankmajer, Jan (1994), *Transmutace smyslů: Transmutation of the Senses*, Prague: Středoevropská galerie a nakladatelství.

Švankmajer, Jan (2014), *Touching and Imagining: An introduction to Tactile Art*, London: I. B. Tauris.

Viveiros De Castro, Eduardo (1998), 'Cosmological Deixis and the Amerindian Perspectivism', *The Journal of the Royal Anthropological Institute*, Volume 4, No. 3, pp. 469–88.

Viveiros De Castro, Eduardo (2004), 'Exchanging Perspectives: The Transformation of Objects into Subjects in Amerindian Ontologies', *Common Knowledge*, Vol. 10, No. 3, pp. 463–84.

Part 2

Immersions into Memory, Culture and Intermediality

CHAPTER 5

Trickster Narratives and Carnivalesque Intermediality in Contemporary Romanian Cinema
Christina Stojanova

> *Trickster's essential participation in humanity is the core of his enduring appeal.*
> (Helen Lock 2002)

The popularity of the Russian-Soviet linguist and philosopher, Mikhail M. Bakhtin, in the 1960s, brought about discussions of dialogism and dialogical structures, prompting a creative surge in semiotics, linguistic, structuralism and philosophy. Little known, however, is that about the same time, when Bakhtin was laying the foundations of his metaphysical theories about the 'unfinished' (or rather the 'unfinishable' self) – the dialogical interaction between self and other, monologism, polyphony and the carnivalesque in literature – Carl Gustav Jung was pursuing the in-depth dialogism between the conscious and the unconscious mind (Rowland 2005, Smythe 2018). Interestingly enough, both thinkers were primarily concerned with the limitless creativity of the mind, which always already transcends the confines of 'monologism' – considered by Bakhtin to be either a 'single-thought discourse', specific of conventional (epic) writings, or unique 'transcendental perspective or consciousness', informing 'all signifying practices, ideologies, values and desires that are deemed significant' (Robinson 2011). Furthermore, as Jungian scholar William Smythe notes, Bakhtin's dialogism comes quite close to Jungian thought as it 'makes room for "hidden" or "concealed" linguistic voices that are inaccessible' to the conscious 'I-positions', allowing for what was to be later defined by Northrop Frye as the 'moral unconscious' (2017: 193) and by Ian Burkitt as the 'dialogical unconscious' (quoted in Smythe 2018: 447).[1] Thus, although Bakhtin's 'dialogic imagination' emphasised the manifest 'dialogical nature of language and the social other', and Jung focused on the hidden 'dialogical psyche and the imaginal other', they both 'made clear that the one realm flows into, and is inflected through, the other' (Smythe 2018: 453). They both prioritised the creative and sharing aspect of the dialogical exchange, where "'the social and the imaginal are contrasting priorities rather than mutually exclusive positions'" (Rowland quoted in Smythe 2018: 453).

Similarly, the figure of the Trickster has a prominent role in both Bakhtinian carnivalesque and Jungian discussion of archetypes. In Jung's *Collected Works* – a 'dialogical field' in its own right – 'there is something unmistakably tricksterish in the way that dialogue plays out, where theoretical claims are often at odds with their mode of expression', and his ability to find eloquent – and subversively carnivalesque – expressions within this 'sea of unconscious creativity' (Smythe 2018: 451).

Based on similarities in Bakhtin's and Jung's ideas concerning dialogism and the Trickster, this chapter discusses intermediality generated by the inclusion of sequences featuring conspicuously heterogenic audio-visual media – the shooting of a film, TV reportage, a home video – and the key role it plays within the works by veteran Romanian directors Mircea Daneliuc and Lucian Pintilie, as well as in films by Corneliu Porumboiu and Gabriel Achim from the New Romanian Cinema generation. Indeed, as Ágnes Pethő writes, 'the dynamic of intermedial relations [. . .] is most often presented as a *dialogue* between arts and media, repurposing Bakhtin's term that came into focus with the theories of intertextuality' (2010: 59). Furthermore, in her view, intermedial dialogism 'manifests relationships of respect and rivalries', while 'highlighting the differences' of the various audio-visual media in 'an astute and hierarchical manner' (2010: 59). Building on her claim, the interaction between the heterogenic audio-visual media sequences and the master cinematic narrative yields a comparison to a dialogical exchange in its original meaning of '*dialogos* (literally, "speaking through")', meaning in Greek 'to create something *in common*' (Smythe 2018: 445, italics in the original). Thus – while 'highlighting the differences of the various audio-visual media in an astute and hierarchical manner' – this type of dialogism could work as a veritable trickster trope vis-à-vis the master narrative where, as mercurial agents of change, the various audio-visual media could serve as intermediaries, which '*enact* or *perform*' the dialogue between the conscious and the unconscious, the sacred and the profane, the official and the dissident, the revealed and the hidden, as well as catalysts for their reversal into the opposite (Smythe 2018: 452, italics in the original).

This chapter will therefore argue that the films under discussion highlight the convergences of Bakhtinian and Jungian dialogism within what could be defined as the intermedial carnivalesque.[2] Strongly remindful of the ways iconoclast folk culture in Bakhtinian carnivalesque challenged monologial medieval thought, the intermedial carnivalesque – by virtue of its unorthodox and non-institutionalised origins – enriches, upends and sabotages, the aesthetic, ideological and cultural expectations posited by the master narrative.

Generally known as a mythical-folkloric personage, the Trickster, for Jung, epitomises a psychic experience of 'an earlier ... stage of consciousness', a manifestation of the shadow – the primitive and animalistic, irrational side of the unconscious, which always already interferes with the conscious mind, sabotaging its intentions – but also, because of his creativity and inventiveness, he also serves as a catalyst for change, even a forerunner of positive figures, such as the cultural hero-saviour. In mythology and the arts, the Trickster is likely to appear in time of crisis and in the no-man's land between two epochs, cutting an uncanny figure, both 'subhuman and superhuman, bestial and divine, whose chief and most alarming characteristics is his unconsciousness' (Jung [1954] 1990: 263). 'Tricksters are not only characters, they are also rhetorical agents, who infuse narrative structures with energy, humor, and polyvalence, producing a politically radical subtext in the narrative' (Smith 1997: 2). Yet Tricksters could also produce texts that are traditionalist and conservative, since their significance in world cultures depends on their ability to sustain sacrosanct traditions and people's lore, decisive for the survival of the community. To be sure, folkloric Tricksters like the Romanian Păcală – whose name is derivative of 'to trick' or dupe – embody not only the myth of an-other, but also collective survival tactics vis-à-vis that 'other'.

In modernity, 'the Trickster figure has been relegated to the collective and individual shadow' – that is, to the personal and collective unconscious (Jung [1954] 1990: 270. Indeed, unlike Jung who insists that all spontaneous changes, conceived in the collective unconscious, lead to positive renewal as myths and folk tales suggest, Rowland believes that changes in the modern world are increasingly imposed without much consideration for 'the superior spontaneity of the collective unconscious', which remains relegated to art and dreams (2005: 5). This may explain the proliferation of Trickster figures in cultural and political discourses, and the recent rise of scholarly discussions on 'Tricksterism' (Fine 2014, Bassil-Morozow 2016). Jung also sees the modern-day Trickster not so much in his traditional role of a folkloric comedian, jester or shapeshifter, but rather as a harbinger of a dangerous situation or a calamity that is about to manifest itself, which makes the modern Tricksters and his postmodern epitomes less and less funny, but bordering instead on the uncanny. Therefore, despite of their immense popularity, Romanian films, inspired by Păcală – namely, Geo Saizescu's *Păcală* (1974) and *Păcală Returns* (*Păcală se întoarce*, 2006), are not included in this study.[3]

As a rhetorical agent, the Trickster figure engenders the Trickster narrative by mediating the 'dialogical relationship of [the unconscious] archetypal image and its manifestation within the [culturally specific] narrative frame' (Rowland 2006: 294). Hence Jungian scholars value film highly for its potential to reproduce the structure of myth as a form of communication between the conscious and the unconscious psyche. And, as the films below demonstrate, the inserted shooting process could be seen as a time-specific media tool for excavating 'inner images', both mimicking and commenting on how 'the psyche produces meaning out of a dialogue between an inner image and an [outer] narrative frame' (Rowland 2006: 286). The featured audio-visual artefacts, on the other hand, dramatise the 'marginal or excluded material' (Rowland 2006: 286) buried in the personal or collective unconscious, thus inviting a multitude of interpretations. Therefore the Trickster figure – usually personified by a director's stand-in of ambiguous cultural, ideological and ethical standing – both facilitates and necessitates the inclusion of (meta) media inserts within the master narrative as part of the intermedial carnivalesque. Moreover, the insertion of audio-visual found footage in the films under scrutiny emphasises the lower professional quality of the shooting process and the produced thereby artefacts – which – as suggested above – amount to veritable carnivalesque actants, whose purpose is to enrich, upend and ridicule the master narrative by exposing repressed meanings of sensitive psychological, ideological or ethical nature. As in the mousetrap scene of Shakespeare's *Hamlet*, they enter into an intermedial dialogue with the master narrative and 'catch the conscience' of the antagonist, but also that of the audience.

Pintilie, the Quintessential Trickster and His Narratives

Lucian Pintilie (1933–2018) was himself a powerful Trickster figure in Romanian cinema by virtue of his life as a free-minded artist, engaged in a perennial game of hide-and-seek with the authorities during communism. His life-long fascination with Trickster narratives, launched with *Reconstruction (Reconstituirea*, 1968), culminates with *Niki and Flo (Niki Ardelean, colonel în rezervă*, 2003), his penultimate film, considered also part of the New Romanian Cinema by way of its scriptwriters Cristi Puiu and Răzvan Rădulescu. Along with *Carnival Scenes (De ce trag clopotele, Mitică?*, 1981) and *The Oak (Balanța*, 1992) his works display inordinate Trickster figures, which help excavate repressed ideological and psychological contents, symptomatic of the anxieties, characterising the Eastern European human condition both before and after the fall of communism.

While a lot has been written about the intermedial, self-reflexive, meta-cinematic and dialogical textuality of *Reconstruction*, its Trickster characters have – as has the tricksterish nature of Pintilie's whole *oeuvre* – gone unnoticed. The Tricksters in *Reconstruction* mark the starting point of an intriguing evolutionary curve, which moves from conservative, status quo protecting Trickster figures, to harbingers of change, and finally to omens of an impending calamity. Thus although Professor Paveliu could qualify as a Trickster as he does 'make visible the invisible' the guilty conscience of Romanian communist intelligentsia, no one takes him seriously due to his perpetual inebriation. His 'cruel games and pranks' fail to challenge the totalitarian status quo, just as the Girl, who shrugs off even her own rape fails to make a dent on patriarchal prejudices (Fine 2014: 5). The only successful Trickster figure in *Reconstruction* therefore is Vuica, one of the boys involved in the police reconstruction of the restaurant brawl. His 'games and pranks' dispel briefly the morbid seriousness of the reconstruction process, yet – being of the clownish, comic-relief nature – they fail to challenge it either. Nonetheless Vuica is tightly kept in check throughout the film by the Policeman, and persistently sought after during his short disappearance, until he is ultimately, albeit accidentally, killed. The director thus also fails – or due to censorship considerations was unable – to harness Vuica's powerful Trickster libido, whose 'polyvalence and humour' could have energised the film's cold allegorical tableaux, replete with morose existentialist symbolism.

Pintilie's *The Oak* features a couple of formidable Trickster characters – and director's stand-ins – manifested as spontaneous harbingers of positive changes in post-communist Romania. Mia Morgenstern's Nela is an unusually creative female Trickster, who – if we do not count Gabita (from Cristian Mungiu's *4 Months, 3 Weeks, 2 Days/4 luni, 3 săptămâni și 2 zile*, 2007) with her propensity to 'trick' her way out of unpleasant situations – has so far remained an isolated occurrence in Romanian Cinema. Mitică, on the other hand, is Răzvan Vasilescu's first appearance as a proficient Trickster figure, to be followed by such quintessential New Romanian Cinema Tricksters as Marcel Ivanov (*Stuff and Dough/Marfa și banii*, Cristi Puiu, 2001), Station Master Doiaru (*California Dreamin'*, Cristian Nemescu, 2007). And certainly, Florian from *Niki and Flo*, where – on the backdrop of Romania circa 2000, plagued by economic chaos, political uncertainties and moral abstruseness – the crisis of the collective consciousness is played out in the symbolic stand-off between two powerful psychological types – Niki, the conservative Senex, and Flo, the mischievous Trickster.

Vasilescu's arrogant and extroverted go-getter Florian – who goes by the youthful and westernised nickname Flo – is cast against Victor Rebengiuc's much older protagonist, the dejected introvert Niki Ardelean, a retired colonel of the defunct Romanian communist army. Brought together by the marriage of Niki's daughter Angela to Flo's son Eugen, they personify the destructive clash between the old and the new forms of collective consciousness. Flo's 'adolescent fixation with eternal youth' makes him a 'tremendously powerful individual [. . .] with an extraordinary talent for causing trouble and disrupting the social order in which he lives' (Henderson 2005: 25). Yet his tricksterish behaviour is reduced here to parochial aping of anything western and 'cool', while his potential to upset the status quo by fostering rabid confrontations and oppositions seems to serve only his opportunistic proclivities. And these are certainly indispensable in his nearly metaphysical determination to destroy Niki by questioning everything he stands for and ultimately 'evicting him out of his own life' (Ioniţă 2010: 40). Thus, Flo signals the constellation of the Trickster archetype in the collective unconscious as a catalyst for the 'organized renunciation of the [communist] Law-of-the-Father' as backward and totalitarian, and of its replacement with the post-1989 conformist culture of 'consumption, organized around an inversion of the superego' and 'its injunction to enjoy' (Žižek quoted in Restivo 1997: 201).

Florian's video-making activities – strategically interwoven within the opening funeral ceremony for Niki's son Mihai, who has died in a ludicrous domestic incident, and within the wedding of Angela and Eugen, seen only through his camera lenses – lay bare the growing moral ambiguity and cultural eclecticism of these moving images inserts. The incessant filming establishes Flo as the more powerful actant vis-à-vis the protagonist – he even demands that Mihai's casket be reopened so he could take a better shot – and affirms him as a true champion of supercilious voyeurism and 'injunctions to enjoy' of the post-communist Trickster culture of 'disengagement, discontinuity and forgetting' (Bauman 2004: 117).

The seven parts of the film are connected to dates of traditional importance for Romanians – Mihai's funeral takes place on 1 April, the international Fool's Day – which supports the polyvalent dramatic modes, ranging from macabre irony and satire, to tragedy, and also throws in high relief the Trickster nature of the narrative. The stand-off between Niki and Flo comes to a climactic resolution on the last emblematic date – 25 October, Romanian Army Day during communism – with Niki piercing Flo's head with a hammer. What pushes him over the edge are the wedding videos revealing his daughter's uninhibited flirting with, and undressing for, Flo's camera. Here, as in *The Oak* – where next to her father's corpse, Nela is watching home videos from her privileged childhood in the family of a prominent party satrap – media artefacts are deployed as uncanny Lacanian objects of desire, meant to shock with voyeuristic material, verging on the incestuous.

While the inserts of shooting processes and audio-visual artefacts in *Niki and Flo* is remarkably well balanced, favouring either one or the other, in *Reconstruction* – in tune with high modernist ideas about the social responsibility of filmmakers and the leading role of cinema in creative media hierarchy – the shooting process, as an allegory of the repressive regime, overtakes the narrative. Conversely, in *Carnival Scenes*, made at the bleakest moment of Ceaușescu's tyranny, it is the audio-visual artefact-cum-simulacrum that takes over. The Fellini-inspired introduction and coda reveal that the film, based on Ion Luca Caragiale's eponymous *drama-à-clef* from the late 1800s, actually represents but a parallel universe, animated by an all-mighty yet invisible Director-cum-Trickster, thus mirroring Romania under the rule of an equally all-mighty Leader.[4]

The fall of communism brought to an end the need of elaborately coded language of Aesopian audio-visual tropes, yet the perennial need of uncovering the 'evil from which others and society suffer' (Henderson 2005: 25) has remained, best met by the capacity for socio-psychological insights, enabled by the Trickster as rhetorical figure. Thus, if Flo could be defined as an 'obscene jouisseur' (who while not enjoying his own daughter's rape as Žižek would have it, is still 'obscene' enough to enjoy being his own son's sexual rival), then the final scene could be read as a re-enactment of the oedipal situation with a foretelling twist (Žižek 1999: 368). Flo is assassinated not by his son, but by his daughter-in-law's father, thus staging the clash between the old communist consciousness and the new, consumerist one not as a renewal but as a regressive rivalry between a Senex and a Trickster, stuck in an incestuous conflict. On a symbolic level, this clash results in a victory – albeit Pyrrhic – of the 'old' over the 'new', leaving however the 'not-quite-dead' Father incapable of enforcing his 'symbolic prohibition' (Žižek 1999: 368). And therefore the 'increasingly narcissistic [postcommunist] subject', as Žižek has it, becomes dominated instead by the uncontrollable influx of 'ferocious superego figures' from the unconscious (1999: 368).

DANELIUC, THE SELF-REFERENTIAL TRICKSTER

Nearly a decade after the ban of *Reconstruction* – which made it virtually impossible for Romanian directors to handle contemporary subjects out of the confines of Socialist Normative Aesthetics[5] – Mircea Daneliuc's moody debut *The Long Drive* (*Cursa*, 1975) appeared. It offers a radically different deployment of the Trickster narrative, facilitating Daneliuc's first foray into a world made invisible in Ceaușescu's Romania. The film opens amidst the dispatch ceremony of an oversized boiler, produced at a big machinery plant, across the Carpathian Mountains. The dialogical interplay of the master narrative and the shooting of a TV reportage, generates the energy of the prologue, thus making it the most interesting part of the film.

The TV crew, under the inept guidance of a young and ambitious Reporter – a veritable Trickster figure played by Daneliuc himself – is shooting what is supposed to be the heroic beginnings of a difficult journey, undertaken by two truck drivers. In their fervour to deliver an ideologically perfect reportage, crew and Reporter get nothing right and, while screaming at each other, chase around with equal zeal self-conceited bosses and incidental workers, doing their best to avoid them and thus undermining the intended momentousness of the event. Such a situation, strongly suggestive of the constellation of the destructive Trickster archetype, both carnivalises the monologic didacticism of the official ideology, and exposes the propensity of Ceaușescu's media to pump ideological hype into otherwise trivial events. On the aesthetic level, Daneliuc harnesses the dialogical tensions between the monological Socialist Normative aesthetics, negotiated by the fluid camera movement style of the master narrative, inspired paradoxically by ideologically frowned-upon Western modernist movements, and the clumsy hand-held amateurish camera of the TV reportage. Indeed, the carnivalesque intermediality in Daneliuc's early films foregrounds the aesthetic and ideological connotations of the swiftly growing media diversity of the 1970s. By having the featured TV crews utilise aesthetically cruder, yet more mobile TV equipment, Daneliuc implies that new technologies – while standing a better chance as tools for manipulating the representation of reality – are much more liable to inadvertently reveal its hidden dark sides, a paradox which was to be amply confirmed two decades later by *Niki and Flo*.

Thus, through the unstable and blurry TV images, the strictly forbidden topic of the official propaganda ineptitude is brought into contact with the collective consciousness. And while the hapless reporter mouths in wooden officialese the propaganda message about 'real-life working-class heroes' and the 'epochal meaning of the event', the two 'heroic' drivers are captured unawares within the shaky TV frames as poking fun, making faces at the camera and hollering one-liners in response to the reporter's insipid questions. Here, the intermedial carnivalesque brings to light the Aesopian language of concealed meanings in the artistic practice of Eastern European auteur cinema during communism to show one thing, while implying a different, subversive meaning: a double entendre which is yet another manifestation of the Trickster narrative potential to bridge opposites. In this line of thought, the prologue can be seen as a sarcastically self-reflexive illustration of Daneliuc's own struggle to reconcile the 'irresolvable frictions' of the 'impossible aesthetics' of socialist realism and its derivatives – arising here between the ideologically 'functional' didactic story of two socialist heroes the TV crew struggles to get out – and the artistic 'fictionality' of the master narrative, trying to smooth over the messy reality on the ground (Robin 1992: 298).

The prologue resolves yet another, ethical friction – that between the Reporter as Daneliuc's opportunistic (alter) ego and his ethical self. Therefore, once the truck leaves the TV camera's shaky viewfinder, Daneliuc could finally focus on the authentic, low-key psychological and artistic pluralism of the 'fictional', ignoring as much as possible the ideological straightjacket of the 'functional,' which explains the three-year ban on the film's release, but also its longevity.

This intermedial carnivalesque feat was to be repeated with a twist in *Microphone Test* (*Proba de microfon*, 1980). Thus, whereas the prologue of *The Long Drive* serves as a precis of Daneliuc's aesthetic and ethical programme, the Trickster narrative of *Microphone Test* helps mediate on a personal level psychological tensions in society at large. The intermedial inserts – featuring the shooting of a controversial investigative TV reportage on migrants from the provinces, who come to work in Bucharest without a residence permit – are embedded within the master narrative. The latter follows Nelu, the reportage cameraman, and his increasingly ambiguous role in this problematic endeavour, complicated by a love affair with the illegal migrant Ani, one of the reportage subjects. Unlike the clownish Reporter from *The Long Drive*, whose impetuous pranks leave the status quo intact, Nelu cuts a promising Trickster figure, potentially able to reconcile the prescribed ideological monologism of the reportage with the polysemous reality. Played again by Daneliuc with a self-reflexive abandon, eased by the casting of his then wife Tora Vasilescu as Ani, Nelu however keeps forfeiting his mediator's role because of the obdurate agendas of the powers-that-be, but mostly because of his non-committal nature. The streamlined contrapuntal dialogicity exposes the mechanism of Nelu's demise and social castration by mirroring the psychological mechanism through which his well-meant acts of spontaneous rebellion get warped by his former lover Luize – the opportunistic Reporter he works with – until they begin to look like (self) destructive tricksterism. Thus, the reportage, which Nelu ambitiously shoots in the free camera style of the 1970s documentary fictions, then popular with Eastern European directors, gradually degenerates into audio-visual eavesdropping, whose sole purpose seems to be ruining migrants' lives. His botched rebellion culminates in the destruction of Ani's interview tapes, whose symbolic meaning heralds the innate unity of ethics and aesthetics – of truth and beauty, poetically speaking – which the New Romanian Cinema would demonstrate so eloquently a quarter of a century later. Unable to overcome the ubiquitous infantilisation he is subjected to by Luize and his controlling family, Nelu remains stuck in the no man's land between the *puer aeternus* he is, and the Wise Old Man he would never become, thus heralding the constellation of the Trickster archetype as an early sign of the forthcoming post-communist crisis of masculinity (see Kalmár 2017, Mazierska 2003, Stojanova 2005 and 1998).

Porumboiu and the Trickster Narrative Polyphonies

Unlike the linear and chronological dialogicity of Pintilie and Daneliuc, with *12:08 East of Bucharest* (*A fost sau n-a fost?*, 2006) Corneliu Porumboiu introduced a new carnivalesque simultaneity of polyphonic interactions, set in motion by his two stand-ins, engaged in a debate of their own, thus making visible an additional, autobiographical layer of meaning. In *12:08*, as in *Reconstruction*, the shooting process of a TV talk show takes over the narrative once the prologue vignettes introduce the three main characters – the anchor and local TV station owner Jderescu and his two guests, retiree Pişcoci and history teacher Mănescu – and provide the backstory, which is set in a small Romanian town (the film was shot in Vaslui, Porumboiu's birthplace) during Christmas week. Jderescu – Porumboiu's Trickster stand-in of the conservative-preservative type – is the moderator of a show, commemorating the anniversary of Ceauşescu's ousting in December 1989. The title of the show, broadcast live from Jderescu's shabby studio, is 'was there or not [revolution in town]?' – which is actually the meaning of the film's original title in Romanian – pretty much summarises its subject. According to the script of the show, after establishing whether spontaneous public activities had taken place on that day in the town square before 12:08, the exact time Ceauşescu fled Bucharest – the panel is to decide whether or not these activities qualify as revolutionary. Like Daneliuc's Reporter, the conformist Jderescu is desperate to get out a story, corroborating the official version of the events, according to which the revolution was not only limited to Bucharest, but widespread across Romania. Yet like the Reporter, he is professionally unequipped to control the message, and the studio camera – operated by the rebellious Cameraman as Porumboiu's second Trickster stand-in – registers mercilessly his helplessness vis-à-vis his guests. Thus, while the first part of the film is shot from a neutral, objective-realist point of view, with internally edited long takes – the second – placed logically after the intermission – is recorded from the Cameraman's subjective point of view. It features amateurishly blurred and canted images, and even a break of the fourth wall, showing the Cameraman's hand snatching the paper ship old man Pişcoci has been modelling while on camera. As Porumboiu claims, he has 'aligned himself with the much-derided cameraman' not only because of his 'overall faulty camerawork', but mainly because of his 'failure to find the truth in all the different versions of the story he is given' (quoted in Bardan 2012: 141). And while the ongoing intermedial frictions epitomise symbolically the tensions between the murky and inconvenient historical truth and the smooth official version of the events, Jderescu plunges into his own trap by taking in-studio phone calls, which – as is typical for the mythological Trickster and his travails – he has set up for others. Bodiless and mostly anonymous, the audial inserts work as *psychopomps*,[6] whose abject intrusions 'drag' both protagonists and viewers 'over the threshold and into the liminal zone' of memories, repressed in the collective unconscious (Bassil-Morozow, 2011: 46–7). It thus becomes known that not only there was no revolution in town, but that old man Pișcoci and family were disappointed when Ceaușescu was prevented from making good on his last-minute promise to present each Romanian with a cash bonus. Yet while the revelation of this carefully hidden sentiment of Pișcoci's – most likely shared by many – does not come through as such a big surprise, it is history teacher Mănescu who drops the bombshell. It turns out that despite his loud anti-communist posturing, this spokesman of the intelligentsia, traditionally considered conscience of the nation in Eastern Europe, was most likely inebriated and could not remember when, if at all, he went to the square. Neither is Jderescu spared the denunciation of his shady dealings during the early days of democracy, to which he owes his career leap from a minor communist apparatchik to studio owner and chief reporter.

The nature of the shooting process and its artefact – where the monological official discourse is upended and ultimately taken over by the unruly spontaneity of amateur media and its unpredictably iconoclast message – amounts to a virtuoso Trickster narrative, baroque variations of which Porumboiu would offer in *When Evening Falls on Bucharest or Metabolism* (*Când se lasă seara peste București sau metabolism*, 2013) and in *The Second Game* (*Al doilea joc*, 2014). In the former, Paul – Porumboiu's stand-in – is in preparation of a film shoot, which is being imagined, planned, discussed, and even rehearsed in detail by him and his principal actress, yet perennially postponed due to Paul's creative block. Overcome by tricksterish shadow content and 'irritated by his own ineptitude', Paul increasingly believes that 'fate is playing tricks on him', and feels therefore justified to trick the others (Jung ([1954] 1990: 267). Thus, the endoscopy he presents as proof of his alleged metabolism troubles and a legitimate excuse for the production delay, is ironically the sole artefact he ever delivers. Yet because of its unproven provenance – it remains unclear whether the endoscopy is authentic – this most likely plagiarised artefact serves as an uncanny snapshot of the Real – that is, of his unconscious – bringing to light Paul's moral and artistic ambivalence. Another *puer aeternus* of the non-committal type, Paul – unlike Nelu who, due to the repressive society he inhabits is more or less absolved of personal guilt – is seen within the ethical framework of New Romanian cinema as solely responsible for his downfall.

The unity of ethics and aesthetics, essential for the New Romanian cinema, is made further explicit by the unusual polyphony of *The Second Game*, where the audio-visual artefact – the archived TV recording of a football match between the most popular Romanian teams of that time, played amidst wet snow and mud in the winter of 1988 – constitutes the first layer of meaning. The audio track – in addition to the muffled original sound – features a commentary, recorded a quarter of a century later by Porumboiu and his father, who was the chief referee of the match, thus providing another two layers of meaning, which enter in a contrapuntal interaction with the first. There is nothing surprising or terribly original in the artefact nor in the accompanying discussion, yet this intermedial layering is mesmerising because of the associations it evokes. By taking out of context the artefact, it reduces its historical importance as a record of the match of the year between the Army team Steaua and the Securitate team Dinamo – Ceaușescu's and his son Valentin's favourite teams respectively. This plays up the ignored and repressed power of the people to overcome relentless manipulation. Hence discursive frame of the Porumboius enhances the folkloric Trickster elements, related to collective survival tactics vis-à-vis an oppressive political regime, but also to keeping perennially alive the contents of a bitter historical experience. The film thus brings together the routine heroics of badly equipped players on that slippery field; Porumboiu Senior's equally daring ability to brave his referee colleagues, dabbling as Securitate informants; and the original cameramen's amusing tricks, aimed at avoiding politically incorrect scuffles by turning the lenses towards the viewers flocked in the stadium despite the forbidding weather in the hope of spending a couple of propaganda-free hours.

CODA: JUDE, ACHIM, AND THE POSTMODERN TRICKSTER TROPES

It has become clear that the Trickster narratives in *Reconstruction*, *The Long Drive*, and to some extent *The Second Game* are forms of Aesopian language, whose main purpose is to make visible not only hidden collective and individual endeavours under communism but, like traditional Trickster myths, to remind contemporaries that the more things change, the more they stay the same. Similarly, *Niki and Flo* and *12:08 East of Bucharest* apply Trickster narratives to bring forth not only hidden problems, plaguing the brave new post-communist world, but also the dialectic interrelatedness of social and personal responsibility for solving them. *Metabolism*, on the other hand, focuses on the creative individual's hang-ups, and their serious ethical implications. Furthermore, while Pintilie and Daneliuc – true to the self-reflexive, intertextual referentiality of high modernism – rely more on streamlined, contrapuntal juxtaposition of master narrative and inserted moving images, Porumboiu – in truly postmodern fashion – experiments with baroque forms of the carnivalesque. His films thus feature intermedial inserts of shooting processes that are either running consecutively to each other and to the master narrative (*12:08*), or appear as imaginary (*Metabolism*), or, in the case of *The Second Game*, take completely over the master narrative. Moreover, these Trickster narratives owe much of their energy to easily identifiable Trickster characters, who are either clowns of the conformist-opportunistic type like the trio in *12:08*, or of the type that signals pending calamity (Paul in *Metabolism*), and even positive change (Porumboiu Sr in *The Second Game*).

In this context, Radu Jude's *The Happiest Girl in the World* (*Cea mai fericită fată din lume*, 2009), and Gabriel Achim's *Adalbert's Dream* (*Visul lui Adalbert*, 2011) could be seen as bookmarks, offering – respectively – a contrapuntal modernist, and a postmodern baroque version of the intermedial carnivalesque. In Jude's straightforward aesthetics, the shooting of a TV commercial for orange juice – inspired by the Cinderella mythologeme and starring the eponymous 'happiest' girl, who happens to be the winner of an expensive car awarded by the orange juice company – is but a parallel universe. It is linked structurally yet tangentially to the master narrative about the escalating tensions between the 'happiest girl' and her parents on account of the prize car, which she wants to keep and they want to sell. Nonetheless, the shoot – as a metonymy of consumerism – becomes a Trickster narrative device, which enters into a complex sociocultural dialogue with the master narrative, thus bringing to the fore the post-communist crisis of patriarchal authority and the disintegration of traditional family (Stojanova 2019, Pop 2014).

Achim's film, in its turn, captures the ubiquitous tricksterism from the late communist era, summarised succinctly by the Eastern European saying 'They lie to us that they are paying, and we lie to them that we are working.' The master narrative is structured as a string of episodes from what turns out to be the last day in the life of the maladroit Iulică Ploscaru, in the marvellously understated interpretation of Garbriel Spahiu. An amateur filmmaker and a safety instructor at a large factory from the second half of the 1980s, Ploscaru's Trickster skill in handling opposites is introduced at the very beginning of the film when he shares amicably – first with his wife, and later in the morning with his mistress – his fatalistic premonitions, prompted by a dream of a fox. The evocation of the fox as a seminal Trickster allegory, sets the tone of the film between comedic irony and macabre sarcasm. Yet despite its traditional ambiguity, the fox dream – in tune with the uncanny role of contemporary Tricksters – signals the constellation of a calamitous situation.

Ploscaru's Trickster skills are best revealed at work, where – while engaging in almost no job-related activities – he is constantly involved in the barter and exchange of deficit goods and services. A lucky owner of a private vehicle and a highly sought-after video player and tapes, which he uses as exchange commodities, Ploscaru comes across not so much as a shrewd opportunist who capitalises on the universal shortages during communism, but as an attention seeker, desperately trying to belong – with his colleagues, his boss, even with the boss's mother, whom he takes to doctor's appointments – and is therefore not taken seriously.

Yet Ploscaru's amateur filmmaking activities are designed as the ultimate way of negotiating his vital and 'safe belonging' to 'the sociopolitical framework that contains and controls' any Trickster (Bassil-Morozow 2016). Unbeknownst to him, however, and in a truly carnivalesque fashion, his shoddy and childishly cruel audio-visual artefacts upend the monologism of the official totalitarian art by virtue of their enantiodromic lapses into the ridiculous and the grotesque. The Trickster narrative thus cracks open the collective unconscious, 'turned dark through neglect' for more than three decades now for, if unattended, it could easily 'engulf' the fragile achievements of democracy (Rowland 2006: 292).

The first inserted artefact is an excerpt from Ploscaru's docu-dramatic re-enactment of a work-related accident, in which his mistress – a former colleague – loses her eye. It comes through as an incongruously insensitive horror vignette, soliciting *Schadenfreude* voyeurism rather than compassion, thus relating to the irrational side of his entertainment-starved viewers. The inclusion of the artefact in the Communist Party Anniversary celebration, taking place that very day at the factory, has consequently little to do with work-safety considerations, and everything to do with gratifying this atavistic side of the collective unconscious.

The other artefact insert is the title video *Adalbert's Dream*, shown in full. After having a nightmare about his death due to safety regulations negligence, the protagonist Adalbert becomes an exemplary New Man, who strictly observes all regulations. The video is an ominously sardonic *mise en abyme* of Ploscaru's own demise later that day, featured in the master narrative. Moreover, thanks to its trash aesthetics and overstated naivety, the video comes across as a biting parody of Socialist Realist film propaganda, enhanced by time-specific media and film language, thus further exposing Ploscaru as a conformist-conservative Trickster, inextricable of his socio-historical context.

In a sinister turn of events worthy of Ionesco, Ploscaru is asked to participate in the re-enactment of a work-related accident he has involuntary caused, since the worker he bartered a private favour from has lost his hand in the process. A chilling parody of Pintilie's *Reconstruction*, but also of the numerous official reconstruction films from the 1950s and 60s, popularised recently by the New Romanian Cinema,[7] Ploscaru's accidental death occurs as a result of what Dostoevsky calls 'administrative enthusiasm' – a demonstrative desire to please the authorities by making his participation in the re-enactment as realistic as possible (1871: 55). It also amounts to a grotesque commentary on the fate of the Trickster as a director's stand-in. With the notable exception of the Cameraman in *12:08* and the behind-the-scenes commentators of *The Second Game*, whose non-corporeality encodes Porumboiu's ethical dispute, the other stand-ins either involuntarily or deliberately engage in various types of conformist interactions with the powers-that-be. By simultaneously mimicking, exposing and commenting on these interactions, the Trickster narratives discussed so far keep, in Jung's words, 'the shadow contents from our collective and individual psyche before our eyes as a conscious referent' (quoted in Rowland 2006: 294).

The intermedial carnivalesque enhances the artistic impact of the films by virtue of its intrinsic attachment to the Trickster narrative built on the interaction of the included moving images and the master narrative. Moreover, the intermedial carnivalesque throws in high relief the innate tricksterish propensity of cinema to take the guise of any extant amateur, improvised, non-professional, or institutional audio-visual media, and benefit artistically from the contrast of its sophisticated – master narrative – look, to their 'unrefined' appearance and even 'vulgar' status. Indeed, the innate medium tricksterism of cinema, while highlighting the differences with the other audio-visual media, also accentuates their rivalries. And it relegates the sequences featuring other media – police re-enactment, TV reportage and show, commercial advertising, amateur and home movies – to production outlets outside of major production studios, believed to be the exclusive domain of sleek master narratives. This self-reflexive and *meta-médiatique* versatility of Trickster narratives explains the fascination of three generations of Romanian film auteurs with re-enactments and intermedial inserts, proven to be effective vehicles for Aesopian cinematic encoding. For, as Marie-Louise von Franz writes, the Trickster effect is essential in undoing the 'hardening of consciousness'(1995: 97), mirrored by the (mono)logical tendencies of the master narrative, through simulating – and stimulating – the creative spontaneity of the collective unconscious, thus predicating the active participation of the audience.

Notes

1. As Smythe writes, Jung's 'dialogism' is best demonstrated in his 'seminal essay on "The Transcendent Function"', where he describes the interactions with the avatars – or the 'others' – of the unconscious 'as if a dialogue were taking place

between two human beings with equal rights, each of whom gives the other credit for a valid argument and considers it worthwhile to modify the conflicting standpoints by means of thorough comparison and discussion or else to distinguish them clearly from one another' (Jung qtd in Smythe 2018: 447).
2. I am deeply indebted to Ágnes Pethő for helping me clarify the link between intermediality and the carnivalesque.
3. According to Doru Pop, the 'mixture of folk tales and ill developed narratives', inspired by 'popular sayings (*zicători și proverbe*)' was first exploited as a tool of propaganda under communism, and then as a form of populist defiance of democracy (2012: 262).
4. In Romanian, he was referred to as 'Conducător', which – ironically – was used before him by King Carol II, and the pro-fascist Marshal Antonescu.
5. My moniker for opportunistic modifications of Zhdanovist Socialist Realism after the so-called cultural 'thaw', precipitated by the twentieth congress of the CPSU in 1956 (Stojanova 1998).
6. A *psychopomp* is a guide, whose primary function is to escort souls to the afterlife, but could also serve as guide through the various transitions of life. Available at <http://www.psychopomps.org/> (last accessed 12 January 2019).
7. For example, Alexandru Solomon's documentary *The Great Communist Bank Robbery* (*Marele jaf communist*, 2004) and its fictional remake *Closer to the Moon* (2011) by Nae Caranfil.

Works Cited

Bardan, Alice (2012), 'Aftereffects of 1989: Corneliu Proumboiu's *12:08 East of Bucharest* (2006) and Romanian Cinema', in Anikó Imre (ed.), *A Companion to Eastern European Cinema*, London: Wiley-Blackwell, pp. 125–47.

Bassil-Morozow, Helena (2011), *The Trickster in Contemporary Film*, London: Routledge.

Bassil-Morozow, Helena (2016), 'Gonzo Tricksterism versus Politics: Anarchy, Sabotage and Self-Sacrifice', IAJS seminar. Available at <http://jungstudies.net/category/onlineseminars/gonzo-tricksterism-versus-politics/> (last accessed 12 January 2019).

Bauman, Zygmunt (2004), *Wasted Lives: Modernity and Its Outcasts*, Oxford and Malden, MA: Blackwell.

Dostoevsky, Fyodor M. (1871), *Demons* [Бесы], Collected Works, Volume 7, <http://rvb.ru/dostoevski/01text/vol7/29.htm> (last accessed 12 January 2019).

Fine, Elizabeth C. (2014), 'Wearing the Trickster Mask in the Contemporary Social Movements of Anonymous and Occupy', in Eric E. Peterson and Annette Mönnich (eds), *Opportunities and Responsibilities in Volatile Times*, Proceedings of the 2012 International Colloquium on Communication, Blacksburg, VA: Virginia Tech, pp. 4–19.

Frye, Northrop (2017), *The Bush Garden*, Toronto: House of Anansi Press.

Henderson, Joseph L. (2005), *Thresholds of Initiation*, Wilmette, IL: Chiron Publications.

Ioniță, Maria (2010), 'Niki and Dante: Ageing and Death in Contemporary Romanian Cinema', *Film Criticism*, 1 January, Vol. 34, No. 2/3, pp. 37–50.

Jung, Carl Gustav [1954] (1990), 'On the Psychology of the Trickster Figure', in C. G. Jung (ed.), *The Archetypes and the Collective Unconscious: The Collected Works* (trans. R. F. C. Hull), Vol. 9A, Princeton: Princeton University Press, pp. 255–74.

Kalmár, György (2017) *Formations of Masculinity in Post-Communist Hungarian Cinema: Labyrinthian Men*, London: Palgrave Macmillan.
Lock, Helen (2002), 'Transformations of the Trickster', *Southern Cross Review*, USA, No. 18. Available at <http://www.southerncrossreview.org/18/trickster.htm> (last accessed 12 January 2019).
Mazierska, Ewa (2003), 'The Redundant Male: Representations of Masculinity in Polish Postcommunist Cinema', in *Journal of Film and Video*, Vol. 55, No. 2/3 (Summer/Fall, 2003), pp. 29–43.
Pethő, Ágnes (2010), 'Intermediality in Film: A Historiography of Methodologies', *Acta Universitatis Sapientiae, Film and Media Studies*, Vol. 2, pp. 39–72.
Pop, Doru (2012), 'Dark Humor and the Imaginary of the New Romanian Filmmakers', *Echinox*, Vol. 23, pp. 259–66.
Pop, Doru (2014), *Romanian New Wave Cinema: An Introduction*, Jefferson, NC: MacFarland.
Restivo, Angelo (1997), 'Lacan According to Žižek', *Quarterly Review of Film and Video*, Vol. 16, No. 2, pp. 193–206.
Robin, Régine (1992), *Socialist Realism: An Impossible Aesthetic*, Stanford: Stanford University Press.
Robinson, Andrew (2011), 'In Theory Bakhtin: Dialogism, Polyphony and Heteroglossia', Ceasefire, UK. Available at <https://ceasefiremagazine.co.uk/in-theory-bakhtin-1/> (last accessed 12 January 2019).
Rowland, Susan (2005), *Jung as a Writer*, New York, London: Routledge.
Rowland, Susan (2006), 'Jung, the Trickster Writer, or what Literary Research can do for the Clinician', *Journal of Analytical Psychology*, Vol. 51, No. 2, pp. 285–99.
Smith, Jeanne Rosier (1997), *Writing Tricksters: Mythic Gambols in American Ethnic Literature*, Berkley: University of California Press.
Smythe, William E. (2018), 'Jungian Dialogism and the Problem of Depth' *Journal of Analytical Psychology*, Vol. 63, No. 4, pp. 444–61.
Stojanova, Christina (1998), 'Le film de genre américain dans le cinéma post-communiste: "Le Mafiosi Thriller"', in Ciné-Bulles, Vol. 17, No. 2, pp. 38–43. Available at <https://www.erudit.org/culture/cb1068900/cb1119772/34363ac.pdf> (last accessed 12 January 2019).
Stojanova, Christina (2005), 'Post-Communist Cinema: The Politics of Gender and Genre', in Linda Badley, R. Barton Palmer and Steven Schneider (eds), *Traditions in World Cinema*, Edinburgh: Edinburgh University Press, pp. 95–114.
Stojanova, Christina (2019), 'Historical Overview', in Christina Stojanova (ed.), *The New Romanian Cinema*, Edinburgh: Edinburgh University Press, pp. 243–82.
Von Franz, Marie-Louise [1972] (1995), *Creation Myths*, Boston, MA: Shambhala.
Žižek, Slavoj (1999), *The Ticklish Subject: The Absent Centre of Political Ontology*, London: Verso.

CHAPTER 6

Photographic Passages to the Past in Eastern European Non-Fiction Films
Melinda Blos-Jáni

In the contemporary post-media landscape re-assemblage has become a memory practice that is omnipresent in amateur media and also within experimental art projects. In 'the new post-historical reign of the technical image' (Ruchel-Stockmans 2015: 40) found footage films have become generic templates to rethink or narrate past events. Contemporary filmmakers mine the audio-visual archives in order to shape and explore world-memory, thus they become 'metallurgists' 'bending the material images and sounds that contribute to our political consciousness' (Pisters 2016: 150). Meanwhile in documentary cinema first-person narratives and home-made images have become powerful political tools, methods of reclaiming collective memory or history (see Renov 2004).

This essay investigates the re-shaping of audio-visual material and the re-assembling of history in a group of recent Eastern European non-fiction films (or more precisely, what could be called 'memory films') that resort to personal memory to revitalise past cultural experiences by bringing together archival photographs and film footage with painterly artifice in visually stimulating ways. Some of them belong to the genre of animated documentary, like Anca Damian's *Crulic. The Path to Beyond* (*Crulic – drumul spre dincolo*, 2011), Vladislava Plančíková *Felvidék. Caught in Between* (*Felvidék. Horná zem*, 2014) or the short film *I Made You, I Kill You* (2016) by Alexandru Petru Bădeliță. These films renegotiate the way photographs can point to past experiences. In a similar experimental vein, Zbigniew Czapla meditates upon the fading of the photographic memory in *Paperbox* (*Papierowe pudełko*, 2011). Radu Jude, on the other hand, constructs his film exclusively from archival photographs and experiments with the boundaries of cinema in *Dead Nation* (*Țara moartă*, 2017).[1]

These films remediate photographs as 'prostheses of memory'[2] in hyper-mediated contexts in order to meditate upon history and time, personal and collective identity, so as to give voice to the unheard, to unearth repressed traumas or to produce an alternative version of Eastern European history. But the ways in which photography is inserted in the first-person narrative of these films displays a heterogeneity that goes far beyond the 'indexical verifier' (Rozenkrantz 2011) or the evidentiary status associated most commonly with repurposed photographs in a documentary. These found footage films that combine photographs, films and videos or other type of visual documents can be understood as a dialogical form between 'competing, unstable signs' (Dalle Vacche 1996: 6), of media that are being in the process of being defined in their interaction with other media.[3] Animated documentaries have many things in common with compilation films, or collage films in this respect. One of the hypotheses of this essay is that photographs are not merely inserted in a cinematic text, rather they enter into a set of relations between the indexical and the non-indexical, stillness and motion, between sound and vision, between the haptical and the optical. Through the analysis of the medial hybridity of the selected films, I would like to understand what it means to be a photographic image in the post-media age[4] documentary.

Reframing Photographs in Non-fiction Films

Films recycling archival or found footage seem to perform many things: to open up the institutional archive, to open up ways of representing history and to 'open up' media itself. The gesture of re-using pre-existing visual material is often a reflexive one, as the recycled images are significant not only due to their iconic features (i.e. the things they are rendering visible), but also due to their attachment to a certain kind of materiality, and a particular image making practice (e.g. amateur, professional or propagandistic). In William Wees's words, they 'present images as images' (1993: 53) 'by reminding us that we are seeing images produced and disseminated by the media, found footage films open the door to the examination of media's use of images' (1993: 32).

The selected Eastern European non-fiction works build 'remembrance environments'[5] around photographs – they compile, juxtapose, structure photographs within the medium of film: they carry this out sequentially through montage, or form a multimedia collage within the confines of a single frame. The moving image (and its mode of exhibition) thus becomes a realm of transfiguration: photographs as still pictures and material objects become means to decode or encode personal memories and transform them into a mnemonic device of collective memory. Simultaneously, by being filtered through the moving image, they are inserted in a temporal flow which bestows on them a new dimension: duration and movement.

Literature on the relationship between stillness and movement often questions the binary opposition of the still photograph and the film, redefining them as 'synthetic image states', as they both display aspects of stasis and movement (Hölzl 2011: 106). Should these heterogeneous objects be watched from the perspective of the medium of film, as photographs inserted in the film, or should we rather step out of the dichotomy of the still/moving image and consider them as a whole, as photo-films? Hölzl analyses the Ken Burns effect as an example of our everyday image culture that generates 'moving views of a statuary scene': 'moving stills reflect the contemporary experience of photography where immobile and immutable prints are replaced by malleable images that "unfold" across electronic screens that have become the universal image display medium for still and moving images' (2011: 5). These malleable, unstable media forms that are present in our contemporary visual culture have introduced intermediality into our perception in multiple ways, which is considered by Ágnes Pethő as 'a two-way porosity of the moving image [. . .] reflected in a kind of intermedialization of the image: in its being perceived "as if" filtered through other arts (like painting) or being reframed, disassembled by other media' (2011: 5).

Within the selected films photographs appear to be static and resist the urge of the contemporary visual culture to produce dynamic images. Thus, while they function as indexical links to, or fragments of, reality, photographs are re-established as 'obsolete/old media' inserted into a post-cinematic visual realm. In their own way, they all strive to emphasise a sense of a past tense. While the medium of photography has been fundamentally associated with the semiotic term of the index, Martin Lefebvre has persuasively shown that restricting photographs to their indexical status is unproductive 'for it reduces the image's contribution to knowledge and limits any potential semiotic growth' (2007: 221), and it shouldn't be isolated from its iconic and symbolic dimensions. Photography is connected to the world in a potentially limitless number of ways, but in order to point at something it needs to be interpreted as a sign of fact. Jens Schröter calls this the difference between medium and sign: the medium of photography is usually described with indexicality, 'suited to the specific, singular and past; nonetheless it can signify things that are unspecific, general, and future' (2013). In a more open semiosis a tension between the medium and the sign is generated, like the process of working on and opening up the forms and meanings of photographs, thus the possible semiotic growth of the photographic index as Lefebvre calls it, requires a new consideration of its mediality.

Photography needs to be explored outside the concept of the index and beyond the framework of semiotics as well to account more fully for our fascination with the photographic image (see Gunning 2007): as a kind of magic that puts us into the presence of something (for Roland Barthes this meant especially the emanation of a past time) or in a 'sense of perceptual richness and nearly infinite detail that strikes us as somehow more direct than other forms of representation' (Gunning 2004: 45).

A strong model for the interpretation of photographs as open-ended, unstable signs is provided by Georges Didi-Huberman's phenomenological reading of four images taken in the August of 1944 in Auschwitz by a member of the *Sonderkommando* (2008). He distinguishes in his analysis a paradoxical, dual mode of all images: truth and obscurity. In the first mode images are seen as metaphors for totality, albeit their status is much more complex, they are in the meantime subjective and inaccurate: 'they have a fragmentary and lacunary relation to the truth to which they bear witness, but they are nonetheless all that we have available to know and to imagine concentration camp life from the inside' (Didi-Huberman 2008: 32). Didi-Huberman proposes that archival images should be read as reflections on a certain event, and their meaning should be the result of an elaborate process:

> [the archive] must always be developed by repeated cross-checkings and by montage with other archives. One must neither overestimate the 'immediate' character of the archive nor underestimate it as a simple accident of historical knowledge. The archive always demands to be constructed. (2008: 99)

Therefore, the laconic character of the images, their blacks and blurs induce the viewer to create a distance from what seems to be an instant view of the past and also open up the image for the imagination. Such cases of visual understanding create what László Tarnay (2017) calls the paradox of visibility: there is the lacunary image which preserves only a residual indexicality that challenges imagination.

Photographs in non-fiction films can assume a lacunary character on the grounds of medial differences (as being still images in a film) and ontologically as fragments of the real due to their residual indexicality. As they are revealing and concealing at the same time, artworks using archival images need to address the obscurity of the frames in order to construct a meaning, or a narrative. In the aforementioned Eastern European films I have found at least three ways in which the lacuna of photographs are rethought by/through other images in order to convey at least a temporary passage to the real.

Photographs as Extendable Frames

The analogue-digital turn generated a rethinking of indexicality that contested also the dichotomy of the non-indexical animation and photographic imagery. As a consequence, the epistemological boundaries of documentary film have been expanded towards inner realities: 'reaching those existential domains that the camera cannot excess, such as states of mind, memories and subjective experiences' (Rozenkrantz 2016: 189). In animated documentaries different imagery can be used to evoke reality iconically (e.g. animation becomes a figurative stand-in for the photographic images that are missing, see Honess Roe 2013), yet the indexical bond to a pro-filmic reality remains an expectation.

From the perspectives of this essay, the hybrid world of the animated documentary is conceived as a storytelling device, where the photographic indexical verifiers are supplemented in order to convey an idea about what is missing from their field of vision. While in Didi-Huberman's reading the blacks and blurs of images indicate what is left out of the Sonderkommando photos, animated documentaries use highly hypermediated, abstract images to fill in the 'obscurity' of the indexical fragments. Consequently, photographs become indexical anchor points in the painterly animation, like an intarsia on a decorative surface.

In Anca Damian's *Crulic. The Path to Beyond* (2011) family photos are placed in an animated environment so as to illustrate the main character's traumatic experiences which led to his tragic death. Animation creates a multilayered narrative world where past events, memories and subjective states of mind are visualised, while on the soundtrack Claudiu Crulic's lifestory is told, which is idiosyncratically connected to the problems of the post-communist Eastern Europe. Crulic's parents divorce shortly after he is born. As an adult, he cannot find a proper job in his hometown, so he decides to try his luck abroad, and moves to Poland, where he is stigmatised for being a guest worker and eventually is arrested for a crime he did not commit. Prejudices prevail in the Polish jurisdiction which lead to his fatal hunger strike.

The film begins with a paradoxical situation: the speaker reveals himself to be already dead, thus the unfolding diegesis is established from the start as belonging to the subjective, inner world of the narrator. The posthumous narration is performed by the widely known Romanian actor, Vlad Ivanov, whose pronunciation of the first-person voice-over in heavy Moldavian dialect adheres to the conventions of animated documentaries which are usually considered as illustrated interviews (see Honess Roe 2013). There is also a strong reciprocity between photography and orality[6] through the evocation of the situation of viewing a photo-album with the guiding voice of a narrator, which affects the presentation of the personal photographs within the animated world of *Crulic*.

The different media types in *Crulic* constitute a far more complex hybrid structure than the dichotomy of the photographic and the graphic could account for. There are various animation techniques employed: 2D and 3D computer animation, stop motion photography and the rotoscopic tracing of live-motion picture footage. One could even say that there is a whole range of variations between computer-generated images, and painterly or photographic traces in the film through which animated drawings are folded over the photographic and vice versa.

Photographs appear for the first time in the film as a flashback to Crulic's childhood, after we learn about his death. The story of one's life is equated here with a handful of photographs, which appear hanging on clothes lines in a three-dimensional virtual space, a vast blackness of a yet unshaped, grainy matter. In this space photographs are more than just optical illusions, they appear as physical supports of the image: curved pieces of paper, flat surfaces bending in the wind. The succession of still images is halted at a photograph representing the door of a room, which morphs into a graphic image and opens up as an aperture on the world that lies behind the flat image. The door leads the viewer into the childhood memories of Crulic, who is abandoned by his parents, raised by his aunts, moves from relative to relative, and spends his days in the company of domestic animals instead of playground friends.

In *Crulic* the initial virtual space of the black is filled with drawings, even the back side of the photograph is an animated world. In contrast to the four Auschwitz photographs, it is not the black frame, the blurred vision that challenges imagination. Instead of the disruptive presence of the black void, there are things to see; the viewer doesn't need to imagine and reconstruct from scratch what is missing from the conventional family pictures. The animated world develops into a whole diegetic universe that supports the narrative, but it also stems from the need to create a 'face' or a mask to expose realities that are not photographable.[7] In *Crulic* this mask highlights its artificiality in multiple ways: by emphasising the techniques of proto-animations and by foregrounding the texture of the paper, the watercolour brush strokes or pencil marks, the materials that constitute the image physically. This reflexive style suggests that reality is constantly under construction, but also reintroduces a sensible materiality into the film, as an alternative to Didi-Huberman's idea of obscurity (2008: 32). Hence the marks of the paintbrush, the figures drawn and coloured by hand generate a sense of precarity.

In this visual context the mediality of photographs is marked by their stillness and their indexicality, complementing the moving images of the animation. Fragments of photographs are often collaged in the animated world, as a gesture of giving faces to the human figures. Such images become similar to surfaces laboriously decorated with intarsia. Instead of the collision of elements that form a collage, these diverse media parts are moulded to complement each other. Medial differences are blurred through the sensuous impression of texture that establishes photographs as similar haptic objects to be animated as the textured (cut and crumpled) paper. In other instances, photographs of Crulic as a little boy are literally transformed into a drawing, which escapes from the surface of the photographic paper and runs into the diegetic space of the film. Drawing, on the other hand, also imitates the photographic when the protagonist's nostalgia for his home is presented as a drawing of a photograph presenting his aunt's house (Figure 6.1). Animation techniques like rotoscopy and stop motion also remediate the photographic, in the manner of a 'sensual mode' of intermediality that opens up images toward sensuous, synesthetic interfaces (Pethő 2011: 95–178).

Photography is barely present as an autonomous medium; it fills the frame of the cinematic image only once. At the turning point of Crulic's life story a series of photographs are presented which were made during his last Italian

Figure 6.1 Crulic. *The Path to Beyond* (2011): Crulic's longing for his home is represented with a drawing of a house that imitates a photograph

holiday, and kept on his digital camera confiscated during arrest. The casually dressed protagonist poses in well-known public spaces and tourist sites, looking into the camera and occupying the centre of the frame. In contrast with the collaged-in and drawn-over faces, these conventional holiday pictures become a powerful testimony of the singularity of the living human being, of the Barthesian 'this has been' (1981: 96) which is even more reinforced by the orange time stamp burnt on the image, marking the exact minute when the picture was taken. The frailty of human life is condensed within this moment of heightened indexicality, while all other uses of photos in the film employ a restrained indexicality and foreground the iconic.

Animated documentary has managed to expand photographs beyond their frames and to make the indexical and the abstract work together in the visualisation of external and inner realities. One could even argue that precisely because of this 'paradox visibility' it could become a popular template to narrate Eastern European memories within a global cinema. In *Crulic*, 'paradox visibility' is achieved through the confluence of media which generates a diegetic world. In this sense, most of the film fits into the category of the veil-image, a term introduced by Didi-Huberman which corresponds to the Lacanian imaginary (Didi-Huberman 2008: 81). While the veil-image maintains the spectatorial illusion, and a sense of whole-ness, in opposition to it the tear-image represents a rupture in the visual field, when a 'fragment of the real escapes' (Didi-Huberman 2008: 81). Crulic's holiday photographs are in fact tear-images that disrupt the coherency of the animated veil-image, performing a kind of metaleptic leap between the artificial and the unmediated. The films presented in the next chapter build heavily on such ruptures and fragmentation, also marked by intermediality.

Photographs as Fragments of the Real

A certain confluence of the photographic and the cinematic occurs also in Vladislava Plančíková's *Felvidék. Caught in Between* (2014), but instead of expanding the frame of photographs, these films capitalise upon their fragmentary character, and their incapacity to give comprehensive historical information is used to challenge the viewer's imagination. While the director of the film embarks on a journey to fulfil a promise that her grandmother made, the emphasis is on the photograph as a fragment of time[8] to be retrieved and understood by a new generation. The grandmother's generation is marked by the trauma of displacement experienced during World War II when Slovakians and Hungarians were forced to resettle after the borders were redrawn. For the third generation this traumatic experience is tangible only through family pictures and survivor's accounts, which is why the director's/granddaughter's quest implies the understanding of family albums, a pile of portraits representing unknown relatives. The search for her ancestor's house transforms into a hybrid documentary form, where talking-head interviews, stylised re-enactments, stop motion animation and archival documents are intertwined. This type of memory work consists in the assemblage of disparate media and objects to construct a passage to the past, as if fulfilling the imperative for meaning construction through montage formulated by Didi-Huberman.

At most *Felvidék* resembles a patchwork in progress, where the process of putting together the pieces is just as important as the final product. New meanings are constructed through the linear montage of the film (as a succession of different types of media, live action scenes and animation), but also within the cinematic frame through the collaging of different materials. Archival photographs and objects such as a watch, leaves and bark are assembled on the surface of a damask cloth, which stands for the abstract space of memory that is permanently rearranged by the visible hands of the director.[9] The uneven surface of the soil becomes the backdrop for reanimating past events with real-life objects such as beans, peas, maze, cut-outs of photographs and embroidery. These playful compositions try to establish new connections between the objects, or place them in a symbolic realm (the bark forms a family tree, later on it transforms into roots). New meanings are disclosed also through the projection of images on unusual surfaces: clips of archival footage and photographs become superimposed images on house walls, railway carriages, or on the handwritten pages of a diary (Figure 6.2). These patchworked and layered

Figure 6.2 *Felvidék. Caught in Between* (2014): photographs and moving images are projected on real-world surfaces in order to construct their meaning in the present

images shown in a permanent process of construction can be considered as a 'structural mode' of intermediality, which 'involves fragmentation and the breaking down of the cinematic into a collage of medial components or the experience of some kind of juxtapositions, jumps, loops or foldings between the media representations' (Pethő 2011: 5). While animated documentaries employ a 'sensual mode' of intermediality, the gesture of re-assembling archival images seems to be definitely an example of the structural template.

Moreover, these collages show a tendency to work with real objects and emphasise matter and texture. Vladislava Plančíková explains her choice of animation technique as follows:

> I knew which animation techniques I wanted to use and what I wanted to achieve with them: to revive the past in a finer form, retaining sufficient emotional charge. I focused on animation of real objects [. . .] I just conjured up the past, maintained a certain playfulness, but without excessive ornamental quality and naïveté. I did not want my animation to be too perfect, I wanted to convey a part of myself and my perspective with it. (Bosáková 2013)

As a result, this is also a case of paradox visibility: haptic vision and sensual experience display an otherwise invisible reality, detached from its ontological sources, and instead of instigating to imagine call for 'pure' perception (Tarnay 2017: 27). The haptic quality of the cinematic images seem to correlate with a recurrent motif of the film: images of hands are framed by close-ups during the talking-head style interviews, while holding the photographs, but also in animated scenes, when the director plays a role similar to a puppet master. As a consequence, in this film, past events and family stories become a patchwork of elements to get in touch with, or to be rearranged and interpreted.

The following film also shows the intellectual quest of a young protagonist trying to understand his identity, trying to connect to a past accessible only through the mediation of photographs and home videos. *I Made You, I Kill You* is an experimental short directed and animated by Alexandru Petru Badeliță and released in 2016. In its 15-minute duration the short film recounts the traumatic childhood experiences of the artist, who becomes in this film a non-conventional male character, whose presence is felt through the excessive use of voice-over and as the subject who joins together different image types. The starting point of the film is a collaged family picture; photos of a woman, a man and their child are glued together, the group photo is faked, their togetherness is not a real, indexical image. The film uses this technique of raw collage (emphasising rupture and fragmentedness) throughout, but in this first instant it is used as a means to uncover the dysfunctional aspects of family life, to create tension not only between different media, but between a normative family life and a traumatic childhood. Thus, the amalgamation of different media (photography, film, drawings, TV-clips, home video) is used to create a disturbance in the conventions of a family photograph. The film becomes a voyage into the childhood self of the director with fragments of dialogues and pop songs. Childhood drawings and family photographs work together to build the visual equivalent of trauma, of a nightmare (Figure 6.3).

Figure 6.3 *I Made You, I Kill You* (2016): one of the few childhood photographs of the director is collaged into a hypermediated landscape

This collage is highly indebted to the artistic gestures of the historical avant-garde and surrealism. Here death becomes a recurring motif both on the level of the voice-over narration, and in image sequences as well. Childhood memories about funerals and the horrific verbal threats of an ever-drunk father are translated visually through rough cuts within frames and a very harsh montage between shots as well. The appeal of the images derives from the tension and collision of different elements. Every element seems uncanny, and the common way of reading the family photographs is detoured.

PHOTOGRAPHS AS EMBLEMS OF OBSCURITY

Several essay films contest established versions of history just as much as traditional views of photography. In such films it is not a disruptive effect that challenges the spectator to see the image as fragmentary, because these works address the issue of invisibility and loss directly from the start.

The loss of one's memories caused by the destruction of personal photographs is the central topic of Zbigniew Czapla's short film entitled *Paperbox* (2011). After a flood destroys his grandparents' home, the director returns to the muddied house to recover some of the belongings, among them the family photographs, but he finds the pictures in a much-damaged state. Extreme close-ups of the running river and of the director's hands emphasise the gesture of retrieval, but these haptic images foregrounding the palpable materiality of water, mud and paper through framing also prefigure the mortality/fatality of the photographs. While sensual images show the family pictures being rescued in a cardboard box, we also learn that the decay of the photographic paper cannot be halted, only temporarily delayed. From this point on the short film follows the slow disappearance of the images by using the technique of stop motion animation. In this case animation is more than just a cinematic means to add a temporal dimension to still images, it is rather like a photo-processing in reverse as it presents the transformation of visible images into latent ones (which are there but not fully comprehensible), and finally into textured surfaces and non-figurative stains. In this way, the film examines the photographic medium as such, as a type of prosthetic memory which was used by the director's family to establish a contact with a wider world and their genealogical roots, but as decomposition takes its course these images gradually lose their iconic dimension and become objects that cannot perform the act of pointing anymore (see Lefebvre 2007). The waning of the human figures is reinforced by the soundtrack of the film consisting of unfinished sentences from oral history interviews, short remarks made by relatives looking at the remains of their photographs.[10] Mumbled voices uttering 'I can't remember', 'I don't know, because I can't see them' create an analogy between the vanishing of images and the fading of memories.

This is why the missing or fading segments of the photographs take on a different role than the obscurity of the image described by Georges Didi-Huberman. The murkiness and fragmentedness resulting from the physical process of putrefaction do not designate the phenomenological aspect, the gesturality of the image,[11] nor do they rupture the 'veil-image' in order to challenge imagination. The lacuna of the photographs is brought into focus in order to challenge the notion of the medium hailed as a container of memory, a fixed image that endures time. The film becomes a meditation on the contradictory, dual nature of photographs which entails tracing and effacing. It is an analogy of memory but also of forgetting. From another perspective it is not the obscurity of the image that induces forgetting, but the blackouts of the medium as a container of images.[12]

As the director observes how images disappear from the paper surfaces and become physically weathered, the medium of cinema fulfils an important but subtle role. Cinematic re-framing, the montage of photographs and the animation of hand-drawn figures are used to depict the very nature of forgetting with photographs. The cinematic frame is filled by the close-up of photographs depicting faces and events. Since we never get to see the full photographs, the animation seems to simulate the subjective point of view of a person looking at a photo album, scrutinising faces, gestures and other details. The major junctures in the ongoing process of decomposition are signalled by handwritten annotations on scraps of paper, the viewer becomes aware of the passage of time as the same images are repeated in the animated montage in order to measure the quantity of loss (Figure 6.4).

The transitional moment when photographs are deprived of their iconicity and turn into dysfunctional indexes is marked by the introduction of animation. Hand-drawn animation is called into play to emphasise the moment when the iconic escapes the photographic object: certain parts of the photographs 'come alive' as drawings. Photographs morph into hand-drawn contours of hands, gestures and faces, which in contrast to their photographic stillness, come alive and start to move, and in certain cases even leave the frame. After the images cease to make things visible, only the texture of the time-worn paper, the washed-out caption from their back side remains. Images layered on top of one another become frames that display texture and materiality as substitutes for the iconic sign that vanished. They become 'pure indexes' as Lefebvre suggested, which compensate for the objects lacking in the image with highly sensory qualities,[13] they point at loss, they become indicators of a lost connection with the world. According to Lefebvre even a blurred, undiscernible photograph is indexical, but it will be interpreted differently, 'as a sign of some existing, though absolutely vague and undifferentiated thing' that can be neither true nor false (2007: 240).

Figure 6.4 *Paperbox* (2011): close-up of still visible details on a photograph in decomposition. This image focusing on the hands of the soldiers returns several times during the film, until its recognisable parts vanish totally

In *Paperbox* cinematic strategies remediate such states of vagueness of the photographic medium as a painting: faceless portraits, fragmented figures and washed out colours are unfolded as paintings. This can be seen as the opposite of what happens in the animated documentary *Crulic*, where photographs and drawings seem to contaminate each other until even the photographic can manifest itself as a drawing. Thus, what cinema does in *Paperbox* is to reinstate the frail, fleeting nature of photographic images, and, as Sulejewska argues, the film itself acquires the status of a 'paper box' (2014: 117).

The art of pointing with a photograph becomes even more intricately entangled with a sense of loss in Radu Jude's *Dead Nation* (2017). While in *Paperbox* the loss of iconicity of the photographs is motivated by the flood which, had destroyed the signs' 'anchorage in the world' (Lefebvre 2007: 226), *Dead Nation* has to construct visually the story of the Romanian Holocaust, of which no photographic vestiges exist. Just as the subtitle of the film, *Fragments of Parallel Lives*, indicates, the film consists of three different types of documents interwoven throughout the film, all of them originating from the period between 1937 and 1946. Excerpts from the diary of Emil Dorian, a Jewish doctor from Bucharest are read by Radu Jude as a kind of voice-over narration; we hear fragments of sound documents from the period such as Romanian radio journals, official speeches and propaganda songs, and we are shown a series of photographs made by a studio photographer in the small Romanian town, Slobozia. These three types of documents are used as indexes of alternative versions of the same historical period, and seem to encode very different, even contradictory human experiences. There is the official narrative represented by the public speeches, radio news and songs supporting the political ideology of the Legionary Movement, and that of the Soviet-affiliated Socialist Party after 1945. Emil Dorian's diary entries read in a chronological order stand for the viewpoint of the victim in this historical context, who filters the historical events and his everyday life through his restricted, subjective point of view, that of the Jew who is gradually deprived of his practice as a physicist, who becomes the eyewitness of the eviction of the Jews from central Bucharest, who relates his everyday actions like standing in a queue or taking a taxi, and records stories that he hears or reads about abuse, persecution, executions or train deportations. The sound documents collide with the autobiographical narration, thus forming a sonorous collage, which speaks of a historical taboo in contemporary Romanian society, and gives voice to the unimaginable experiences of World War II.

For the argument of this essay it is most relevant to describe how these stories that stir up imagination are visualised. At first glance Radu Jude's film seems like a slide show of randomly chosen archival photographs meant to illustrate the autobiographical voice-over narration. Most of the photographs are portraits of people staged in frontal poses in a studio or in open air, without any supplemental information. They were selected from a recently digitised collection of glass plates, made by Costică Acsinte, Slobozia's photographer in the same years covered by the diary entries. The everyday faces of the small town bear the traces of their times, as they wear the military uniforms or as they perform the Nazi salute, but they don't seem to be affected at all by the persecutions related in the diary, nor by the tragedies of war. Thus, the film associates the audible historical record and traumatic reality that has no visible evidence with the visible external reality of the studio photographs that seem to be ignorant of the atrocities of war. As the synopsis of the film points out: the film is about what pictures do and do not show. They do show the everyday life of Slobozia, but they do not show the war and the rising anti-Semitism that marked the era. It is a special case of paradox visibility, to use Tarnay's term, as the traumatic experience of history, the blackness of the unimaginable is filled with black-and-white photographic images of another reality. With the analogue images of Acsinte pointing to the world of Slobozia, actually it is the parallel historical reality of a Jew from Bucharest that acquires visibility.

As the missing picture of the Romanian reality from the 1940s is substituted by a series of archival photographs, it is also important to look at the role cinema plays in this process of visualisation. Photographs are embedded as still, unmoving images, the mediality of which is emphasised by the direct look of the portraits, and also by details foregrounding the materiality of the glass plates. Broken, fractured plates as well as different flaws in their dry gelatin coating feature often in the film, accentuating the image as a surface. As most of the portraits were composed in the vertical format, they cannot fill the cinematic frames, they appear against a black backdrop. Photographs appear in a succession, avoiding any simulation of movement (such as the Ken Burns effect), or continuity (rough cuts are used instead of fade-in or fade-out). Moreover, the cinematic frame doesn't reframe the photographs, and it keeps their original aspect ratio. Photographic stillness is also highlighted with the slow succession of the frames on the screen: the very first and the very last image lasts ninety seconds on screen, while the length of the other pictures oscillates between twenty and forty seconds. The non-cinematic nature of the remediated images is emphasised, like ratio, flatness and stillness, while the cinematic endows them with a temporality reminiscent of slow cinema, which challenges the viewer to meditate upon the text in the voice-over and its relation to the photographs.

The first photograph of the film is a landscape, a long shot of a wasteland with no life in it while on the soundtrack of the film a record of a patriotic speech can be heard, praising the soldiers who fought for the unification of the country. As the speech goes on, it arouses different associations and presumptions concerning the image: it becomes an ironic commentary, but it also connotes the 800,000 dead soldiers of World War I mentioned by the speaker, and gives an interpretation to the Romanian title of the film (*Țara moartă*), which slightly differs from the English version, as its exact meaning is *Dead Country* and not *Dead Nation*, as it is used in the international distribution. Thus, the landscape becomes the metaphor for a country which is already dead because of the casualties of war, or just because it is an image of the past, moreover because it is represented by photographs.[14] The photographs that constitute the montage are offered for interpretation in a similar way; although they have no direct connection to the audible text, the possibility of a metaphoric meaning or an ironic association is created. A meditation on the unbearable memories of the Great War is supplemented by an image of three men drinking and smoking at a garden table, or the gruesome stories about the thirst of the people transported in train wagons are accompanied by images of people bathing in a river. Some of the metaphors are reproductions of conventional allegories such as the image of a slaughtered pig or a sheep that illustrates stories about death. Even material aspects of the image are called into the play of metaphoric meaning production. A portrait disfigured by the putrefying gelatin coating becomes the avatar of the story of a wounded soldier who concludes that his life is more sacred than the country. On another occasion an image of men posing with their horses and bulls creates a pretext to reflect on the rigidity and stillness of images. While the photograph appears for twenty-five seconds, the following commentary can be heard: 'A minute of silence leaves our country breathless at the supreme moment when Bessarabia

Figure 6.5 *Dead Nation* (2017): an example of the gelatin coat in decay. The photograph of the men standing in front of their carriage becomes a metaphor for stillness due to the voice-over

is ripped from its body' (Figure 6.5). At times a meaningful silence accompanies the photographs in order to shift attention to their absurd, grotesque take on the world, like in the case of children posing with guns. There is one instance in the film, when the opposite occurs; while the journal entry about the uses of gas during the war is read, instead of an Acsinte photograph a black screen appears, apparently a direct reference to the myth of the unimaginability of the Shoah.

Dead Nation is a film about shifting, fluid meanings that are fully dependent on the stills from the Costică Acsinte archive. It is the intermediality of film and photography that creates a context where the 'opening up' of history occurs. In the context of the diary notes indexicality is weakening,[15] images cease to point at the unique reality of Slobozia from the 1930s and 1940s, instead they become signs of possible realities from that era. They are not exactly pointing at the past evoked by diary either, they rather create atmosphere and a time frame for contemplation, and they give the spectator the task of deciphering the real object of pointing. Photography holds up the flow of time, puts the spectator in a limbo phase, between the now and then, and between the sensual material of the dry gelatin glass plates and the pristine, high-resolution digital versions of visual documents. The film showcases the sensual mode of intermediality, but without the aesthetic of interruption exemplified by *Felvidék* and *I Made You, I Kill You*.

Conclusions

Contemporary theories of documentary agree that a key to the documentary is that it uses reality as its referent, but they seem to draw the conclusion 'that the inevitable manipulation inherent in any process of signification renders one signifier as good as the other' (Rozenkrantz 2011). But how does medium really matter? As we have seen the in the filmic examples indexical status of the photograph is morphed and detoured according to the artists' agenda. According to André Bazin (1967: 166) there is another way to distinguish photography from painting. He argues that actually only painting has a frame, or edges that emphasise the existential divide between the outside and the inside world. Photographic images only mask the outside world, the screen is not a frame. Animated documentaries like *Crulic* build frames around indexical images, they build a diegetic reality around the blur, the noise or the fragmentary photograph. They create a space for the imagination that the viewer needs in order to compose the story from the photographs. In the photo-collage of *I Made You, I Kill You* there is no homogenous world around the edges of the cut-outs, it actually emphasises the rough edges of the pictures, it wants to disrupt any attempt to accept these images as real, as having any relationship to the outside world. In Radu Jude's *Dead Nation* photographs are indexical documents with a twist: they become traces/proofs of the world that is missing from it, and is represented by the voice-over narration in the film. Emphasising the material, haptic quality of the analogue material of the glass plates in decay, indexical photographs become symbols of the lacuna and also the spaces of the imaginary, they fill in the black screen of the audio track – thus photographs become frames.

Artworks recycling archival imagery have to face the problem of the lacunary, residual character of photographs as images that cannot represent their object in totality (the real, the past, the unimaginable). In found footage films this problem is revealed in a montage that shapes meaning, and in doing so images become ambiguous: they reveal and cover up the truth at the same time: 'they are like folds: they should be unfolded' (Tarnay 2017: 25, based on Didi-Huberman 2011). In the case of photographs this unfolding occurs within the context of the assemblage; while they are partially pointing at the real (to the external world beyond the image), at the same time they are rethought by other images and sounds that make up the hypermediated world of the film. As soon as we see a photograph as 'just an image', the fragments of reality captured by the image are extended through the means of other images and media. Thus, in photo-based documentaries, both the act and the art of pointing become intermedial, addressing the middle ground between pure indexicality and visibility.

This work was supported by a grant of the Romanian Ministry of National Education, CNCS – UEFISCDI, project number PN-III-P4-ID-PCE-2016-0418.

NOTES

1. This example can be linked to Chris Marker's experimentations with photography and film in his famous 1962 film, *La Jetée*, but Radu Jude's film is different, as it uses archival images in a non-narrative succession.
2. Alison Landsberg defines the term prosthetic memory as the process through which individuals can internalise mediated images of the past as personal experiences and this has the capacity to produce empathy. 'This new form of memory [. . .] emerges at the interface between a person and a historical narrative about the past, at an experiential site such as a movie theatre or museum. In this moment of contact, an experience occurs through which the person sutures himself or herself into a larger history' (2004: 2).
3. Drawing on Ágnes Pethő's (2011) theories about the perception of the intermedial differences as a process, the interweaving of photographic images with moving images can be understood as a performative act or action.
4. The cinematic post-media condition has been hailed as a new state of hybridity resulting from the challenges of the digital age, like the relocation of moving images, the extensive processes of remediation or the passage from the analogue to the digital. See the discussion of this post-media hybridity in the book *Film in the Post-Media Age* (Pethő 2012).
5. The term originates from Zerubavel Eviatar's sociological works on memory, which was later adapted by Martha Langford to indicate how the loss of the original context of photos is compensated by the new ways to preserve memories, such as archives (Langford 2006: 223).
6. Martha Langford in her seminal work on albums, has introduced the concept of the oral-photographic framework based on the similarities between 'what Ong calls the "psychodynamics of orality" and photographic experience, beginning with the evanescence of sound and photographic instantaneity, and continuing in the album's predictable patterns of content, structure and presentation' (Langford 2006: 225).
7. The concept of masking with respect to animated documentaries is thoroughly discussed by Nea Ehrlich as a question of visualisation that 'facilitates a convergence of exposure and concealment' (2011).
8. Even the live action shots of the film are 'contaminated' by the photographic; while the director is shown as being 'on the road' to memories of the past, the moving images of the film are converted into photographs through the means of freeze frames and optical printing.
9. The recent documentary by Şerban Georgescu entitled *Being Romanian: A Family Journal* (*Jurnalul familiei Escu*, 2019) – which presents the past hundred years of Romania through a mixture of talking heads, archival film clips and animated photographs – ends with a similar scene starring the director of the film, who

arranges the photographs of the last century on an immense wall decorated with a dark red damask cloth.
10. In Justyna Sulejewska's interpretation of the film these utterances have a universal character, they don't belong to a specific person, even the members of the family appear as the alter egos of the filmmaker (2014: 116–17).
11. Regarding the mass of black around the four *Sonderkommando* photographs, Didi-Huberman states that: 'this image is, metaphorically out of breath: it is pure "utterance", pure gesture, pure photographic act without aim' (2008: 37).
12. Hans Belting has made a seminal distinction between image, medium and body. He understands medium as a host or a carrier of images: 'No images reach us unmediated. Their visibility rests on their particular mediality, which controls the perception of them and controls viewer's attention' (2005: 304). *Paperbox* deals with the dysfunctional medium, and not the image.
13. This idea is reinforced by László Tarnay: 'we can formulate the principle that the more blurred the object of vision is, the more haptic the sensation becomes' (2017: 26).
14. The use of photography can also be understood as a proto-cinematic device, as an integral part of the director's preoccupation, within his *oeuvre*, with the historicity of the medium (see Mironescu 2017: 104).
15. Lefebvre based on Pierce likens this to a kind of semiotic growth when a sign interpreted as a sign of fact (*dicent*) becomes the sign of a possibility of fact (*rheme*). 'No single photograph can entirely exhaust the determination of its object. Consequently, if every photograph is a potential dicent sign by virtue of its indexicality, it is also a potential rheme by virtue of the vagueness that haunts it' (Lefebvre 2007: 240).

Works Cited

Barthes, Roland (1981), *Camera Lucida. Reflections on Photography*, New York: Hill and Wang.
Bazin, André (1967), *What is Cinema?* Vol. 1, Berkeley: University of California Press.
Belting, Hans (2005), 'Image, Medium, Body. A New Approach to Iconology', *Critical Inquiry*, Vol. 31, No. 2, pp. 302–19.
Bosáková, Žofia (2013), '*Felvidék – Horná zem.* Interview with Vladislava Plančíkova', *Homo Felix*, Vol. 2, <http://homofelixjournal.com/onlinefulltexts/felvidek-horna-zem> (last accessed 12 January 2019).
Dalle Vacche, Angela (1996), *Cinema and Painting: How Art is Used in Film*, Austin: University of Texas Press.
Didi-Huberman, Georges (2008), *Images in Spite of All. Four Photographs from Auschwitz*, Chicago: University of Chicago Press.
Didi-Huberman, Georges (2011), 'La conditions images. Entretien avec Frédéric Lambert et François Niney', in Frédéric Lambert (ed), *L'expérience des images*, [*The Experience of the Images*], Bry-sur-Marne: INA, pp. 6–17, <http://documents.irevues.inist.fr/bitstream/handle/2042/28239/MediaMorphoses_2008_22_6.pdf?sequen> (last accessed: 15 September 2019).
Ehrlich, Nea (2011), 'Animated Documentaries as Masking', *Animation Studies Online Journal*, Vol. 6, <https://journal.animationstudies.org/nea-ehrlich-animated-documentaries-as-masking/> (last accessed 12 January 2019).

Gunning, Tom (2004), 'What's the Point of an Index? Or, Faking Photographs', *Nordicom Review*, Vols 1–2, pp. 39–49.

Gunning, Tom (2007), 'Moving Away from the Index: Cinema and the Impression of Reality', *differences*, Vol. 18, No. 1, pp. 29–52.

Hölzl, Ingrid (2011), 'Moving Stills: Images That are no Longer Immobile', *Photographies*, Vol. 3, No. 1, pp. 99–108.

Honess Roe, Annabelle (2013), *Animated Realities*, New York: Palgrave Macmillan.

Landsberg, Alison (2004), *Prosthetic Memory: The Transformation of American Remembrance in the Age of Mass Culture*, New York: Columbia University Press.

Langford, Martha (2006), 'Speaking the Album: An Application of the Oral-Photographic Framework', in Annette Kuhn and Kirsten Emiko McAllister (eds), *Locating Memory. Photographic Acts*, New York and Oxford: Berghahn Books, pp. 223–46.

Lefebvre, Martin (2007), 'The Art of Pointing: On Peirce, Indexicality and Photographic Images', in James Elkins (ed.), *Photography Theory*, New York: Routledge, pp. 220–44.

Mironescu, Andreea (2017), 'In-Between Histories: Intermedial Configurations in Radu Jude's Collage Film "The Dead Nation"', *Jazyk a kultúra*, Nos 31–2, pp. 103–111.

Pethő, Ágnes (2011), *Cinema and Intermediality. The Passion for the In-Between*, Cambridge: Cambridge Scholars Publishing.

Pethő, Ágnes (2012), *Film in the Post-Media Age*, Cambridge: Cambridge Scholars Publishing.

Pisters, Patricia (2016), 'The Filmmaker as Metallurgist: Political Cinema and World Memory', *Film-Philosophy*, Vol. 20, No. 1, pp. 149–67.

Renov, Michael (2004), *The Subject of Documentary*, Minneapolis and London: Minnesota University Press.

Rozenkrantz, Jonathan (2011), 'Colourful Claims: Towards a Theory of Animated Documentary', *Film International*, <http://filmint.nu/?p=1809> (last accessed 12 January 2019).

Rozenkrantz, Jonathan (2016), 'Expanded Epistemologies: Animation Meets Live Action in Contemporary Swedish Documentary Film', *Journal of Scandinavian Cinema*, Vol. 6, No. 2, pp. 189–97.

Ruchel-Stockmans, Katarzyna (2015), *Images Performing History: Photography and Representations of the Past in European Art after 1989*, Leuven: Leuven University Press.

Schröter, Jens (2013), 'Photography and Fictionality', *Mediascape* (Winter), <http://www.tft.ucla.edu/mediascape/pdfs/Winter2013/Photography.pdf> (last accessed 12 January 2019).

Sulejewska, Justyna (2014), 'Self-reflexiveness in Photo-film Form as Illustrated by Zbigniew Czapla's *Paper Box*', *Images*, Vol. 15, No. 24, pp. 113–17.

Tarnay, László (2017), 'Paradoxes of Visibility', *Acta Universitatis Sapientiae: Film and Media Studies*, Vol. 14, pp. 7–30.

Wees, William C. (1993), *Recycled Images: The Art and Politics of Found Footage Films*, New York: Anthology Film Archives.

CHAPTER 7

Trauma, Memorialisation and Intermediality in Jasmila Žbanić's For Those Who Can Tell No Tales

Katalin Sándor

The deferred, incomprehensible and unrepresentable aspect of trauma (see Caruth 1996; Elsaesser 2001; Rutherford 2013) haunts and challenges the theoretically heterogeneous approaches of trauma studies. The representability or communicability of trauma is most often dealt with as an aporetic issue: as addressing something that resists representation or memorialisation. Commenting on 'the popular scepticism towards the visual representation of historical trauma' Frances Guerin and Roger Hallas argue that 'trauma studies consistently return to an iconoclastic notion of the traumatic event as that which simultaneously demands urgent representation but shatters all potential frames of comprehension and reference' (2007: 3).

The communicability of trauma may be precluded by the corporeality and inaccessibility of traumatic memory that dislocates cultural and discursive practices of meaning making and the self-understanding of the subject. In a dissociated type of trauma – as in Cathy Caruth's approach (1995: 4–7) – the memory of a traumatic experience that is too overwhelming to be cognitively processed is delayed and becomes a special form of bodily memory that 'tries to find a way into consciousness, but ends up only leaking its disturbing and ambivalent traces in the typical traumatic symptoms of flashbacks, hallucinations, phobias, and nightmares' (Kaplan and Wang 2004: 5). However, the most debatable aspect of this approach is that it focuses 'on the impasse of the psyche and on the paralysis of the subject' and consequently it 'is at risk of ignoring the possibilities of working through [trauma] and historical change' (Kaplan and Wang 2004: 5).[1]

Mick Broderick and Antonio Traverso in their edited volume surveying alternatives for critical trauma studies consider that 'it is the analogical physicality of the traces left by the past in traumatic memory – a violent latency of the past in which memory is imagined as a wounded body – that complicates attempts to understand trauma in terms of cultural representation' (2011: 5). Since trauma disrupts cultural strategies of memorialisation, narrativisation or symbolisation, attempts to integrate traumatic events into a narrative that confers a coherent sense or (historical) significance to them might eventually domesticate them within the comprehensible (or the teleological). Thus, an ethical account of trauma needs to acknowledge the unsayable and the unseeable within the traumatic, the 'gaps, elisions and impossibilities of speech, the partial nature of it' (Rutherford 2013: 85).

Theories of the affective turn acknowledge what is outside of language, of conceptual, discursive categories and recognisable cultural patterns (see Atkinson and Richardson (eds) 2013). These are concerned with affect as unqualified 'intensity' aroused by sensation that is 'not ownable or recognisable' – contrarily to the qualified, codifiable, narrativisable intensity of emotion that can be inserted into function and meaning[2] (Massumi 1995: 88). For trauma studies, the concept of traumatic affect that differs from emotional or moral response might be relevant 'as the mode, substance and dynamics of relation through which trauma is experienced' crossing the boundaries 'between personal and political, text and body, screen and audience, philosophy and culture' (Atkinson and Richardson 2013: 11). Relating the influence of the affective turn to the study of trauma in cinema, Ann Rutherford considers that narrative and affect, or semantics and somatics should not function as simple binaries in critical, theoretical approaches, but should be identified simultaneously 'as dimensions of film through which affect can draw spectators into a heightened sensory-affective engagement' when addressing traumatic experience (2013: 93–94).[3]

In cinema, the question of representing trauma may point to a 'crisis of indexicality with regards to the photographic mode of the moving image' (Elsaesser 2001) but, in a much broader sense, also to a necessity of revising concepts of referentiality and the relation between film and the construction of (historical) reality. Nevertheless, the crisis of referentiality related to the traumatic encounter with the 'real' may pose a challenge to films that confront the aporia of addressing that which disrupts representation. In such films, intermediality may 'enact' the emergence of this aporia.

According to Ágnes Pethő, intermediality that disrupts the transparency of the filmic image can be perceived not only in evident cases of stylisation but 'also within a cinema that maintains the illusions of realistic representation' (2011: 4). Pethő distinguishes two, often intertwined modes of cinematic intermediality. The 'sensual' mode offers the viewer an embodied synesthetic experience by making cinema perceivable through sensations of music, photography, painting, sculpture, architecture or palpable textures. In this sensual mode, cinematic imagery often becomes textural, 'tangible' enabling a haptic, immersive gaze. The 'structural' mode of intermediality reflexively discloses the media components of cinema, as well as different layers of multimediality that make up the cinematic medium. The 'structural' mode often entails a more optical imagery (with distinguishable, clear-cut, or geometrical forms) that involves the (aesthetic) distance of the spectator's gaze (Pethő 2011: 99, 140).

I argue that through foregrounding the opacity of the medium or the act of mediation and displacing cinema towards other media, cinematic intermediality may enact the evasiveness of trauma, as well as the aporia of its representation. The experience of intermedial in-betweenness may enable both the reflexive and the embodied engagement of the spectator and may point to the dis-place-ment of the traumatic in-between being 'possessing but nonpossessed, somatic but without visible signs [. . .], "real" and "spectral"' (Elsaesser 2001: 200). Intermediality may engender what Laura Rascaroli calls 'interstitial thinking' (2017: 51) in relation to the essay film, which performs a 'radical calling into question of the image' (Deleuze, quoted by Rascaroli 2017: 52), 'necessitated by the crisis of rationality and of representation instigated by the Holocaust' (Rascaroli 2017: 52). In Rascaroli's view, interstitial thinking 'is also a way of moving thought beyond the impasse of the Holocaust's unthinkability' (2017: 52). Following this line of thought, I suggest that 'intermedial thinking' and the heterogeneity of media practices it implies may approach the argument of the unrepresentability of trauma by addressing not only traumatic memory but also the question of its representation in a both reflexive and sensory-affective way.

Intermediality appears to be a productive concept in approaching several recent Central, Eastern or South-Eastern European fiction films and documentaries[4] about individual or collective traumatic experiences embedded into particular socio-historical contexts. To memorialise (historical) trauma and to address the crisis of representation it induces, films may foreground the opacity and the sensuality of the cinematic medium. In László Nemes's highly awarded film, *Son of Saul* (*Saul fia*, 2015), the argument of the unrepresentability of the Holocaust is both addressed and displaced through the excess and the textural layeredness of the soundscape, as well as through the blurred, haptic imagery that presupposes the corporeality of the gaze. The mobile, vertiginous 'over the shoulder' shots skim the space of the concentration camp from an unstable, vacillating perspective that may often (though not always) be linked to the point of view of the protagonist, Saul Auslander, a member of the Sonderkommando.[5] László Nemes constructs the world of the concentration camp with almost documentary precision. According to Georges Didi-Huberman, Nemes does not choose either 'radical silence' or 'radical blackness' (in Adorno's terms) as an answer to the unrepresentability of the Holocaust, but impurity, colours and an acoustic whirl of multilingual speech fragments (2016: 13–14). The film questions the conditions of seeing and focus through the unstable 'panic image' that distorts distance

(Didi-Huberman 2016: 28) and visibility. The film enables the immersive, 'heightened sensory-affective engagement' (Rutherford 2013: 93–4) of the viewer, which is, nevertheless, inseparable from the diverting, dissociating effect of the limited accessibility of the visible (due to shallow focus and small depth of field). Through turning sight into a kind of visual palpation or inhalation of the visible environment, the film allows for an embodied spectatorial experience, a visceral encounter with the mediated memory of the Holocaust, enacting at the same time the inaccessibility and incommensurability of trauma that disrupts representation itself. Whether the narrativisation/memorialisation of (personal or collective) trauma is performed through the disclosure of the opacity and sensuality of the medium or through the intermedial displacement of film towards a non-cinematic medium, the suspension of the transparency of the image may be symptomatic of the aporia of representing something that shatters representation itself.

In what follows, I will discuss in detail the way in which the memory of collective trauma is addressed through intermedial discourse in Jasmila Žbanić's[6] film, *For Those Who Can Tell No Tales* (*Za one koji ne mogu da govore*, 2013). In the film, the acts of memorialising silenced past traumas of atrocities and mass rapes committed during the 1992–5 Bosnian war are performed through an intermedial cinematic discourse that intersects other artistic practices (such as performance art), non-cinematic image-making (such as amateur video diary) that construct and reflect on the 'real' in different ways.

Before her 2013 film, Žbanić tackled the question of war trauma, traumatised female subjectivity and the after-effects of the Bosnian war in her 2006 Golden Bear-winning *Grbavica: The Land of My Dreams* (*Grbavica*). The female protagonist of the film, Esma and her twelve-year-old daughter, Sara live in post-war Sarajevo exposed in the film as a wounded city echoing the corporeality of traumatic memory through its architectural body. Esma's secret (as one of the English versions of the film's title highlights) is that during the war she was held prisoner in a Serbian rape camp, where her daughter was conceived against her will. Esma tries to protect her daughter from this trauma but Sara finally learns that her father is not a martyr killed in the war (as she used to think), but one of the Serb soldiers who raped her mother. Certain aspects of Žbanić's understanding of trauma in *Grbavica* will recur in her 2013 film with somewhat different overtones, mainly in the conception of the gendered condition of war rape trauma and the role of affect in addressing traumatic memory, as it will be pointed out later.

Based on real-life, quasi-autobiographical events, *For Those Who Can Tell No Tales* focuses on the memorialisation of war trauma through an Australian performance artist, Kym Vercoe's perspective.[7] Vercoe, who plays herself in the movie, travels to Bosnia in 2011 as a tourist. When she visits the town of Višegrad (being 'directed' there by the English translation of Ivo Andrić's novel, *Na Drini ćuprija/ The Bridge on the Drina*), she spends a night in Vilina Vlas Hotel, recommended by a tourist guidebook authored by Tim Clancy, without knowing that it was used as a rape camp where Bosnian Muslim and Croatian women were held captive and were tortured and raped by Bosnian Serb paramilitary soldiers during the war. The famous sixteenth-century Mehmed Paša Sokolović *Bridge of the town* also turns out to have been a site of horrendous war crimes. Vercoe returns to Višegrad in winter, and despite the official, institutional denial and the lack of public memorial[8] of the atrocities and the mass rapes, she engages in a private, intimate memory work. Not having access to the names of the two hundred raped and tortured women, she counts two hundred flowers for the victims, and, through uttering numbers instead of names, she recollects their unrecorded memory on a bed of the infamous hotel. Meanwhile the camera performs memorialisation by showing the numbered doors of the hotel rooms as if marking each of them as a site of traumatic memory.

The critical reception highlights the socially transformative potential of the film and also a few problematic gestures of addressing war traumas in a multi-ethnic environment still strongly marked by tensions and the remnants of war. Olivera Simić and Zala Volčić acknowledge that Žbanić's film works as 'a strategy for resistance, intervention and justice' and becomes 'not simply a witness but an interpreter that transmits the painful process of traumatisation and its historical legacy, while promoting symbolic reparation' (2014: 377, 396). However, they are more sceptical about the capacity of the film to 'cross ethno-national lines of division strongly instilled in BiH [Bosnia and Herzegovina]'[9] and consider that 'the representations of perpetrators and victims remain one-dimensional' (Simić and Volčić 2014: 389, 391).[10] In her recent monograph, *Dislocated Screen Memory: Narrating Trauma in Post-Yugoslav Cinema*, Dijana Jelača considers that Žbanić's film is a 'cinematic enactment of memorialization' (2016: 44) of suppressed war crimes within an 'ethically driven cinema that actively seeks to fill the gap of forgotten trauma and insert it back into active, knowable cultural memory' (2016: 47). Jelača aptly argues that the memorialising practice of the film seems to resonate with Young's ideas about 'counter-monuments': 'the surest engagement with memory lies in its perpetual irresolution'[11] (Young 1992: 270).

In the hotel room and around the bridge, Vercoe's memorialising work precluded by the male force of authority (through both implicit and explicit threats) is related to the forcefully silenced trauma of many and unfolds as a performative, investigative, corporeal memorialisation. Unlike the (institutionalised) acts of laying flower wreaths with national-flag ribbons on ideologically enclosed memorial sites of Višegrad (as shown in the film), the protagonist's encounter with past traumas remains irresolute, open and self-questioning.

But what role does cinematic intermediality play in articulating the displacing experience of memorialisation? I argue that the corporeality and the evasive character of memorialising the trauma of rape camps and massacres are enacted by a film that acknowledges the unsaid, the inaccessible and non-representable within the discourse on trauma. The intermedial juxtaposition of optical and haptic imagery, of well-framed images and short non-cinematic inserts (from the protagonist's amateur video diary) together with the reflexive exposure of the act of filming and performing may disclose an unsettled, irresolute engagement with traumatic memory.

The protagonist's 'accidental' encounter with the site of collective trauma is all the more disquieting in that it happens first in a belated way, and only through the medium of the body exposed to something that is not yet known. The uncannily intimate corporeality of the encounter is articulated on one of the posters of the film (that functions as an intermedial paratext):[12] it shows a human figure in a vulnerable, embryo-like position covered by a white sheet that sticks to the body.[13] The sheet (evoking the hotel bed as the site of rape but also the image of both a womb and a burial shroud) appears as a prosthetic skin, a haptic medium of corporeal encounter between the female body and the site of past female traumas. (When the protagonist spends a night in the hotel, not knowing that it was used as a rape camp during the Bosnian war, she feels an inexplicable corporeal disquiet.) In the later scene of the solitary commemoration at the hotel, the sheet will appear as a both inscribable and palpable surface of memory taking up the whole frame for a few seconds, when the protagonist arranges the flower-memorial on its whiteness. The conventionality of commemorating with flowers might appear as an integration of the trauma of mass rape into the dimension of the comprehensible. Nevertheless, the torturous, long process of uttering two hundred numbers for the victims[14] (not having access to their names) is a transient, performative, oral commemoration that might have an affective potential, unlike official commemorative practices of engraving names into immutable monuments. (The length of the process is only inferred by the viewer who is not shown the commemoration in real time but in an edited, shorter, more 'digestible' form.) When the cleaning woman of the hotel catches sight of the flowers on the bed the next day, her sudden, uncontrolled, spasmodic corporeal reaction reveals the affective potential of the improvised, intimate memorial.

The film, performing an unsettled memory work, does not endow the rape victims with a voice, nor does it attempt to reconstruct the traumatic events themselves, but through staging a foreigner's relation to these events, it intervenes into the (institutionalised[15] and private) silencing of war crime memories. *For Those Who Can Tell No Tales* adopts a foreigner's gaze that will be displaced from an initial quasi-touristic[16] engagement with the foreignness of a cultural landscape[17] towards questioning the touristic, ethno-cultural appropriation and commodification of this landscape and the silencing of war traumas inscribed into it.

Jelača argues that through introducing 'the outsider's gaze as a diagnostic, but also distancing device', the film 'elides the more complicated aspects of local knowing and not knowing, which often exist simultaneously, in a seemingly paradoxical way' (2016: 45). Thus, the protagonist is likely to reproduce 'an outsider's sense of moral outrage that war crimes are not being acknowledged in a more proactive way' (Jelača 2016: 45).

At times, the protagonist's outsider gaze appears to constrict her investigative[18] and intimate memorialising acts to reductive or judgemental gestures, as it is reflexively revealed by the film itself. In a scene, she alludes to the risk of a homogenising, judgemental gaze or of the certainty of some kind of moral superiority: 'When I walk through the town, every person that I see, I think: What did you do during the war? Did you participate or you just watched? And then I hate myself for looking at people in such a way.' When Vercoe promises herself never to cross the old Višegrad bridge again as a gesture of acknowledging it as a site of silenced war atrocities, she finds out that the new bridge is also marked by war crimes, which consciously exposes the naivety of her previous promise. The site of trauma is not localisable in representative, emblematic places only, but – in an unconfinable way – it expands to the architectural layers of the whole cultural landscape.

Vercoe makes a video diary of her first and second visit to Bosnia and confesses that 'seeing Višegrad through the lens makes it digestible'. Thus, according to Jelača, the protagonist acknowledges 'the distancing that is allowed to her through a technological embodiment of her outsider's perspective' (2016: 45). The diegetic video diary, however, does not only allow distancing: through enacting a non-cinematic, private image making practice, it discloses the embodiedness and the mediality of memorialisation. Through breaking the fourth wall, the protagonist's direct look into the (diegetic or non-diegetic) camera may enable spectatorial engagement and may also foreground the corporeal, sociocultural and media conditions of perceiving what counts as 'real'. From the perspective of media-reflexivity, the diegetic hand-held camera and the video diary do not only engage the viewer into a more intimate relation with the image but also disclose the mediality of film, revealing the process of memorialisation – and that of filmmaking – as unsettled cultural and media-technological labour.

Through wide shots, close-ups and 'amateur' images, as well as through discursive contextualisation, the film attempts to relocate[19] the famous Višegrad Bridge, exposing it as an emblematic cultural and historical heritage site of the country, as a popular tourist destination, but also as a locus of memory of war crimes. The appropriation and cultural commodification of the bridge by touristic and national/cultural self-representational practices entails that it is to some extent decontextualised, ripped off from the socio-historical processes that have shaped its discursive and architectural body (for example, Vercoe finds out only after going back to Australia that on the bridge she admired, horrific crimes were committed during the recent war). Thus, the bridge may become a kind of 'gem object'.[20] The film, contesting this 'gem object' status, partially unravels the discursive architecture of the bridge shaped by historiographic, cultural, literary, institutional and local, personal knowledge, as well as by particular ideological struggles/negotiations of meaning. (In a somewhat overplayed, insistent manner, a Serbian inhabitant of the city emphasises the 'truth' to Vercoe, according to which the bridge was built by his Serb ancestors under Turkish rule, a domination lasting for five hundred years.)

The bridge is reinserted into the cultural landscape as a site of traumatic memory through (inter)medial interventions. It is the medial heterogeneity of enunciation and the discontinuous narrative that enact the gaps, the partial, unsaid aspect of commemoration within a politics of memory that attempts to question ethno-nationalist practices of constructing the past.

The film frames the protagonist looking at the bridge first through a tourist's/traveller's gaze, then through the knowledge about war crimes that redraws the map of the town for her. Both frames incorporate not only the sight of the bridge but also the act of looking, in which the reality and the meaning of the bridge are negotiated at the intersection of differing gazes (Figure 7.1). In another wide shot, the slowly approaching camera (detached from a specific diegetic point of view) is accompanied by a perplexing, wuthering (non-diegetic) sound that infuses the breathtaking image of the bridge and its reflection on the water with a particular atmosphere of impenetrability, of compressed, spatialised historical temporality. The sound-design of this sequence might be an instance of transposing the uncontainability of the traumatic into the aural.[21] The wide shots that frame the bridge presuppose optical visuality and a kind of visual mastering of the image requiring distance and abstraction (see Marks 2002).[22] However, in a short scene, optical imagery is dissolved into haptic visuality involving corporeal proximity: through a point-of-view shot of the protagonist, the embodied gaze of the camera appears to skim the uneven surface of the stones of the bridge with pores, cavities, 'wounds' accumulated throughout time. The image of the bridge 'unfolds' as

Figure 7.1 For Those Who Can Tell No Tales (2013): framing the gaze

a porous, textured, palpable surface through a haptic (camera) gaze. At the same time, it becomes a performed space of memory through the corporeal encounter of the remembering subject with a site of trauma. In another shot, the image of the bridge reflected by water dissolves the optical visuality of architecture into ambiguous fluidity. The stretched, waving reflected image unfolds on the surface of water in a tactile manner, enabling not primarily the identification of forms but rather the sensation of an image in its becoming in the non-place of a liquid mirror. As Laura U. Marks argues, through the movement 'from one form of sense-perception to another [e.g. from optical to haptic and vice versa], the image points to its own caressing relation to the real and to the same relation between perception and the image' (2002: 20). The static wide shots construct a carefully framed, aestheticised image of the bridge. This image is dislocated by a short insertion of a sequence recorded by the protagonist's unstable hand-held camera. The poorly framed, shaking, 'amateur' images, resonating with the moving body, unframe (and literally displace) the image of the bridge as an architectural and cultural icon, opening it up to the contingency of gazes and to the uncontainable dimension of the real. Lúcia Nagib – drawing on Bazin's, Lyotard's and Badiou's ideas about impure cinema or a-cinema – argues that non-cinematic traces in a film such as 'fortuitous, dirty, confused, unsteady, unclear, poorly framed, overexposed' images (Lyotard, quoted in Nagib 2016: 142) can be 'endowed with the evidential quality and political power of the unembellished real' (Nagib 2016: 142) and the potential of becoming transformative.

The last static long take of the film lingers on the winter image of the bridge in a photofilmic frame that fuses the stasis of the camera and the immense stillness of the bridge with the slow, heavy flowing of the river and the frail movement of the snowfall. The performativity of the photofilmic is manifest in arresting and de-dramatising the narrative into an image that presents 'what happens when nothing happens', through recording the 'small occurrences of movement within the still picture' (Pethő 2016: 248). Thus, the aestheticised photofilmic shot of the bridge enfolds stasis and movement, immutability/continuity and transience, grandeur and terror, forgetting and remembrance within the vicissitudes of historical conditions. Through intermedial interventions, the image of the Višegrad bridge is re-articulated at the intersection of a more sensual/haptic and a more structural/optical imagery (see Pethő 2011), and is relocated as a site of cultural architecture and traumatic memory whose meaning is negotiated among differing 'gazes', discourses and spatial practices.

The becoming real of the film that memorialises trauma implies a 'moving away from itself' as Nagib would put it, in which 'the medium disregards its own limits in order to politically interfere with the other arts and life itself' (Nagib 2016: 132). In Žbanić's film, this involves not only a displacement towards the photofilmic or the non-cinematic but also a metaleptic fold between the cinematic and the 'real'. The protagonist, Kym Vercoe, the performance artist who co-scripts the film with Žbanić, plays herself in the movie, and in a short sequence 'rebuilds' the Višegrad bridge through a performance[23] in a space shared with other artists. In the performance, the building material of the bridge is not some kind of enduring stone but soft, dispersible, earth-like material arranged on the ground in a transient bridge-pattern produced through the iterative movements of the hand and accompanied by staccato sounds. Displacing the concept of an (ideologically and spatially) fixed monument, the memorialisation of trauma becomes here an irresolute corporeal-discursive process enacted through the performative intermediality of body, material, movement and sound. The monumentality of the bridge, the density of its cultural and historical signification is refigured into a small-scale re-enactment of the protagonist's encounter with a site of trauma. Through the tactility, corporeality and transience of the performance, the film questions the practices that fix the architecture of the bridge within (commodifiable) touristic imagery or ethno-cultural discourses only, and relocates it as performed, negotiated memorial space redrawn by the choreography of the body (Figure 7.2).

During her first visit to Bosnia and Herzegovina, Vercoe films a street dancer in Sarajevo (Suvad Veletanlić, who plays himself as well), and she is fascinated by the 'totally liquid' movement of his body, as she comments on the images to her Australian friends. During her second stay, she does not film him, but (as a performer herself) enters this process of liquid movement, and establishes a corporeal, affective connection through the gestures and the rhythm of the body. Putting down the camera might be a gesture

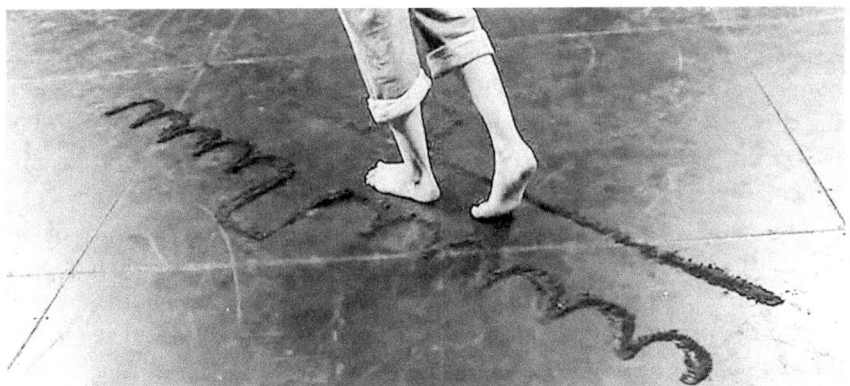

Figure 7.2 *For Those Who Can Tell No Tales* (2013): performing a site of trauma

of juxtaposing the practice of observation (and at times distanciation and judgement) with a more participatory and affective encounter between two foreigners in the ambivalent, both liquid and spasmodic rhythm of the dance, where conceptuality and interpretation are not the privileged modes of relating to the other. As a relational, trans-corporeal intensity, affect 'is concerned with what occurs in the currents and exchanges between bodies, not just what happens within them' (Atkinson and Richardson 2013: 11). Affect also appears in Žbanić's earlier film, *Grbavica* as a significant factor in addressing trauma beyond the discursive or the conceptual. Connection through affect may become a modality of working through trauma. At one of the meetings of the support group for women who were raped during the Bosnian war, the strange, tense laughter of a woman who cannot control her behaviour triggers the uncontainable, ambivalent laughter of the whole group expanding from painful smiles to more liberated voices. The scene displays the connective potential of a non-discursive, affective occurrence that may be described as not ownable, corporeal, unqualified 'intensity' (as in Massumi's concept of affect drawn from Deleuze 1995).

In *For Those Who Can Tell No Tales*, the protagonist's gesture of filming and performing reveals the joint efforts of a film director and a performance artist to intervene into the silencing of war traumas and mass sexual violence. The film does not perform a memorialisation that would question homogenous categories of victimhood and ethnicity, nor does it endow the victims of wartime rape with a voice in an empowering manner. The victims are evoked through their disquieting absence and namelessness: one of the most striking images of the film is the shot of a large restaurant, presumably in a hotel, with laid tables and no guests. In this image, the physical place becomes a non-place of memory, a figuration of absence.

Nevertheless, the movie disturbs the public invisibility of war crimes, and enacts an intimate memorialisation of trauma that might cross the institutional boundaries of the medium.[24] Olivera Simić and Zala Volčić point out that in the aftermath of the Bosnian war, judicial discourses focusing only on retributive justice have not been able to address the traumatic memory of wartime atrocities and mass rapes. That is why 'many local organisations and artists employ various forms of symbolic reparations to acknowledge victims of the war' (2014: 384). Thus, in Žbanić's film, the different discursive, intermedial interventions into the institutional or private silencing of war traumas, as well as into the iconic cultural landscape of Višegrad might be considered in the broader context of politically transformative cultural practices that necessitate a rethinking of the concept of intermediality along the poetics and the politics of representation. The gesture of incorporating Šejla Kamerić's work, *Bosnian Girl* (2003) into the diegetic space of the film (in Edina Omerovič's office) may also point to the (politically) transformative potential of (intermedial) artistic practices. Kamerić's poster, as part of a larger project (with street posters, magazine covers), expands beyond the boundaries of the museum and of institutionalised artistic practices and attempts to contest prejudices about ethnicity and the female body (related in this case to the 'Western' gaze). The poster shows a black-and-white photograph of the artist herself looking into the camera. The text written over the image says: 'No teeth . . .? A mustache . . .? Smel [*sic*] like shit . . .? Bosnian girl!' As the poster itself specifies, the text is graffiti written by an 'unknown Dutch soldier on the wall of the army barracks in Potočari, Srebrenica 1994/95. Royal Netherlands Army troops, as a part of the UN Protection Forces (UNPROFOR) in Bosnia and Herzegovina 1992–95, were responsible for protecting of Srebrenica safe area.'

From a gendered perspective, the film performs not only memorialisation, but also exposes the power mechanisms within the private and institutional suppression (or forgetting) of female traumas of mass rape. However, the film does not completely avoid the trap of the ethnicisation of wartime rape, which, as historian Andrea Pető points out, may often conceal the structural aspect of sexual violence as an act of power that can be committed due to the structure and the values of militarism – irrespective of ethnic boundaries (2018: 26). In the film, the representation of Bosnian Serbs sometimes reinforces ethnonationalist preconceptions and posits them as subjects who deny or silence the memory of war rapes and war crimes. Žbanić's film showcases how ethnonationalistic discourses may be inscribed into the architectural, cultural and social 'landscape' of a place with traumatic history and may disable an inclusive, socially negotiated politics of memory.

By incorporating short inserts of non-cinematic image-making (from the protagonist's amateur video diary), carefully framed photofilmic pictures, and haptic imagery, as well as fragments of performance art, Žbanić's *For Those Who Can Tell No Tales* 'acknowledges' discontinuity and non-representability *within* the discourse of/on trauma. The intermediality of the film in which the corporeality of performance art is juxtaposed with the intimate practice of private video diary enables both an affective and a reflective spectatorial engagement and discloses memorialisation and filmmaking itself as forms of irresolute labour with traumatic memory.

Žbanić's film together with Nemes's *Son of Saul* display various ways in which historical trauma and the crisis of representation it engenders may be addressed by 'acknowledging' the unrepresentable, the unspeakable *within* representation. By disturbing the transparency of the medium and foregrounding the aporetic, non-homogenous, interstitial and corporeal aspect of trauma discourses, intermediality may become – from the perspective of the politics of representation – a strategy to challenge social, political and artistic practices of memorialising (collective) trauma and to engage the viewer in potentially transformative memory work.

This work was supported by a grant of the Romanian Ministry of National Education, CNCS –UEFISCDI, project number PN-II-ID-PCE-2012-4-0573.

Notes

1. Dominick LaCapra considers that working through trauma is an attempt of breakout: not by completely unbinding oneself from trauma, but by enabling 'a measure of critical purchase on problems and responsible control in action which would permit desirable change' (La Capra quoted by Kaplan and Wang 2004: 6).
2. Drawing on Deleuze, Brian Massumi describes affect as 'something that happens too quickly to have happened', and as something 'resistant to critique' (1995: 88).
3. A further challenge for trauma studies would be to question the universal, ahistorical conceptions of trauma and relocate them in particular socio-political and economic contexts. Drawing on Ann Cvetkovich's attempt to acknowledge quotidian forms of trauma besides (large scale) catastrophic events and to contextualise trauma within specific socio-economic conditions, Dijana Jelača considers that 'an answer to the risk of making trauma into too homogeneous an experience – thereby depoliticizing it – might be to locate it within specific historicities and, even then, not to assume its uniform meaning' (2016: 9).
4. For a detailed discussion of intermediality in contemporary Eastern European documentaries see Melinda Blos-Jáni's chapter in this volume.
5. The film traces Saul's impossible quest to bury a child he believes to be his son according to Jewish traditions.

6. Jasmila Žbanić was born in 1974 in Sarajevo. Besides the Golden Bear for *Grbavica* at the 2006 Berlinale, she received the prestigious Kairos award in 2014 as a recognition of her cinematic work and activism for women survivors of the Yugoslav war.
7. After her visit to Bosnia and Herzegovina in 2008, Kym Vercoe wrote and staged the performance *Seven Kilometres North East: Performance on Geography, Tourism and Crime* (Version 1.0, 2010). The closing credits of Žbanić's film acknowledge the performance as one of the inspirational sources of the film.
8. To understand the socio-political context of Žbanić's film, it should be pointed out that after the Yugoslav war 'it was before the International Criminal Tribunal for the Former Yugoslavia ("ICTY") that, for the first time in history, rape was recognised as a war crime' (Simić and Volčić 2014: 380). In July 2009, Milan Lukić was sentenced to life in prison and Sredoje Lukić to thirty years. Both were involved in the mass rapes and tortures at Vilina Vlas Hotel, but 'despite numerous allegations that Milan and Sredoje Lukić committed war crime rapes, they have never been charged with rape. [. . .] The survivors had to wait almost 20 years for the first indictment for crimes committed against young women kept in the Vilina Vlas rape camp', many members of Lukić's former paramilitary unit still remaining free in Višegrad (Simić and Volčić 2014: 381, 383).
9. Olivera Simić and Zala Volčić rightfully argue that Bosnian Serbs are often pictured in the film as 'evil and ignorant' (2014: 391) without challenging ethno-nationalist preconceptions.
10. Unlike in *Grbavica*, this may reinforce dichotomies along constructions of ethnicity. Jelača argues that '*Grbavica* stubbornly denies the coopting of gender and, particularly, of women's war trauma into ideologically (in)formed ethnic divisions', and thus it 'opens up spaces for cross-ethnic spectatorial alignment along the lines of feminine trauma as a means to negate ethno-national(ist) politicizing of women's bodies' (2016: 84).
11. See Young's ideas about the memorialisation of the Fascist period in Germany: 'In fact, the best German memorial to the Fascist era and its victims may not be a single memorial at all, but simply the never to be resolved debate over which kind of memory to preserve, how to do it, in whose name, and to what end. Instead of a fixed figure of memory, the debate itself – perpetually unresolved amid ever-changing conditions – might be enshrined' (Young 1992: 270). Thus, 'by defining itself in opposition to the traditional memorial's task, the countermonument illustrates concisely the possibilities and limitations of all memorials everywhere' (Young 1992: 277).
12. Since the film does not contain such an image, the poster may offer an additional insight to interpreting the corporeal encounter with the site of trauma.
13. The position of the bent body seems to echo the image of the protagonist's naked body in the restroom of the notorious hotel.
14. For example, 'Woman number six, woman number seven.'
15. The Bosnian Serb regime does not allow the public commemoration of war rapes.
16. Drawing on James Buzard, Ewa Mazierska argues against a strict dichotomy of the tourist with less authentic cultural experiences and the traveller with more

authentic encounters with foreignness. See: 'Rather than being a description of objective differences, the tourist/traveller dichotomy has functioned primarily, to convince oneself that one is not a tourist [. . .] the desire to distinguish between tourists and real travellers [being] part of tourism – integral to it rather than outside it or beyond it' (Buzard quoted in Mazierska 2013: 123).

17. During the second visit, when Vercoe identifies herself as a tourist to the authorities and to Višegrad or Sarajevo inhabitants, she in fact reacts to their presupposition that she is not one.
18. In the film, Vercoe's investigative work aims to reassemble past events through inquiring about war atrocities from a woman, Edina Omerovič, who fled the town in 1992 and whose articles Vercoe read before returning to Bosnia, from a Višegrad history teacher who also left the town during the war and from the author of the tourist guidebook that recommended Vilina Vlas Hotel.
19. Žbanić aims to 'to re-introduce the bridge as a site of remembering and memorializing the pain and loss of many' into a landscape 'where such memories have been denied' (Jelača 2016: 45).
20. Eva Mazierska drawing on Naripea uses the term 'gem object' to describe famous buildings, monuments 'of which the country or region is most proud, and represent them in a flattering way, in a special light, from a particular angle, often obfuscating the way they are normally seen' (2013: 123).
21. As Andrea Virginás considers, 'traumas which are hard or impossible to represent through images or filmic narration might be displaced into the aural in the form of innovative, non-conventional, or experimental sound design' (2014: 162).
22. See: 'Optical visuality requires distance and a center, the viewer acting like a pinhole camera. In a haptic relationship our self rushes up to the surface to interact with another surface. [. . .] But just as the optical needs the haptic, the haptic must return to the optical. To maintain optical distance is to die the death of abstraction. But to lose all distance from the world is to die a material death, to become indistinguishable from the rest of the world. Life is served by the ability to come close, pull away, come close again' (Marks 2002: xvi).
23. This act is also a paraphrase, a quotation of Kym Verco's 2010 performance, *Seven Kilometres North East: Performance on Geography, Tourism and Crime*.
24. After having a conversation with Verco about Vilina Vlas Hotel as a rape camp during the war, Tim Clancy, the author of the Bosnia and Herzegovina tourist guidebook decided to take out the hotel from the list of recommended accommodations. Žbanić's film, *Grbavica* led to legal reform: in 2006 'a Federal law was enacted that conferred on women rape survivors the status of civilian war victims, [. . .] entitling them to small, but regular, welfare payments' (Simić and Volčić, 2014: n. 46).

Works Cited

Atkinson, Meera and Michael Richardson (2013), 'Introduction: At the Nexus', in Meera Atkinson and Michael Richardson (eds), *Traumatic Affect*, Newcastle upon Tyne: Cambridge Scholars Publishing, pp.1–19.

Broderick, Mick and Antonio Traverso (2011), 'Interrogating Trauma: Towards a Critical Trauma Studies', in Mick Broderick and Antonio Traverso (eds), *Interrogating Trauma: Collective Suffering in Global Arts and Media*, London and New York: Routledge, pp. 3–11.

Caruth, Cathy (1995), 'Introduction,' in Cathy Caruth (ed.), *Trauma: Explorations in Memory*, Baltimore and London: Johns Hopkins University Press, pp. 3–12.

Caruth, Cathy (1996), *Unclaimed Experience: Trauma, Narrative, and History*, Baltimore and London: Johns Hopkins University Press.

Didi-Huberman, Georges (2016), *Túl a feketén: Levél Nemes Lászlóhoz, a Saul fia rendezőjéhez* [*Beyond the Black: Letter to László Nemes, the Director of* Son of Saul], transl. Forgács András, Budapest: Jelenkor.

Elsaesser, Thomas (2001), 'Postmodernism as Mourning Work', *Screen*, Vol. 42, No. 2, pp. 193–201.

Guerin, Frances and Roger Hallas (2007), 'Introduction', in Frances Guerin and Roger Hallas (eds), *The Image and the Witness: Trauma, Memory and Visual Culture*, London: Wallflower Press, pp. 1–20.

Jelača, Dijana (2016), *Dislocated Screen Memory: Narrating Trauma in Post-Yugoslav Cinema*, Basingstoke: Palgrave Macmillan.

Kaplan, E. Ann and Ban Wang (2004), 'Introduction: From Traumatic Paralysis to the Force Field of Modernity', in E. Ann Kaplan and Ban Wang (eds), *Trauma and Cinema: Cross-Cultural Explorations*, Hong Kong: Hong Kong University Press, pp. 1–22.

Marks, Laura U. (2002), *Touch: Sensuous Theory and Multisensory Media*, Minneapolis: University of Minnesota Press.

Massumi, Brian (1995), 'The Autonomy of Affect', *Cultural Critique*, Vol. 31, pp. 83–109.

Mazierska, Ewa (2013), 'Tourism and Travelling in Jean-Luc Godard's *Allemagne 90 neuf zéro* and *Éloge de l'amour*', in Michael Gott and Thibaut Schilt (eds), *Open Roads, Closed Border: The Contemporary French-Language Road Movie*, Bristol and Chicago: Intellect, pp.119–36.

Nagib, Lúcia (2016), 'Non-Cinema, or the Location of Politics in Film', *Film-Philosophy*, Vol. 20, pp. 131–48.

Pethő, Ágnes (2011), *Cinema and Intermediality: The Passion for the In-Between*, Newcastle upon Tyne: Cambridge Scholars Publishing.

Pethő, Ágnes (2016), 'Figurations of the Photofilmic: Stillness versus Motion – Stillness in Motion', in Brianne Cohen and Alexander Streitberger (eds), *The Photofilmic: Entangled Images in Contemporary Art and Visual Culture*, Leuven: Leuven University Press, pp. 221–43.

Pető, Andrea (2018), *Elmondani az elmondhatatlant: A nemi erőszak története Magyarországon a II. Világháború alatt* [*Speaking the Unspeakable: The History of Sexual Violence in Hungary during the Second World War*], Budapest: Jaffa.

Rascaroli, Laura (2017), *How the Essay Film Thinks*, Oxford: Oxford University Press.

Rutherford, Anne (2013), 'Film, Trauma and the Enunciative Present', in Meera Atkinson and Michael Richardson (eds), *Traumatic Affect*, Newcastle upon Tyne: Cambridge Scholars Publishing, pp. 80–102.

Simić, Olivera and Zala Volčič (2014), 'In the Land of Wartime Rape: Bosnia, Cinema and Reparation', *Griffith Journal of Law and Human Dignity*, Vol. 2, No. 2, pp. 377–401.

Virginás, Andrea (2014), 'Female Trauma in the Films of Szabolcs Hajdu, David Lynch, Cristian Mungiu and Peter Strickland', *Studies in Eastern European Cinema*, Vol. 5, No. 2, pp. 155–68.

Young, James E. (1992), 'The Counter-Monument: Memory against Itself in Germany Today', *Critical Inquiry*, Vol. 18, No. 2, pp. 267–96.

CHAPTER 8

An Immersive Theatrical Journey through Media and Time in Alexander Sokurov's Russian Ark
Fátima Chinita

GETTING IMMERSED IN THEATRE

Alexander Sokurov's film *Russian Ark* (*Russkiy kovcheg*, 2002) is considered a technical tour de force, since the film was shot in one uninterrupted segment of ninety minutes. This implied positioning and choreographing over 4,700 cast members (867 actors, hundreds of extras and three live orchestras), all dressed in garments from several periods of history and moving between thirty-three different all-lit rooms of the State Hermitage Museum in St Petersburg.[1] From an aesthetic perspective, however, the accomplishment lies in the *mise en scène* and the impression of flowing through both time and space. One of the characters in the film remarks 'it feels like we are floating', and the last sentence spoken, in voice over, is 'we are destined to sail forever, to live forever'.[2] Works of art (and the human beings portrayed in them) are fixed in eternity, living through preservation or memory, but, somehow, implicitly they also contain movement. As a character points out in relation to El Greco's painting of Saints Peter and Paul: 'they are covered with the dust from their long road to appear in this painting'.

The film is structured as a walk through part of the Hermitage complex (museum and Winter Palace) and shows many of its celebrated rooms. There are two main characters in the film: a French Marquis simply named The Stranger in the end credits, but modelled upon the historical Marquis Astolphe de Custine,[3] and an anonymous present-day man whom we never see but hear in a continuous dialogue with the Marquis. The two protagonists walk through the State Hermitage, especially the areas most related to Imperial Russia, and encounter diverse people along the way. Such characters may be historically remote personalities (the Tsar Peter the Great, Catherine the Great seen in two different periods of her life, Nicholas I and his wife, Nicholas II and his family, the poet Alexander Puskhin), as well as anonymous and long-deceased ordinary citizens, such as a custodian during the 900-day siege of Leningrad during World War II, several guards and officers, courtiers and aristocrats, servants, a troupe of masquerading performers, musicians and simple visitors in bygone centuries. The film also contains present-day characters, either alive on the actual day of the shooting (23 December 2002) or having lived not too long before that. Like the more historical characters, these may either be renowned figures, some of them playing themselves (Mikhaïl Piotrovsky, the current director of the Hermitage; the ballet dancer Alla Osipenko; the blind sculptress Tamara Kurenkova; the pathologist Oleg Khmelnistky and the actor Lev Yeliseev), or anonymous people, such as contemporary museum personnel, visitors and tourists. There is also a mysterious man in coat-tails and white gloves, referred to in the end credits as The Spy, who follows the protagonists around the museum and oversees the other characters. Along the way, the two protagonists stop to watch re-enactments of historical events, sometimes interacting with them, and to observe artworks, all the while talking about art and history.

This journey feels like a wandering, happening as if in real time during an actual visit to the museum. The structural device of an impromptu guided tour holds together a narrative played out by a hierarchy of characters with different personalities and roles. The film recounts the history of the museum itself and several specific stories that are inseparable from it. The physical journey undertaken in the rich, diverse and large architectural site of the Hermitage starts as the invisible protagonist seemingly infiltrates a group of aristocrats, following them down some dark stairs. The path is not clear, as there are so many alleys available. The breaking down of the overall action and space into micro-events and micro-settings, despite the fluidity of the single long take, is highly fragmentary in diegetical terms, but intentional from an artistic point of view.

Russian Ark is a metaphorical representation of theatrical performativity, i.e. of an act of theatre. Both the protagonists' physical wandering and the historical characters' motion and interaction amongst themselves provides a narrative anchorage that is highly performative. It is this performative nature of the film that links all the elements that it contains: the different times, the diverse spaces, the characters from different ontological planes, the sensorial experience of art in general, and the resultant immersion of the film viewers. Indeed, by following the two protagonists (and the camera) around the Hermitage, spectators are exposed to a narrative, which they need to follow, mentally as well as spatially, and in which the characters, either historical or contemporary, are not presented all at once: they are discovered in time. Some of the protagonists' verbal exchanges allude to theatre directly. At some point, the invisible protagonist asks: 'Is this a spectacle?' The Marquis, for his part, later on, observes: 'Russia is like a theatre' A theatre [. . .] What actors! And the wardrobe!' I propose to use this metaphor of Russia as a theatre that the historical Marquis de Custine also wrote about,[4] and turn it on *Russian Ark* itself, approaching the film from the perspective of theatricality instead of emphasising the relationship between cinema and painting that most commentators construe as the key to Sokurov's *oeuvre*. Ravetto-Biagioli (2005: 24) mentions that the film contains multiple layers of theatricality, one of them being the film as an artistic performance in itself. I propose to take this assumption farther, claiming that it is precisely the theatricality, viewed under a positive light, that is responsible for the experience of immersion in the film.[5]

I am aware that conjoining 'theatricality' and 'immersion' might seem problematic, but in proposing the term 'immersive theatricality', I would like to emphasise both the singularity and importance of this phenomenon in Sokurov's film. The noun 'theatricality' has been pejoratively connoted with artificiality, exhibitionism, excessive drama and unreality at least since Plato's Cave (Weber 2004: 5–8; Carlson 2002: 240–1). However, Samuel Weber observes that the notion of theatricality has changed over time, from a negative conception, that viewed theatre as a bounded space where all the events and the role of the viewers were determined upfront (2004: 4), to a highly positive one, in which the place is mobile and in which 'it is not so much what is said or shown as the way that showing takes place' (2004: 12). The Beijing Opera performances, for instance, are like 'linking pearls with a thread' (Weber 2004: 25), the thread being the plot and the pearls standing for the scenes. Féral and Birmingham, too, distinguish between a more traditional theatre occurring 'in a framed theatrical space' where a performance is subjected to a (viewer's) gaze that validates it as fiction (2002: 97–8) and a more innovative, albeit still institutional variety, where all the aspects are subordinated to the actor, who creates the fiction (2002: 101). In *Russian Ark*, a kind of mobile stage is erected wherever the protagonists go, catching glimpses of ongoing events as they penetrate several rooms or palace areas and interact, with different degrees of discretion, with other bodies in space. What they do not witness is left entirely out of the film. So, in a way, they diegetise the actions: their choices do create the fiction and guarantee its fragmentary nature, ensuring that each event perceived by the film viewers is precious.

Although film viewers do not experience immediacy (to the space, the events and the characters), as they would if they were really inside the Hermitage at the time of filming, they experience, nonetheless a relationship of proximity to the events through the aforementioned aspects of the film, and become privy to some of the historical personages most intimate moments. Some of them, like the elderly Catherine the Great keeping her grandchildren company, and the princess Anastasia being late for supper because she was playing with her friends, are the sort of things that hardly ever get into the history books. By playing these characters against their 'symbolical status' and letting us see what happens behind 'closed doors' (Nasirov 2016: 30), whether metaphorical or literal, the spectator has a feeling of 'being there'.[6] Thus, *Russian Ark* also manages to impart the impression of immersiveness to the film viewers. This is accomplished through some narrative devices, namely the development of a hermetic and mythic universe whereupon the viewer can feel absorbed. Oliver Grau defines immersion as the 'diminishing [of] critical distance to what is shown and [the] increasing emotional involvement in what is happening' (2003: 13). Yet, for Grau, immersion does not preclude distance: 'Obviously, there is not a simple relation of "either-or" between critical distance and immersion; the relations are multifaceted, closely intertwined, dialectical, in part contradictory, and certainly highly dependent on the disposition of the observer' (2003: 13). In *Russian Ark* the perpetual motion of the camera and the actors, combined with the abrupt scene changes in which the viewer has no control, also calls attention to the apparatus.

MOVING THROUGH SPACE AND TIME

Although it was essentially recorded in a continuous long take, narratively *Russian Ark* is far from being an indivisible film. On the one hand, every time the Marquis and his unseen companion climb or descend a staircase or cross a doorway, there is an implicit change of scene, because we enter a different place within the museum. Along the way, the protagonists meet diverse characters moving in other directions, but as long as the two of them (and the camera) stay where they are and do not follow them, the scene does not change. In some of the rooms that the protagonists enter – furnished in styles belonging to other eras and inhabited by characters from a certain historical period – they come across several actions already in progress (tableaux). On the other hand, the temporal layers are combined in visual metalepsis, further enhancing the performative nature of the whole film and its immersive theatricality. The episodic nature of *Russian Ark* divides into different temporal strata the creatures joined on a single spatial platform. Since the invisible narrator and the Marquis are always on the move, there is no return to a previous temporal stratum. All the other characters are also motion-prone, for whatever ridiculous reason, as when the younger Catherine the Great rushes off from the theatre balcony in order to go and relieve herself.

Tableaux are meant here in a theatrical sense, although they may occur in films as well. According to Brewster and Jacobs (1997), tableau-like shots are, above all, uncut scenes in which the setting acquires both visual and narrative prominence. The style based on those shots is referred to by the authors as 'pictorialism' and involves a broad staging, i.e. a 'large space beyond the proscenium "window" and a long temporal unit, constituted by a theatrical scene' (1997: 13). This cinematic technique emphasises media artificiality and, therefore, in films highly dependent on continuity editing is considered the exception and not the rule. In *Russian Ark*, however, as in some other art-house European films that use the long take, the rule is based on the exception (Figure 8.1).

An Immersive Theatrical Journey   167

Figure 8.1 Tableau-like shot showing an affinity to theatrical practices

Figure 8.2 *Tableau dramatique*: allegorical theatrical stasis

In eighteenth-century France, Denis Diderot advocated the tableau as visual effect (a 'pregnant moment') taking place at the end of each act and produced by the seemingly accidental grouping of actors in a visually satisfying and silent pose. 'The spectator in the theatre, he maintained, ought to be thought as before a canvas, on which a series of tableaux follow one another as if by magic' (Fried 1980: 78). For Diderot these moments were the artistic highlights of the play. In *Russian Ark*, such a moment is illustrated (Figure 8.2) in the play-in-the-film attended by the younger Catherine the Great.

In the nineteenth-century theatre, a tableau was chiefly the equivalent of a scene, produced by the change of scenery on stage.

The combination of visual still effects and narrative scene is to be found in the related practice of the tableau vivant, which can be either a theatrical phenomenon, or a high society private entertainment. Conventional tableaux vivants require that a group of people pose exactly as depicted in a pictorial work of art, of which the tableau is deemed to be a three-dimensional reproduction (Vouilloux 2002: 32). In these circumstances, the models do not move, unless it is to adjust their positions or change the pose. For that reason, they cannot really be considered characters, they must remain forever figures. Besides, the story they impart is not theirs, since it was already contained in the painting they are merely reproducing. Consequently, the staged inner scenes of *Russian Ark*, where the historical characters are perceived going about their business, cannot be considered as actual tableaux vivants since they are not reproducing a given work of art. Such scenes, corresponding to a *mise en scène* inside the *mise en scène,* are three-dimensional historical depictions in motion. However, the visual similarity to an actual tableau vivant is here more than a coincidence. Tableaux vivants were part of a European culture, extremely fashionable among the elites of the Second Empire in France (at the court of Napoleon III), thus reinforcing the cultural period and style primarily conveyed and debated in *Russian Ark*. Besides, in this film, the use of the tableau and its visual affinities with real tableaux vivants bring the said characters out of their time frame and doubly animate them. The stylisation of static moments operates as a frozen moment in time, reinforcing another possible affinity with painting. As Ágnes Pethő contends in the case of tableaux in general, people 'do not walk into rooms, they walk into "spatial arrangements", or enter visual environments resembling paintings' (2015: 58). Ultimately, as Pethő claims: 'the *tableau* shot reframes a "slice of life" within the aesthetic constructedness of a picture' (2015: 43).

Such a hybrid use of the tableau accommodates, in *Russian Ark*, the existence of some symmetrical and artificial-looking images which, however, are not framed frontally from a distance, as long shots derived from the tableaux of theatre or early cinema. Also, in them we can see more than just strictly pictorial and rather static 'moments' for they combine the theatrical depiction with an internal *découpage* structured around moving actions. For example, in the tableau of Nicholas I receiving the Persian emissaries in the large throne hall, the film viewers partake of the grandiosity of the scene from up close, as the camera walks amongst the ranks of dignitaries, officers and nobility, as well as right across the hall close to the foreign emissaries. On other occasions, the film viewers seem to stand on the axis of the camera, swirling around the aristocrats dancing the mazurka in the dance hall, or they may feel to be literally on stage (and backstage) in the company of diegetic actors playing an allegorical scene for Catherine the Great (Figure 8.2). The two conditions that are the most relevant in *Russian Ark* and which are shared by all of its tableaux are: the artificiality (stylised aspect) and the nature of re-enactment. Both are found in immersive theatre productions, where the participants, actors or spectators, enter artificial narrative and visual settings (scenes or tableaux), but, because they can move freely in space are not bound to one framing only.

The division in tableaux of the actions portrayed in *Russian Ark* cannot be separated from their narrative function as well as their sensorial impact on the viewer, being quite appropriate to convey the glamour of Imperial Russia and its emulation of European culture from the Petrine era onwards. 'I love the 18th century, a time of genius and manners', says the Marquis. This re-staging of history by Sokurov, exercised from a contemporary perspective, works as an enhanced reality, or 'hyper-realism', which, ultimately is not realistic at all (see Youngblood 2011: 126). The visual embellishment accomplished through the most accurate depiction of details, notably the garments worn by the characters, places the Tsars depicted on a par with the works of art exposed, as if they too were somehow irreplaceable and therefore worthy of preservation. The dinner scene with the last Romanov family was deliberately worked over in post-production in order to give it an accentuated rosy tone (Figure 8.3). It is, indeed, 'a slice of life' and 'a poetic construction' that erases some harsh truths about the past (Ravetto-Biagioli 2005: 20). Steven Jacobs is right when he says that tableaux usually convey melancholy (2011: 96). This is apparent even in images which were not recoloured.

Figure 8.3 *La vie en rose*: Nicholas II and his family

Russian Ark, which was once meant to be an elegy, is contaminated by the nostalgic atmosphere and all the aesthetic traits of that filmic genre as practised by Sokurov: there is a subjective and plaintive narrator, a sorrowful tone, and a contemplative stance regarding aspects of the past that helps to mitigate a general feeling of loss and pain in the face of unavoidable death. In this case death is foremost that of Imperial Russia, 'not a celebration of [its] grandeur, but a sad song to its extinction' (Szaniawski 2014: 178). The whole film conveys a profound nostalgia for an unrecoverable past, underscored by the decision of the Marquis to no longer be a spectator who keeps on going 'straight ahead', but to join the world of the other characters and become a true figure of the past. In all of Sokurov's films, but particularly in the elegies, time is of the essence. The elegy, like the metalepsis, brings several times together in the same lyrical space. According to Szaniawski, the goal of the elegy is to remember the past while the object of mourning is still alive (2014: 165), but the subjectivity of the narrator also steeps these films in an oneiric atmosphere. Although multiplied, time is abstracted and transformed into a happy past (a 'then') and a not too bright present (a 'now'). In *Russian Ark*, the Petrine era represents the glorious Russian past and is made the object of subjective nostalgia by the Marquis and the invisible narrator alike. Instead of imagining the events, both characters get to watch them in the performance of tableaux. Through the theatrical performativity, the past is conceived as a perpetual present, yet one that is unrepeatable per se.

So much so that in *Russian Ark*, the representation of historical scenes as three-dimensional tableaux is more cogent than in other Sokurov's films dealing with history, for example, *Francofonia* (2015), a film which has the same museological topos. *Russian Ark*, unlike *Francofonia* – a documentary set in the Louvre museum in Paris, the European counterpart to the Hermitage – contains no archival footage. Although in this one-take film Sokurov revives historical figures, of whom diverse archival material actually exists, he avoids the appearance of authenticity that use of such materials would provide. This omission contributes to the maintenance of immersion throughout *Russian Ark*: the diegetic world of the Hermitage (its narrative frame and corresponding oneiric atmosphere) is not broken, even if the technical artifice is revealed. Inversely, in *Francofonia* the two characters roaming around the Louvre (Napoleon Bonaparte and Marianne, the French Republican symbol of freedom) are merely treated as icons, rather than historical figures. Bonaparte's role is reduced to his contribution to the history of the Louvre alone, instead of the larger role he played in the destiny of France. The two historical characters who are dealt with in depth in the film are Jacques Jaujard, the French director of the Louvre during the Occupation, and Franz von Wolff-Metternich, the German military art historian, responsible for the protection of works of art in France during World War II. They are the subjects of re-enactments which are separated from the rest of the film in a completely artificial, albeit *cinematic*, way. The scenes in which they appear were aged in post-production and are presented to the viewers with a fake analogic sound track flamboyantly visible on one side of the film (imitating a celluloid strip). Whereas in *Francofonia* Sokurov's main aim is to expose the cinematic apparatus, being less interested in creating the illusion of theatrical immersion, in *Russian Ark*, the interconnection of several people from different time periods in one single location is self-reflexive, but endowed with a theatrical nature.

In *Russian Ark* the border crossings between art (represented by the past) and reality (symbolised by the present) help to convey the thematic importance of memory, history, death and the atmosphere of nostalgia that impregnates Sokurov's fictional films, elegies and sonatas, and also address the nature of art as something which is unperishable. As the Marquis de Custine pointedly observes in relation to a person depicted in the painting *A Young Woman in the Morning* (by Frans van Mieris the Elder, 1660): 'Eternal people. Live and go on living. You'll outlive them all.'

Russian Ark engages several varieties of metalepsis, which for Gérard Genette implies the existence of two different ontological strata. The first and most important type of metalepsis to deserve scrutiny in this film is the insertion of the Author in the world of the diegesis. According to Genette (2005: 32), the 'metalepsis of the author' can be figural whenever the author makes him- or herself present in the artwork, either as a narrator or as a character. By deciding to remain invisible in this film, unlike some elegies where his body does appear, such as *Elegy of a Voyage* (*Elegiya dorogi*, 2001), Sokurov maintains a certain distance from the action in which he, nonetheless, takes part as a voice-over narrator/character. As such, he is possibly present in the film not only figurally, but as a multi-layered narrator who reinforces the overall self-reflexiveness. Although his voice corresponds literally to the actual/real life author who directed and wrote the film,[7] his dialogue with the Marquis is entirely fictional for the two men are not, strictly speaking, coincident in the same time-space continuum. Besides, the Marquis is no less a mouthpiece for Sokurov than the invisible narrator. Sokurov's invisibility seems, therefore, to be more in tune with a stand-in for the real-life author, known in narratology as 'implied author' (Branigan 1992: 91–111). However, since the film viewers' perceptions are, from beginning to end, aligned with the invisible protagonist, he is also an implicit diegetic narrator who lives in the story world and takes a mild part in the events therein (Branigan calls such a narrator 'the storyteller' and considers him or her a bystander, 1992: 95). According to Genette, however, the metalepsis can be fictional as well, in cases where the work of art comes alive, crossing the borders of the 'reality' frame in either direction, from the viewing site into the diegesis or vice versa (2004: 79–93).[8] Genette perceives the anachronistic intrusion of characters who do not belong in a certain sphere as a sort of micro-fiction inside a larger fictional work. Applying this principle to *Russian Ark* leads me to contemplate the historical tableaux as fictional metalepsis. The Tsars live on in people's collective imagination and are the natural objects of much fantasising. The references to dreams which abound in *Russian Ark* point to a fabulatory dimension.

Russian Ark's cohabitation of characters from different historical times emulates the archivist nature of a museum space, where works of art of different provenances, periods and types coexist in one single site. However, in neither of the aforementioned situations one can incontestably speak about 'narrative levels', since the characters do not inhabit hermetic worlds of their own. Put another way, because of the permanent motion of people in space, there is no framing device to explicitly embed realities within other realities – as Genette's meta-diegetic level(s) require – or to present them in a way that the beginning and ending of their actions could be clear and indisputable. When proceeding along the museum, the invisible narrator and the Marquis do not enter realities, they transpose architectural frames (doors) and encounter situations, *in media res*. Even the contemporary characters playing 'themselves' are personae in that they were given lines to speak and guidelines on how to behave, imparting the film viewers with no exact knowledge of their lives outside of the Hermitage. It could be argued that they too take part in re-enactments, that they too are part of a primarily fictional event with a spectacular status.

Jean Bessière (2005: 280) actually claims that the purpose of all fiction is to place in one single ontology beings and events considered imaginary and beings and events taken to be real. In other words, the context of fiction is always 'unreal', just as in an immersive performance everything that goes on in the premises is part of the spectacle. According to Bessière (2005: 283), a historical piece can only be shown from outside of that circumstance, which implies a meta-level corresponding to the work of art in the making, that is, its enunciation. In this view, the episodic tableau structure implies a double de-contextualisation of the fictional narrative: the historical tableaux are current presentations of the past; they are both past and present (Bessière 2005: 285), since they are lived in a spatial 'now' but portray events already elapsed.[9] The historical credibility of a film depends exclusively on the credibility of the representation as such, and, in fact, 'every narrative fiction is a play of communicating vessels of time' (Bessière 2005: 291, my translation), independently of how worked-over by legend the characters have been.

Re-enacting Intimacy and Identity

Due to its theatrical elements, *Russian Ark* is an extremely immersive project: it is not a film to watch, it is a film to experience, just like a space-based theatrical performance which it seemingly emulates. The import of the film's structure is twofold: on the one hand, it combines motion with occasional stops, affecting the viewers sensuously; on the other hand, the segmentation typical of narrative and fictional constructs impacts on the spectators' power of recognition and engagement at a cognitive level. According to several commentators and practitioners, the expression 'immersive theatre' describes a certain type of theatrical attendance 'that combine[s] the act of immersion – being submerged in an alternative medium where all the senses are engaged and manipulated – with a deep involvement in the activity within that medium' (Machon 2013: 21–2). The spectators are thrown into a strange environment, different from their everyday life, in the expectation of physical interaction with the actors, participation in the theatrical scenes and role playing. Moreover, these performances are highly inter-artistic in nature (Machon 2013: 27–8).

Some theatre companies, such as Punchdrunk, Dreamthinkspeak and Shunt[10] develop space-based performances, which resemble *Russian Ark*'s aesthetic conception. In their highly engaging shows, the performance begins at a certain pre-designated point and the actors scatter throughout the space, which is usually large, labyrinthine, mysterious and full of architectural recesses and dissimilar rooms. These found spaces 'provide ready-made exploratory landscapes, redolent of other stories and generate their own atmosphere' (White 2012: 223). Catherine Bouko agrees that many of these productions are based on narrative, albeit a non-linear one and which '[multiplies] ways in which events being recounted can be chained together to produce "the" narrative itself' (Bouko 2014: 264–5 quoting Stern 2011), much like a string of pearls or a sequence of tableaux. The spectator is forced to follow a character or group of characters, or else he or she will have nothing to look at as the characters move on. The performance is, therefore, a movement through space which lasts a certain time. Machon uses the metaphor of the journey to describe the relation of the spectators to the spectacle, which is configured as 'an individual journey throughout the work' (2016: 36).

No two attendances of the same spectacle are likely to produce the same result, since naturally the spectator, moved by curiosity, chooses different characters to follow the second time around. Group scenes within the performance are watched by many people, others are seen only by a lucky few who dare to venture through the space on their own and have 'one-to-one' contacts with isolated diegetic figures, located in some specific points of the building. These one-to-one encounters are an opportunity for the performers to officially acknowledge the presence of the spectators and are considered by White as an additional layer of immersion, both in geographical and dramaturgical terms (2012: 230). For example, in *Russian Ark* the encounter with the ravenous Hermitage custodian who is making his own coffin to be buried in during the 900-day siege of the Hermitage and assesses the Marquis as a possible source of nourishment falls into this category.

Machon argues that immersive theatre involves a mixture of internal and external space and interactions. On the one hand, there is an all-encompassing world with specific features, an 'in-its-own-world'-ness where space, scenography, sound and duration are palpable forces (2016: 35). On the other hand, the event, holistically perceived by the spectators, 'inspires a sense of occupying the experience as much as the space' (2016: 43). Spectators (may) have a double identity, being incorporated in the fictional world as characters for the performers to interact with, and as themselves, endowed with their own social identity brought on from the real world (Bouko 2014: 266). This entails a double perspective, as they perceive themselves as both participants in that event and as detached observers of the fictional world around them (Machon 2016: 43). This leads Machon to opt for the designation of 'immersive interactor' instead (2016: 39). In *Russian Ark*, for instance, the Marquis is acknowledged by his invisible companion as being a published author and asked to sign a book by some female members of a theatrical troupe. The work of art is entered into, yet a certain distance is kept because the immersion is simultaneously physical – the audience moves in the same space of the performers – and metaphorical – being equated with deep involvement. As Gareth White puts it: 'To be immersed is to be surrounded, enveloped and potentially annihilated, but it also is to be separate from that which immerses' (2012: 228). The metaphors of the camera, of the voyeur and of the ghost used by Bouko to allude to the distance maintained between performers and spectators point to the fact that, for the most part, no direct contact between the two instances is allowed (2014: 262). The duo of protagonists in *Russian Ark* express this phenomenon as clearly they are in different modes of immersive relationship to the work. The Marquis is seen most often, as when he makes faces at a custodian lurking through a door, whereas the contemporary narrator is hardly ever seen and kept from the film viewers' eyes. He is literally a ghost among characters as spectators in immersive performances are expected to act. In all fairness, *Russian Ark* combines a theatrical immersive practice with a more traditional narrative engagement. The film viewers start by getting acquainted with a disembodied voice, belonging to the Marquis's unseen companion, which plunges them into the space (and the story). Through an internal focalisation process,[11] the film viewers are aligned with this unseen character's immediate visual perception: first the absolute darkness with which the film begins, and then, as the image fades in and the character walks on, also the corridors and other micro-spaces of the inner sanctum which is the State Hermitage. In fact, for most of the film the viewers only see what he sees while he moves along a certain physical path. This subjective coincidence is reinforced by the emotional content of the internal focalisation process. The film viewers are meant to feel the Hermitage just as this voice emotionally perceives it and talks about it in his dialogue.[12] In strictly narrative terms, in *Russian Ark*, the invisibility of one of the protagonists may be explained by the fact that the character could actually be dead, dreaming or simply fantasising, and comes to realise his condition as a ghostly one. His initial discomfort equals our own, and he too starts a voyage of discovery. Initially, he follows a group of four people, who will reappear at different points of the film: two ladies, one of them dressed in white, another in purple, and two officers, one of them blonde and the other dark-haired. One of the women's laughter provides the continuity between the literally dark moment of the beginning of the film, when we only hear sounds, and the first images, which are of her stepping out of the carriage in which she has arrived. This entrance into the 'story world' is meant to be mysterious in order to activate the sensorial and cognitive abilities of the film viewers. In immersive theatrical practices the eyes as well as the other senses (including hapticality, kinaesthesia, viscerality and proprioception) of the spectators are directed towards the performance taking place all around them. Some companies block a self-image of the audience (Punchdrunk, for instance, makes the audience members wear masks), others block the image altogether by actually blindfolding the spectators, in order to reinforce the other senses.

The place, the time and the action of the beginning of *Russian Ark* are all unrecognised by the invisible protagonist as well as by the film viewers (especially if they are not Russian and are unfamiliar with the buildings of the Hermitage). The woman in white declares herself anxious at the prospect of not being let into the building, which prompts the idea that something illegal is happening; the fact that the men divide the women among themselves ('Don't forget: the girl in white is mine') casts a shadow over their female partners' reputation. There is no establishing shot, as the camera stays very close to the characters; quite the opposite, there is a lot of confusion, provided by some additional extras who walk into the building with the characters. At this point the invisible protagonist, speaking in voice-over, is simply trying to understand the events around him, a task made more difficult by the presence of masquerading characters, apparently belonging to some theatrical troupe. The two officers do not know the way and, consequently, they walk up and down staircases, along narrow and dark corridors. Narratively, they might be trying to force their way into the Great Ball, but physically they contribute to a mystifying experience of spatial and sensual discovery which, besides being ontological ('Can it be that I'm invisible? Or have I simply gone unnoticed?', wonders the voice), is also visual (the corridors are poorly lit); haptic (one of the officers falls down and is helped up by the others); and aural (muffled music is heard in the distance). All of this creates false expectations in the invisible protagonist, who suspects he is in a theatrical show ('Could this be theatre?') but does not understand its nature or his role in it: 'Am I expected to play a role?'

The other protagonist of *Russian Ark*, the Marquis, is also another lost spectator metaphorically walking in the midst of an immersive performance. Yet, since he is corporeally visible he interacts with other characters, sometimes very intimately: in a one-on-one encounter the blind artist takes the Marquis by the hand, and in another scene the ballet dancer embraces him; in the communal Great Ball he dances the mazurka with some of the female courtiers. Although the Marquis calls the disembodied voice his 'cicerone', it is the Marquis who turns out to be the film viewers' real guide; not only is he the one that the camera prefers to follow from the moment he first appears in the film onwards, thus leading the way in this journey of physical discovery through the artistic labyrinth, but, being extremely knowledgeable in art history and history in general, he also acts as a curator providing contextual explanations (in which he is aided, here and there, by some other characters in the film). Early in *Russian Ark* he realises he has acquired a new skill: 'Russian? How strange! I never spoke Russian before.' Indeed, entering the fictive universe of an immersive performance means adhering to some house rules; in this case it is literally speaking a different language. The first time this character is seen by the film viewers, he is already immersed in the show, for he is gazing at something happening off frame, which is immediately revealed as an action involving a re-enactment of Peter the Great in the Winter Palace, one of the tableaux of this space-based performance. The Marquis's nature is dual: as he is already inside the diegesis, he represents both a character in the performance itself – even more so than the narrator, who has no body – and a symbolic companion to the spectator (since some of the immersive theatrical practices imply going into the performance alongside strangers, with whom the experience is shared).

The mysterious man called 'the Spy' does not seem to have any role to play in the performance, except to watch over things and the two protagonists. He is seen everywhere in the Hermitage. Narratively, he could be a zealous custodian of the museum, but in the context of an immersive performance he is very likely to be the member of the troupe who guarantees the spectators' safety and only intervenes in case of danger to them. There is, indeed, danger lurking about in the recesses of the State Hermitage (Voice-over: 'Sir, be careful! Don't betray our presence'). Literally, it is not clear what these dangers might be, since the Marquis, who is already dead, cannot be killed again. Symbolically, though, there are two types of danger: one of them is being evicted from the theatrical experience by the performers; the other is to break the frame of suspended disbelief and, therefore, dismiss the cinematic tableaux by revealing them as mere staged constructs instead of 'slices' in the life of grandiose personages. Both dangers amount to the same thing: the end of the spectacle. Metaphorically, the Spy also represents the twenty-two assistant directors employed in shooting *Russian Ark* in one single take.

During an immersive performance the troupe members act in front of (and around) a live audience, who observes the action but cannot touch the actors or address them unless they are touched or addressed by the company members first. At one point, in *Russian Ark*, the invisible protagonist is worried that they are talking too loudly and the Marquis replies: 'No matter. They're completely deaf. I'm careful. I won't touch anyone.' The tableau of Peter the Great bullying his wife and a General in his quarters is observed by the film viewers from outside the room in which the scene takes place, while the Marquis and the camera peep through the window that leads to the compartment. There is a markedly architectural dimension in this particular tableau which creates a safe distance from the violent monarch (Figure 8.4). In other tableaux physical boundaries are absent but there are always rules and limitations to an actual contact. Museum personnel, guards and servants block certain paths. This is occasionally confused by the protagonists with a restraint on their freedom, but narratively the purpose is to enable the film to move forward in the manner of an immersive theatrical performance. Metaphorically, it also reinforces the idea, voiced by the Marquis, that 'Russia is a stage'. Indeed, the State Hermitage in *Russian Ark* is a physical location but also a narrative world filled with a certain atmosphere (at once, a theatrical site and a container of a diegesis). The space-based immersiveness is connected with time in a manner that combines duration with succession because the events portrayed (the tableaux or scenes) are not presented in

Figure 8.4 Historical tableau: watching the spectacle from the outside

their complete form: the film viewers do not see the whole action, only part of it, since the Marquis and his invisible companion want to cover as much ground as possible, driven by an insatiable curiosity. Both protagonists are simultaneously overrun by a rush of sensations and a time pressure, in accordance with the immersive theatre practices.

INTERMEDIALITY AS PERPETUAL REMEDIATION

Russian Ark is part of a deliberate and recurrent meta-cinematic discourse permeating Sokurov's *oeuvre*. The film may be interpreted as a statement, not only about history, art and media in general, but also about cinema. The State Hermitage in St Petersburg contains artistic masterpieces depicting famous people, therefore disclosing affinities with Noah's Ark, dedicated to a zoological preservation of species for future use, and the Ark of the Covenant, a rich container of sacred relics. In Sokurov's *Russian Ark* these two arks come together into a single vessel dedicated to the preservation of the past, especially in its artistic dimension. However, *Russian Ark* stands out in Sokurov's *oeuvre* as a rare intermedial achievement, for two reasons: the quantity of media involved and the theatrical nature of the whole enterprise.

To begin with, *Russian Ark* is a 'remediated space' (Bolter and Grusin 2000) permeated with media in a way that it replicates the embeddedness of the Matryoshka dolls. Actually, the film itself is a cinematic ark that contains another museological ark, the Hermitage, which can also be considered a complex medium. On the one hand, it is an architectural display, a labyrinth of corridors, aisles, rooms, exhibition halls, staircases, interior gardens, patios, doors, windows, chandeliers, furniture and paintings. On the other hand, it is an architectural ensemble inside of which we find a palace, several museum buildings and also a theatre, all of which are housing picture galleries and various exhibition spaces. These museum spaces hold other media in place through the artefacts they exhibit, notably spatial art forms such as painting and sculpture, which, in turn, point to additional temporal art forms pertaining to the actors' motion through several spaces: theatre, music and dancing. All the artistic media are simultaneously covert, in that the motion permeating the film makes the viewers forget the technique inherent to their production, and overt, in that the effects of that technique – speed of motion, two- and three-dimensionality, texture and artifice – are quite apparent.[13] This way *Russian Ark* reconciles the spectatorial involvement with the characters and the situations presented (as if they were 'real') with the audio-visual excess of the permanent movement through space and time. Both aspects create immersion, but, paradoxically, they do so in opposing ways: on the one hand, the film viewers feel that they are 'there', transported into other historical periods, and, on the other, that, somehow, they are still mere spectators to the events depicted.

Both Alaniz and Beumers recognise the importance of intermediality in this film and the role of theatre in that equation, but they are not willing to give theatre the upper hand. Alaniz thinks of the film as a mixture of cinema, theatre, stunt performance, travelogue and farce (2011: 165). For Beumers theatre conveys enactments in motion, whereas painting exhibits fixed representations; the image thus alternates between the acts of staging and framing (2011: 177). Beumers does not perceive the film's framing of staging and the importance of the temporal dimension for the achievement of that goal. She also mentions that the 300 years of history recreated in the film are depicted chronologically (2011: 178), missing the point of the encounters with the historical personages. In *Russian Ark*, characters and spaces are discovered as theatrical tableaux by the film viewers; the apparent chronological order of their presentation in the film serves as a mere tool for better identifying the people in question.

Sokurov's cinema is utterly unreal, and consciously so. He calls art the 'other life', for it has no direct and real relationship with our daily one (Szaniawski 2014: 292). For cinema to become closer to art it needs to call upon other pre-existing, and, in Sokurov's view, higher art forms. Despite all the conversations that the two protagonists entertain about the historical time, ultimately it is their own situation in space, in their present (the phenomenological time of the film recording), that drives them through the labyrinth in a sort of chronological suspended temporality akin to legendary time. Theatre as an art form differs from painting in that it requires the present moment; the expression 'live theatre' is both redundant (as theatre is always a live performance) and the truest definition of the medium in question (since theatre requires the coexistence of spectators and performers to achieve its fullest impact). Yet, in *Russian Ark*, theatre is no less capable of operating a suspension in time than painting.

At the end of the film, the Marquis stays behind, inside the museum, among the artefacts that do not move, because he is truly a-temporal. As a published writer, he has outlived his own time and has become a work of art. People in general, however, do not have such luck and there is nowhere to hang them or exhibit them except for the viewers' memory. The exit of all the extras from the Hermitage, following the last ball, is excruciatingly poignant (and sentimental) because it enacts a double death: the end of an era and the closing of the spectacle that represents it. 'In Sokurov's world, all days are last days', as Condee observes (2011: 188). If one decides to perceive *Russian Ark* as a meta-artistic film, allegorically pointing to the nature of high art, there is a solution for the sadness that is left hanging in the air: a re-visitation of the film, just as aficionados of immersive theatre go in for another try at another performance. What both have in common and what both are looking for is the immersiveness of the experience, whether they get exactly the same content or not. Ultimately, the viewers long for the eternity of the spectacle, performed always at the threshold of death and as a rite against it. Each re-visitation is a metaphorical return to the Home, a crucial leitmotif in Sokurov's cinematic career; each actor of the drama is an 'immortal' person.

Research for this work was supported by FCT – Foundation for Science and Technology (Portugal), under the Post-Doctoral fellowship programme SFRH/ BDP/113196/2015.

Notes

1. See further technical information about the production of the film in Alaniz (2011: 155–60).
2. This and all other quotations from *Russian Ark* were taken from the English translation contained in the subtitles of the Artificial Eye edition of the DVD.
3. He was a French liberal aristocrat and travel writer, author of the book *Empire of the Czar* (published in French as *La Russie en 1839*). De Custine spent a considerable part of his voyage in St Petersburg.
4. According to Szaniawski, the metaphor of life as a stage or a masquerade contained in *Russian Ark* appears in de Custine's description of the courting staff attending upon the Tsar and his family: 'In this frame, it was the czar who appeared as the ultimate *metteur-en-scène* of this never-ending production' (2014: 169).
5. Dragan Kujundzic (2003) does compare the one-take shoot to a theatre performance, but considering that it reproduces history as a unique event, unrolling 'live' *in front of* the spectators and for their gaze. He leaves out the possibility of immersion, albeit metaphorical. Other commentators approach theatre from the perspective of intermediality, as I will agree in the concluding section of this chapter.
6. This is usually associated with digital worlds. The virtual 'presence', typical of video games, is more easily produced when there is a coalescence of the characteristics of the system (i.e. its technological base) with the mental absorption brought about by narrative immersion (Nilsson et al. 2016: 120).
7. According to the synopsis of the film, he is 'a contemporary filmmaker' (although no exact mention of the name is provided). See the official press sheet of the film. Available at <https://people.ucalgary.ca/~tstronds/nostalghia.com/TheNews/RussianArk_SevillePressNotes.pdf> (last accessed 12 January 2019).
8. This so-called reality is perceived by comparison and usually refers to another layer of fictionality, separated from the first by a different narrative space or time.
9. For Bessière, metalepsis is, therefore, a necessary condition of fictional narratives.

10. See descriptions of their projects on their websites. Available at <https://www.punchdrunk.org.uk/>, <http://dreamthinkspeak.com/about> (last accessed 12 January 2019) and <http://cargocollective.com/nigelandlouise/shunt> (last accessed 12 January 2019).
11. According to Edward Branigan, internal focalisation 'ranges from "simple perceptions" (the point-of-view shot), to "impressions" (the out-of-focus point of view shot depicting a character who is drunk, dizzy or drugged), to "deeper thoughts" (dreams, hallucinations and memories)' (1992: 103).
12. The very few moments of the film which are not internally focalised are semi-subjective, a process also known as external focalisation, causing the viewers to infer that what they have seen corresponds to a character's sight. This happens more for technical reasons than narrative ones. The only exception occurs at the end, when the extras exit the Hermitage: the camera backs off in a tracking shot, which would imply that the invisible narrator is walking backwards.
13. Media in the film can be further divided: certain types of movement can be discerned within movement (forming specific forms of spectacle such as a masquerade, an operatic drama, two concerts and a ball), as well as certain types of images within images (the tableau as a historical reconstruction of several situations, pictures hanging on the walls, statues adorning the corridors, and so on). These are responsible for the intermedial vitality of the film.

Works Cited

Alaniz, José (2011), 'Crowd Control: Anxiety of Effluence in Sokurov's *Russian Ark*', in Birgit Beumers and Nancy Condee (eds), *The Cinema of Alexander Sokurov*, London and New York: I. B. Tauris, pp. 155–75.

Bessière, Jean (2005), 'Récit de fiction, transition discursive, présentation actuelle du passé: ou que le récit de fiction est toujours metaléptique', in John Pier and Jean-Marie Schaeffer (eds), *Métalepses, entorses au pacte de la représentation*, Paris: École des Hautes Études en Sciences Sociales, pp. 280–94.

Beumers, Birgit (2011), 'And the Ark Sails On . . .', in Birgit Beumers and Nancy Condee (eds), *The Cinema of Alexander Sokurov*, London and New York: I. B. Tauris, pp. 176–87.

Bolter, Jay David and Richard Grusin (2000), *Remediation: Understanding New Media*, Cambridge, MA and London: The MIT Press.

Bouko, Catherine (2014), 'Interactivity and Immersion in a Media-based Performance', *Participations: Journal of Audience and Reception Studies*, Vol. 11, No. 1, pp. 254–69.

Branigan, Edward (1992), *Narrative Comprehension and Film*, London and New York: Routledge.

Brewster, Ben and Lea Jacobs (1998), *Theatre to Cinema: Stage Pictorialism and the Early Feature Film*, Oxford and New York: Oxford University Press.

Carlson, Marvin (2002), 'The Resistance to Theatricality', *SubStance*, Vol. 31, No. 2/3, issue 98/99, pp. 238–50.

Condee, Nancy (2011), 'Endstate and Allegory', in Birgit Beumers and Nancy Condee (eds), *The Cinema of Alexander Sokurov*, London and New York: I. B. Tauris, pp. 188–99.

Féral, Josette and Ronald P. Birmingham (2002), 'Theatricality: The Specificity of Theatrical Language', *SubStance*, Vol. 31, No. 2/3, issue 98/99 pp. 94–108.

Fried, Michael (1980), *Absorption and Theatricality: Painting and Beholder in the Age of Diderot*, Chicago and London: The University of Chicago Press.
Genette, Gérard (2004), *Métalepse: De la figure à la fiction*, Paris: Éditions du Seuil.
Genette, Gérard (2005), 'De la figure à la fiction', in John Pier and Jean-Marie Schaeffer (eds), *Métalepses, entorses au pacte de la representation*, Paris: École des Hautes Études en Sciences Sociales, pp. 21–35.
Grau, Oliver (2003), *Virtual Art: From Illusion to Immersion*, Cambridge, MA and London: The MIT Press.
Jacobs, Steven (2011), *Framing Pictures: Film and the Visual Arts*, Edinburgh: Edinburgh University Press.
Kujundzic, Dragan (2003), 'After "After": The "Arkive" Fever of Alexander Sokurov', *ArtMargins* <http://www.artmargins.com/index.php/6-film-a-video/272-after-qafterq-the-qarkiveq-fever-of-alexander-sokurov> (last accessed 12 January 2019).
Machon, Josephine (2013), *Immersive Theatres: Intimacy and Immediacy in Contemporary Performance*, New York: Palgrave Macmillan.
Machon, Josephine (2016), 'Watching, Attending, Sense-Making: Spectatorship in Immersive Theatres', *Journal of Contemporary Drama in English*, Vol. 4, No.1, pp. 34–48.
Nasirov, Yasin (2016), 'Eulogy for Art, Elegy for History: Aura, Museification and Memory in/of *Francofonia* (2015) and *Russian Ark* (2002)', in *Avanca Cinema* 2016, Avanca: Edições Cineclube de Avanca, pp. 28–36.
Nilsson, Niels Christian, Rolf Nordhal and Stefania Serafin (2016), 'Immersion Revisited: A Review of Existing Definitions of Immersion in their Relation to Different Theories of Presence', *Human Technology*, Vol. 12, No. 2, pp. 108–34.
Pethő, Ágnes (2015), 'Between Absorption, Abstraction and Exhibition: Inflections on the Cinematic Tableau in the Films of Corneliu Porumboiu, Roy Andersson and Joanna Hogg', *Acta Universitatis Sapientiae: Film and Media Studies*, Vol. 11, pp. 39–76.
Ravetto-Biagioli, Kriss (2005), 'Floating on the Boarders of Europe: Sokurov's *Russian Ark*', *Film Quarterly*, Vol. 59, No. 1, pp. 18–26.
Stern, Nathanael (2011), 'The Implicit Body as Performance: Analyzing Interactive Art', *Leonardo*, Vol. 44, No. 3, pp. 233–8.
Szaniawski, Jeremi (2014), *The Cinema of Alexander Sokurov – Figures of Paradox*, London and New York: Wallflower Press.
Vouilloux, Bernard (2002), *Le tableau vivant. Phryné, l'orateur et le peintre*, Paris: Flammarion.
Weber, Samuel (2004), *Theatricality as a Medium*, New York: Fordham University Press.
White, Gareth (2012), 'On Immersive Theatre', *Theatre Research International*, Vol. 37, No. 3, pp. 221–35.
Youngblood, Denise J. (2011), 'A Day in the Life: Historical Representations in Sokurov's "Power" Tetralogy', in Birgit Beumers and Nancy Condee (eds), *The Cinema of Alexander Sokurov*, London and New York: I. B. Tauris, pp. 122–37.

Part 3

*Reflections upon Reality,
Representation and Power*

CHAPTER 9

The Real and the Intermedial in Alexander Sokurov's Family Trilogy

Malgorzata Bugaj

Alexander Sokurov's *Mother and Son* (*Mat i syn*, 1997), *Father and Son* (*Otets i syn*, 2003) and *Alexandra* (2007) share many narrative and stylistic similarities. Their stories are simple and dialogue sparse: in the first film, a son cares for his dying mother; in the second, a father and son explore their emotional bond knowing that the latter will soon leave; in the last, a grandmother visits her grandson, most probably for the last time. As allegories of idealised familial relations, these films give a concrete, physical form to powerful emotions translated into audio-visual representations. In addition to their minimalist narrative, each film unfolds at a meditative pace reminiscent of the conventions of slow cinema in which typically 'narrative interaction is dissolved in favour of sensory experience and aesthetic apprehension' (de Luca 2014: 10). This contemplative approach opens the space necessary to observe, on the one hand, the details of the presented world and, on the other, the artificiality of its cinematic construction.

The family trilogy constitutes an intensified investigation into the trace of the material presence on screen by connecting the sensual to the physical-biological and the socio-political in three distinct ways. Firstly, haptic images – which 'search the image for a trace of the originary, physical event' (Marks 2002: xi) – emphasise the multisensory experience of the world and accentuate bodily sensations. Secondly, references to the discourse of medicine (particularly in *Father and Son*) introduce a scientific analysis of the physicality of the body. Thirdly, the films insistently examine presented worlds from different angles and proximities, frequently coming intimately close to their subjects. These techniques combine to produce moments when the materiality of the on-screen reality is heightened; in this sense, the trilogy echoes de Luca's discussion of 'sensory realism' (2014: 1) – an attempt to represent the sensual which takes precedence over the purely representational functions of images and sounds.

Mother and Son, *Father and Son* and *Alexandra* consciously underscore the simultaneous awareness of film as a medium carrying the story along with references to other means of expression. Beumers and Condee point out that Sokorov's work

> is often a non-narrative visual experiment, somewhere between photography and painting, rather than film in the traditional sense of the term. Basically, we would suggest, Sokurov challenges that cinema conceived as a method either to capture or narrate reality. (Beumers and Condee 2011: 1)

The cinematic medium is rendered opaque by conspicuous distortions and manipulations of the visual elements of the films. The references to painting and medical images play a similar role; they are remediations – the representations of one medium in another – that echo Bolter and Grusin's (1999: 45) discussion of literary texts viewed online or Dutch painters incorporating maps in their works. Through repurposing other arts, Sokurov's family trilogy enters into a dialogue with other forms of expression.

In my consideration of *Mother and Son*, *Father and Son* and *Alexandra*, I am drawing on Brigitte Peucker's *The Material Image: Art and the Real in Film* (2007), a study of intermediality interrogating the relationship between cinema and 'the real' and referring to a variety of works from the broader field of visual arts. In particular, this analysis is an attempt to answer Peucker's question: 'in cinematic experience, what promotes the impression of reality, and when does medium awareness come into play?' (2007: 1). Each section investigates a discrete part of the family trilogy, examining the oscillation between the material and the stylised, the immediate and the mediated that is characteristic of these works.

MOTHER AND SON

Mother and Son, the film opening Sokurov's family trilogy, is the poetic tale of a son (Aleksei Ananishnov) who tends to his dying mother (Gudrun Geyer). The story takes place within a single day during which they begin a journey through an ethereal landscape. Most shots in *Mother and Son* are broad painterly panoramas of landscapes, the figures of characters lost in overwhelming nature. Less frequently, the camera frames them in medium shots. In contrast, the film finishes with prolonged extreme close-ups of the characters' skin, carefully drawing attention to the recognisable physical features of the human body. The bodily surface of the aged mother is juxtaposed with that of her young son to create skinscapes constructed out of layers of human skin.

While Sokurov's *oeuvre* has been considered exemplary of slow cinema (Jaffe 2014; de Luca and Barradas Jorge 2016; Lim 2014; Flanagan 2008), *Mother and Son* is one of the most pronounced representatives of the genre. The film operates within what Hänsgen calls the 'aesthetics of still images'

(2011: 44), with stillness created through long takes and long shots, minimal movement both of the camera and within the frame, repeated silence and depictions of landscapes fixed on screen. Other traits particular to slow cinema present here include the focus on the characters who 'sidestep the frenzy and modernity' (Jaffe 2014: 6) and 'the minimal narrative structure' (Flanagan 2008). *Mother and Son* follows characters living on the fringes of civilisation through their walks, punctuated by frequent rests and reminiscences. This part of the family trilogy can be classified as belonging to what Davis describes as 'a body of films that are purposefully concerned with waiting' (2017: 393). The slower pace renders the subjective perception of time almost palpable, which makes the film an exploration of experience: the approaching death of one of the characters.

According to Botz-Bornstein, Sokurov's cinema can be discussed in a way akin to traditional oil paintings: the landscapes chosen by the Russian director, the organisation of figures, the particular focus on texture and the use of colour make his films look 'more painterly than typically "cinematic"' (2007: 32). These tendencies are particularly prominent in *Mother and Son*, with scenes 'condensed to a few shots like cinematic paintings' (Hänsgen 2011: 50). Szaniawski, in turn, finds parallels in the works of classical painters, primarily Caspar David Friedrich whose influence is recognisable in the film (2014: 128). Friedrich's atmosphere of stillness, limited range of colours, nostalgic tone and focus on landscape rather than the human figure are echoed throughout the film. We see this in the similarities between *Mother and Son*'s shots of light and textures playing across fields and the ripe, yellow crops and the forms and colour palette of Friedrich's *Sunrise over the Sea* (1836), or in the scene with the hilly, misty landscape and *Riesengebirge Landscape with Rising Fog* (1820).

Mother and Son frequently deploys an array of experimental techniques, such as shooting through painted glass, or using mirrors and anamorphic lenses. In the film – 'stylised and aesthetically controlled to the extreme' (Szaniawski 2014: 127) – distortions of the image are introduced from the very first shot where we see the stretched silhouettes of the protagonists. The film explores skewed perspectives (for example in a scene when the son walks down the path), and unreal colours in landscape (e.g. in the depiction of the wind moving crops); it also emphasises a flatness of composition as well as its focus on textures. Distorted on screen, nature in the film is distancing and alienating 'as a result of which the audience's emotional engagement may be retarded, if not arrested' (Jaffe 2014: 60).

If, as Bolter and Grusin claim, 'the goal of remediation is to refashion or rehabilitate other media' (1999: 56), *Mother and Son* can be considered a cinematic experiment adapting the methods of painting along with the very experience of viewing the still image on canvas. Long takes coupled with particularly strong stylisation attempt to recreate an engagement with the on-screen image which is similar to that experienced with a painting: the slow, deliberate gaze of the camera encourages the viewer to ponder and admire the details such as varied hues and textures. A succession of nearly static images in the film invites a meditative approach to the visuals rather than a focus on the progressing narrative. In this way, the film translates the modality of the painting into the aesthetics of cinema, which confirms Szaniawski's remark that 'with *Mother and Son*, the medium procuring the commentary (film) comes several steps closer to the medium commented upon (painting)' (2014: 128). By highlighting the presence of the new medium (film) and entering into a dialogue with the older medium (painting), *Mother and Son* draws attention to the self-reflexive potential of film.

Painterly references in *Mother and Son* are also emphasised through the film's reliance upon long takes and long shots to place its subjects within a wider context (Figure 9.1). Here, the scenery plays the lead role; the silhouettes of the characters often lost in the landscape. The camera frequently abandons its focus on the human figure to explore the space that surrounds it. For instance, in a scene when the mother and son discuss their memories, the camera assumes a more distanced position in order to concentrate on their surroundings leaving the characters' silhouettes relegated to a third of the screen. Another example here is the sequence where the son carries his sick mother on a walk in which the characters are presented as if they were

Figure 9.1 Painterly influences in *Mother and Son* (1997) are highlighted through the film's reliance upon long takes and long shots employed to place the subjects within a wider context

travelling through a painting and can be distinguished from the background only through their movement. The rich texture of the surface, the limited colour palette, and reduced depth of the image resolve the silhouette and background into a single plane.

A similar de-emphasis of the human figure can be observed in the scenes depicting the mother against a backdrop of conspicuous surfaces. In these, she is presented in medium shots or close-ups focusing on her face. After the son sits her on the bench beneath the tree, their bodies and clothes in varied hues of grey and brown appear to merge with the background. As the woman rests, her eyes half closed, the bark of the tree mirrors her dry, wrinkled face. Later, when she lies amongst the crops, her pale face echoes the colour of the field behind her. Towards the end of the film, we watch the pale, sickly face of the mother melt into her surrounding: a stonewashed wall and the white sheet the son covers her with. In most scenes, composition, light and colour function to valorise the setting and purposefully avoid distinguishing or isolating the figure from the background.

In contrast to de-emphasising the figures of the characters, the three-minute-long final scene comes intimately close to their bodies and compels viewers to focus on the texture of their skin. The son mourns after the death of his mother: the close-up of her wrinkled, still hand against a backdrop of rough fabric fills the screen. The man's face comes close to his mother's inert body, first only as a shadow. His hands, young and glistening, travel slowly over the uneven surface of the woman's pale fingers, examining the delicate folds of her skin. As he moves further, an image of his throat stretched over the hand of the mother is brought to prominence and the film focuses on the trembling muscles and tendons of the sobbing son. The heavy silence of the final fragment is punctuated by the son's cries while the steady camera corresponds to the stillness of this moment.

Shown in extreme close-ups, the surfaces of the mother's and son's bodies are de-familiarised through scale and the attention they receive. This artificial amplification accentuates recognisable properties of skin: its roughness and dryness along with pores, hair and wrinkles. Here, the film focuses on skin as a raw material constructing an image with varied colours and textures. The surfaces of the individual bodies – that of the son and the mother – fill the screen. In this scene the film recalls the hilly scenery it presents in the preceding scene with the image constructed from varied typographical features, however, the geography of the landscape is replaced with that of the body. By presenting in close-ups the contrasting surfaces of the body, Sokurov creates 'surface-scapes' (Quinlivan 2012: 99), or the aforementioned skinscapes.

This extreme close-up contrasts with the previous depictions of the characters as either lost in overwhelming landscape or merged with their surroundings. In the closing scene, the bodies become the centre of attention (with almost no other elements present) and bring to the fore their material nature through the emphasis on the texture and hues of the skin along with the breath of the protagonist. Strikingly, this turn to materiality occurs in the moment of mother's death; death ultimately reveals the physicality of the flesh; this is the part of a human being that is sure to be turned into a lifeless form. The on-screen space is transformed to reflect the emotional state of the character – it is the mother's dead body that overwhelms the son.

Hänsgen claims that 'to Sokurov, the traditional medium of the fine arts serves as an inspirational reservoir of image motifs, shot compositions as well as perspective, light and colour arrangement' (2011: 50–1). *Mother and Son* is the most stylised part of the family trilogy: the presence of a new medium (film) and references to an older one (painting) are intertwined throughout the film. However, the use of an extreme close-up in the final scene, concentrating on the texture and colour of skin, represents an emphasis on the materiality of the body. By coming intimately close to its characters, *Mother and Son* opens a space in which it can engage with the trace of the physicality of the characters' bodies and produces what Peucker calls 'the material image' (2007: 8), that is the way the real is suggested by visual metaphors.

FATHER AND SON

Father and Son is a story of a war veteran father (Andrei Shchetinin) and his son, Alexei (Aleksei Neymyshev), a cadet in a military school. Shot between St Petersburg and Lisbon, the second part of the family trilogy is set in what Szaniawski aptly describes as an escapist, imaginary realm (2014: 207). Equally allegorical is the relationship of the father and son: it is loving and tender, frequently translated into physical closeness. The harsh military ethos of their shared army background contrasts strikingly with the trilogy's 'deep, visceral desire to restore the idyllic fusion between children and parents' (Iampolski 2011: 109).

The opening scene of the film – the recollection of a dream – links us back to *Mother and Son* with images of similarly stretched silhouettes and the same desolate scenery in an identical colour palette. Moreover, the presence of the medium is here also clearly accentuated through a number of techniques: colour filters, soft focus, anamorphic lenses and chiaroscuro effects, as well as filming through transparent objects, such as glass or X-ray photos. Jose Alaniz sees another link between both parts of the family trilogy: their allusions to the paintings of the great masters. While in the case of the former film, the reference point is mainly Caspar David Friedrich, in the case of the latter, it is Rembrandt (Alaniz 2010: 290), particularly considering Sokurov's use of colour along with shadow and light. Crucially, however, *Father and Son* moves mostly between close-ups and medium shots. In contrast to the first part of the family trilogy, *Father and Son* explores the bodies of its characters at varied proximities: from the investigation of their muscular figures, through extreme close-ups registering the skin (and breath), to an exploration of the father's bodily interior inscribed in the medical discourse. Such juxtaposition of different perspectives – as well as intertwining of medical (detached and objective) and haptic (close and engaged) images – enhances an illusion of the materiality of the presented bodies.

Father and Son pursues its preoccupation with the human corporeality by focusing on the sculpted bodies of two soldiers. The exploration of their physical figures begins with the opening scene where the main characters are presented half-naked and in each other's embrace. Throughout the film, we watch the father weightlifting on rooftops, or the son stepping out of the shower (Figure 9.2). Alexei is observed during martial arts training, or exercising on a ladder. The father and son play football and talk about their physical fitness; their muscular physiques are accentuated by sleeveless tops and tight T-shirts. Such underscoring of muscularity, in turn, implies strength and fitness. This echoes Dyer's analysis of male pin-ups in which he notes that muscles are generally associated with 'hard bodies' (1992: 274); strikingly, in Sokurov's film this hardness is nonetheless presented through soft focus.[1] The film's frequent references to sport (e.g. football, wrestling and gymnastics) provide the illustration of Dyer's note that 'sport is the area of life that is the most common contemporary source of male imagery' (1992: 271). Additionally, the camera and lights highlight

Figure 9.2 *Father and Son* (2003) pursues its preoccupation with the human corporeality by focusing on the sculpted bodies of two soldiers. The film can be viewed as a certain glorification of the male physique, but remains ambiguous as to whether these are displayed for the erotic gaze

the physicality of characters who are usually submerged in saturated sunlit yellows and oranges or subdued sepias which emphasise the skin, and frequently in close-ups underscoring texture and proximity. Repeatedly, subjects within the frame are partially obscured by a shadow which creates a chiaroscuro effect that sculpts the bodies.[2] *Father and Son* can be viewed as a certain glorification of the male physique, but while the film offers spectacles of corporealities turned into bodies-to-be-looked-at, it remains ambiguous as to whether these are displayed for the erotic gaze.[3]

This ambiguous eroticism is particularly prominent in the opening scene. *Father and Son* begins with a few seconds of a blank screen before we are able to distinguish the anguished breath[4] of two men, one trying to console the other. In the ensuing sequence, the soundtrack continues the close exploration of breath, while an image appears. We can see the distorted surface of the bodies presented in close-ups and through a soft lens: the depiction of struggling hands and naked chests pressed to one another. The next cut is to an image of open lips stretched on screen through an anamorphic lens; it is the space where the sound comes from. Finally, the image resolves into the clear figuration of two embracing men.

The beginning of *Father and Son* presents a certain incompleteness: first, it is the lack of images, then distorted close-ups fragmenting the bodies. The sonic and, later, visual puzzle, offering, to use Elliott's words 'a vague sensation rather than specific information' (2011: 171), refers us to Marks's notion of haptic visuality and her statement that 'rather than making the object fully available to view, haptic cinema puts the objects into question, calling on the viewer to engage in its imaginative construction' (2002: 16). Here, the spectator needs to create mental pictures based on sound while the concealed image is gradually revealed. After the image appears, the camera draws close, as if probing the body. Like the final scene of *Mother and Son*, the exteriors of two different corporealities create layers that construct the image; our eyes linger on the corporeal surfaces that fill the screen. With these skin-scapes, the close-ups of the father and son's bodies register their intimacy, as well as the muscularity of their silhouettes (which is similarly emphasised later in the film). This scene exemplifies vividly the family trilogy's play between the immediate and the mediated. It is vibrantly sensual and immerses the audience in the bodily experience of the characters. Yet, as Szaniawski pointed out, this fragment is 'verging on abstraction through close-ups and distortions' (2014: 193). This apparent attempt at creating haptic immediacy is connected with conspicuous artificiality of the scene, which points to the presence of the medium.

Father and Son considers the surface of the body not only as the site of sensations, but also as a cover, its appearance belying the condition of that which is beneath. By introducing medical elements, *Father and Son* comments on the bodies of the characters from the perspective of medicine. The use of medical images revealing the bodily interior, an X-ray and an anatomical poster, can be considered in terms of remediation, 'representation of one medium in another' (Bolter and Grusin 1999: 45). Here cinema enters into a dialogue with medical science retaining the awareness of the original scientific discourse. Medicine – with its focus on measuring and regulating (see Foucault's *Birth of the Clinic*) – understands an individual primarily as a material and biological entity. Under the auspices of science, the human body is turned into a biological specimen and investigated in the same way as an object of any other scientific observation; in Leder's words: 'the human body, while perhaps unusual in its complexity, is taken as essentially no different from any other physical object' (1990: 5).

An illustration of such intersection of the medical with the cinematic is the scene when Alexei returns home from the military academy and finds an X-ray of his father's ribcage. The medical photograph is first presented in close-up, the hand of the son slowly, almost tenderly travelling across its surface: the screen is filled with a black-and-white image of the corporeal interior. The film then cuts to the young man's blurred portrait shot in soft focus. The camera briefly dwells upon the father's silhouette as it 'appears behind him [Alexei], ghostlike, more a hazy reflection of Aleksei's inner thoughts than a concrete figure' (Alaniz 2010: 297). It then quickly returns to an examination of the son's expression that changes from a smile to a distressed frown as he investigates the roentgen representation. This time the face of the son is shown through an X-ray photograph which softens it even more: at this point the image is not clear – it is blurred and partially hidden in the shadow. 'It is your portrait', explains Alexei to his parent, 'it is still a photograph. Just a little more revealing. You are not hiding behind clothes . . . nor your muscles.' The son, who studies medicine as a part of his course, is capable of reading the photo, yet refrains from discussing it with his father.

As the hand of the son moves slowly across the surface of the radiographic photograph, almost caressing it, the film juxtaposes the exterior of the body with its interior. This close-up of the hand, with its focus on human skin and the act of touching, echoes the emotional overtones and intimacy of the opening scene. Additionally, the strong stylisation of this fragment – it is filmed through soft lenses with subtle hues – adds a personal and artistic touch to the image created in the detached and objective context of medical analysis.

Generally, X-ray images denote certain impersonal (that is medical) reality of the body. By penetrating the skin and unveiling the viscera, medical imaging technologies, such as roentgen rays, offer views that are unavailable to the naked eye. Skin ceases to be the boundary of the visible, the gaze of the observer is able to reach deeper, 'the border of the self is no longer the skin, the shape of the body no longer just the outline in the mirror, and the story of an individual body no longer just an autobiography' (Helman 1991: 99). In *Father and Son* the X-ray contributes to a more comprehensive biography of individuals by adding yet another dimension to their story. While photos shown later in the film and the dialogues throughout characterise the father and son by revealing the history of their relationship and the parent's war experiences, the X-ray conveys information about the father's old injury and reveals a mystery hidden within a seemingly healthy body.

Another reference to the medical perception of the body can be found in a scene which follows a game of football between the father and son. Alexei, pictured in medium close-up, is shown standing almost still between the spread arms of a painted figure in the background (Figure 9.3). This image is of a flayed human form portraying a gymnast on rings, his skin removed in order to demonstrate the anatomical position of muscles. The son smiles, appearing lost in his thoughts, his face lit by soft hues of sunlight as he listens to his father calling his name. The camera moves slightly around the Alexei's head, revealing more of the *écorché* figure and then, abandoning it, follows him as he walks around the apartment. Again, this scene is filmed through soft-focus lenses and sepia-tone filters, shadows and light playing within the image.

The scene discussed above harks back to early anatomical drawings and their distinctive aesthetic take on medicine. With a complete human face

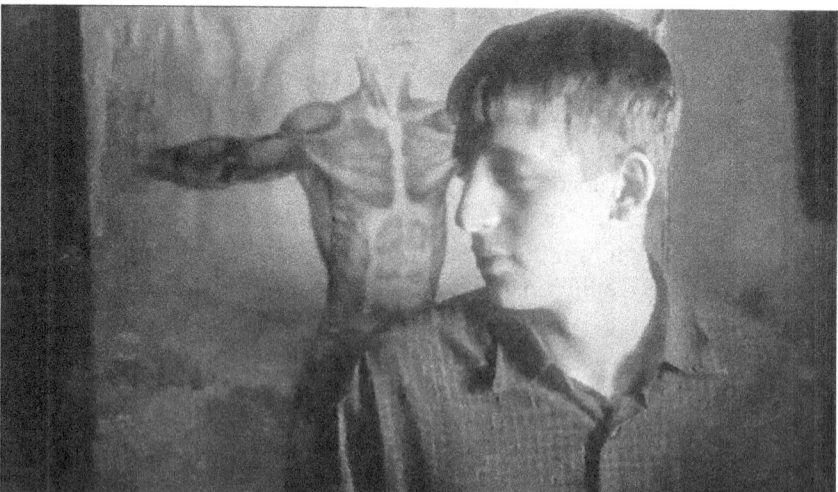

Figure 9.3 This image of a flayed human form in *Father and Son* (2003) points to early anatomical drawings and their distinctive aesthetic take on medicine intertwining the scientific with the artistic. It is also yet another way of emphasising the body of the character

(as the locus of the self), a stylised pose, and a prop (the rings, which place the body in context), the picture of the flayed figure appeals to the imagination of the lay audience. Anatomical drawings dating from the sixteenth to the eighteenth century – the most significant examples of which were created by Andreas Vesalius, Charles Estienne and Juan Valverde de Amusco – intertwine the scientific (distanced and objective) with the artistic (painterly and stylised) (Benthien 2002). In such depictions, bodies demonstrating certain aspects of human anatomy frequently assume the poses of classical sculptures, and are presented against the background of a landscape, or supplied with a prop (Rifkin et al. 2006: 16). These images were designed to correlate the human body as it appears every day with the human anatomy within.

In *Father and Son*, the fragment presenting Alexei exercising on the rings draws parallels between the anatomical image of the flayed figure and the son's body, as both are portrayed in the same position. This is also another way the film underscores the perfect physical form of the son. The X-ray, in turn, is similarly associated with the hidden depths of his father's body. Through the introduction of the medical realism, the film examines the characters from yet another angle – that of scientific, quantifying medical analysis, which points to the biological materiality of the human body.

The second part of Sokurov's family trilogy accentuates the stylised and the constructed through its use of colours, light, soft focus as well as distorting lenses. However, these manipulations of the image emphasise the physicality of characters, juxtaposing haptic images of the body with pictures captured with scientific detachment. The penetration of the inside and outside, as well as the juxtaposition of the haptic and medical, draws attention to the material and biological dimension of the human body and thus emphasises the trace of the physical presence on screen.

Alexandra

Continuing the military theme of *Father and Son*, this time in a Russian army camp in Chechnya, *Alexandra* sketches a portrait of a grandmother (Galina Vishnevskaya) who visits her grandson, Denis (Vasily Shevtsov), a captain in the Russian army. The titular elderly woman travels together with a group of military men and stays with them in a camp. *Alexandra* extends the trilogy's preoccupation with family ties, but is less concerned with myth and contains fewer intermedial references than the previous films. As Szaniawski notes, 'it certainly boasts the most transparent, "televisual" style of *mise en scène* and editing in his [Sokurov's] corpus, and is very "realistic" in every other aspect: shot on location, with real props and costumes' (2014: 242). Indeed, the fact of mediation is here less conspicuous, but still present: an example is *Alexandra*'s employment of a limited palette of desaturated greens, greys and yellows strengthened by the use of filters. Also, in contrast to previous parts of the family trilogy, this film is situated in a definite socio-political context and can be read as a comment on the Chechen war (Szaniawski 2014: 241–2). Additionally, by exploring the materiality of the presented world and by offering vivid depictions of the landscapes, objects and human bodies interpreted through multiple senses, *Alexandra* lends greater immediacy to the cinematic experience.

The final instalment of Sokurov's family trilogy begins with a sequence introducing Alexandra. She is portrayed in medium close-up from the back (she sits inside a bus, her hair pinned in a bun), the camera pans down to focus on her feet (she leaves the bus), it shows her from the front (she examines her surroundings) and then moves slightly around the character. Finally, a zoom-out reveals her whole figure: she stands against the background of a desolate landscape, looking slightly lost. With its insistent gaze, the camera examines Alexandra's body from different angles and proximities.

In the next scene Alexandra, accompanied by a few soldiers, walks to a train station. Upon entering the carriage, she is greeted by men in military uniforms: the camera is fixed on the woman's face while the recruits only appear in a flash by as they pass. After the young men assume their places, the camera scans their features: we look at similar bodies, in the same uniforms and with identically organised sets of activities. The soldiers stare at Alexandra emphasising her incongruence (Figure 9.4). This part of the family trilogy

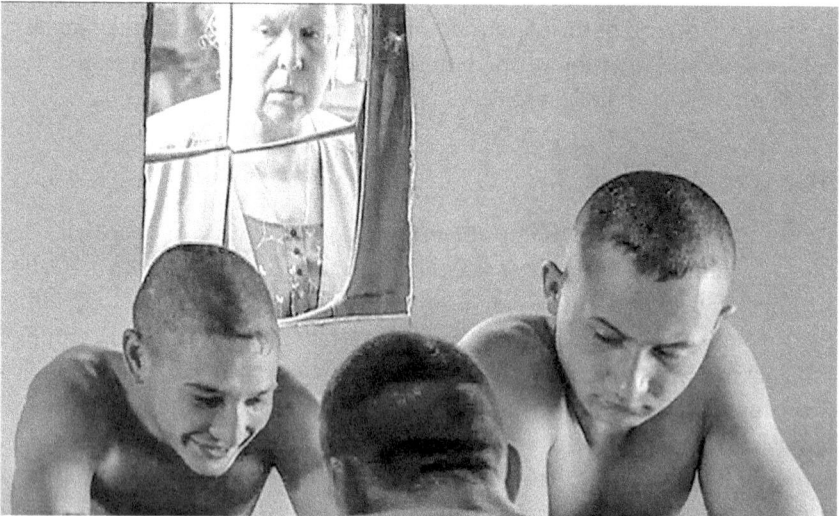

Figure 9.4 *Alexandra* (2007): juxtaposing the elderly woman with young soldiers. A series of opposing pairs explored in the film calls attention to the physical properties of the main character's body

is founded on contrasts: the elderly titular character is compared with the young soldiers; her wrinkled, dry skin is contrasted with their sweaty muscles. The film juxtaposes the individual and the group, youth and maturity, women and men. This series of opposing pairs calls attention to the physical properties of the main character's body.

The investigation of materiality continues through the film's attention to diverse surfaces. As Donaldson claims, 'some films are prominently textured, featuring elements of clothing, environment and bodies that appeal to our tactile sense' (2014: 1); *Alexandra* is one of those densely textured cinematic works. Its narrow colour range calls attention to the textures of objects (steel, wool, wood and rubber), bodies (skin) and landscape (dry and sandy). Rough surfaces clash with smooth ones, slick and glossy with coarse and dusty. Alexandra has ample opportunity to investigate the space in close proximity. After the first night spent in the army camp, she wakes up in bright daylight and notices a man curled on the bed on the other side of the room. He is asleep which gives the woman a chance to examine his body and his belongings. The camera assumes her point of view and offers close-ups of the objects she investigates: a pair of boots and socks along with a military uniform. As Alexandra leans over her sleeping grandson, she focuses on the head and arms of the soldier. Her gaze slowly moves down to Denis's bruised feet. This scene pays particular attention to the conspicuous textures: the uneven surface of the unpolished wooden floor, mud on the leather boots, the roughness of his woollen socks and the fabric of the military uniform.

Alexandra scans the objects soldiers interact with; the camera mimics her gaze through persistently repeated close-ups registering 'haptically charged surfaces' (Elsaesser and Hagener 2010: 124). The film explores military vehicles and weapons: the metal of tanks and cars – greasy and glistening just like the skin of soldiers – and the rubber of the tyres. In one of the scenes, Alexandra is seen inside a tank surrounded by steel, cables and rubber; these are slowly investigated at intimate proximity. In another sequence, we watch soldiers cleaning their weapons; the camera observes the clash of textures – those of oil and stone – and examines the roughness of a cloth presented against a background of unpolished wood. Here, the shiny, greasy surfaces of guns collide with those of leather and wood. These scenes vividly illustrate Balázs's statement that 'the magnifying glass of the cinematograph brings us closer to the individual cells of life, it allows us to feel the texture and substance of life in its concrete detail' (2010: 38). They also recall Doane's remark that the close-up 'supports the cinema's aspiration to be the vehicle of presence' (2003: 93). Through frequent use of tactile close-ups, texture in *Alexandra* becomes central to the viewer's experience and heightens the awareness of the materiality of the presented world.

Although the final instalment of family trilogy is set in the masculine domain of the overtly detached army camp, the film features numerous moments presenting – or alluding to – gentle touch. In one of them, the grandmother begins unplaiting her hair and Denis helps her. In two repeated, almost identical scenes, the camera closes in on his hands and follows the movements of his fingers in extreme close-up as they play with the woman's hair. The image, composed of hair and skin against a background of textiles, fills the screen. The focus, again, is on the textures: of Alexandra's dry hair, of her dress, and of Denis's rough hands. After a while, when the haptic returns to the optical, we can see the woman in the embrace of her grandson. A few moments later, following an intimate conversation, Denis combs and plaits Alexandra's hair. As the grandmother and grandson recall tactile memories from the soldier's childhood, he repeats a ritual from when he was a little boy.

In her meditations on film's power to call on senses other than vision and hearing, Marks considers cinema's capacity to appeal to touch. For Marks, 'the vision itself can be tactile, as though one were touching a film with one's eyes' (2000: xi). Tactile vision imitates touch, or rather, constitutes a certain attempt at evoking traces of the tactile. The gaze 'moves along the surface of the object' (Marks 2000: xiii), thus, as a viewer, one is (figuratively) 'touching a film with one's eyes' (Marks 2000: xi). In the scene discussed above, the close-ups of contrasting textures – the dry skin of Alexandra and the young shiny skin of Denis – encourage the vision to linger on the surface of the characters' bodies. Additionally, the depictions of the characters immersed in tactile experiences index physical and emotional proximity and appeal to the memory of the sensation (Marks 2000: 113). This evocation of touch and textures captures not only the closeness, but also emphasises the on-screen trace of the physical.

As a newcomer and outsider, the titular character explores new and unfamiliar places with very acutely tuned senses; these include not only touch but also smell. *Alexandra* pays ample attention to olfactory sensations in the army camp. Military life is characterised by a variety of smells: of male bodies, weapons, tents, wooden structures, machines, military vehicles and food. The titular character is immersed in odours that are new to her and, as a visitor, she perceives them more intensely. Inside the tank that Denis shows to her, she remarks: 'It smells.' 'It's the guns, the iron, the men. You'll get used to it', replies her grandson. In another of her excursions, the woman comes upon a sentry post and encounters two soldiers. They reluctantly allow her to sit down in their hut: 'It stinks of dog in here', warns one of the soldiers. 'It always smells of something here. I am getting used to it', answers Alexandra. The act of smelling features next to the experience of touch in a gentle encounter between Alexandra and her grandson. Denis smells his grandmother's hair in order to evoke memories from his childhood.

Through her references to the soldiers' heat-oppressed and sweaty bodies we are constantly reminded that they are not indurate. 'You can wash your clothes', Alexandra states when a soldier helps her leave the train, and upon meeting Denis for the first time since her arrival, she jokingly comments: 'You're all sweaty! Where are your manners?' Such remarks make us aware that this setting should be understood also through the sense of smell; the film suggests the olfactory qualities of the images. References to odours can also enhance the viewer's experience and understanding of the on-screen space. This resonates with Marks's description of haptic visuality as inspiring 'an acute awareness that the thing seen evades vision and must be approached through other senses – which are not literally available in cinema' (2000: 191).

With the opening scene exploring the body of the main character from different angles and proximities – and placing it firmly both within a clear socio-political context and in contrast to other bodies – *Alexandra* establishes itself as a film preoccupied with the material. Such an approach is strengthened by the film's investigation of the proximal senses of touch and smell as well as its contemplation of details and conspicuous textures via the close-ups of the camera. *Alexandra* encourages spectators to 'almost touch' the places and objects its central character explores contributing to a heightened illusion of the physicality of the presented world and evoking what de Luca calls 'sensory realism' (2014: 1).

Alexander Sokurov's Family Trilogy: Self-Conscious Stylisation and the 'Reality Effect'

Mother and Son, Father and Son and *Alexandra* consciously employ techniques that underscore both the presence of the medium and what de Luca describes as 'realities highlighted in their sensory, phenomenal and material plenitude' (2014: 11). In the case of *Mother and Son*, the conspicuous opacity of the medium is brought to the fore throughout the film, with characters often lost in the painting-like landscape. However, the final close-up draws attention to the material properties of the presented bodies and the intimate nature of the experience depicted in this sequence. In contrast, *Father and Son* is preoccupied with the physicality of on-screen bodies, insistently investigating them from a variety of perspectives and proximities. By juxtaposing haptic images with medical appropriations, this part of the family trilogy focuses on the sensual along with the biological by enhancing the perspective of the viewer with medical images of the body's interior. However, here the medium does not attempt to be transparent: the image is often presented through distorting lenses and bathed in bright, unreal colours. Meanwhile, *Alexandra* is set within a clear socio-political context and shows the reality of army camp life by drawing attention to the multisensory aspects of the presented world, especially through references to touch and smell. It too is heavily stylised, particularly in terms of the colour treatment, light and grain of on-screen images. Hence the duality of the trilogy: it successfully opens a dialogue with other media not only by featuring them directly, but also by appropriating their techniques. Viewed together, these films create what could be interpreted as an orchestrated search for the trace of the material in cinema.

Notes

1. Here Szaniawski's observation that the film 'is bathed in hues that connect it to at least one major landmark of queer cinema' (2014: 185–6) might open new avenues for interpretation.
2. This prompted Alaniz to point to the similarities of the opening scene to Rembrandt's *The Sacrifice of Isaac* (2010: 290).
3. The ambivalent sensual and erotic charge of the film evoked contrasting responses from the critics: Iampolski, for example, dismisses reading of the film as homoerotic (2011: 116), while Szaniawski points that Sokurov's previous films feature strong homoerotic representations of beautiful male bodies (2014: 185–7).
4. The proximity of the camera to the bodies of the father and son is additionally emphasised by evoking breath. For Quinlivan, 'hearing the "grain" of a breathing body posits a dimension of breathing visuality informed specifically through sound and its haptic implication' (2012: 137). To foreground breath is to engage in intimacy, to recall the trace of the material object on screen and to 'offer a profound sense of the palpability of the body' (Quinlivan 2012: 139).

Works Cited

Alaniz, Jose (2010), 'Vision and Blindness in Sokurov's *Father and Son*', in Helena Goscilo and Yana Hashamova (eds), *Cinepaternity. Fathers and Sons in Soviet and Post-Soviet Film*, Bloomington: Indiana University Press, pp. 282–309.

Balázs, Béla (2010), *Early Film Theory: Visible Man and The Spirit of Film*, transl. Rodney Livingstone, New York and Oxford: Berghahn Books.

Benthien, Claudia (2002), *Skin: On the Cultural Border between Self and the World*, New York: Columbia University Press.

Beumers, Birgit and Nancy Condee (eds), (2011), *The Cinema of Alexander Sokurov*, London: I. B. Tauris.

Bolter, J. David and Richard Grusin (1999), *Remediation: Understanding New Media*, Cambridge, MA and London: The MIT Press.

Botz-Bornstein, Thorsten (2007), *Films and Dreams: Tarkovsky, Bergman, Sokurov, Kubrick, and Wong Kar-Wai*, Lanham, MD: Lexington.

Davis, Glyn (2017), '"Waiting as Such": The Politics of Tarrying', *Aniki. Portugese Journal of the Moving Image*, Vol. 4, No. 2, pp. 392–410.

de Luca, Tiago (2014), *Realism of the Senses in World Cinema. The Experience of Physical Reality*, London: I. B. Tauris.

de Luca, Tiago and Nuno Barradas Jorge (2016), 'Introduction: From Slow Cinema to Slow Cinemas', in Tiago de Luca and Nuno Barradas Jorge (eds), *Slow Cinema*, Edinburgh: Edinburgh University Press, pp. 1–21.

Doane, Mary Ann (2003), 'The Close-Up: Scale and Detail in the Cinema', *Differences: A Journal of Feminist Cultural Studies*, Vol. 14, No. 3, pp. 89–111.

Donaldson, Lucy Fife (2014), *Texture in Film*, Basingstoke: Palgrave Macmillan.

Dyer, Richard (1992), 'Don't Look Now: The Male Pin-up', in Mandy Merck (ed.), *The Sexual Subject. A 'Screen' Reader in Sexuality*, London and New York. Routledge, pp. 265–76.

Elliott, Paul (2011), *Hitchcock and the Cinema of Sensations: Embodied Film Theory and Cinematic Reception*, London: I. B. Tauris.

Elsaesser, Thomas and Malte Hagener (2010), *Film Theory: An Introduction through the Senses*, New York: Routledge.

Flanagan, Matthew (2008), 'Towards an Aesthetic of Slow in Contemporary Cinema', *16:9 in English*, No. 29 (November) <http://www.16-9.dk/2008-11/side11_inenglish.htm> (last accessed 12 January 2019).

Foucault, Michel [1963] (2003), *The Birth of the Clinic*, London: Routledge.

Hänsgen, Sabine (2011), 'Sokurov's Cinematic Minimalism', in Birgit Beumers and Nancy Condee (eds), *The Cinema of Alexander Sokurov*, London: I. B. Tauris, pp. 43–56.

Helman, Cecil (1991), *Body Myths: The Werewolf, Medusa and the Radiological Eye*, London: Chatto & Windus.

Iampolski, Mikhail (2011), 'Truncated Families and Absolute Intimacy', in Birgit Beumers and Nancy Condee (eds), *The Cinema of Alexander Sokurov*, London: I. B. Tauris, pp. 109–131.

Jaffe, Ira (2014), *Slow Movies: Countering the Cinema of Action*, London: Wallflower Press.

Leder, Drew (1990), *The Absent Body*, Chicago and London: University of Chicago Press.

Lim, Song Hwee (2014), *Tsai Ming-Liang and a Cinema of Slowness*, Honolulu: University of Hawaii Press.

Marks, Laura U. (2000), *The Skin of the Film: Intercultural Cinema, Embodiment, and the Senses*, Durham, NC: Duke University Press.

Marks, Laura U. (2002), *Touch: Sensuous Theory and Multisensory Media*, Minneapolis: University of Minnesota.

Peucker, Brigitte (2007), *The Material Image: Art and the Real in Film*, Stanford, CA: Stanford University Press.

Quinlivan, Davina (2012), *The Place of Breath in Cinema*, Edinburgh: Edinburgh University Press.

Rifkin, Benjamin A., Michael J. Ackerman and Judy Folkenberg (2006), *Human Anatomy: Depicting the Body from the Renaissance to Today*, London: Thames & Hudson.

Szaniawski Jeremi (2014), *The Cinema of Alexander Sokurov: Figures of Paradox*, London: Wallflower Press.

CHAPTER 10

This is Not Magritte: Corneliu Porumboiu's Theory of Representation
Zsolt Gyenge

> *Porumboiu is a filmmaker obsessed with definitions and signs.* (Alice Bardan 2012: 127)

Minimalism, Realism, neo-Realism – these are the terms most often used to describe the Romanian New Wave in the critical and scholarly discourse. Maria Ioniță describes this 'distinctive brand of realism' as a 'type of realism [that] demonstrates a gift for the patient observation of characters and surroundings, and an attraction towards the more unvarnished, marginal or muted aspects of reality' (2015: 176). This emphasis on different aspects of Realism is definitely a novelty and a defining feature of films produced after 2000, especially when compared to the metaphorical-allegorical mode of expression that dominated the Romanian cinema of the 1980s and 90s. However, one of the main goals of this essay is to transcend the discourse of Realism on Romanian cinema, because if we consider Realism as a general characteristic for the whole New Wave, the meaning of the term will become too broad and the differences between filmmakers will disappear.

Though most scholars agree that despite some similarities, the cinema of Corneliu Porumboiu represents a distinctive voice within the Romanian New Wave, they are still reluctant to abandon the terminology and the theories of Realism.[1] Andrei State (2014), for example acknowledges that Porumboiu's cinema differs from the approach of other Romanian directors, but will only go as far as analysing his works through a more nuanced spectrum of Realism.[2] Contesting this discourse on Realism, I will argue that Porumboiu is not a realist filmmaker, he is merely theorising the possibilities of Realism, more precisely those of the representation of reality.[3] Although his stories are deeply rooted in the social realities of contemporary Romania, they provide a cinematic and narrative discussion of some major theories of representation. After analysing the most important topics and scenes where Porumboiu's interrogations regarding representation can be identified, I will briefly investigate on the 'philosophic' nature of Porumboiu's cinema. I will try to answer the question whether his films can be interpreted as 'direct theory' – a term introduced by Edward S. Small (1994: 5) to describe the way in which experimental cinema can be seen as a kind of implicit philosophical discourse. Furthermore, do Porumboiu's films provide perhaps a substantial philosophy of audio-visual representation in cinema in a similar way as we see in René Magritte's 'philosophical' paintings, for example?

As we will see, in Porumboiu's films the investigations regarding the theory of representation evolve around two major issues. The first one is related to the mediality of representations, as the Romanian director quite often creates situations where the difference between the media characteristics of representations, especially their verbal or visual nature lies at the heart of a situation of conflict in the narrative. The ways in which images, signs and symbols can communicate and the difference between the possibilities and limits of the various systems of signification seem to be crucial in almost all of his films. The second major issue addressed by Porumboiu is the relation of representation to reality and truth. How can one be sure that a representation (be it verbal or visual) is an actual and truthful rendering of a reality that exists independently of that representation? What happens to representations when fictional or non-existing entities are being represented? In what follows I will discuss Porumboiu's cinematic theory of representation around these two major issues.

THE MEDIALITY OF REPRESENTATIONS

The protagonist of *Police, Adjective* (*Polițist, adjectiv*, 2009) is a small-town detective whose task is to follow three high-school teenagers smoking weed during school-breaks, and after collecting enough evidence, to prosecute them. The conflict of the story emerges from the fact that Cristi, the detective, considers that smoking weed is not worth the severe punishment prescribed by Romanian laws. This is why after each day of stalking and observation he tries to give such an account of the events to his superiors that could suggest that nothing serious has happened. The problem he is facing is that of representation and communication: each night he has to deliver a linguistic description of the events he has observed, but the judiciary terminology and the formal rules of the report do not seem to allow him to accurately formulate his interpretation of the situation. He observes a few kids fooling around, but the kind of 'phenomenological' description of the events that he produces afterwards leads his superiors to the conclusion that youngsters have committed a crime that is punishable according to the law.

Maria Ioniță starts her analysis of the film with a comparison to two Magritte paintings that question the visual representability of reality and, also, reveal the fundamental incompatibility of the visual and the linguistic. She argues that in a similar way to Magritte, the first two films of Porumboiu 'represent a deliberate exploration of the limits of cinematic realism and a polemic engagement in cinema's ability to present an objective snapshot of the real' (Ioniță 2015: 173–4). One important feature of Porumboiu's cinema – which uses long takes like Cristian Mungiu or Radu Muntean – is that major events that involve the protagonists in the narrative take place outside of the frame: the revolution in *12:08 East of Bucharest* (*A fost sau n-a fost?*, 2006), the drug dealing of the teenagers in *Police, Adjective*, the shooting of the film within the film in *When Evening Falls on Bucharest or Metabolism* (*Când se lasă seara peste București sau metabolism*, 2013), and finally the actual discovery of the treasure in *The Treasure* (*Comoara*, 2015). 'All that is left in the frame is a sense of form and organization – an apparently accurate rendition of reality from which meaning has been somehow excised: a pipe which is not a pipe' (Ioniță 2015: 178). In what follows, I will contextualise and interpret Porumboiu's cinematic analysis of verbal and visual signs through the discussion of Foucault's and Mitchell's semiotic approach to Magritte, and through Roland Barthes's and Gadamer's description of the relation of signs, images and symbols.

In his famous paper entitled *This is Not a Pipe* Foucault argues that Magritte's painting *La trahison des images* (1928–9) can be understood through the analysis of the peculiar phenomenon of the calligram.

> The calligram uses that capacity of letters to signify both as linear elements that can be arranged in space and as signs that must unroll according to a unique chain of sound. [. . .] Thus, the calligram aspires playfully to efface the oldest oppositions of our alphabetical civilization: to show and to name; to shape and to say; to reproduce and to articulate; to imitate and to signify; to look and to read. (Foucault 1983: 21)

We can draw the conclusion that Magritte's strategy of bringing the relation of the verbal and visual representation into focus is based on the derailment of the functioning of the two systems of signification. According to W. J. T. Mitchell, *La trahison des images* is a third order metapicture, where

> it isn't simply that the words contradict the image, and vice versa, but that the very identities of words and images, the sayable and the seeable, begin to shimmer and shift in the composition, as if the image could speak and the words were on display. (Mitchell 1994: 68)

There is a scene in *Police, Adjective* when the protagonist tries in vain to convince his bosses (first the prosecutor, then the commander) that contrary to what one might deduce from his official reports, there is nothing serious (like drug dealing) taking place among the teenagers. As we will see shortly, he challenges the limits of written and visual communication and acknowledges the incompatibility of the two, and thus faces a problem of (visual) representation characteristic of modernist art. Only that his conclusion is somehow opposite to that of Magritte, who in the twelfth issue of the journal *La Révolution surréaliste* published a kind of visual dictionary through which he argued that in visual representation the images are as arbitrary as the linguistic signs and the material of (written) words and images is identical (Magritte 1929). The detective of Porumboiu's film believes in the authenticity of his direct (visual) experience, but, with his limited verbal means, he is incapable of articulating his uncertain feelings and intuitions based on his immediate experience of the events. For him, until the last scene of the film, the real chasm is between reality and its representation in a system of significations, where meaning seems to be encoded in advance in the very nature of the pre-established set of signs that can be used (i.e. definitions in a dictionary, the language of the law).

Analysing a Panzani advertisement, Roland Barthes argues that if we remove all verbal signs from the picture, we will remain with a message that uses signs which do not originate in any institutionalised set of signs, and thus we get to a paradoxical 'message without a code'. These messages, says Barthes, and in fact

> all images are polysemous; they imply, underlying their signifiers, a 'floating chain' of signifieds, the reader able to choose some and ignore others. Polysemy poses a question of meaning and this question always comes through as a dysfunction [. . .]. Hence in every society various techniques are developed intended to fix the floating chain of signifieds in such a way as to counter the terror of uncertain signs; the linguistic message is one of these techniques. [. . .] The denominative function corresponds exactly to an anchorage of all the possible (denoted) meanings of the object by recourse to a nomenclature. [. . .] When it comes to the 'symbolic message', the linguistic message no longer guides identification but interpretation, constituting a kind of vice which holds the connoted meanings from proliferating. (Barthes 1987: 38–9)

Such a technique is observable in *Police, Adjective*, where the protagonist is forced to fix the 'proliferating' connotations of his direct experience within the precise grammar and vocabulary of the judicial language when he is writing his surveillance reports. The only thing to report regarding his workday is that the three teenagers have actually smoked weed together. This process becomes even more evident, when his superiors (first the prosecutor, then the commander) as representatives of the institution and thus of the institutionalised semantics, make him precisely define the meaning of the words. The commander actually accuses him of 'being sick' if he does not know the meaning of the words he is using. Cristi's strategy seems to be to avoid this kind of anchoring of his direct experiences into the linguistic system. At the beginning of the film, when explaining the case to the prosecutor he starts by trying to make his boss avoid the use of the label 'dealer', arguing that the guy is not selling the drugs, he just shares it with two of his friends. But this leads him to a dead end, because when he tries to argue the inadequacy of the Romanian law to the European ones, they both get involved in a funny conversation on pretentious labels given to cities in Eastern Europe (The Golden City, The Little Paris), thus creating the illusion that labels are not so important. While – as Cristi will find out – in the judicial procedures they are crucial. He realises this in the famous final scene, where the police commander corrects him every step of the way, even when he uses slang terminology instead of the adequate linguistic terms of the law. Cristi's case to protect the teenagers is lost not on the field, not during the investigation, not even due to the hierarchical position towards his bosses, but in the moment when he is forced to accept to precisely define every word he is using with the help of a dictionary. From that moment on he is completely unable to use a more subjective, sometimes metaphorical language to express 'a floating chain of signifieds'.

Cristi's central struggle in *Police, Adjective* is to translate his undefined visual and direct experience into the conventionalised system of language, and while doing this, he makes several efforts to understand the functioning of representation with the help of his wife. One evening arriving home he finds her in front of the computer listening endlessly to a Romanian pop song; after having finished dinner, he sits near her, and begins to mock the song analysing the banal but poetic lyrics with the same semiotic rigour that will be exercised soon on his words by his bosses. First she replies that verses such as 'What would the sea be without sun? What would the field be without flower?' are images, but when he asks if she is picturing any image while listening, she corrects herself by saying that these are in fact symbols, because they refer to love as an absolute. Thus, in her account the song tries to define the ideal love with the help of words used as symbols, in the sense that their referent is much larger than the strict sense of the word: sea means the infinite, the sun refers to light, the field stays for birth and creation, while flower means beauty.

I suggest trying to understand Cristi's and his wife's semiotic inquiry following Gadamer's taxonomy of signs, symbols and images. According to him the two extremes of representation between which every form of representation can be identified are the sign and the symbol. 'The essence of the picture is situated, as it were, halfway between two extremes: these extremes of representation are pure indication (*Verweisung*: also, reference), which is the essence of the sign, and pure substitution (*Vertreten*), which is the essence of the symbol. There is something of both in a picture.' The sign completely effaces itself in order to indicate something else 'in such a way that the absent thing, and that alone, comes to mind'; while the symbol does not only indicate or refer, but also represents in the sense that it makes immediately present something that is not here (Gadamer 2004: 145, 147). Thus, for Gadamer the picture is situated between these two extremes in the sense that it is capable of indicating something, but in a certain way it also stands in the place of the represented thing: it causes us 'to linger over it' but without disappearing 'in pointing to something else' (Gadamer 2004: 146).

Though acknowledging its revelatory characteristic, I argue for a different schema of the three elements of representation, where the two extremes would be the sign – that is, complete indication and self-deletion – and the picture that invites us to linger over it, that is capable of conveying something about the represented without 'sending us away' from the picture itself. The antithesis of complete self-deletion and indication is the emphasised 'lingering over', the attraction of attention towards itself – which is the definition of the picture, according to Gadamer. In this schema the symbol is to be found in the middle, for its appearance has a certain informative value in itself, but its ontological status is still strictly connected to the thing it is standing for. This structure can also be argued for by looking at the arbitrariness of representation: the complete freedom of choice in the case of signs is opposed to the close relation of the picture to the pictured thing. The symbol is to be found in the middle in this respect too, because though there is a certain arbitrariness in choosing the symbols, a kind of analogous relation to the represented thing is always present.

Returning to *Police, Adjective* one can observe that Cristi's direct visual observation clearly belongs to the category of pictures, his and our 'lingering over' is evident during the painstakingly long shots. Interestingly enough he never takes photos to illustrate his reports, so he is constrained by the use of linguistic signs, that are not capable in any way of making the described things or phenomena present, and thus observable for those who have not been able to actually see what he is talking about. In the argument with his wife developed around the lyrics of the pop song, Cristi says that instead of complicated and fuzzy symbols like the sea or the field, the word used in the song should have directly been 'the infinite'. This will prove to be crucial in the development of the events, as this is the moment where he seems to accept that signs and thus verbal representations are the most adequate means for precise communication. Another argument for using the distorted Gadamerian schema to describe the relationship between different forms of representation is provided in the same scene by the wife, who corrects her own description of the song (that it consists of images) by saying that they are in fact 'images that have become symbols'. This makes it clear that she also pictures images and symbols as being similar, but different instances of the same system of signification. Thus, we can say, that actual images can sometimes become symbols through their (over)use – as the image of the Eiffel Tower has become the symbol of the French capital. The same trio of representations seems to be at work in the final scene of the film. Here Cristi argues that the police should overlook the general rules of the law, and instead pay attention to the individual details, to 'linger over' the image of the actual people in question, while the Commander is on the side of the precise definitions offered by the verbal communication. Whereas at the end of the scene, when Cristi is forced to plan the sting operation, he draws a map, which should be considered as something in between the two, being a symbol that uses conventional signs, but also resembling the space of which it is the map.

A somehow similar shift in type of representation can be observed in Porumboiu's 2015 film, *The Treasure*. The story revolves around a treasure that was supposedly hidden somewhere in the garden of the protagonist's neighbour, who asks him to help find it. The semiotic interest is manifested already when the men make several efforts to decode the metal detector's system of signification. But what is most relevant to us here is the last twist of the story, when after having found a treasure in the form of old, but seemingly quite valuable Mercedes bonds, in order to make the story of the treasure credible for his son, the protagonist transforms the signs of wealth (that is, the bonds) into another form that can also be interpreted as a more universally recognised symbol of wealth (jewellery), thus creating a new type of representation. The plain paper bonds meant nothing to the protagonist's young son, to whom his father had been reading the story of Robin Hood every day; thus he needed an actual treasure that could be seen on the one hand as wealth in itself, as an object, but would also appear as the symbolic representation of richness in the mind of the child.

Cristi's struggle to express his experiences in *Police, Adjective* leads us to one of the main questions of phenomenology. As László Tengelyi explains, Husserl is concerned with the relationship of the perceptual experience and its expression when he talks about an apparent contradiction. First, he argues that even the simplest perception of an object contains a categorical surplus of meaning, that is, something that goes beyond the simple apperception of the object lying ahead of us. From the other perspective, however, Husserl also acknowledges that every linguistic phrase contains a surplus of meaning compared to the appearing object (Tengelyi 2007: 49). This means that the word and the appearance of the object it describes overlap only partially. Drawing on Husserl, Tengelyi argues for the understanding of the experience 'as an event in which new meaning emerges by itself' (2007: 345, my translation). However, he also adds that in the life of human beings, experience without expression, language and concept does not occur. This, however, does not change the fact that experience contains a surplus compared to the linguistic meanings that express it and that, by their own nature, can never perfectly overlap with it (see Tengelyi 2007: 347). Maria Ioniță's interpretation regarding the issue of perception revolves around the comparison of vision and language, as she contends that in *Police, Adjective* 'in the absence of vision, words take over' – even though the protagonist, as his reaction to his wife's song analysis shows, is sceptical towards the expressive power of language. This is how

> the trajectory of *Police, Adjective* goes from subjective vision (inaccessible to the audience), to traces of this vision (Cristi's stakeouts), to poetic language mixed with music, which still maintains a certain flexibility, as well as the promise of some sort of vision [. . .], to handwritten reports (a subjective attempt at reducing a subjective vision), to printed language – the dictionary in which the rigidity of words eliminates any need for the real. (Ioniță 2015: 180–1)

Finally, the film ends with the sublimation of reality into the abstract code of the map.

Porumboiu's heightened interest in various media (and media differences) can be recognised also in his representation of text on screen. In *Police, Adjective* there are three instances of text on screen: the handwritten reports of Cristi that are shown in detail (two times), his personal definition of conscience written on the blackboard by his colleague, and finally the printed text of the definitions in the dictionary of the Commander. Following Sean Cubitt's taxonomy (1999), first we have to state that on all these three occasions we are dealing with compositions where the texts are neither in front of the screen nor on the screen, but in the image, and they are an integral part of the diegesis, which means that the characters are aware of them and they can always see them (as opposed to films where intertitles or subtitles are invisible for the diegetic world). In this regard, however, we have to observe the handwritten reports separately, as they are presented to us neither in the process of their writing (as it is in the case of Nana's letter, for example, in Godard's *Vivre sa vie*, 1962), nor in the process of their reading. Though we can clearly see that the reports are exactly the same ones that

Cristi carries around in a folder, at the moment of the spectatorial reading the already finished texts are laid out in such a way in front of the camera that the paper completely fills the frame eliminating every reference to the diegesis. The camera pans over the letter slowly, which makes it possible for most of the spectators to read the handwritten text, thus transforming cinema 'into a medium of reading' and partially disconnecting the written text from the diegetic realm (Holmberg and Rossholm 2015: 467, 465). The presentation of these reports destabilises the boundary between the diegetic and the non-diegetic in a similar way as it happens in Ingmar Bergman's *Persona* (1966). Holmberg and Rossholm point out that Elisabet's letter that is secretly read by Alma, looks different in the diegetic space (where in Alma's hand the whole text is in one block), while moments later it is broken into shorter segments like in a silent film insert, in order to make the letter easily readable on screen (see Holmberg and Rossholm 2015: 468–70).

However, if we consider the screening of the reports as being part of Porumboiu's investigation of mediality, we have to take into account the fact that the reports – surprisingly enough for a story set in our times – are handwritten, which usually is 'an intimate form of writing and reading, [that] belongs to a personal sphere' (Holmberg and Rossholm 2015: 471). What makes this worth a closer analysis is the tension created by the contradiction between the intimacy of the medium (the handwriting) and the distant, official formulation and choice of words of the text. The reason this seems important for the understanding of Porumboiu's cinema is that the tension delivered by the choice of medium represents the tension that is at the centre of the whole story, a tension that exists between Cristi's personal apprehension of the events and their official interpretation and handling by the authorities (that as a policeman he is also part of).

In the scene towards the end of the film where the Commander tries to convince Cristi through a 'linguistic lesson', handwriting and printed text are confronted. Cristi's personal definition of 'conscience' is handwritten on a chalkboard (Figure 10.1), thus suggesting its subjective and ephemeral nature; the definition of 'police officer', on the contrary, is presented to us on the printed page of the dictionary, suggesting its institutional prestige and validity. Ironically, though Cristi has previously read aloud several definitions from the dictionary, which were all accepted by the Commander, only this one, that is finally shown in print is considered 'bullshit' by him. Regarding the place of these texts within the narrative we have to note that both types of text are presented within the diegesis through the continuous presence of the sound of the scene, where the written texts are read aloud by one of the characters. However, visually they are both shown in separate, static shots, where the blackboard and respectively the page of the dictionary fill the whole frame. Moreover, in the

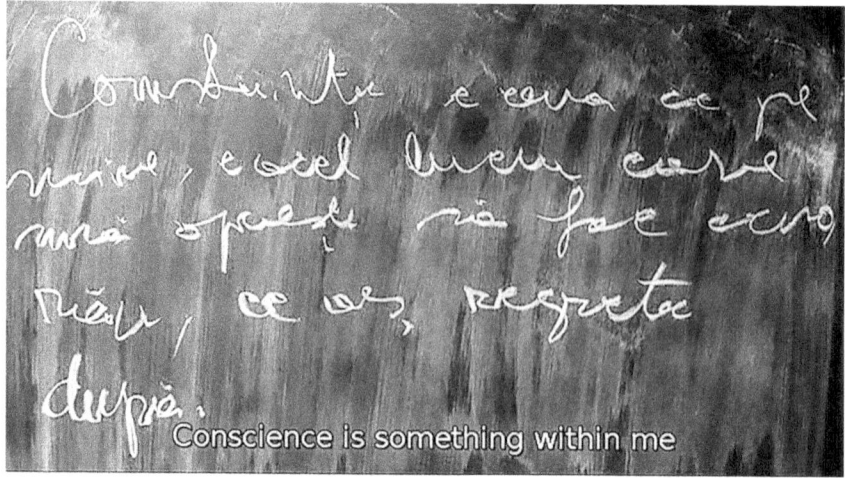

Figure 10.1 *Police, Adjective* (2009): the chalkboard and the definition of 'conscience' in the handwriting of the detective

case of the latter, the disruption from the scene becomes evident through the fact, that just before the cut we see Cristi following the text he is reading aloud with his finger, while when the printed text is on-screen, his hand is missing from the image. Thus we can conclude that Porumboiu follows a similar tactic in all three cases of text on screen in order to destabilise the boundary between the diegetic and the non-diegetic layers of the narrative.[4]

The mediality of representations seems to be a crucial issue in *When Evening Falls on Bucharest or Metabolism* too, where the two protagonists discuss the classical problem of form and content on several occasions. The film relates one day of a film director and his actress during a shooting, when the former fakes stomach problems in order to be able to spend a whole day with the woman who has just become his lover. In the first shot Paul, the fictional director, explains the difference between films that can be shot on analogue and on digital stock; later in a restaurant he exposes his theory, that the evolution and characteristic of each national gastronomy is based on the cutlery they are using (i.e. chopsticks or forks and knives); finally, in another scene, set in a car, the director argues that no matter how perfectly the actress speaks French, she would never be able to play a French person because her mind and behaviour have been formed elsewhere. All these dialogues, and especially the first one, expose the fact that Paul – who might be considered Porumboiu's alter ego – is concerned in every situation with the fact that the choice of a medium or of a technology can determine to a great extent what can be told (and echoing McLuhan's technological determinism, see McLuhan 1994: 7–21).

Reality Represented

The issue of the reliability of representations is brought up most clearly in *When Evening Falls on Bucharest or Metabolism*, where Paul, the director has to produce evidence of his illness to the producer worried about the costs of the delay in shooting, and who seems to distrust him. Semiotic theories of representation discuss very often the issue of denoting both in representations of real-world entities and of fictional, non-actual things. Goodman in his well-known passages in *Languages of Art* argues that due to the fact that 'no degree of resemblance is sufficient to establish the requisite relationship of reference', 'denotation is the core of representation, and is independent of resemblance'. (Goodman 1968: 5, 6) However, he quickly adds that in the case of visual representations resemblance is still important, as this makes them different from denotations of other kinds.

Towards the beginning of *When Evening Falls on Bucharest or Metabolism* Paul calls in sick to his producer, and just before talking to her in a suffering tone, he presses hard a spoon to his stomach in order to create the reality that is being verbally represented. In this case the pain in the stomach is not fictional – though it is self-inflicted by the protagonist – so the verbal expression of it can be accepted as being a representation of a bodily sensation existing independently from the representation. However, due to the inherent subjective nature of every verbal representation of inner states, the producer is not satisfied with Paul relating his illness, and asks for visual evidence in the form of an endoscopy. Like Goodman, Gombrich (2000: 239–62, 291–3) also argues that a major problem of representations is that even in the case of images there is no such thing as the innocent eye, thus every representation is affected by thoughts, emotions, goals and interests both during their process of creation and of reception/interpretation: 'content cannot be extracted by peeling off layers of comment' (Goodman 1968: 8). However, technical images, such as an endoscopy, ideally should be able to provide an unaffected, objective representation of reality, as during its production there is no conscience or intentionality that could distort the image for any reason. To fulfil the producer's request Paul uses an old endoscopy taken when he was actually ill, and forges it by omitting the date of the recording before presenting it to the physician brought by the producer to analyse it. As in the case of the self-inflected pain, this situation either cannot be understood with the help of the theoretical discussion of the fictional representation, as the endoscopy does represent Paul's actual stomach. The situation created here by Porumboiu brings in the temporal side of representations, an issue that is quite neglected within the theoretical discourse. It is again Goodman whose ideas can be applied here through the concept 'representation-as', a concept that is exemplified by a picture of the Duke of Wellington as an infant, where the picture 'denotes a certain [. . .] temporal part or "time-slice" of him' (Goodman 1968: 27). The endoscopy can be considered as a completely faithful representation of Paul's stomach at a certain moment some years ago. From an ontological point of view, no one can deny that Paul's endoscopy depicts, denotes and thus represents his stomach, in the same way as we cannot say that a picture of the infant Churchill (another example of Goodman's) does not represent him any more when he became older, or even dead. Thus, the conflict between the director and the producer is not about the nature of the representation, but its use, its context, its description: Paul presents it as a recent image. So, contrary to the approach we have observed in *Police, Adjective*, where the medium of the representation defined and constrained its content, in *When Evening Falls on Bucharest or Metabolism* – somehow in contradiction also with what the protagonist has been explaining to his actress on many occasions – it is not the chosen medium, but the authorial intention and the use of the representation that defines its meaning. The trick here is that though we have a representation presenting itself as resembling the original, no one can verify this resemblance, as only this type of technical image is capable of recording an image inside a body. Lacking any possibility of verifying resemblance or matching, we are left with verbal descriptions, but as Susan Sontag claimed when discussing photographs that show casualties of war, which are almost always appropriated by the different sides, 'all photographs wait to be explained or falsified by their captions' (Sontag 2003: 10). Kibédi Varga considers that in almost all cases when images and words are presented together, it is the word that dominates, the exception being only those very well-known images where we do not need words to identify them and their content: 'in the image-title relation, the word explains the image; it restricts its possibilities and fixes its meaning' (Kibédi Varga 1989: 42). This is why the producer of *When Evening Falls on Bucharest or Metabolism* finally has to accept Paul's argument, though – as her final remark suggests – she is still convinced that she has been fooled.

A different approach to the reliability of representation can be identified in Porumboiu's first feature, *12:08 East of Bucharest*, where the television talk-show host questions the existence of a real revolution in the small provincial town where the action is located. During the show one of the guests, the alcoholic schoolteacher, relates his memories of the day of the revolution, and makes the statement that he and his friends had already been protesting on the main square of the town before the dictator escaped, this meaning that there was a real revolution, sixteen years before. Afterwards, through the comments of several spectators calling in, the reliability of the teacher's verbal accounts is shattered based on the subjectivity of any verbal representation, exactly in the same way as the producer of *When Evening*

Falls on Bucharest or *Metabolism* doubted the director's statement on his stomach pain.

DIRECT THEORY?

Many of Porumboiu's films present situations that make the viewer reflect on the role of images and texts in processing, interpreting and sharing everyday experiences. But has Porumboiu managed to also reflect on the possibilities of the cinematic representation through the filmic expression itself? This would be something similar to what Edward Small called 'direct theory' regarding experimental films and video art, in the sense that, due to their 'remarkable reflexivity', such works can function as 'a manifest, immediate, direct theory that bypasses the limiting intervention of separate semiotic systems, especially the spoken or written language' and thus can reflect on their 'own intrinsic semiotic system(s)' (Small 1994: xv, 5). Can a filmmaker, who is focusing on such theoretical problems throughout his whole *oeuvre*, transcend conventional filmic expression through the creation of a cinematic experience that is able to convey in itself something similar to the issues addressed in the narratives? Analysing Porumboiu's *oeuvre* I have found one instance in *Police, Adjective* where the possibility of such an intention might be present. In the long scenes of the stake-out we may observe how Porumboiu is playing with the illusion of the POV shot. Many times, we get to see the teenagers in various situations (smoking in the school-break, arriving at and leaving a house, walking in the streets) from a point of view that seems to belong to Cristi. However, after a certain amount of time the detective appears within the same frame, thus clearly marking the difference between what the detective sees and what the camera shows, cancelling the visual identification of the spectator's point of view with that of the protagonist. There is a clear lack of consistency here, as there are five shots where this entering in the frame does not take place, which could indicate that the construction of the shot described above is more an accident than a conscious device meant to reflect on representation through perception. Thus, despite the director's obvious interest in the problematic nature of representations, questions of the mediality and the reliability of representations seem to be present only on the level of the script, the narration, they do not permeate the cinematic expression, the visual compositions of the films. In this sense, we can say that Porumboiu's cinema can be categorised neither as direct theory, nor – as it has been suggested by Maria Ioniță (2015) – as a cinematic equivalent of Magritte's paintings.

This work was supported by the project entitled Space-ing Otherness. Cultural Images of Space, Contact Zones in Contemporary Hungarian and Romanian Film and Literature (OTKA NN 112700).

NOTES

1. Alex Leo Șerban was one of the few critics who rejected the label of Realism with regards to Porumboiu (2009) in his response written to a series of articles published by Andrei Gorzo (2009) in which he describes how Porumboiu defies the rules of conventional filmic language, reaching an 'anti-spectacular realism'.
2. State (2014: 80–7) identifies three forms of Realism in Porumboiu's films: situational realism in *12:08 East of Bucharest* (*A fost sau n-a fost?*, 2006), semantic realism in *Police, Adjective* (*Polițist, adjectiv,* 2009) and conceptual realism in *When Evening Falls on Bucharest or Metabolism* (*Când se lasă seara peste București sau metabolism,* 2013) and *The Second Game* (*Al doilea joc,* 2014).
3. Porumboiu's uniqueness among filmmakers considered to be part of the Romanian New Wave and the outstanding complexity of his cinema, which goes beyond questions of Realism, is also proven by scholarly articles and analyses which have interpreted it in the broader context of contemporary world cinema. See, for example, Ágnes Pethő's article (2015) focusing on the cinematic tableau in which she compares Porumboiu's cinema to that of Roy Andersson and Joanna Hogg; Ira Jaffe (2014) in the last chapter of his book on slow cinema analyses Tarr's *Werckmeister Harmonies* and *The Turin Horse* together with *12:08 East of Bucharest* based on their ironic take on revolution.
4. Handwriting is also quite often used as a self-reflexive auteuristic gesture by many filmmakers, like Bergman or Godard through the use of their own handwriting in their films. However, I have found no information on the handwriting in *Police, Adjective* belonging to its author.

WORKS CITED

Bardan, Alice (2012), 'Aftereffects of 1989 Corneliu Porumboiu's *12:08 East of Bucharest* (2006) and Romanian Cinema', in Anikó Imre (ed.), *A Companion to Eastern European Cinemas*, Chichester and Malden: Wiley-Blackwell, pp. 125–47.

Barthes, Roland (1987), 'Rhetoric of the Image', in Stephen Heath (ed.), *Image, Music, Text*, London: Fontana Press, pp. 32–51.

Cubitt, Sean (1999), 'Preliminaries for a Taxonomy and Rhetoric of On-Screen Writing', in Jonathan Bignell (ed.), *Writing and Cinema (Crosscurrents)*, New York and London: Routledge, pp. 59–73.

Foucault, Michel (1983), *This Is Not a Pipe*, Berkeley: University of California Press.

Gadamer, Hans-Georg (2004), *Truth and Method*, London and New York: Continuum.

Gombrich, Ernst Hans (2000), *Art and Illusion: A Study in the Psychology of Pictorial Representation*, Princeton: Princeton University Press.

Goodman, Nelson (1968), *Languages of Art: An Approach to a Theory of Symbols*, Indianapolis: Hackett.

Gorzo, Andrei (2009), 'Despre îndrăzneala lui *Polițist, adjectiv*' ['About the Boldness of *Police, Adjective*'], *Dilema veche*, Nos 279, 280, 281, <http://agenda.liternet.ro/articol/9406/Andrei-Gorzo/Despre-indrazneala-lui-Politist-adjectiv.htm> (last accessed 12 January 2019).

Holmberg, Jan and Anna Sofia Rossholm (2015), 'Screened Writing: Notes on Bergman's Hand', *Word & Image*, Vol. 31, No. 4, pp. 459–72.

Ioniță, Maria (2015), 'Framed by Definitions. Corneliu Porumboiu and the Dismantling of Realism', in Janelle Suzanne Blankenship and Tobias Nagl (eds), *European Visions: Small Cinemas in Transition*, Bielefeld: Transcript, pp. 173–86.

Jaffe, Ira (2014), *Slow Movies: Countering the Cinema of Action*, London and New York: Wallflower Press.

Kibédi Varga, Aron (1989), 'Criteria for Describing Word-and-Image Relations', *Poetics Today* Vol. 10, No. 1, pp. 31–53.

McLuhan, Marshall (1994), *Understanding Media: The Extensions of Man*, Cambridge, MA: The MIT Press.

Magritte, René (1929), 'Les mots et les images', *La Révolution surréaliste*, No. 12 (December), <http://gallica.bnf.fr/ark:/12148/bpt6k58451673> (last accessed 12 January 2019).

Mitchell, W. J. T. (1994), *Picture Theory: Essays on Verbal and Visual Representation*, Chicago: University of Chicago Press.

Pethő, Ágnes (2015), 'Between Absorption, Abstraction and Exhibition: Inflections of the Cinematic Tableau in the Films of Corneliu Porumboiu, Roy Andersson and Joanna Hogg', *Acta Universitatis Sapientiae: Film and Media Studies*, Vol. 11, pp. 39–76.

Șerban, Alex. Leo (2009), 'Despre realismul lui *Polițist, adjectiv* (scrisoare pentru Andrei Gorzo)' ['About the realism of *Police, Adjective*. A letter to Andrei Gorzo'], *Dilema veche*, No. 285, 29 July 2009, <http://agenda.liternet.ro/articol/9531/Alex-Leo-Șerban-Andrei-Gorzo/Despre-realismul-lui-Politist-adjectiv-scrisoare-pentru-Andrei-Gorzo.html> (last accessed 12 January 2019).

Small, Edward S. (1994), *Direct Theory: Experimental Film/Video as Major Genre*, Carbondale: Southern Illinois University Press.

Sontag, Susan (2003), *Regarding the Pain of Others*, New York: Picador.

State, Andrei (2014), 'Realismele lui Corneliu Porumboiu' ['The Realisms of Corneliu Porumboiu'], in Andrei Gorzo and Andrei State (eds), *Politicile filmului: contribuții la interpretarea cinemaului românesc contemporan* [*The Politics of Cinema: Contributions to the Interpretation of Contemporary Romanian Cinema*], Cluj-Napoca: Tact, pp. 73–87.

Tengelyi, László (2007), *Tapasztalat és kifejezés* [*Experience and Expression*], Budapest: Atlantisz.

CHAPTER 11

Intermedial Détrompe l'Oeil *and Contemporary Polish Narrative Cinema*
Gabriel Laverdière

Video and film have turned digital, and digital technology has significantly informed the way we think about cinema. It seems to command us to revise even our most basic understanding of what film is or of how it operates. However, the full extent of the digital era has probably yet to be grasped. Most writing about – or even the most common sense of – digital cinema is concerned with special effects and technological innovation, which can be notably observed in Hollywood blockbusters. Digital aesthetics and possibilities are flourishing in many areas (from film to advertisement, design and science). Almost everyone now has the technical tools and basic skills needed to produce moving images; by casually holding a (now digital) camera of some kind, everyone is potentially a filmmaker or videographer. The smartphone and the digital video camera are the more portable, perhaps more intuitive heirs to the 8mm, 16mm, and video cameras of the past. The history of the portable camera dates back to the beginning of film (from Marey's 1882 photographic gun to Prószyński's 1909 compressed-air-powered Aeroscope, to his later 120mm domestic camera, the Oko, and so on). If digital cinema is often understood as a break with past film aesthetics, this essay rather sees continuity. Digital culture preserves and prolongs video culture. Indeed, amateur images produced by domestic cameras are also part of digital culture, or of the culture of digital moving images. These 'domesticated' uses of digital technology have been investigated by numerous studies (e.g. visual anthropology, focusing on private, non-industrial usages of moving images, or the aesthetics of the so-called 'poor image' as opposed to the obsession with high-resolution digital image), and have been contributing to visual artistic practices (e.g. new media art, video installations). The aim of this essay is to investigate the use of video and digital images in the context of minor national cinemas (through the Polish example), and to note how digital filmmaking is also a continuation not only of argentic filmmaking but also of video aesthetics, of video not as art (video art) but as common practice.

Digital cinema is not a Hollywood affair only. Minor national cinemas are also part of the landscape of digital culture. Polish cinema certainly qualifies as a minor cinema given its somewhat fragile industrial bases: until 1989, the film industry was state-owned, often successfully operated and regulated (though submitted to censorship); and, following the initial turbulence of early post-communist society, only in 2005 did the government invest in a significant support structure, the Polish Film Institute. Film production had until then been left under the wavering guidance of the new and understandably precarious free-market economy. Given that post-communist societies have been adapting to new models of work and life, and that digital culture in film is now a staple of worldwide cinema (but especially, or most obviously, of costly American productions), the ways minor world cinemas handle the digital should be of particular interest as it can further our understanding of the possibilities of digital cinema as a whole.

Intermedial practices have long been used to create perceptual ruptures, breaching the illusion of reality and spurring the awareness of seeing. Video, whether analogue or digital, has added to the ways in which these ruptures may occur, or in which these two seemingly contradictory effects (illusionism and reflexivity) are intertwined. For this essay, I will suggest that in certain Polish films the use of analogue and digital video cameras can be considered as aesthetic strategies of unveilment, assisting the critical discourse that these works engage in regarding the (social) reality they represent or reference. Although my investigating the use of video in fictional narratives (and how it can reproduce or extend other distancing effects) points to a widespread phenomenon in cinema, my analysis will be restricted to three post-communist films that are overtly critical of contemporary Polish society and culture: *The Wedding Banquet* (*Wesele*, directed by Wojciech Smarzowski in 2004), *The Egoists* (*Egoiści*, by Mariusz Treliński, 2001) and *Suicide Room* (*Sala samobójców*, by Jan Komasa, 2011). Their subject matter can be connected to a socio-economic and political situation for which the transition from communism to capitalism has been not only decisive, but divisive. The films chosen evince how socio-political volatility can invest cultural and symbolic objects or artefacts. Furthermore, these films speak to how the aesthetics and practices of analogue video help establish those of digital video, and to the mixed – if imperceptible – interactions of analogue and digital video with argentic film and digital film.[1]

Alternating between a 'master' film track (that is, the majority of the scenes and sequences, filmed in a professional and meticulous way) and shots produced by a video camera (from analogue video to digital webcam), these three films could call attention to the critical relevance of using video and especially digital technologies in a 'minoritarian' national cinema[2] – which can't possibly compete with the technological prowesses of Hollywood – and to the challenges (technological, aesthetic, ideological) of adapting a communist society to a capitalist regime.

In these films, through an effect of *mise en abyme* the cinema screen is expanded into various types of screens, or images of screens, and this intermedial design presents the cinema screen itself as a surface, as an object to be noticed and examined. This use of other screens, or mediating screens, sometimes lends itself to a character's intimate testimony, or helps to reveal what they cannot see or refuse to see, individually or as a community. For the purpose of conceptualising the form under study and of linking it to the visual arts, I will consider this aesthetic pattern as a *détrompe l'oeil*, a way to 'disabuse the eye' by joining images of varying nature and meaning. Based on the pictorial *détrompe l'oeil* this argument implies at least the following: that the history of the continuing development of film is not divorced from the history of the arts; that film has not only relied upon realism more intensely than any other modern or contemporary art form, but that strategies of realism and of spectacle have bonded in cinema with great success; and that we can consider this inclination towards dramatic verisimilitude as a variant on the pictorial *trompe l'oeil* (or the misleading of the eye), which is itself an extreme stylistic manifestation of the inclination toward realism in the visual arts.

FILM AND *TROMPE L'OEIL*

Trompe l'oeil, a French expression, is a painting technique, style, effect and movement that intends to imitate the reality of inert objects, of surfaces and flat space in order to deceive and trick the unsuspecting watcher. The *trompe l'oeil* painting involves playing with the watcher, who (it is expected) will yield to a feeling of bewilderment 'that brings them to reflect upon the nature of the world of appearances' (Marlier 1964: 105, my translation). For this temporary effect to occur, the painter must reproduce as realistically as possible a given subject (and strategically place the picture in adequate space). This approach to painting exaggerates the mimetic line and tradition that has been more or less abandoned since the late nineteenth century and the advent of modernism.

Realism itself is an inexhaustible problem in the history of the visual arts. From its beginnings, cinema has also been engaged in the idea of reproducing reality, and it has, as such, effectively reactivated the realist pictorial tradition. The filmic apparatus can produce a realistic effect contingent on the photographic image, on the later presence of sound and colour, and especially on movement, which is always real in itself, since 'reproducing the appearance of movement is in fact to reproduce its reality: a movement reproduced is a "real" movement, since the visual manifestation is identical in both cases' (Aumont et al. 1983: 106, my translation; see also Aumont 1990: 31–4). However, photographic reproduction and the apparatus itself never were quite sufficient to fully ensure realism. Several techniques (of framing, editing, etc.) and norms (of storytelling, verisimilitude, etc.), elaborated since the early years of film, made possible the spectacle of realism. Video has added to the realism of especially certain modes of filming. The recent use of digital technology adds new tools to complete the realistic illusion of motion pictures. Digital enhancement and special effects can quite literally mislead the eye by creating shapes and textures that no audience member can recognise as computerised constructs. In this way, digital technology can operate as a kind of *trompe l'oeil*.

Regardless of digital technology, there are numerous other ways to consider film as *trompe l'oeil*. Film has consistently developed recreationally delusive modes of representation: being deceived can indeed be entertaining. Some films deliberately mislead the viewer in creating a semblance of reality (e.g. in the case of mockumentaries), or incorporate narrative reversals that alter the conditions of the fictional illusion (e.g. in so-called metafictional narratives, see: Ledoux 2012). Techniques of *mise en abyme* and intermediality can produce effects of perplexity, possibly leading to the transgression of the usual boundaries of fiction. In painting, there is the so-called *Détrompe-l'oeil* series of the avant-garde visual artist Daniel Spoerri, in which objects are crudely attached to realistic genre paintings, violently breaking any sort of illusion they might have created, extending the canvas and expanding the meaning of the single image. In *The Shower* (*La Douche*, 1961) a showerhead, faucet and hose have been attached to a painted landscape: water has been figuratively diverted from the painterly, romanticised vision of a past agrarian, pastoral equilibrium to the palpable presence of the brash, industrialised showerhead that signals our present, practical though wasteful use of water resources. The painting therefore becomes part sculpture, an art installation where imitation recedes in favour of action and, ostensibly, of commentary. The protruding objects are the undeniable signs of artistic intervention. Incorporating other arts and practices can function similarly in film as an infraction of traditional realistic norms. The domestic video image may prompt the viewer to briefly detach from the film's referential construction. Digital aesthetics are here expanded from special effects to include video.

Film, Video and the Digital

In aesthetic terms, digital technology in contemporary cinema seems to follow two main lines of development, each with its own codes and tradition. The new digital possibilities for visual alterations supplement the usual methods of realistic cinema (invisible cutting, audio-visual synchronicity, etc.), or help to make them either more efficient or more in tune with the requirements of current popular tastes. Following video practices and, therefore, aesthetics, the second trend of digital cinema aims to create effects of contingency that encourage intimacy or disclosure. It takes advantage of the mobility and convenience that lightweight and portable digital video cameras allow. Such effects can be produced through the introduction of various types of images into the narrative and visual design of a film (i.e. images produced by cameras handled by the fictional characters, typically used as a kind of portable and electronic confessional booth).[3] While one of Hollywood's aims in using digital technology is a mixture between sophisticated spectacle and the enhanced reproduction of reality (and often impressing audiences by the expensive efficiency of the effects on display), for independent films or those produced outside of the large-scale film industry, another mode of representing reality is sometimes preferred, no doubt encouraged by the lightness of the video camera.

The rough sort of realism that is characteristic of video images, analogue or digital, can be rather different from the one provided by the classical narrative film. Here, film technology and practices intersect: fiction films are often shot with (argentic or digital) film cameras, whereas video is usually considered adequate for documentary, amateur or family films (or, quite differently, for video art and experimental film). The special gloss of film stock or high-end digital cameras seems to correspond with the singular reality of fiction, whereas the grittiness of video (digital or not) appears to show a truer face of reality. The viewer will tend to interpret video footage using codes commonly associated with documentary or amateur film, modes generally considered to be non-fictional and truthful. But, of course, documentary is itself partly fictionalised in the sense that the process of making a film will necessarily transform any reality captured by the camera. Codes generally associated with video footage include the seemingly random use of the camera, and a sense of improvisation or lack of *mise en scène* (space and characters appear haphazardly, framing is less centripetal), visuals and sounds are less smooth (blurring, failing light, grain, resonance, sound instability).

In classical narrative cinema, such footage is usually justified in the fictive realm by being associated with characters who are handling cameras, or more recently, smartphones. The images created by non- or semi-professional cameras that are included in otherwise classically structured movies[4] can suggest points of view that, at least momentarily, appear to be foreign to the one presented by the other shots. While today's digital film cameras used for major motion pictures produce images of high quality (dependant on technical specifications, but also on adept staging and lighting), the low-end non-professional cameras generally produce images of comparatively poorer quality. In motion pictures, the graininess and grit of inserted video footage make more noticeable the visual nature of the images, whereas uncompressed high-resolution digital (or quality film) images tend to focus our attention on their content. Also, the filming techniques for video sequences will often mimic, in fiction, the less glamourous style of the documentarian or the freer style of the amateur. Compared to the glossy, prepared frames and images of the other, main parts of these professional fiction films, the inserted and seemingly spontaneous gritty scenes appear (perhaps paradoxically) to be even more real. Contingency is indeed a significant feature of this visual realm full of pixelated close-ups and blurry hand-held shots (which is undoubtedly why the horror genre – specifically the subgenre of the found footage – has been so quick to embrace this aesthetics: contingency is most effective in creating an atmosphere of insecurity).

In other words, realism operates also, in the films studied here, by virtue of the aesthetic divide between images of obvious fictionality (the shiny and polished creations of expertly crafted pictures) and video images where fictionality somewhat recedes. Surely this is instantly recognised by the viewer, whose own everyday life is now brimming with similar-looking images, whether through phones or websites. Film and video interact as rival media, both sprouting from the same stem of aesthetic and technological development. This interaction is a form of intermediality, one that speaks particularly to contemporary visual culture. As Lucie Roy points out, 'intermediality is a cultural phenomenon [. . .] in so far as it depends on the viewer's knowledge of the cultural museum that is made up of artworks and means of expression, of forms and figures associated with various means of expression' (2015: 170, my translation). Today's viewer is, as are today's filmmakers, familiar with the codes of both upscale motion pictures and rudimentary homemade audiovisual productions.

In such a case where the two types of images or footage described above alternate in a single fiction film, the erratic framing or stark colours of the gritty video image, rather than strengthening fictional illusion, or *trompe l'oeil*, can cast doubt on the fictional universe, disrupt its stability, briefly, by the intrusion of a different type of visual rendering. The fictional realm of a film generally requires uniformity. The gritty video images' irregularity never quite goes unnoticed. Alien to the uncanny but familiar realism of the fictional world presented on the screen, they may appear to 'burst' out of the otherwise predictable flow of film, and produce an effect that could be described as *détrompe l'oeil*.

Some contemporary Polish productions use video images to draw the viewer in closer to certain characters or to reveal key moments otherwise hidden from view. As I previously said, the three films described in this essay are all critical of modern Polish society and values. Western-style materialism, old-style (but lasting) Polish hypocrisy, and the new globalised web-world of today are all lampooned in these films. For the most part, the characters are swallowed up by ideological and technological quagmires, and can see clearly only when time has run out for them. Critical discourse is partly accomplished through the intermedial use of the analogue or digital video cameras that the characters handle. These images or shots display fragments of reality in which the illusion of social acceptability and unity can no longer hold itself together. Weaknesses are revealed or emphasised; characters' and society's faults are exposed or ridiculed. The intermedial effects of video within the films achieve a kind of *détrompe l'oeil* that denounces society as a *trompe l'oeil*, which ultimately cannot contain the orgiastic-sacrificial night of *The Wedding Banquet*, the sexual-suicidal crisis of *The Egoists*, nor the digitally induced demise in *Suicide Room*.

The Wedding Banquet

I will begin with Wojciech Smarzowski's 2004 film *The Wedding Banquet* (*Wesele*), not as an analytical blueprint for the others, but because it features both a clear critical discourse and a consistent use of the video camera throughout. In this loose adaptation of a classic Polish play by Stanisław Wyspiański, Smarzowski produces a scorching caricature of Polish society, where tropes of nationhood are debased one after another (Andrzej Wajda's own 1972 film was a closer adaptation of the play). The film begins with the wedding ceremony of a young couple, but quickly moves on to the wedding party (the *wesele*), where most of the narrative is set up. In the 1901 play, an 'assault on traditional patriotism' (Eile 2000: 170), the foundational literary, cultural and ethical paradigm of valorous Polish romanticism is subjected to Wyspiański's criticism, which is characterised by 'his conviction that [Polish national mythology's] illusions uphold quixotic dreams and the consequent inability to act' (Eile 2000: 172).[5]

Smarzowski intends to shock Polish audiences: 'This film is a provocation, one that is, in my view, done with good cause' (Pietrasik 2009, my translation). Smarzowski relentlessly exposes what he views as Polish society's moral shortcomings through symbols of nationality and culture, which are adapted to fit a modern context (and which are complicated by capitalist values, or rather by the failure to treat them as values): the priest, the policeman, the accountant are all corruptible, the institution of marriage crumbles as a result of pervading amoral gambits, the newly wed couple and families are torn apart, the *bigos* (an iconic national dish) will nauseate most of the guests, a patriotic chant sung with alcoholic ferver turns to farce, and so on. Of course, as noted by Monika Nahlik about the film,

> any attempt to illustrate national identity through characters from a particular group of people and their interactions in a limited time frame always implies a certain schematism. Although it doesn't mean the negative scope of the stereotypes should be lessened, there is no doubt that to some extent they represent reality. Poles see themselves as religious, patriotic, honorable, hospitable and sociable, prodigal, thriftless, remiss, undisciplined and abusing alcohol. (Nahlik 2009: 323, my translation)

The film presents these stereotypes and more, emphasising the desire to keep up appearances, as well as the greed and hypocrisy of self-interested characters. As cases of vodka bottles are emptied and as general abjection increases, it is made obvious that the sacred union has been perverted. With a hand-held camera, a guest shoots 'everything', as he is ordered to do by his employer, the father of the bride, Wiesław. The film shifts between more than fifty shots filmed using this amateur video camera and numerous others filmed with a professional movie camera; the amateur shots stand out because of rough visuals and jittery framing. These images sometimes unexpectedly reveal more vividly the characters' flaws.

After the ceremony, as the married couple receives wishes of happiness from the guests, in a shot taken from far away with the video camera we hear some of them gossiping: 'It's because he got her pregnant. He did quite well for himself.' Shortly after, in a faraway shot of the father talking on the phone while standing near a portable toilet, we hear a voice-over dialogue of guests lamenting the buffet: 'This sausage is cheap, green and smelly . . . And this cake, I won't touch it.' Although these comments seem trivial, appearances matter greatly to Wiesław as the rest of the sequence makes perfectly clear. A brand-new luxury car soon approaches: his gift for the couple, proudly displayed before the guests. 'Shoot everything, you hear? Everything', Wiesław says to the cameraman as he proudly approaches the car.

In the rented space where the wedding party and the rest of the film take place, video footage shot from a distance shows the married couple smiling, unaware of the guests, once again heard in a voice-over, commenting on the unplanned pregnancy that supposedly pressured the woman into marriage (those rumours will turn out to be true). And so the party can commence, featuring much alcohol and raunchy sex games. The video footage shows some of these rituals, and the annoyed young wife required to participate: a balloon is placed between her and her husband's pelvis, the man pushing his hips forward to make it burst in a gross display of intercourse simulation;

next, between her thighs the bride holds an empty bottle in which a blindfolded man must introduce a long phallic object hanging from his waist; women must insert an egg through the bottom leg of a man's pants, carry it along the leg and pull it out unbroken from the participant's unzipped fly, etc. In all these cases, the camera is almost intrusively close to the action and the characters. These scenes seemingly show up apart from the main narrative; they are cultural vignettes, showing the celebration as an irritating challenge for the new bride.

Throughout the film, guests offer wishes of happiness directly to the video camera, often in an artificial or clumsy way (a tipsy maid of honour laughs through it; a visibly drunken man, standing next to the bathroom door through which people are coming and going, records his message using foul language and commenting on Poland where, he says, one is 'ankle deep in piss'). Near the end of the film, the bride faints after discovering her grandfather's corpse hidden in the instrument case of a musician. The cameraman – her secret lover, we soon learn – takes her outside where he shows her images he secretly recorded of the altercation preceding the old man's passing. The viewer is simultaneously informed of this part of the story. The footage shows the grandfather and his son quarrelling over a piece of land Wiesław had promised a gangster in exchange for the luxury car. He admits that the car was the condition required by his son-in-law to accept to marry his daughter. Wiesław leaves; the grandfather suffers a stroke, also on camera since the cameraman remained hidden and filming after Wiesław's exit.

Catching the guests off-guard, the video camera helps to disturb the initial stilted appearances. It follows that the unravelling of the sacred institution of marriage, and of other notable national figures of moral authority, is helped along by this added point of view which enriches the viewer's perception of the characters and events unfolding as well as their critical reading of the film.

The Egoists

Mariusz Treliński's film *The Egoists* (*Egoiści*, 2001), it could be argued, is part of a revival of the cinema of 'moral concern'. These films are characterised by 'their setting in contemporary Poland and sensitivity to social issues that are nevertheless represented from the perspective of an individual faced with important moral choices' (Mazierska 2007: 143). Like other films of its time, *The Egoists* offers a biting look at materialistic urban youth, a new elite that has benefited economically from the change of political regime, as opposed to much of the rural population or working class. The material or professional success achieved by the four characters whose fates are intertwined in this mosaic-like film do not keep them from disillusionment. After his gay lover has left him, Filip, an architect, willingly burns to death in his own home following a night of delirium. Anka and Młody are overwrought addicts. At the centre of the plot is Smutny ('sad', literally), a musician disgusted by his employment as a jingles composer.

Stylish, wide panoramic overhead shots of Warsaw open and close the film, and also separate inner sections, suggesting that the filmmaker's criticism applies to more than just these characters: the inhabitants are of a similar ilk as the city, immersed in an almost permanent darkness, a moral darkness – at least for those who blindly subscribe to the new ideology of success without its necessary ethical or spiritual foundations. The film mocks traditional Polish symbols, particularly in a surreal scene where Filip and Smutny go on a rampage in the city with a crew of soldiers, occupying the space of a monument dedicated to dead soldiers and a church-like setting dominated by a big raised cross. In this city, symbol of the New Poland, only a premature and feeble infant can be born, the film tells us, as shown in the penultimate scene which brings this moody film to a close on an expectedly sour note.

After the first extreme long shot of Warsaw, the story begins with the attempted suicide of Smutny's girlfriend. She's seemingly gone mad, watching a recording of her own face being broadcast on the TV screen: this footage is filmed with a small video camera that an early shot clearly displays laying on a table. A series of close-ups produced with the video camera alternate with other shots in which we see Anka egotistically observing herself on the screen. Her melodramatic confession is directed at Smutny; with her face contorted, she cries and screams. The scene is meant to be outrageous (and comes off as contrived pathos).

Rather than directly confronting her boyfriend – she later will – Anka opts for the transmediation provided by the video camera's revealing, blunt image, through interposed screens: Smutny will view the recording later. Anka's actions and histrionics are overly dramatic. The close-up framing of the face, the insistent gaze at the camera and the image's coarseness all magnify her solitude and despair, but it also burdens the viewer with a plaintiveness made especially unbearable by the realness and roughness of the video image. The scene fully indulges Anka's crisis, but it also feels somehow detached, possibly because of aesthetics (editing, framing, inclusion of the video image as separate from the normal flow of film) and staging (Anka looking at herself on the screen, alternatively fascinated and withdrawn). The video camera, such as it is used narratively and aesthetically, serves paradoxically as a means of communicating a message (from Anka to Smutny) and as a way to distance oneself from it (looking at oneself), allowing both intimacy and detachment.

Later on, the film will continue to question the obsessive relationship of people to objects, especially electronics or any other material property by which a high social status can be ascertained. This introductory 'suicide attempt' scene initiates this criticism with suggesting the idea of the commodification of human suffering – now more mediated than ever through various screens – but also the narcissism associated with human pathos, when it is disconnected from the imperative of personal responsibility, and with capitalist values and property, when they are disengaged from their ethical standards or historical significance, a perversion of modern ideals which the film's characters all represent. Incidentally, the digital video camera stands both as a luxury item in the Polish socio-economic context and as 'one of the most potent symbols of postmodern culture' (Mazierska 2007: 162), in which the practice of self-examination has turned obsessive (in the form of the selfie).

Suicide Room

While *The Egoists* criticised the newly formed Polish consumerist society through the shallow greed and spiritual misery of the financially successful – represented by a generation of thirty- and forty-year-olds – (a criticism at times laboriously overemphasised), Jan Komasa's polished *Suicide Room* (*Sala samobójców*, 2011) questions the power dynamics and emotional disorders that can affect teenagers while they mindlessly stroll the Internet and its social networks (Figure 11.1). Smartphones and their extensions – the Internet and Facebook-like software – stand here for the new *logos*, the new social matrix, fast, entertaining, vectorial, mesmerising, all-knowing, as well as gripping, inescapable, open to the realms of fantasy, feelings, perversion and cruelty, which all permeate social media (e.g. ruthless PC policing and crude trolling;

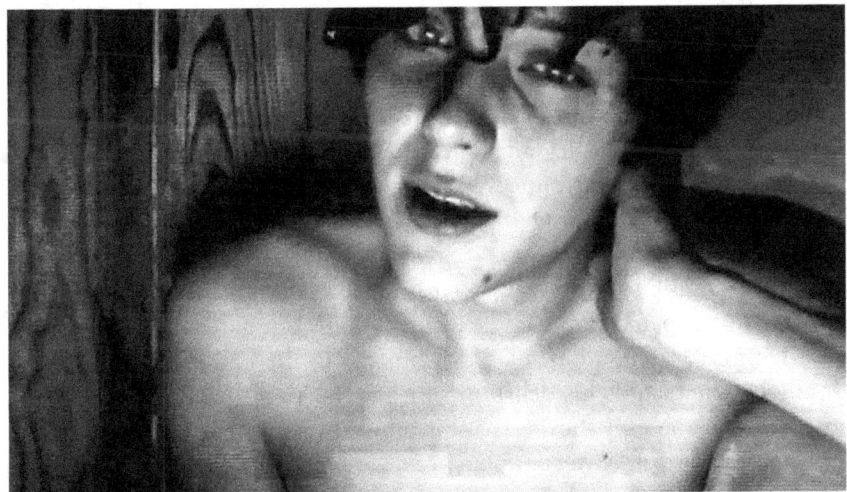

Figure 11.1 Suicide Room (2011): the grainy digital images of webcam communications convey the troubled teenage protagonist's fears

the obsession of liking, being liked, disliking, seen liking, and so forth; in other words, existing as bristling emotional beings in this advanced technological marvel of cold scientific ingenuity). In so far as web images often take up the entire film screen in *Suicide Room*, whether as rough webcam conversations or as computerised and fully animated 3D worlds, the story thematises the problem of proliferating screens, the permanent or endlessly repeated representing of the self through them, and the unbalanced human relationships that this swelling of images and virtual life can result in.

The film tells the story of an offbeat teenager's sexual discovery and of his later public shaming. Longing to belong, he becomes an unwilling sexual dissident, having been drummed out of his bourgeois social circle. From a socio-economic Polish perspective, Dominik and his family's luxurious lifestyle is truly exceptional (his parents are immersed in the bustling higher spheres of politics and fashion). Although Poland's economic situation has apparently improved since the early 1990s, unemployment is still high and the country has experienced a serious brain drain. This of course does not preclude a certain elite group from gathering in large cities, and this social context is where the film takes place. Unsurprisingly, the elites are derided, as they were in *The Egoists*. Material success and wealth are shown to be delusions, failing to preserve citizens from moral decay. The teenager's fruitless revolt against everything will symbolise a dearth of the values that would be necessary to humanise both the world of material prosperity and the practice of digital wandering. Both are shown, instead, as minefields or traps.

Early on, lack of communication is manifest as Dominik turns away from his parents, who are busy with their professional lives and extramarital sexual affairs. He attends high school with no particular problem until he kisses a male classmate at a party and then discovers his attraction to him – he is soon after ridiculed online and at school. In despair, he shuts himself in his room and spends most of his time surfing the Internet, chatting and exploring. Through the degraded image of a webcam, he communicates with a young woman who introduces him to the Suicide Room, a bizarre website inviting suicidal teens to take part in a virtual experience (not unlike the famous virtual world of *Second Life*). After his first suicide attempt (and rescue), Dominik soon shuts himself in once again. His parents hire a psychologist who manages to convince him to come out of his room. Nevertheless, Dominik later successfully kills himself in the bathroom of a club; a young couple records his delirium and death with a smartphone. The very last frame of the film shows that this morbid footage has ended up online (where visitors can leave comments), and therefore will forever inhabit the digital sea of innumerable videos cluttering the web (Figure 11.2).

The film brings together various types of images: the slick ones of a master film track (enhanced by the setting of opulently constructed or furnished

Figure 11.2 *Suicide Room* (2011): the final images of the film show the footage of the boy's suicide posted online, with the comments of the viewers below

milieus); computer and website screen captures (including the vibrant and all-animated sequences of the Suicide Room simulation); coarse web videos; grungy images produced by the protagonist's webcam; videos produced by a smartphone. The film recreates through cinematic means and movie logic the social experience of these now commonplace practices. The kind of visual excess this entails here recalls both cinema's representational tradition (films have inclined toward realism rather than abstraction) and contemporary society's obsession with the visual, more and more prone to self-representation (and self-contemplation). Nowhere, it seems, is this truer than in today's digital mapping of our lives through visuals: an established habit that can be pleasurable and creative, but also risky and monomaniacal. Teenagers and young adults, whose identities are now deeply rooted in the use and production of images, are especially affected. Their identities – that is, how they are seen and thought of by others, but also how they see and think about themselves – have become almost fully united with their multivisual, digital and intermedial existence. Their visual identities have become a narrative – a narrative identity (to evoke, in passing, Paul Ricœur's work). In such a faulty fusion of the state of being and of the visual presence of self, there is no longer such a thing as virtual harm: the online homophobic mockery aimed at Dominik cuts through him like a knife.

The virtual space of the Suicide Room is built in a series of fully computer-animated sequences where participants, reincarnated as avatars of their choosing, interact apart of the social norms that alienate them. The animated images feature as a new medium of communication operating on the fringes of the social or familial spheres and, to a certain extent, operating outside of the main narrative. The film is shifting between images of the master track and various kinds of digital transmediations. The small digital video cameras give way to the possibility of concealed filming (as was the case in *The Wedding Banquet*) and to a sense of exposed privacy (which was also made evident in *The Egoists*); the vectorial virtual world of the Suicide Room gives way to a concealing of the users, who 'physically' (that is, visually) appear not as themselves. However, the user can paradoxically create a strong and sincere bond with others, that which they can't seem to accomplish in real life, with family or friends. It follows that authenticity and deception are intertwined, and that the technological means of reproducing reality (or of setting up a new virtual reality) are here shown to be as cutting-edge as they can be misleading. In effect, the bonds that Dominik ends up creating in the Suicide Room will be beneficial in appearance only. If the grainy digital video images of webcam conversations divulge Dominik's concealed fears, the animated sequences, to which the video scenes lead to, only *appear* to offer a whole new, freer world. They function as distractions, but actually turn out to be as prescriptive, contrived and deceiving as the real, social world. Only too late will Dominik see 'the shower head on the landscape', that which *we* can see because of the filmmaker's careful handling and editing of these various visual systems the characters interact with or inhabit. The gritty DV images directly reveal the failings of the social realm by unmasking the emotional reality it hides, while the seductive creations of the virtual world indirectly do likewise by proving themselves to be more or less an extension of the social realm, in the guise of fantasy and emotional freedom.

One of the first digital transmediations of importance happens when a video of Dominik's gay kiss appears on the web. For obvious reasons, this upload and its subsequent sharing through social networks will have more of an impact than the kiss itself. By exposing Dominik's sexual ambiguity, the video initiates the sequence of events to follow. One day in gym class, Dominik unwillingly gets an erection (and an orgasm) after having been pinned to the ground by the boy he kissed at the party. Soon, the news get out and a second video emerges, a crude shadow-theatre parody of Dominik's misadventure. As soon as Dominik's feelings are revealed to be authentic and not only part of a game, they are rejected by the student community. The digital video footage acts as an indicator of character. Dominik himself does not seem particularly aware of his own sexual desires. For the rest of the film, they will be mostly sublimated through his virtual exploration of the Suicide Room and a destructive friendship with a young woman. All of this could be understood as a response not only to the rejection he experienced, but more profoundly as a response to his own conflicted sexual feelings. The moral implications of this issue – social and internalised homophobia – are rather lightly threaded by the film, and understandably so given that the subject of homosexuality has been a hot-button issue in Poland since the beginning of the twenty-first century. (Komasa's film was intended to be a commercial, popular film, and it did succeed in that regard:[6] by associating it with themes of digital representation and communication, as well as teen depression, unrest and suicide, *Suicide Room* underlines the contemporaneity and relevancy of gay identity as a potent figure for Polish cinema.)[7]

Another key digital transmediation takes place at the end of the movie, when a young couple decides to film Dominik's final agony. Having swallowed a bottle of pills, he is soon struck with severe pain. In a sequence full of camera jerks and jump cuts, he is shown trying to induce vomiting, crying, looking straight at the camera and pitifully screaming for his mother. This pathos is once again, as in *The Egoists*, rendered unbearable on account of its emphasis through the (close) framing and, possibly, the coarse video visuals. Using the ordinary DV image to represent this ultimate desperate act (and the film's denouement), the filmmaker indicts the new predatorial paradigms of mass media and society (or of social media), and their potential for deception and entrapment. Dominik's (mental) eye has been lost in a strange enrapturing gaze from beyond; through his recorded death, his parents and friends have the cruel opportunity to witness (over and over again, if they would so choose) the cold and inhumane design of technological worlds, for which some are fatally ill-prepared.

Unlike Hollywood's mainline paradigms of spectacle or realism, these contemporary Polish films explore the reflective potentialities of intermedial video images. Through *mise en abyme* and intermediality, the eye sees the intrinsic duality of images: displaying reality or imagined realities and displaying themselves as images. Similarly, we are of a dual nature, with both a secret and complicated inner world, and an outer, social self, which relies on any number of constructions (or, as Erving Goffman famously discussed in his 1956 book *The Presentation of Self in Everyday Life*, performances). These kinds of reflective practices are not new to cinema. Nevertheless, it must be noted how relevant they are today, as the concern for representation is constantly reactivated, questioning the ethical standards conveyed by the images we produce and, moreover, the social behaviours we choose to adopt.

Seeing the unmasking effects of *détrompe l'oeil* in a larger scope, the use of video images and of the now proliferating digital images as potential *détrompe l'oeil* can aid us to consider with more suspicion (and aesthetic appreciation at the very same time) the glitzy surface of self-promotion that our modern societies seem to favour. Life has become increasingly technological, ever since man has seen the benefits of the awe-inspiring innovations that make our comfortable lives possible. But technology has progressed further and further, reaching our body and our soul, attaching itself to the hand and the face, populating our minds with images, fascinating screens and alternate versions of ourselves and of the world. Now fully connected to new technologies, intermediality goes beyond aesthetics.

Notes

1. *The Wedding Banquet* was shot with an Arriflex 35 BL (a 35mm film camera), and the video footage was shot with a Sony Hi8 camcorder (according to Feliks Pastusiak, producer for Film It, the company who produced the film: personal email communication, 2019). *The Egoists* was shot with an Arriflex 35 BL 3, and the video footage was shot with a Sony PC 1000 (according to Grzegorz Kuczeriszka, director of photography for the film: personal email communication, 2019). As is now generally the case, *Suicide Room* was shot digitally in its entirety: for the main film track, a Red One production camera was used; for the smartphone and webcam footage, a simple Canon HD camcorder was used (according to Radek Ładczuk, director of photography for the film: personal email communication, 2019).
2. Deleuze and Guattari distinguish 'the majoritarian as a constant and homogeneous system; minorities as subsystems; and the minoritarian as a potential, creative and created, becoming [. . .] whose value is to trigger uncontrollable movements and deterritorializations of the mean or majority' (Deleuze and Guattari 2004: 117). Though there is little reason to expect small national cinemas of the world to substantially 'deterritorialize' anything of cinema in general, filmmakers have (as artists in other fields have) been influencing each other irrespective of political, social, moral, financial, linguistic or any other worldly considerations. (To state an obvious example, the influence of minoritarian German Expressionism can be felt still in majoritarian Hollywood cinema.) Deleuze and Guattari's theoretical proposal brings to mind the natural evolution of the arts, through cultural appropriations and transformations for which the creative potential of the minoritarian remains indispensable to artists everywhere.
3. This is truer today, considering the popularity of confessional style YouTube channels.
4. Other than the obvious fact that non-professional cameras can be used in professionally produced films, it must be noted that the quality of non-professional digital cameras is fast increasing.
5. Polish culture has been moulded by the literary and ideological-philosophical duality of a sacrificial-mystical romanticism (emotionalism) and an empirical-scientific positivism (rationalism). Poland was suffused with this familiar pattern of European history at the pivotal time of its 123-year-long subjugation (the Russian, Austrian and Prussia Partitions). Veteran Polish scholar Maria Janion views this pulsation of national identity as continuing to this day and also as rooted in the early (966) Orthodox East and Latin West division: 'the

Romantic writers [. . .] were deeply affected by the disconnection from Slavdom and [. . .] with the use of native folk art and its transformations, [they] attempted to restore its forgotten greatness. [. . .] In Romanticism, the uncanny Slavdom was a sign of a torn identity' (Janion 2014: 19–20).
6. A sequel to the film, titled *Suicide Room: The Hater* (*Sala samobójców: Hejter*), was produced in 2020 (also directed by Jan Komasa).
7. However relevant, the film's critical reception in Poland generally avoided commentaries on gay identity or minimised its importance, unlike foreign critics of the film (Jagielski 2013: 481–3; Laverdière 2017: 259–67).

Works Cited

Aumont, Jacques (1990), *L'image*, Paris: Fernand Nathan.
Aumont, Jacques, Alain Bergala, Michel Marie and Marc Vernet (1983), *L'Esthétique du film*, Paris: Fernand Nathan.
Deleuze, Gilles and Félix Guattari (2004), *A Thousand Plateaus*, London: Bloomsbury Academic.
Eile, Stanislaw (2000), *Literature and Nationalism in Partitioned Poland, 1795–1918*, New York: Palgrave Macmillan.
Goffman, Erving (1956), *The Presentation of Self in Everyday Life*, Edinburgh: University of Edinburgh Press.
Jagielski, Sebastian (2013), *Maskarady męskości. Pragnienie homospołeczne w polskim kinie fabularnym* [*Masquerades of Masculinity: Homosocial Desire in Polish Fiction Films*], Cracow: Universitas.
Janion, Maria (2014), 'Poland Between the West and East', *Teksty Drugie. Teoria literatury, krytyka, interpretacja*, Special Issue English Edition, Vol. 1, No. 5, pp. 13–33. <http://tekstydrugie.pl/wp-content/uploads/2016/06/t2en_2014_1webCOMB.pdf> (last accessed 25 May 2019).
Laverdière, Gabriel (2017), *Figures de l'homosexualité dans le cinéma polonais contemporain*, Thesis, Québec: Université Laval.
Ledoux, Aurélie (2012), *L'ombre d'un doute. Le cinéma américain contemporain et ses trompe-l'œil*, Rennes: Presses universitaires de Rennes.
Marlier, Georges (1964), 'C. N. Gysbrechts l'illusionniste', *Connaissance des arts*, No. 145, pp. 96–105.
Mazierska, Ewa (2007), *Polish Postcommunist Cinema. From Pavement Level*, Oxford: Peter Lang.
Nahlik, Monika (2009), 'Katyń w czasah popkultury' ['Katyń in the Time of Pop Culture'], in Tadeusz Lubelski and Maciej Stroiński (eds), *Kino polskie jako kino narodowe* [*Polish Cinema as National Cinema*] Cracow: Korporacja Ha!Art, pp. 321–49.
Pietrasik, Zdzisław (2009), 'Rozmowa z Wojciechem Smarzowskim' ['Interview with Wojciech Smarzowski'], *Polityka*, 4 November 2009.
Roy, Lucie (2015), *Le pouvoir de l'oubliée. La perception au cinéma*, Paris: L'Harmattan.

CHAPTER 12

Superhero Genre and Graphic Storytelling in Contemporary Hungarian and Russian Cinema

Bence Kránicz

We live in the age of superheroes. Films involving superheroes – mainly adaptations of stories from another medium, such as comic books – are highly successful on the global market, and can be considered an important trend of contemporary mainstream cinema. Before the 2000s only one comic-book adaptation reached the status of the top-grossing film of the year on the American domestic market. After 2000 this happened eight times, and all eight of those films were superhero movies.[1] The tendency is also visible on the international market: since 2000 five comic-book adaptations (all of them superhero movies) have gained the position of the highest-grossing film of a given year.[2]

Without exception, these films were produced by major Hollywood studios on a high budget, and they are distributed globally on as many markets as possible. This also means that they have the potential to influence popular cinema outside of the United States. This chapter focuses not on American superhero movies, but the ones produced outside of the US, by smaller national film industries which can be considered peripheral from the point of view of American audiences and distribution. By adapting American superhero stories, however, the national film industries open a 'third space' through hybridity, mixing elements of both cultures, thus attempting to destroy the oppositions between 'centre' and 'periphery' (Wang and Yueh-yu Yeh 2005).

I aim to examine how the superhero genre and characters are interpreted, adapted and changed in the context of the Hungarian and the Russian film industry. How do the writers and directors create an American-type superhero in their own national environment and local culture? Are there any stylistic elements kept in the respective films from comic books, the original medium of the most famous superheroes? Do the resulting films function as superhero parodies or 'serious' superhero movies (meaning superhero stories played for a dramatic effect instead of comedy)? And last but not least, do these national superheroes function as tools for criticising and opposing the West?

Who Are the Superheroes and What Do They Do in Eastern Europe?

All nations, ethnicities and cultures create their own superheroes. In fact, certain mythic figures and characters of national folklore can be considered superheroes, from Gilgamesh and Hercules of the ancient Akkadian and Hellenic myths, to the hero of British folklore, Robin Hood, the latter being an early example of costumed vigilantes. Most English-language theoretical works on the subject mainly consider comic-book characters created from the 1930s onwards when defining superheroes, without emphasising or, sometimes, even mentioning the importance of earlier national myths in the popularity of the genre. The bulk of these academic works define superheroes as fictional characters with extraordinary physical and/or mental abilities who use their skills protecting not just their loved ones, but large groups, even societies of average people. As Fingeroth argues, among the defining characteristics of superheroes 'the most obvious things are: some sort of strength of character (though it may be hidden), some system of (generally-thought-to-be) positive values, and a determination to, no matter what, protect those values' (Fingeroth 2004: 17). Another definition states that 'the main theme that can be applied to superhero narratives is the cult of the individual; that is the focus on a single person with a great kind of power, usually a combination of mental and physical strength, who succeeds against all odds' (Gray II and Kaklamanidou 2011: 4).

However, there is a certain theoretical gap or ambiguity here: if we consider Batman a superhero, a man with above-average physical skills, a detective's mind and of considerable wealth, who vows to protect his fellow men after his personal loss, why do we not consider Zorro a superhero as well? After all, he can be described with exactly the same words. The similarities in their costume and their lack of supernatural powers invites comparisons between the two characters, even if Zorro is more deeply rooted in Spanish-Californian folklore. This conflict between different definitions remains unresolved. One can only assume that American scholars tend to forget about the fact that the concept of superheroes can also be connected to other nations' folklore, fables and popular culture beside the more immediate American context. Larger-than-life characters who vow to protect society are not necessarily superheroes, but the evolution of the superhero genre – based primarily on the popularity of early twentieth-century book series like Tarzan and Conan who might be considered as inspirations for superheroes – brought possibilities in popular literature and film to redefine national folklore tales as 'superhero stories'. On the other hand, the popular American superheroes can also be adapted to local contexts. Analysing these different approaches to adaptation may call for the use of post-colonial theoretical concepts and methods, both because of the nexus between the peripheral and the globally present Hollywood film industries, and the symbolic role of the superheroes as pop cultural agents of American military, cultural and ideological dominance over the rest of the world (DiPaolo 2011).

Adapted, 'nationalised' superheroes can serve multiple purposes. Their creators are tempted by the promise of financial success: since superhero movies form a globally popular group of films, it is only natural that film industries outside of Hollywood also try to create their own superheroes. Ideally, the new characters will interest local audiences (because their adventures take place in local spaces and contexts), and will be marketable on the global market (because the superhero genre is popular almost everywhere). The more superhero films are made, their distinction becomes inevitable, and this process might also be in favour of the national, non-Western superheroes. Recently, female characters (*Wonder Woman*, 2017), antagonist-type superheroes (*Deadpool*, 2016; *Deadpool 2*, 2018) and ethnicised ones (*Black Panther*, 2018) have also achieved financial success, indicating a global interest in characters who were previously considered 'niche' superheroes.

The promise of success on both the local and international markets clearly led the distribution plan of a number of recent non-American superhero films. The big-budget Bollywood production of *Krrish* (Rakesh Roshan, 2006) and its sequel, *Krrish 3*[3] (Rakesh Roshan, 2013) were distributed on many foreign markets, in eight and thirteen countries, respectively.[4] *Krrish* grossed 1.4m US dollars in India, and another 16m worldwide, which shows the film's worldwide appeal.[5] The Russian superhero movie *Black Lightning* (*Chernaya molniya*, Dmitriy Kiselev, Aleksandr Voytinskiy, 2009), which I will be examining in fuller detail later on, was produced by the internationally well-known Timur Bekmambetov, had a budget of roughly 15 million US dollars – certainly a big sum in Russian terms –, and it was distributed in thirty countries either in cinemas, on DVD or on television. A key element in the success of these movies might be their connection to well-known American superheroes: *Krrish* is largely inspired by the Superman origin story[6] with elements of many Spider-Man stories, while *Black Lightning* evidently remakes Spider-Man's origin story in contemporary Russia.

However, the iconic characters of Western, particularly American popular culture have a different significance in national-peripheral cultures: they can be interpreted as symbols of Western cultural dominance. As the author of a paper on a recent Mexican superhero comic book puts it:

> the modern moral code inherent in the superhero profile was not originally built on philosophical universals, but on a national ethos. Thus, a close relationship can be discerned between a national, status quo vision of modernity

and the emergent twentieth century cultural figure of the superhero: 'the American Way' of individualism and capitalist democracy in superhuman form, dressed up in tights for good measure. (Campbell 2009: 29)

An 'ethnicised' superhero (of American origin, but operating in local spaces and contexts) means something different in countries with historical pasts as colonies, or historical and ideological opposition to the West. In the cases of Indian, Russian or Japanese superheroes, the symbolic-ideological position of the protagonist becomes essential. The adaptation of the American superhero in non-Western contexts is definitely a form of the post-colonial mimicry, which effectively points out the imperialist logic behind the superhero narratives. As Campbell argues, superheroes are the symbols of the capitalist way of protecting a society, thus, mimicking and refashioning them eventually contributes to the deconstruction of Western cultural hegemony (Dudrah 2006).

A mixture of concepts of the superhero genre, the post-colonial and the postsocialist theoretical frameworks can be applied when dealing with Eastern European superheroes. The method is the same with both films chosen for analysis: I will argue that the hybrid narrative forms created by adapting American superhero motifs in national contexts are used to articulate the global positions of postsocialist nations. In our case, both the Hungarian short film *Sha-Man Vs. Ikarus* (*Táltosember Vs. Ikarus*, György Pálfi, 2003) and the Russian feature film *Black Lightning* follow the same narrative method: they use the archetypical character and storyline of the American superhero to define their relation to the Soviet past.

SHADOWS OF OUR LIFE IN THE EASTERN BLOC

Sha-Man Vs. Ikarus[7] is an 18-minute Hungarian short film directed by György Pálfi. It was screened as part of the omnibus project *A Bus Came . . .* (*Jött egy busz*, 2003), which consisted of five short films directed by five then-upcoming Hungarian directors. In a sense, *A Bus Came . . .* was a showcase of Hungarian talent in film and new directions of Hungarian cinema, which highlights the importance of the fact that Pálfi used the superhero genre, then unknown in Hungarian cinema.

His film is inspired by the ancient Greek myth of Ikarus and his father, Daedalus. In Pálfi's version Daedalus, here called Daeda and presented as a comic-book supervillain, tries to resurrect his son, Ikarus, and presumably gain control over the world. His son, though, is not a person but the collective entity of the bus vehicles used for public transport in present-day Budapest – a special brand of Socialist-era buses still in use, called Ikarus. The only one who can stop Daeda is Sha-Man, the superhero of Budapest, a middle-aged, caring father in his daily life, and a fearless superhero at night. Sha-Man's name comes from the word 'sámán' – shamans were medieval priests of Hungarian tribes before the country adopted Christianity, and are part of Hungarian national folklore. Thus, the film connects local and 'international' myths, tales of old times and the twentieth century.

Even the narrative summary of Pálfi's film reveals that *Sha-Man Vs. Ikarus* is indeed a superhero parody, which partly explains why Pálfi was so keen on using self-reflexive, comic-book-inspired stylistic elements throughout the film (Figure 12.1). According to the director's approach, superheroes cannot be other than parodistic characters in the Eastern European context, both because of the different cultural background, the lack of present-day mythic tales in a country which endured so much suffering during the twentieth century, and the insufficient financial and technical background to present on-screen superheroes, using up-to-date special effects. *Sha-Man Vs. Ikarus* argues that superheroes are perceived as mighty but flawed and ultimately ridiculous creatures in the Eastern European context: 'false gods' instead of genuine saviours. In Pálfi's vision parody is a fitting genre for a Hungarian superhero tale, and because parodies are inherently self-reflexive films (mixing different genres, playing with narrative tools and visual elements), Pálfi is not afraid to apply a self-conscious, often alienating visual inventory. As Gehring argues, 'self-consciousness represents the ultimate parody prick, since nothing affectionately deflates a celebrated genre or auteur faster than a comic reminder that this is, indeed, only a movie' (Gehring 1999: 16).

Figure 12.1 György Pálfi's *Sha-Man Vs. Ikarus* (2003), a self-reflexive superhero movie made in a style inspired by comic books

The self-reflexive style in question comes directly from the visual inventory of comics. The elements of comics in the film are part of Pálfi's postmodern mashup aesthetic, since *Sha-Man Vs. Ikarus* is not an adaptation of a single comic book. Mainstream comic-book adaptations usually tend to leave behind most stylistic elements of the original medium, because certain visual tools, which are perfectly normal in comics, become transgressive and alienating on screen. Comic-book films which use some of these techniques are typically parodies, e.g. the American *Scott Pilgrim vs. the World* (Edgar Wright, 2010), with its split-screens and visible sound effects, or *Gagamboy* (Erik Matti, 2004), produced in the Philippines, using frequent axial jumps.[8] In these films, as well as in *Sha-Man Vs. Ikarus*, the visual inventory of comic books works as an obstacle of the viewers' immersion in the filmic narrative. This can be seen as a typical postmodern method because the narrative is ironically weakened and might be seen as merely a tool of colliding different media. The focus moves on, in this way, to the interpretations of intermediality, and, in Pálfi's case, an auteur's comment on postsocialist national conflicts.

The dominating visual tools of *Sha-Man Vs. Ikarus* are diegetic frames and the split-screen effect. Pálfi and his cinematographer, Gergely Pohárnok constantly play with split screens of different shapes and numbers, resembling comic-book panels, guiding the audience through an intimate dinner scene in an apartment using at least three split screens with moving cameras and characters, who are drifting from one screen to another from unexpected directions, confusing the audience in their spatial orientation. In other scenes, the director creates diegetic frames: the space inside of a bus, divided into different sections by the stanchions, or the long shot of a bus garage, where the separate garage doors form separate on-screen frames. These visual tools and some computer-generated images constituting the visual excess of *Sha-Man Vs. Ikarus* move the film closer to a self-reflexive approach of the superhero genre.

The unique way of how a comic-book narrative is formed was labelled 'graphic storytelling' by Will Eisner, one of the pioneers of the medium (Eisner 1996). What Pálfi achieves in his short film might also be called the adaptation of this comic-book-style 'graphic storytelling' in a cinematic context, because the visual elements of comics are not only ornaments in the visual style, but they open the narrative towards the ironic and allegorical interpretations. *Sha-Man Vs. Ikarus* is notable because of its place in Pálfi's auteuristic *oeuvre*, the way it appropriates and introduces superheroes into contemporary Eastern European cinema: as agents of the auteurs' art cinema. The director sets up a mythical war in our everyday world, and uses the dull objects of this world (buses, especially) as symbols of this battle of ancient origins. The name Ikarus connects and mixes two different pasts: the mythic past of Hellenic gods and the real past of Soviet oppression.[9] The parodistic effect partly comes from the fact that the banal, everyday situations of present-day Hungary are stylised into the setting of a supernatural battle – and also from Pálfi's joke about building the 'myth' of the socialist decades of Hungary. Thus, *Sha-Man Vs. Ikarus* puts a postmodern twist on two separate 'heroic ages'. Pálfi constructs a hybrid space where ancient fables collide with modern popular culture, symbols of Western popular culture meet with symbols of Hungarian folklore, and a conflict between national past and present emerges. The visual tools of the comic book are integrated into the film to graphically underline these forms of hybridity.

Stylising real past and real present into mythical, folkloristic time and space is a method Pálfi follows frequently in his films. The story of his debut feature film *Hukkle* (2002) takes place in a timeless, or rather out-of-time Hungarian village, a space where present and past, real and magical, technology and tradition exist at the same time. The borders between real and mythical time and space also fade in *Taxidermia* (2006), in which Pálfi transforms landmark historical moments of the twentieth century into a symbolic family tale of generations. The block of flats in *Free Fall* (*Szabadesés*, 2014), much like the bus garages of *Sha-Man Vs. Ikarus*, yet again becomes the scenery for magical-realist events in present-day Budapest. It is also worth mentioning Pálfi's unfinished project based on *Toldi*, a famous Hungarian heroic saga from the nineteenth century, was envisioned as a 'medieval action film'. The adaptation of the superhero character fits perfectly into this group of films, which build bridges between realistic and mythic worlds and tropes.

Putin's Own Superhero

When analysing Russian superhero movies, a question arises: what theoretical framework may be applied to the films and other cultural products of post-socialist countries, especially Russia, to compare these cases with the typical 'target countries' of post-colonial theory, such as India? The problem is contradictory. The Soviet Union acted as a colonising power in the Eastern Bloc after World War II, while simultaneously the Soviet state oppressed and deformed the Russian culture, along with the national culture of all other member states.[10] Post-colonial interpretation seems to be relevant in the case of *Black Lightning* for two reasons. On the one hand, Russian stereotypes about the peoples of the ex-Soviet countries are still lingering in the film, echoing the colonising attitude of the Soviet Union. On the other hand, contemporary Russia is similar to other Eastern European countries (mainly ex-colonies of the Soviet Union) in the sense that Eastern Europe is often considered a homogeneous geopolitical unit and the Other of Western Europe (Mazierska et al. 2013: 22). After the fall of the Soviet Union, Western cultural influence grew stronger, leaving its mark on the Russian film industry and becoming fierce rivals to the local films, just like in every other country in Eastern Europe. In 1985, forty Soviet films were attended by more than 5 million people, while in 1994 not a single Russian film was seen by more than 500,000 people (Larsen 1999: 193). *Black Lightning* can be seen as part of a project in the new millennium to appeal to Russian audiences with new national popular stories.

The cultural dominance of the United States, mirrored by the attendance numbers of American films screened in Russia, focused attention on the significance of producing genre films. In the 1990s many Russian film critics and other members of the film industry shared the opinion that it was essential to produce genre films to attract audiences, if they aimed to revitalise the Russian film industry (Seckler 2009). Like other national film industries in Europe, Russian filmmakers realised they had to learn the rules of professional genre filmmaking if they wanted to compete with American genre films. This required larger budgets and more sophisticated knowledge of the craft – as the author of an essay on contemporary Russian genre film emphasises, 'not a single Russian film was able to reach high professional standards' (Komm 2002).

Among others, Dmitriy Komm wrote about the demand for a new cinematic national myth, which could serve as the foundation of the local genre film production. To follow his train of thought: the superhero genre is perfectly suitable for creating modern national 'myths', as seen by the present-day popularity of superhero characters created in America in the 1930s. In contemporary Russia, this need for new – predominantly male – heroes is strongly connected to politics, specifically to Putinist strategies. Black Lightning, the superhero saving Russia, emphasises the moral superiority of the 'Russian Way', the refusal of the Western capitalist logic, and thus effectively becomes Russia's answer to American genre films. He emerges as the hero of a 'cultural cold war', so to speak, who derives from the American popular myths but also opposes them. Highlighting the connection to popular American culture, Dmitriy Kiselev and Aleksandr Voytinskiy's *Black Lightning* appropriates motifs from several contemporary American blockbusters, such as the *Transformers* series, but first and foremost, *Spider-Man*: the protagonist's trauma and motivations, the sense of responsibility fuelled by guilt are elements directly lifted from Spider-Man's origin story.[11]

Dima is a university student from a poor working-class family, who lives with his parents and his younger sister. As a birthday gift from his father, he gets a used, dingy Volga car. Soon he realises that the car can fly. Dima starts working as a flower courier to make some money with his marvellous car, which was engineered by Soviet scientists and operates with still-unknown source of energy. One evening Dima is late from a meeting with his father, who is attacked and stabbed by a criminal. Dima hears that someone is wounded, but he does not know his father is the victim. Although a passer-by is urging him to call an ambulance, he fails to call it in time. Because of his carelessness, his father dies. Realising this, Dima decides to use his flying car to patrol the streets and the sky of Moscow, to protect his fellow men and fight for justice.

The protagonist does not have supernatural physical abilities; his power comes from a technological marvel, the flying car (which resembles the robot cars from *Transformers* (Michael Bay, 2007), or Marty McFly's DeLorean from *Back to the Future* (Robert Zemeckis, 1985)). In his everyday life Dima is in many ways similar to Peter Parker (Spider-Man): he is considered a nerd in school, and is frustrated by the economic background of his family. An essential part in Spider-Man's history is the fact that Peter Parker first wants to make money with his supernatural abilities. This motif is also very important in *Black Lightning*, although in Dima's case he is able to act as a superhero merely due to the possession of a supernatural car.

There are two characters in the film who influence Dima to think that if he wants to move up the social ladder, and win the heart of the girl he wants, he needs to focus on financial profit. His schoolmate, Max is bragging about his new toys all the time: his Mercedes car and his iPhone are Western status symbols, which mesmerise girls and which other boys are envious of. Dima fancies his new classmate, Nastya, and thinks he needs the same artefacts symbolising wealth to impress her. As a flower courier, he starts to make money – he is more successful than his colleagues, by using the flying Volga he doesn't have to trudge in traffic – and spends his first wages on an iPhone to get Nastya's attention. There seems to be a clash between Soviet and Western technology, as later in the story, while Dima is fighting to save Nastya and other people, Max can do nothing but follow his friend's actions on the news, staring at the screen of his smartphone. Thus, the narrative role of gadgets and technology is to underline the conflict between two cultures and two ideologies: Russian technology helps fight the good fight, while Western technology only creates a simulacrum, a secondary channel to follow events unfolding in real life.

Another character, a millionaire businessman, Mr Kuptsov, also encourages the protagonist to focus more on material goods and moneymaking. In his lecture given at Dima's class, Mr Kuptsov states that the world only moves ahead if everyone minds their own business, instead of helping others. He offers one million rubles to the student who promises him that when they have a chance next time, they will not help another person in need. The character is perfectly defined by Slavoj Žižek's term, who applied Lacan's dichotomy of intellectuals, the 'fools' and the 'knaves' to members of the European intelligentsia after the fall of the Soviet Union. According to Žižek, the 'knave' is 'a neoconservative advocate of the free market who cruelly rejects all forms of social solidarity as counterproductive sentimentalism' (Žižek 1997: 45).

However, Kuptsov is not only an 'advocate of the free market', he is also the antagonist of the story. He is looking to find the flying car to lay his hands on its core, the 'nanocatalyzer'. With it he plans to drill deeper into the ground than anyone before him, and extract more and more resources from the body of 'Mother Russia'. The psychoanalytical interpretation seems to be plausible also because we find many phallic symbols in the story, which can be considered weapons in the men's battle for saving or ruling Russia. Kuptsov's headquarters is called Diamond Tower, while Dima's father works as a tram driver: the two opposing parties may be defined as representatives of phallic objects which strike through the city in vertical or horizontal shapes. The flying car destroys this opposition, as it is able to move through the city in every direction, on the ground and in the sky. Adapting the conflict between the protagonist and the antagonist to spatial relations also derives from superhero comics, which frequently deal with questions of size and (phallic) shape. The heavily symbolic, iconologically dense image of Black Lightning and Kuptsov before their final fight might also borrow its bombastic quality from superhero comics, which often build up the narrative towards spectacular 'splash pages': pages which do not consist of several panels, only one action-packed image. This might also be regarded as a way of adapting the 'graphic storytelling' of comics into a superhero film.

Upon realising that Dima is Black Lightning, Kuptsov kidnaps the scientists who once built the flying Volga, and commands them to build another car: this time, a flying Mercedes. Thus, Kuptsov becomes an advocate of the West not just in his ideologies, but also by his iconology. In the end, the clash of the Volga and the Mercedes over the Red Square becomes the battle between two ideologies, two world orders (Figure 12.2), recreating the binary logic of traditional superhero narratives. But this time it is the antagonist who is representing capitalist ideology and cultural codes, not the superhero. This is why *Black Lightning* is not only a 'harmless' superhero movie: as I later argue, it is a key production in the battle against Western pop-cultural dominance, symbolised by the popularity of Hollywood genre cinema in international markets.

While the evil businessman – and Dima's dumb but well-meaning classmate, Max – are advocates of an ideology strongly associated with the West and presented as false and unjust, the marvellous car which makes Dima a hero is an innovation of the Soviet Union. Its innovators were scientists working on the technological advance of the Soviet Union, and the Volga is a distinctly Soviet brand, which was distributed in all countries of the former

Figure 12.2 Flying Volga above the Red Square in *Black Lightning* (2009)

Eastern Bloc.¹² The most curious element in *Black Lightning* is that it not only represents innovations of the Soviet Union as useful tools and glorious achievements of the Russian culture, but through these, the film builds continuity between the Soviet past and the present-day Putinist political system. When his father gives the Volga to Dima, he proudly adds that 'Putin has the same car.' This means the creators of the film do not only build an opposition between Russia and the West (mainly, the United States) in the ideological and cultural spaces, but they also add a political interpretation. *Black Lightning* bears proudly the heritage of the Soviet past, and is positioned as a tentpole production among the new Russian genre films, defying the dominance of Hollywood – its role is parallel to Putin's actions who also aims to defy Western interests and create his own 'Russian way'. This problematic and simplified opposition is heavily criticised by Muireann Maguire in her analysis of the film: '*Black Lightning* attacks market capitalism, but it offers no replacement morality besides sentimentality, and no social alternatives except nostalgia' (Maguire 2010).

As Russia fits into the role of the 'colonised' party that rebels against cultural oppression through criticising the capitalist ideology associated with the West, *Black Lightning* also reveals the colonising attitude and reflexes of the late Soviet Union in its storyline and character building. Clearly this is the case with Dima's boss, a Georgian florist called Bahram, who is represented as a penny pincher exploiting his employees. It seems as if this negative stereotyping is also a tool of nostalgia for the Soviet world order. *Black Lightning* is pervaded by enthusiasm for Soviet technological advance, anticapitalist (anti-imperialist) ideology and an ethnicist viewpoint echoing the hierarchy of the former Eastern Bloc. The adaptation of the superhero in this context signals the claim to defeat the Americans with their own pop cultural icon, with their own 'weapons'. The remorse of the protagonist, adapted from the *Spider-Man* stories, is not only felt for the father's death: figuratively, it is a sense of guilt for the fall of the Soviet Union, and the protagonist vows to act as a superhero to give new meaning to the values of the Soviet past in the present.

Black Lightning is not the only Russian film which uses Western genre patterns or adapts other media to appease both the local and the Western market. Bekmambetov's vampire fantasy, *Night Watch* (*Nochnoy dozor*, 2004) and its sequels were also successfully distributed abroad, while *Hardcore Henry* (Ilya Naishuller, 2015), again with Bekmambetov as a producer, aims to exhibit the forms of masculinity supported by Putin's Russia through a POV action film (Sepsi 2016). In this aspect *Hardcore Henry* is very much similar to *Black Lightning*, as the superhero film also demonstrates the contemporary Russian way of masculine hierarchy: *Black Lightning*'s Nastya is constantly floating between different men who try to win her by showing off money, or demonstrating their physical strength. Based on these two films, all a man has to have is power, be it economic or physical, and nothing else.[13]

While *Black Lightning* evidently cannot compete with American superproductions on the international market, the use of the superhero character shows the endeavour to please global audiences. The creators of the film use a Western archetype, a superhero story based largely on *Spider-Man*, to oppose a simplified capitalist ideology associated with the West, and interpret their moral-ideological disagreement in the present-day political and social spaces. This is how the American-type superhero becomes a tool of explicit criticism of the West, and his godlike power merely a weapon in an ideological war.

Old Conflicts, New Superheroes

The need to refashion motifs from American superhero stories in *Black Lightning* might be also explained with the fact that traditionally Eastern European genre cinema is not populated by superheroes. Japan constantly produces a fair amount of 'henshin hero' ('transforming hero') science fictions, and after *Krrish* even Bollywood started to regularly put out superhero films (see *Ra.One*, directed by Anubhav Sinha, 2011; or *A Flying Jatt*, directed by Remo D'Souza, 2016), while European film industries in general are not willing to contribute to the wave of superhero films. This does not mean that the genre cannot find its roots in the popular mythology or folklore of the European countries, as the previous examples have shown. There is also a particular field in Hungarian film, which is even more directly connected with the superhero genre: animation. Hungarian animation has been closely linked to national folklore as many fables were adapted to cartoons, most notably the *Magyar Népmesék* series (*Hungarian Folk Tales*, 1980–2012). The narratives of these tales are often based on individual heroes who go on epic adventures and undertake difficult tasks, using supernatural, magical tools to succeed. However, these are almost exclusively children's films, and the links to a grown-up audience, which are more defined in superhero stories, are mostly missing. There are a few exceptions: the supernatural powers of Grabowski, the protagonist of the cult-classic *Cat City* (*Macskafogó*, Béla Ternovszky, 1986) effectively define the spy mouse as a superhero. The many costumes and aliases of *Mattie the Goose-boy* (*Lúdas Matyi*, Attila Dargay, 1977), a peasant boy who takes revenge on the rich landlord who wronged him, place this folklore hero and literature character close to the superhero genre. Marcell Jankovics's adaptations of famous Hungarian fables, *Johnny Corncob* (*János Vitéz*, 1973) and *Son of the White Mare* (*Fehérlófia*, 1981) can also be regarded as superhero fantasies.[14] Among Jankovics's two films especially *Fehérlófia* stands comparison with *Sha-Man Vs. Ikarus* because it is not made as a fantasy for children, it is rather an art-house, 'grown-up' version of a folklore tale. Moreover, it can be also compared to Pálfi's film in its intermedial quality: Jankovics's visual style is closer to abstract painting than to a Disney-type animation. Once again, intermediality is connected to lifting a canonical narrative – a folklore fable or a superhero story – from its regular basis of interpretation and institutional background.

Just like these animation films, *Sha-Man Vs. Ikarus* builds on national folklore and the historical past. It demonstrates how the elements of the superhero genre can be sewn into a parodistic story about national remembrance of the past – a new goal compared to the efforts of the earlier animation movies. Following Pálfi's method of analysing the ambivalent relationship with the national past, another Hungarian auteur chose to present a contemporary political allegory as a superhero story. In 2017, Kornél Mundruczó, an established art-house director of György Pálfi's generation, premiered *Jupiter's Moon* (*Jupiter holdja*), whose protagonist, a Syrian refugee, has the supernatural ability to fly. Mundruczó's film uses the superhero motifs to create the character of a saviour, a 'contemporary Jesus', who, as an illegal immigrant, is also an enemy of the state. In its narrative, *Jupiter's Moon* follows a superhero's origin story – with the protagonist coming to terms with his supernatural abilities in the end – but it also serves as an allegory of the apocalyptic conditions that the governmental xenophobia might create, not a reflection on its genre roots.

Dealing with the often traumatic national past and present through a fantastic superhero story is the strategy followed both by *Sha-Man Vs. Ikarus* and *Jupiter's Moon*, as well as by *Black Lightning* in a Russian context.

Sha-Man Vs. Ikarus and *Black Lightning* are both exciting objects of study in the context of post-communist memory of the past – an important aspect regarding contemporary Eastern European works, and one connected to nationalist discourses. Within these contexts, the difference between the cultural positions of the two films becomes evident. *Sha-Man Vs. Ikarus* is essentially art-house cinema: it playfully draws parallels between an ancient, global myth and a modern, local one, emphasising that a way of dealing with the past is to convert it to fantastic and, ultimately, harmless mythology. By using the stylistic conventions of comic books, György Pálfi creates a self-reflexive postmodern superhero parody – the intermediality of his short film is a tool to ridicule the symbols of the Soviet past.

On the other hand, *Black Lightning* is a propagandistic effort to establish the power of contemporary Russian popular culture, strongly connected to Russian national identity. The stylistic elements of comic books are less important here than the origin story and guilt-ridden character of Spider-Man, one of the most popular superheroes of the genre. The same motivations which made Peter Parker Spider-Man make Dima the Black Lightning, a superhero who uses the heritage of the Soviet Union to fight for justice in present-day Russia. It is equally as important in this film as in *Sha-Man Vs. Ikarus* to make peace with the past, but the methods and conclusions are different: Soviet times are presented as an era of Russian dominance. It is an era worthy of being remembered with nostalgia and, partly, worthy of being recreated. *Black Lightning* proved to be popular and, since that film's premiere, Russia has produced another big-budget superhero movie. *The Guardians* (*Zashchitniki*, Sarik Andraesyan, 2017) follows up on the project of re-evaluating the Soviet heritage: the film's superheroes come from different ex-Soviet countries, symbolically reuniting the fallen state. In addition, they have to defeat a scientist who terrorises Russia with a satellite weapon built in Ronald Reagan's America. Thus, the film operates with the same 'cold war with superheroes' undertone as *Black Lightning*.

The questions of intermediality are key in these superhero films. The stylistic elements of comic books, which might seem transgressive on film, move *Sha-Man Vs. Ikarus* towards postmodern parody and auteur cinema. The popular 'myth' of a superhero story, following the conventions of superhero comics but rooted in ancient myths and popular literature as well, may serve to redefine national identity in *Black Lightning*. Meanwhile, the use of comic-book elements, be they stylistic or thematic, helps the creators find their way towards new and presumably younger audiences, the main consumers of American superhero films; audiences who otherwise may not be particularly interested in films about their countries' communist past. Beside these distinctly Eastern European conflicts, different patterns of international superhero adaptations emerge even through such a small number of films as examined in this chapter. Integrating the visual elements of comic books in the cinematic context contributes to creating hybrid spaces of postsocialist discourse. The ambivalent relationship between Western and Eastern cultures are effectively highlighted by the adaptations of ideological Western (comic book) characters in Eastern European (filmic) contexts. *Sha-Man Vs. Ikarus* and *Black Lightning* show how these modes of adaptation might also lead to diverging perspectives in national self-identification.

This work was supported by the project entitled Space-ing Otherness. Cultural Images of Space, Contact Zones in Contemporary Hungarian and Romanian Film and Literature (OTKA NN 112700).

Notes

1. See the Yearly Box Office list on the Box Office Mojo website. Available at <http://boxofficemojo.com/yearly/> (last accessed 20 November 2019).
2. Available at <http://boxofficemojo.com/yearly/?view2=worldwide&view=releasedate &p=.htm> (last accessed 20 November 2019).
3. There is no *Krrish 2* as with the release of the *Krrish* sequel the original film was deemed to be already the second instalment of a series that started with *Found Someone* (*Koi . . . Mil Gaya*, 2003), a sci-fi without superheroes.
4. Data according to the IMDb pages of the films. Available at <http://www.imdb.com/title/tt0432637/releaseinfo?ref_=tt_ov_inf&> (last accessed 12 January 2019).
5. See on this Box Office Mojo: *Krrish*. Available at <http://www.boxofficemojo.com/movies/?id=krrish.htm> (last accessed 12 January 2019).
6. The 'bedrock account of the transformative events that set the protagonist apart from ordinary humanity' (Hatfield et al. 2013: 3), i.e. the background stories of superheroes which present how they got their powers are called 'origin stories'.
7. Internet sources differ on the English title of the film, which is sometimes cited as *Shaman Vs. Icarus*. The pun in Sha-Man is obviously a reflection on common superhero names.
8. A notable exception is Ang Lee's *Hulk* (2003), which is not a superhero parody, but uses axial jumps to highlight the split personality of the protagonist.
9. The situation is further complicated by the fact that Ikarus was a brand built under communist rule and encouraged by the Soviet Union. Nevertheless, it was a Hungarian, not a Soviet brand. Ikarus buses were products of the Hungarian industry, and were exported into communist countries as far as Cuba. The brand was a source of national pride at the time of communism.
10. On the differences and similarities between post-colonial and postsocialist theories, and the appliance of a post-colonial theoretical framework in the case of Eastern Europe and the Balkans, see Chari and Verdery (2009).

11. The parallel with the Spider-Man stories is also mentioned by Lee and Ditko (2006).
12. 'The Volga Gaz-21 is very much a Soviet hero-car. Its large-scale production signalled the Soviet Union's post-war economic recovery. Last manufactured in 1979, the car now recalls the good old days prior to perestroika – a living symbol of the sturdiness, durability and economy of Soviet craftsmanship' (Maguire 2010).
13. Looking back at *Sha-Man Vs. Ikarus* from the gender perspective, it's evident that the superhero character is seen as a confident family man and a responsible father, which also builds towards the traditional and conservative male roles associated with the superhero genre.
14. I would like to thank Zsolt Gyenge for the observation about Jankovics's films.

Works Cited

Campbell, Bruce (2009), 'Truth, Justice, and the Critique of Globalization in a Mexican Superhero Parody', *Headwaters*, Vol. 26, pp. 27–43.

Chari, Sharad and Katherine Verdery (2009), 'Thinking between the Posts: Postcolonialism, Postsocialism, and Ethnography after the Cold War', *Comparative Studies in Society and History*, Vol. 51, No. 1, pp. 6–34.

DiPaolo, Mark (2011), *War, Politics and Superheroes. Ethics and Propaganda in Comics and Film*, Jefferson, NC and London: McFarland.

Dudrah, Rajinder Kumar (2006), *Bollywood: Sociology Goes to The Movies*, New Delhi, Thousand Oaks, CA and London: Sage.

Eisner, Will (1996), *Graphic Storytelling and Visual Narrative*, Tamarac: Poorhouse Press.

Fingeroth, Danny (2004), *Superman on the Couch. What Superheroes Really Tell Us about Ourselves and Our Society*, New York and London: Continuum.

Gehring, Wes D. (1999), *Parody as Film Genre. 'Never Give a Saga an Even Break'*, Westport, CT and London: Greenwood Press.

Gray II, Richard J. and Betty Kaklamanidou (eds) (2011), *The 21st Century Superhero. Essays on Gender, Genre and Globalization in Film*, Jefferson, NC and London: McFarland.

Hatfield, Charles, Jeet Heer and Kent Worcester (eds) (2013), *The Superhero Reader*, Jackson: The University Press of Mississippi.

Komm, Dmitriy (2002), 'Adósok és hitelezők. Az orosz műfaj ['Debtors and creditors. Russian Genre'], *Metropolis*, No. 3–4, <http://metropolis.org.hu/?pid=16&aid=409> (last accessed 12 January 2019).

Larsen, Susan (1999), 'In Search of an Audience: The New Russian Cinema of Reconciliation', in Adele Marie Barker (ed.), *Consuming Russia*, Durham, NC and London: Duke University Press, pp. 192–216.

Lee, Stan and Steve Ditko (2006), *Essential Spider-Man Vol. 1*, New York: Marvel Comics.

Maguire, Muireann (2010), 'Black Lightning', *KinoKultura*, Vol. 29, No. 3, <http://www.kinokultura.com/2010/29r-chernaiamolnia.shtml> (last accessed 12 January 2019).

Mazierska, Ewa, Lars Kristensen and Eva Näripea (eds), (2013) *Postcolonial Approaches to Eastern European Cinema. Portraying Neighbours on Screen*, London: I. B. Tauris.

Seckler, Dawn A (2009), *Engendering Genre: The Contemporary Russian Buddy Film*, Unpublished PhD dissertation, Pittsburgh: University of Pittsburgh, <http://d-scholarship.pitt.edu/10213/> (last accessed 12 January 2019).

Sepsi, László (2016), 'Putyin kedvenc videójátéka' ['Putin's Favourite Video Game'], *Filmvilág*, No. 5, pp. 50–1.

Wang, Georgette and Emilie Yueh-yu Yeh (2005), 'Globalization and hybridization in cultural products. The cases of *Mulan* and *Crouching Tiger, Hidden Dragon*', *International Journal of Cultural Studies*, Vol. 8, No. 2, pp. 175–93.

Žižek, Slavoj (1997), 'Love Thy Neighbor? No, Thanks!', in *The Plague of Fantasies*, London and New York: Verso.

Index

12:08 East of Bucharest (*A fost sau n-a fost?*, 2006), 118, 120–1, 123, 205, 214
4 Months, 3 Weeks, 2 Days (*4 luni, 3 săptămâni și 2 zile*, 2007), 113

A Bus Came . . . (*Jött egy busz . . .*, 2003), 240
absorption, 166, 180
Achim, Gabriel, 110, 120–21
Adalbert's Dream (*Visul lui Adalbert*, 2011), 121–2
adaptation, xi, 3, 10, 19, 21, 23, 50, 67, 86, 225, 237, 238, 240, 242, 243, 247, 249, 251
Adriaensens, Vito, 86
Adrienn Pál (*Pál Adrienn*, 2010), vii, 27–8, 32, 33, 35, 38, 40–1
Aesopian language, 115, 116, 120, 123
affect/affective, 9, 15, 31, 34, 41, 54, 62, 65, 72, 85, 89, 148–9, 150, 152, 156–7, 159, 173, 229
Aftermath (*Pokłosie*, 2012), 59
Agamben, Giorgio, 13, 91, 96, 103, 104
Alaniz, José, 179, 180, 190, 193, 200
Alexandra (2007), ix, 17, 185, 186, 195–9
allegory/allegorical, viii, 6, 9, 20, 63, 78, 100, 113, 115, 121, 167, 169, 179, 190, 203, 242, 249
amateur film/amateurish filmmaking, x, 16, 116, 118, 119, 121, 122, 123, 128, 150, 152, 154, 155, 158, 219, 223–4, 226
American Torso (*Amerikai anzix*, 1975), 5
Anatomy Lesson of Dr. Tulp, The (Rembrandt), vii, 9
Andersson, Roy, 216
Andraesyan, Sarik, 250
Andrei Rublev (1966), 71, 87
Anemone, Anthony, 67, 86
Angelopoulos, Theo, 82
animated documentary, 127, 128, 130, 131, 135, 139, 143, 144
animation, 2, 16, 31, 39, 92–3, 98–9, 102, 130, 131–2, 134, 135, 137, 138, 248–9
3D, 131, 230–231
Antonioni, Michelangelo, 56

architecture and/in film, 16, 66, 67, 78, 83, 93, 148, 150, 153, 154–6, 158, 164, 172, 173, 177, 178
archival/found footage in film, x, 5, 112, 127, 128, 134, 143, 144, 170, 224
archival image/photograph, 127, 128, 130, 134, 135, 140, 143, 144
Arcimboldo, Giuseppe, 100, 105
Arnheim, Rudolf, 74
Atkinson, Meera, 148, 157
Aumont, Jacques, 222
avatar, 123, 141, 231

Bad Luck (*Zezowate szczęście*, 1960), 51
Bădeliță, Alexandru Petru, 127, 136
Bakhtin, Mikhail M., 16, 109, 110
Bardan, Alice, 118, 203
Barney, Mathew, 87
Bartas, Sharunas, 12, 13
Barthes, Roland, 40, 46, 85, 129, 133, 205, 206
Bassil-Morozow, Helena, 111, 119, 122
Bataille, Georges, 72–3, 76, 85, 87, 88
Bauman, Zygmunt, 114
Baumbach, Noah, 51
Bazin, André, 50, 143, 155
Becker, Wolfgang, 82
Being Romanian: A Family Journal (*Jurnalul familiei Escu*, 2019), 144
Bekmambetov, Timur, 239, 248
Bellour, Raymond, 57, 63, 86
Belting, Hans, 145
Bene, Adrián, 3
Bergman, Ingmar, 211, 216
Bessière, Jean, 172, 180
Beumers, Birgit, 179, 186
Bibliothèque Pascal (2010), 10, 27–8, 30, 33, 38, 40, 41
Bicycle Thieves (*Ladri di biciclette*, 1948), 50
Black Lightning (*Chernaya molniya*, 2009), ix, 239–40, 243–51
Blos-Jáni, Melinda, x, 4, 5, 14, 16, 127, 159
Bódy, Gábor, 5, 22
Bolter, Jay David and Richard Grusin, 178, 186, 187, 193
Bosáková, Žofia, 135

Bosch, Hieronymus, 12, 20, 70
Botz-Bornstein, Thorsten, 72, 88, 187
Bouko, Catherine, 173, 174
Bourgeois, Louise, 87
Brâncuși, Constantin, 12
Branigan, Edward, 171, 181
Bresson, Robert, 54
Brewster, Ben and Lea Jacobs, 166
Broderick, Mick, 147
Brueghel, Pieter the Elder, 12, 67, 70
Bugaj, Malgorzata, x, 185
Burkitt, Ian, 109
Buzard, James, 160–1

California Dreamin' (2007), 113
Campbell, Bruce, 240
Caranfil, Nae, 4, 124
Carlson, Marvin, 165
Carnival Scenes (De ce trag clopotele, Mitică?, 1981), 112, 115
carnivalesque, 16, 109, 110, 112, 116–18, 121, 122, 123, 124
Caruth, Cathy, 147
Cat City (Macskafogó, 1986), 249
Cézanne, Paul, 88
Chakravorty, Swagato, 3
Chari, Sharad, 252
Chattah, Juan, 34, 38
Chinita, Fátima, x, 17, 163
close-up, vii, viii, 7, 17, 58, 59, 60, 61, 68, 70, 71, 75, 76, 91, 135, 137, 138, 154, 186, 189, 190, 191, 192, 193, 197, 198, 199, 224, 228,
 extreme, 17, 137, 186, 189, 190, 191, 198
 medium, 194, 196,
cinema of moral concern, 227
Cold War (Zimna wojna, 2018), vii, 47, 54–6, 59, 62, 63
Colpaert, Lisa, 86
Come and See (Idi i smotri, 1985), 71
Condee, Nancy, 179
Contempt (Le Mépris, 1963), 56–7
Costa, Pedro, 20
Cubitt, Sean, 210
Cvetkovich, Ann, 159
Czapla, Zbigniew, 127, 137

Dalle Vacche, Angella, 88, 128
Damian, Anca, 127, 131
Dánél, Mónika, 3
Daneliuc, Mircea, 3, 10, 110, 115–18, 120
Dargay, Attila, 249
De Castro, Eduardo Viveiros, 92, 93, 99
Dead Nation (Țara moartă, 2017), viii, 127, 139–43
décadrage, 59
deframing *see* framing/deframing/reframing
Deleuze, Gilles, 13, 39, 149, 157, 159, 234

Descola, Philippe, 99
détrompe l'oeil, 18, 219, 221–5, 233
dialogism/dialogical, 16, 109–10, 112, 115–16, 117, 118, 123, 128
 intermedial dialogism, 110, 112
 Jungian dialogism, 110, 123
Diderot, Denis, 167
Didi-Huberman, Georges, 17, 129–31, 132, 133, 134, 138, 143,145, 149–50
digital cinema/image, ix, xi, 2, 12, 17, 18, 45, 46, 50, 51, 80, 142, 219–24, 231–4
digital mimicry, 46, 51
digital monochrome/black-and-white, 45, 47–8, 50, 57, 58, 62–3
Dimensions of Dialogue (Možnosti dialogu, 1983), viii, 94, 98, 100, 101, 102, 103
DiPaolo, Mark, 239
direct theory, 204, 215
dissensus, 50, 51, 55, 62
distribution of the sensible, 55
documentary, 3, 5, 50, 62, 117, 124, 127, 128, 130, 133–5, 139, 143, 144, 149, 159, 170, 223, 224; *see also* animated documentary
Dostoevsky, Fyodor M., 20, 123
Dreyer, Carl Theodor, 54
Durys, Elżbieta, 48, 51

Eclipse, The (L'Eclisse, 1962), 56
Egoists, The (Egoiści, 2000), 18, 220, 225, 227–9, 230, 232, 233, 234
Ehrlich, Nea, 144
Eile, Stanislaw, 225
Eisenstein, Sergei, 71, 81
Eisner, Will, 242
ekphrasis, 2, 22, 80
Elegy of a Voyage (Elegiya dorogi, 2001), 171
Eliasson, Olafur, 57
Elleström, Lars, 2, 19
Elsaesser, Thomas, 29, 30, 32, 33, 41, 147, 148, 149, 197
Enyedi, Ildikó, 28, 32, 33
Epstein, Jean, 99

Faluhelyi, Krisztián, 3
Father and Son (Otets i syn, 2003), ix, 17, 185, 186, 190–5, 199
Felleman, Susan, 86
Fellini, Federico, 68, 82, 115
Felvidék. Caught in Between (Felvidék. Horná zem, 2014), viii, 127, 134–5, 142
Féral, Josette and Ronald Birmingham, 165
Fine, Elizabeth C., 111, 113
Fingeroth, Danny, 238
Finnegans Wake (James Joyce), 68, 77
first-person narrative/narration, 127, 131
Flat, The (Byt, 1968), viii, 94, 98, 103
Fliegauf, Benedek, 3, 6

Focillon, Henri, 74
fold/intermedial fold, 39, 58, 156
For Those Who Can Tell No Tales (*Za one koji ne mogu da govore*, 2013), viii, 17, 147–73
Forgács, Péter, 6, 10
Foucault, Michel, 193, 205
found footage *see* archival/found footage in film
fragmentation, 8, 11, 17, 68, 79, 84, 86, 93, 129, 130, 131, 132, 133–9, 143, 149, 159, 164, 165, 189, 192, 193, 195, 225,
framing, viii, 34, 51, 58, 137, 155, 169, 172, 179, 222, 223, 224, 226, 228, 233
deframing, 37, 59
reframing, 5, 128, 138
Frances Ha (2012), 51
Free Fall (*Szabadesés*, 2014), 243
Fresh Air (*Friss levegő*, 2006), vii, 27, 28, 37, 38
Fried, Michael, 167
Frye, Northrop, 109

Gadamer, Hans-Georg, 205, 207–8
Galt, Rosalind, 51–2
Garden of Earthly Delights, The (2004), 12, 20
Garden of Earthly Delights, The (Hieronymus Bosch), 20
Gehring, Wes, 241
Gelencsér, Gábor, 3
Genette, Gérard, 171, 172
Georgescu, Șerban, 144
German Expressionism, 234
Gherman, Aleksey, vii, viii, 15, 65, 67–77, 78, 85, 86–7, 88
Gherman, Aleksey, Jr, viii, 15, 65, 66, 77–85, 87
Gilić, Nikica, 3
Glass Lips/Blood of a Poet (2007), 13
Gledhill, Christine, 28, 29, 30, 42
Gliński, Robert, 47, 50
Glissando (1984), 10
Godard, Jean-Luc, 22, 40, 56, 63, 162, 210, 216
Goffman, Erving, 233
Gombrich, Ernst, 213
Goncharov, Ivan, 80
Good Bye, Lenin! (2003), 82
Goodman, Nelson, 213–14
Gorzo, Andrei, 216
Grau, Oliver, 166
Grbavica: The Land of My Dreams (*Grbavica*, 2006), 150, 157, 160–1
Guardians, The (*Zashchitniki*, 2017), 250
Guattari, Félix, 234
Guerin, Frances 147
Gunning, Tom, 129
Gyenge, Zsolt, x, 17, 203, 252
Győri, Zsolt, 3

Hajdu, Szabolcs, 10, 13, 20, 23, 27, 43
Hallas, Roger 147
Hamlet (William Shakespeare), 84
Hänsgen, Sabine, 3, 186, 187, 190
Happiest Girl in the World, The (*Cea mai fericită fată din lume*, 2009), 121
haptic/hapticality, 62, 74, 128, 132, 135, 137, 143, 145, 148, 149, 152, 154, 155, 156, 159, 161, 175, 185, 191, 192, 195, 197, 198, 199, 200
Hard to Be a God (*Trudno byt bogom*, 2013), vii, viii, 16, 65, 67–77, 78, 84–6, 87
Hardcore Henry (2015), 248
Henderson, Joseph L., 114, 115
Hermitage/State Hermitage Museum, 163, 164, 165, 166, 170, 172, 173, 174, 175, 176, 177, 178, 179, 181
Hi, Tereska! (*Cześć, Tereska*, 2001), 47–50, 62
history/historical, ix, 1, 2, 3, 4, 5, 6, 9, 10, 11, 12, 14, 15, 16, 17, 18, 20, 21, 30, 45, 47, 48, 53, 55, 61, 62, 68, 71, 72, 78, 81, 82, 83, 84, 86, 87, 91, 104, 118, 119, 120, 122, 127, 128, 130, 134, 137, 140, 142, 144, 147, 148, 149, 151, 154, 156, 158, 159, 160, 161, 163, 164, 165, 166, 168, 169, 170, 171, 172, 178, 179, 180, 181, 234, 240, 243, 249
Hogg, Joanna, 216
Hollywood, 219–21, 223, 233–4
Holmberg, Jan, 211
Hölzl, Ingeborg, 128
Homunculus (2012), vii, 7
Honess Roe, Annabelle, 130, 131
House, The (*A Casa*, 1997), 13
Hukkle (2002), 243
Hungarian Folk Tales (*Magyar népmesék*, 1980–2012), 249
hybridity/hybridization, 3, 5, 16, 31, 46, 50, 51, 83, 128, 130, 131, 134, 144, 168, 237, 240, 243, 251, 253

I Made You, I Kill You (2016), viii, 127, 136–37, 142, 143
I, Olga Hepnarová (*Já, Olga Hepnarová*, 2016), vii, 47–50, 61–2
Ida (2013), vii, 47, 53–4, 58–60, 62–3
I'm Not Your Friend (*Nem vagyok a barátod*, 2009), 3, 24
image-ness, 48, 59
immersion/immersive, 17, 57, 61, 67, 75, 88, 93, 104, 148, 150, 164–6, 170–80
impure cinema/impurity, 46, 50, 149, 155
in-betweenness, 1, 4, 10, 15, 18, 20, 46, 51–2, 57, 62, 68, 72, 73, 74, 78, 87, 91, 94, 149
index/indexical, 58, 127, 128, 129, 130, 131, 132, 133, 136, 138, 140, 142, 143, 145, 198

informe/formless, 72, 73, 76, 85
installation art and cinema, vii, 2, 3, 7, 12, 13, 14, 16, 66, 78, 81, 83, 84, 219, 222
intermediality, 1–21, 27, 29, 39, 41, 42, 45, 50, 57, 58, 62, 65, 66, 91, 92, 93, 96, 98, 103, 104, 105, 109, 110, 112, 116, 117, 118, 120, 121, 123, 124, 129, 132, 134, 135, 142, 143, 144, 147, 148, 149, 150, 152, 156, 158, 159, 178, 179, 180, 181, 185, 186, 195, 219, 220, 221, 222, 224, 225, 231, 233, 234, 242, 249, 250
   sensual mode of, 62, 132, 135, 148, 156
   structural mode of, 135, 148, 156
Internet, 229–32
Ioniță, Maria, 203, 205, 209, 114
It's Not the Time of My Life (*Ernelláék Farkaséknál*, 2016), 13, 20
Ivanov, Vlad, 131

Jabberwocky (*Žvahlav aneb šatičky Slaměného Huberta*, 1971), 2, 105
Jacobs, Steven, 86, 169
Jaffe, Ira, 216
Jagielski, Sebastian, 235
Jameson, Frederic, 75, 76, 81
Janion, Maria, 234–5
Jankovics, Marcell, 249, 252
Jelača, Dijana, 151, 153, 159-61
Jeles, András, 5
Johanna (2005): 27, 31, 32, 33, 36, 38, 40, 42
Johnny Corncob (*János vitéz*, 1973), 249
Journey to Italy (*Viaggio in Italia*, 1954), 56
Jude, Radu, vii, 4, 8–9, 120, 121, 127, 139–40, 143, 144
Jung, Carl Gustav/Jungian, 16, 109, 110, 111, 112, 119, 123–4
Jupiter's Moon (*Jupiter holdja*, 2017), 249

Kalmár, György, 118
Kaplan, E. Ann, 147, 159
Katalin Varga (*Varga Katalin Balladája*, 2009): 27, 30, 31, 33, 34, 36, 37, 38, 40
Kazda, Petr, 47
Ken Burns effect, 129, 141
Khrustalyov, My Car! (*Khrustalyov, mashinu!*, 1998), 68
Kibédi Varga, Áron, 214
Kieślowski, Krzysztof, 54
Király, Hajnal, x, 3, 6, 12, 15, 20, 27, 42
Kiselev, Dmitriy, 239, 244
Klimov, Elem, 71
Kocsis, Ágnes, 6, 27, 28, 37
Komasa, Jan, 220, 229, 233, 235
Komm, Dmitriy, 244
Kos-Krauze, Joanna, 47, 52, 64
Kosmala, Katarzyna, 3
Kránicz, Bence, xi, 18, 237
Krauss, Rosalind, 66, 72, 76, 77, 81, 83

Krauze, Krzysztof, 47, 52, 64
Kristeva, Julia, 6, 88
Kujundzic, Dragan, 180

La dolce vita (1960), 82
La Jetée, (1962), 144
Lacan, Jacques, 114, 133, 245
LaCapra, Dominick 159
Lamentation over the Dead Christ, The (Mantegna), vii, 6, 8
Landsberg, Alison, 144
Langford, Martha, 144
Lankosz, Borys, 47, 51
Lanzmann, Claude, 59
Las Meninas (2008), 13
Laverdière, Gabriel, xi, 18, 219, 235, Ledoux, Aurélie, 222
Lefebvre, Martin, 129, 137, 138, 145
Lermontov, Mikhail, 80
Lindsay, Vachel, 75, 84
Lipiński, Kamil, 3
Liška, Zdeněk, 96
literature and/in film, xi, 11, 12, 15, 52, 80, 86, 104, 105, 109, 238, 249, 250
Liza, the Fox Fairy (*Liza, a rókatündér*, 2015), vii, 27, 28, 31, 33, 35, 36–9, 40, 42
Lock, Helen, 109
Long Drive, The (*Cursa*, 1975), 115–17, 120
López-Varela Azcárate, Asunción, 2
Lyotard, Jean-François, 155

Machon, Josephine, 173, 174
McLuhan, Marshall, 212
Magritte, René, 94, 203, 204, 205–6
Maguire, Muireann, 247, 252
Majewski, Lech, 3, 12–13, 14, 20, 21, 23, 24
Mantegna, Andrea, vii, 6, 8
Marey, Étienne–Jules, 219
Marker, Chris, 144
Marks, Laura, 28, 154–5, 161, 185, 192, 198–9
Marlier, Georges, 221
Martin, David F., 74, 75
Massumi, Brian, 89, 148, 157, 159
Mattie the Goose-boy (*Ludas Matyi*, 1977), 249
Mazierska, Ewa, xi, 3, 20, 50, 118, 160–1, 227, 229, 243
memory, 7, 13, 16, 33, 47, 127, 128, 134, 137, 138, 144, 147, 149, 150–52, 154–9, 160, 163, 171, 179, 198, 250
   memorialisation, 17, 150–53, 156–160
Merleau-Ponty, Maurice, 98, 99, 104
metalepsis, 166, 170, 171–2, 180
metaphor, viii, 28, 29, 32, 38, 66, 70, 130, 141, 142, 145, 164, 165, 173, 174, 176, 177, 180, 190, 203, 207
Microphone Test (*Proba de microfon*, 1980), 117

Mill and the Cross, The (*Młyn i krzyż*, 2011), 12
Mironescu, Andreea, 4, 145
mise en abyme, 122, 221, 222, 233
Mitchell, W. J. T., 88, 205
modernism, 40, 48, 54, 56, 57, 59, 62, 66, 67, 114, 116, 120, 121, 206, 221
mood cue, 27, 29, 34, 36, 37, 40–41
Mother and Son (*Mat i syn*, 1997), ix, 17, 185, 186–190, 192, 199
Mroz, Matilda, xi, 20, 58
Mrozek, Wiktor, 48
Mukhina, Vera, 88
Mulvey, Laura, 6, 48, 62
Mundruczó, Kornél, 6, 27, 31, 42, 249
Mungiu, Cristian, 113, 205
Munk, Andrzej, 51
Muntean, Radu, 205
music, vii, xi, 3, 5, 11, 15, 16, 27, 28–42, 47, 55–6, 84, 93, 96, 102, 104, 105, 148, 163, 176, 178, 210
My Life to Live (*Vivre sa vie*, 1962), 210

Nagib, Lúcia, 19, 50, 155, 156
Nahlik, Monika, 226
Naishuller, Ilya, 248
Narcissus and Psyche (*Nárcisz és Psyché*, 1980), 10
Nasirov, Yasin, 165
Nemes, László 149, 159
Nemescu, Cristian, 113
Nietzsche, Friedrich, 74, 88
Night Watch (*Nochnoy dozor*, 2004), 248
Niki and Flo (*Niki Ardelean, colonel în rezervă*, 2003), 112–14, 116, 120
non-cinematic 150, 152–3, 155–6, 158
Nowicka, Magdalena, 48
Noys, Benjamin, 72, 76, 88

Oak, The (*Balanța*, 1992), 5, 112, 113, 114
Of Body and Soul (*Testről és lélekről*, 2017), 28, 36, 37, 40
Oosterling, Henk, 19
Ossuary, The (*Kostnice*, 1970), viii, 94, 96, 98, 99, 100, 103
Own Death (*Saját halál*, 2008), 10

Paech, Joachim, 19
painting and/in cinema/references to paintings, vii, ix, 5, 6, 7, 8, 10, 11, 12–13, 15, 20, 42, 45, 46, 57, 59, 66, 71, 74, 88, 94, 96, 99, 100, 102, 105, 139, 143, 148, 163, 164, 168, 169, 171, 178, 179, 186, 188, 190, 204, 205, 215, 221–2, 249
 painterly image, 3, 6, 9, 10, 17, 48, 52, 53, 61, 67, 70, 79, 83, 91, 92, 96, 127, 129, 131, 186, 187, 188, 195, 199, 222
Pálfi, György, ix, 3, 9, 240–43, 249–50

Paperbox (*Papierowe pudełko*, 2011), viii, 127, 137–9, 145
Papusza (*Papusza*, 2013), vii, 47, 52–3, 61–2
paradox visibility, 129, 130, 133, 135, 140
Parallel Lives (*Senkiföldje*, 1993), 5
Pasikowski, Władysław, 59
Passion of Joan of Arc, The (*La passion de Jeanne d'Arc*, 1928), 54
Pasternak, Boris, 84
Paterson, Mark, 74
Path to Beyond, The (*Crulic – drumul spre dincolo*, 2011), 127, 131–3, 143
Pawlikowski, Paweł, 20, 47, 53–6, 63
performance art and/in cinema, 17, 66, 87, 150, 156–7, 159, 160, 161
performative, 6, 16, 66, 73, 74, 78, 84, 144, 151, 152, 156, 164, 166
Persona (Ingmar Bergman), 211
Pethő, Ágnes, xi–xii, 3, 6, 10, 12, 13, 14, 15, 19, 20, 39, 58, 62, 63, 110, 124, 129, 132, 135, 144, 148–9, 156, 168, 216
Pető, Andrea 158
phenomenology, x, xii, 16, 65, 68, 73–7, 129, 138,179, 204, 209
photography and film/photographs in film, vii, 3, 4, 6, 8, 10, 13, 15, 16, 17, 20, 58, 127–45, 158, 193, 214, 219, 221, 222; *see also* archival image/photograph
 photo-collage in film, 16, 143
 photofilmic/photographic quality in film, vii, 6–7, 15, 16, 45, 46, 48, 52, 53, 57–9, 62, 63, 66, 80, 93, 148, 155–6, 158
photography and painting, 186
photography and sculpture, 85, 93
pictorialism, 166
Pieldner, Judit, xi, 3, 5, 10, 12, 42
Pietà (Michelangelo), vii, 7
Pintilie, Lucian, 3, 5, 110, 112–15, 118, 120, 122
Pisters, Patricia, 127
Plančíková, Vladislava, 127, 133, 134, 135
Podolchak, Ihor, 12, 13
Police, Adjective (*Polițist, adjectiv*, 2009), ix, 204–16
Pop, Doru, 121, 124
Porumboiu, Corneliu, 3, 14, 17, 18, 110, 118–21, 123, 204–16
postmodern, 66, 111, 120, 121, 229, 242, 243, 250
Prévert, Jacques, 96, 105
Procession to Calvary, The (Pieter Brueghel the Elder), 12
Puiu, Cristi, 4, 6, 13, 20, 42, 112, 113
Pushkin, Aleksandr, 80

Rancière, Jacques, 50, 55
Rascaroli, Laura, 3, 149

Ravetto-Biagioli, Kriss, 164, 169
realism, 18, 46, 47, 50, 62, 116, 118, 122, 123, 124, 148, 169, 185, 195, 199, 203, 205, 216, 221–4, 231–3, 243
Reconstruction (*Reconstituirea*, 1968), 112–13, 114, 115, 118, 120, 122
re-enactment, 16, 115, 122, 123, 134, 156, 164, 169, 171, 172, 176
reflexivity, ix, x, 3, 5, 6, 12, 39, 54, 56, 58, 61, 62, 63, 112, 116, 117, 120, 123, 128, 132, 148, 149, 152, 153, 171, 188, 215, 216, 220, 241–2, 250
remediation, 56, 144, 178, 186, 187, 193
Renov, Michael, 127
representation, 5, 13, 15, 17, 18, 19, 20, 28, 29, 39, 40, 41, 45, 46, 47, 48, 50, 66, 68, 93, 98, 99, 102, 103, 104, 116, 129, 135, 147, 148, 149, 150, 151, 154, 158, 159, 164, 170, 172, 179, 185, 186, 193, 200, 203–4, 205–10, 213, 215, 222, 231, 233
  self-representation, 154, 231
Restivo, Angelo, 114
Reverse, The (*Rewers*, 2009), vii, 47–8, 51–2, 62
Richardson, Michael, 92, 148, 157
Ricœur, Paul, 104, 231
Rint, František, 96
Robertson Woicyk, Pamela, 34–6
Robin, Régine, 116
Robinson, Andrew, 109
Rodowick, David N., 29
Roe's Room, The (*Pokój saren*, 1997), 13
Romney, Jonathan, 68
Rosen, Philip, 46
Rossellini, Roberto, 56
Rowland, Susan, 109, 110, 111, 112, 122, 123
Roy, Lucie, 224
Rozenkrantz, Jonathan, 127, 130, 143
Ruchel-Stockmans, Katarzyna, 127
Russian Ark (*Russkiy kovcheg*, 2002), 17, 163–82
Rutherford, Anne 147–8, 150

Sándor, Katalin, xii, 3, 5, 6, 10, 17, 20, 147
Sartre, Jean-Paul, 69, 70, 87
Scarred Hearts (*Inimi cicatrizate*, 2016), vii, 8, 9
Schatz, Thomas, 51
Schröter, Jens, 129
Schwarz, David, 36–7
sculpture and cinema/sculpture in cinema, 10, 12, 15–16, 65, 66, 68, 69, 70, 73, 74, 78–86, 87
  sculptural/sculpturality, vii, viii, 16, 49, 66, 67–77, 78, 83, 84, 85, 86, 87, 88, 93

becoming sculptural, 71, 73–7, 85; *see also* sculptural
cine-sculptural, 16, 65; *see also* sculptural
Seckler, Dawn A., 244
Second Circle, The (*Krug tvoroy*, 1990), 89
Second Game, The (*Al doilea joc*, 2014), 14, 119–21, 123, 216
Sepsi, László, 248
Sera, Mareike, xii, 16, 91
Șerban, Alex Leo, 216
Serres, Michel, 77, 84–5
Sha-Man Vs. Ikarus (*Táltosember Vs. Ikarus*, 2003), ix, 240–3, 249–52
Shaviro, Steven, 89
Shoah (1985), 59
Sieranevada (2016), 13, 20, 42
silence, 29, 33, 37, 59, 71, 84, 141–2, 149, 150, 151, 153, 158, 187, 189
Simić, Olivera 151, 158, 160
Sinnerbrink, Robert, 29, 34
Small, Edward S., 204, 215
smartphone, 219, 223, 229–31, 234
Smarzowski, Wojciech, 220, 225
Smith, Jeanne Rosier, 111
Smythe, William, 109–10, 123–4
Sobchack, Vivian, 74, 75
social media, 229, 232–3
Sokurov, Alexander, 3, 17, 80, 163–82, 185–201
Son of Saul (*Saul fia*, 2015), 149, 159
Son of the White Mare (*Fehérlófia*, 1981), 249
Sontag, Susan, 46, 214
sound/sound and image relations, 15, 34, 37, 38, 40, 41, 71, 87, 96, 100, 120, 127, 128, 131, 137, 139, 140, 141, 143, 144, 149, 154, 156, 161, 171, 174, 175, 185, 192, 200, 205, 211, 221, 223, 242
  sonorous envelope, 36–7
spectacle, ix, 28, 30, 58, 82, 164, 172, 173, 177, 179, 180, 181, 192, 221, 222, 223, 233
Staszczyszyn, Bartosz, 52
State, Andrei, 203, 216
Stőhr, Lóránt, 3
Stojanova, Christina, xii, 16, 109, 118, 121, 124
Stone (*Kamen*, 1992)
Streitberger, Alexander, 57, 58
Strickland, Peter, 27
Strugatsky, Arkady and Boris, 67, 68
Stuff and Dough (*Marfa și banii*, 2001), 113
Suicide Room (*Sala samobójców*, 2011), ix, 18, 220, 225, 229–33, 234
Suicide Room: The Hater (*Sala samobójców: Hejter*, 2020), 235
Sulejewska, Justyna, 139, 145
Sutton, Damian, 58
Švankmajer, Jan, viii, 2, 16, 91–105

symbol/symbolic/symbolism, vii, 7, 8, 11, 16, 30, 33, 39, 59, 78, 81, 113, 115, 117, 118, 129, 134, 143, 147, 151, 158, 165, 170, 171, 176, 204, 205, 206, 207–9, 220, 225, 228, 229, 230, 239, 240, 242, 243, 245, 246, 250, 252
Szaniawski, Jeremi, 170, 179, 180

tableau/tableau shot, vii, vii, ix, 6, 7, 8, 13, 17, 45, 49, 53, 58–9, 61–2, 77, 79, 80, 84, 86, 96, 97, 98, 100, 113, 166, 167–8, 170, 172, 173, 176, 177, 179, 181, 216
tableau vivant, 6, 9, 10, 12, 168–9
Tarkovsky, Andrei, 71–2, 87
Tarnay, László, 130, 135, 143, 145
Tarr, Béla, 3, 6, 7, 20, 21, 22, 216
Taxidermia (2006), 9, 243,
television/TV, 11, 13, 14, 110, 115, 116, 117, 118, 120, 121, 123, 136, 214, 228, 239
Tengelyi, László, 209–10
Ternovszky, Béla, 249
Tes, Ursula, 3
theatre/theatricality, 11, 12, 13, 15, 16, 30, 144, 163, 164–8, 172–80, 232, *see also* theatrical performance
    theatrical, vii, 17, 30, 55–6, 164, 165, 170, 172–80
Thompson, Kristin, 57
Thompson, Lara, 46–7
three-dimensionality, 75, 131, 168, 170, 178
Through the Looking-Glass (Lewis Carroll), 2
transmediation, 19, 228, 232–3
trauma/traumatic experience, viii, 17, 30, 31, 34, 41, 48, 49, 54, 58, 61, 79, 127, 131, 134, 136, 140, 147–53, 155, 157–60, 244, 249
Traverso, Antonio, 147
Treasure, The (*Comoara*, 2015), 205, 209
Treliński, Mariusz, 220, 227
Trickster, 16, 109–123
    archetype 114, 116, 117
    as director's stand-in, 112, 113, 118, 119, 123
    narrative, 111, 112, 114, 115, 116, 117, 118, 119, 120, 121, 122, 123
    tropes, 110, 120, 121
trompe l'oeil, 18, 221, 222, 224, 225
Turgenev, Ivan, 20, 80
Turin Horse, The (*A torinói ló*, 2011), 6, 7, 216
Twardoch, Ewelina, 3

Ujj-Mészáros, Károly, 27, 31
Ulysses (James Joyce), 68
Ulysses's Gaze (*To vlemma tou Odyssea*, 1995), 82
unconscious, 109, 110, 111, 112, 114, 115, 119, 122, 123
Under Electric Clouds (*Pod elektricheskimi oblakami*, 2015), viii, 16, 65, 77–86

Van Gelder, Hilde, 57
Varga, Zoltán, 3
Vercoe, Kym, 150, 156, 160, 161
Virginás, Andrea, 34, 161
Volčić, Zala, 151, 158, 160
Vouilloux, Bernard, 168
Voytinskiy, Aleksandr, 239, 244

Wajda, Andrzej, 54, 225
Wang, Ban, 147, 159
Wang, Georgette, 239
webcam, 220, 229–34
Weber, Samuel, 165
Wedding Banquet, The (*Wesele*, 2004), 18, 220, 225–7, 232, 234,
Wees, William, 128
Weinreb, Tomaš, 47
Werckmeister Harmonies (*Werckmeister harmóniák*, 2000), 216
When Evening Falls on Bucharest or Metabolism (*Când se lasă seara peste București sau metabolism*, 2013), 119, 205, 212–15, 216
Whispering Pages (*Tikhiye stranitsy*, 1994), 80
White Ribbon, The (*Das weiße Band – Eine deutsche Kindergeschichte*, 2011), 45, 61
White, Gareth, 173, 174
Williams, Linda, 28, 30
Woodward, Katherine, 40–1
word and image relations, xi, 86, 205–12, 214
Wyspiański, Stanisław, 225

Young, James E., 151, 160
Youngblood, Denise J., 169
Youngblood, Gene, 86
YouTube, 234

Žbanić, Jasmila, 17, 147–73
Žižek, Slavoj, 114, 115, 245–6
Żuławski, Andrzej, 3
Zvonkine, Eugénie, 3
Zvyagintsev, Andrey, 6, 78–9, 85

EU representative:
Easy Access System Europe
Mustamäe tee 50, 10621 Tallinn, Estonia
Gpsr.requests@easproject.com

www.ingramcontent.com/pod-product-compliance
Lightning Source LLC
Chambersburg PA
CBHW071833230426
43671CB00012B/1950